Between Here and There

Between Here and There

Creating the Political Economy of Mexican Migration, 1900–1942

DANIEL MORALES

OXFORD
UNIVERSITY PRESS

OXFORD
UNIVERSITY PRESS

Oxford University Press is a department of the University of Oxford. It furthers the University's objective of excellence in research, scholarship, and education by publishing worldwide. Oxford is a registered trade mark of Oxford University Press in the UK and certain other countries.

Published in the United States of America by Oxford University Press
198 Madison Avenue, New York, NY 10016, United States of America.

Library of Congress Cataloging-in-Publication Data
Names: Morales, Daniel (History teacher), author.
Title: Between here and there : creating the political economy of
Mexican migration, 1900–1942 / Daniel Morales.
Description: New York, NY : Oxford University Press, [2024] |
Includes bibliographical references and index. |
Identifiers: LCCN 2024024064 (print) | LCCN 2024024065 (ebook) |
ISBN 9780197612590 (hardback) | ISBN 9780197612606 (paperback) |
ISBN 9780197612620 (epub) | ISBN 9780197612637
Subjects: LCSH: Mexicans—United States—History—20th century. |
Mexico—Emigration and immigration—20th century. |
United States—Emigration and immigration—20th century. |
Mexico—Emigration and immigration—Economic aspects. |
United States—Emigration and immigration—Economic aspects.
Classification: LCC E184.M5 M656 2024 (print) | LCC E184.M5 (ebook) |
DDC 973/.046872—dc23/eng/20240723
LC record available at https://lccn.loc.gov/2024024064
LC ebook record available at https://lccn.loc.gov/2024024065

DOI: 10.1093/oso/9780197612590.001.0001

Paperback printed by Marquis Book Printing, Canada
Hardback printed by Bridgeport National Bindery, Inc., United States of America

Chapter 5 is adapted from Daniel Morales, "*Tejas, Afuera de México*: Newspapers, the Mexican Government, *Mutualistas*, and Migrants in San Antonio 1910–1940." *Journal of American Ethnic History*, 40, no. 2 (Wntr 2021): 52–91.

Dedicated to my grandparents
Mariana Gonzalez Morales
Fermín Ramón Morales Hernandez
&
Maria Juana Martinez Ramírez
Jose Jesús Martinez Rodríguez

Contents

Acknowledgments

Nobody can write alone. This work could only have been completed with the help and generosity of many people along the way. I became interested in writing Latino History while an undergraduate at the University of Chicago. A long way away from the barrio I grew up in, I increasingly spent more time involved in the city, education programs, and immigrant communities. In the city, I became involved in activism for immigrant rights, and to my surprise found support for my interests in the history department. Through the Mellon-Mays Undergraduate Fellowship, I found a community of students and worked with Kathleen Conzen, Emilio Kouri, and Sarah Osten on immigrant research in Chicago. Later, thanks to the advice from Ramon Gutierrez, I was able to turn that initial paper into my BA thesis.

It was at Columbia University that I learned to take my interest in migration and turn it into what became my book. Mae Ngai took my half-formed ideas for a history of Mexican migration and guided it into this book. I would like to thank the rest of my committee, Elizabeth Blackmar, Pablo Piccato, Claudio Lomnitz, and Jose Moya, for their patience and feedback throughout all of these years, and Pablo Yankelevich for acting as a mentor at the Colegio de México. I would also like to thank all the faculty who read parts and provided advice: Karl Jacoby, Caterina Pizzigoni, Carlos Alonso, John Coatsworth, Eric Foner, and Adam McKeown.

This project has received funding and forums from various organizations that helped refine and revise the project. A post-doctoral fellowship at the American Academy of Arts and Sciences allowed me to expand the project's scope. The Mellon-Mays Foundation has supported this project in various forums, and a fellowship from the Institute for Scholars and Citizens (formerly the Woodrow Wilson Foundation) allowed me time to finish the book. Research and travel grants from James Madison University (JMU) and Virginia Commonwealth University (VCU) made additional chapters possible. I would like to thank the organizers and participants in places where pieces of the book were workshopped. The Bancroft Seminar on Interdisciplinary Latina/o History at the University of California, Berkeley;

the Newberry Seminary in Borderlands History at the Newberry Library; and the Southeastern Latinx History Workshop.

Community is critical in doing research, completing work, reading drafts, and keeping each other company. I want to start with the South El Monte Arts Posse: Romeo Guzman, Nick Juravich, Carribean Fragoza, Yesenia Barragan, Maria John, and Andre Deckrow. Those from the Southeastern Latinx History workshop are Sarah Deutsch, Fawn-Amber Montoya, Benny Andres, and Cecilia Marquez. Those at JMU and VCU, especially the Migration Studies Lab, who have provided an academic home and community: Bill Van Norman, Kristen McCleary, Carlos Aleman, Antonio Espinoza, Gabriella León-Pérez, Rocio Gomez, Robert Mckenna, Paula Rodriguez, Michael Ahn Paarlberg, Carolyn Eastman, Meliz Hafez, Michael Dickinson, and Gabriel Reich. Those who had encouraged this work along the way: Fernando Saúl Alanís Ensico, Mark Overmyer-Velázquez, David Montejano, Jose Alamillo, Emilio Zamora, George Sánchez, Alberto Camarillo, Kelly Lytle Hernandez, and many more. A special thanks to Melisa Borja, Georgina Escoto Molina, Laura Gutierrez, Adam Goodman, James T. Roane, Jessica Ordaz, Jessica Lee, Amy Absher, Mariana Gatzava, Maru Beltran, Nancy Ng Tam, Ian Chin, Masako Hattori, Rachel Newman, Allison Powers, Tracy Goode, and everyone who has helped me throughout the years. There are too many to thank here.

A special thanks is in order for the people at the libraries, archives, and organizations that made this research project possible: Columbia University, El Colegio de México, and the University of Chicago. Collections in the United States: Columbia's Rare Books and Manuscripts Library; the National Archives in Washington, DC; the Bancroft Library at the University of California, Berkeley; the California State Archives; the Archives of the University of California, Los Angeles; the Oral History Archives at California State University, Fullerton; La Historia Society of El Monte; the South El Monte Arts Posse; the Stanford University Archives; the Benson Library at the University of Texas at Austin; Arte Publico Press at the University of Houston; the Oral History Collection at the University of Texas at El Paso; Special Collections at the University of Chicago; the Newberry Library; and the New York City Public Library. Collections in Mexico: Archivo del Instituto Nacional de Migración, El Archivo General de la Nación, Archivo de la Secretaria de Relaciones Exteriores, Archivo Plutarco Calles, Registro Agrario, Biblioteca Nacional de Antropología e Historia, and Los Archivos Municipales de Villa Juárez y Cerritos San Luis Potosí.

I would like to thank Oxford University Press and my editor, Susan Ferber. Her guidance and three anonymous readers helped shape this work into a much more focused and better book. I would also like to thank the research assistants who have worked on various parts of the project: Hannah Rosner, Nidale Zouhir, César Omar Tenorio Nava, Lauren Oakes, Kimberly Garcia, and Louise McDonald.

This project began on the road, journeying across the landscape of Mexico as a child. I grew up in Azusa, California, in a home that knew the meaning of migration. My parents came without documents and had been deported on a few occasions, as have many of my relatives. Once they obtained documentation from the 1986 Immigration Reform and Control Act in the mid-1990s, they began not only to send money back to Mexico as they had always done, but to travel there as well. Going to Mexico and then to Chicago every few months opened up a world of Mexican communities. There, I learned that my maternal grandfather had been a bracero, as had most of the men in his town, Villa Juarez. I also learned that my fraternal grandmother was American born but had been deported in the 1930s and that my great-grandparents had been migrants in the 1910s. It is to the story of my grandparents, especially my grandmother Mariana Gonzales-Morales, that this book is dedicated. Finally, I wish to thank my loving and supporting family, my parents Maria Socorro and Felipe Morales, my brothers David and the late Philip Morales, and my nephews Philip, Issac, and Daniel David. My wife and soulmate Heng Rui has supported this project in ways too many to account for here. Her heroic work on the frontlines of the pandemic has given me a new perspective on the nature of essential work. Our daughters Isabella and Gabriela have given purpose to all our work. May this book one day open up the past to them.

Between Here and There

Introduction

The Roots of Mexican Migration

The church of Santa Gertrudis de la Carbonera is in surprisingly good condition for a centuries-old building. The church looms over the town square of Villa Juárez, San Luis Potosí. The town is mostly empty, with about 5,000 people remaining, and its fields are mostly fallow. More than 15,000 people have left in the past four decades; over two-thirds of them reside in the United States. Most of the men who live in Villa Juárez today have been to the United States—from the old braceros who sit in the plaza sharing stories, to the leadership of the political parties. Migration from the town began during the Mexican Revolution and continues to this day. To listen to the stories of its people is to listen to the history of Mexican migration in the twentieth century.

Every year, from the festival of Santa Gertrudis on November 16th, when a large carnival is thrown, to January 6th, thousands of people return from *El Norte*. While the number of people participating in the annual return has fallen since the start of Mexico's drug war, license plates from California, Texas, Illinois, and other US states in Villa Juárez testify to the spread of the town's migrants. Their material success is visible in the large amounts of cars, consumer goods, and money they bring back and in the large houses that line the town's streets, the rewards for years of labor in America's hardest jobs. There are Villa Juárez town associations in Houston, Dallas, Chicago, and even Nebraska. The largest of these, the Fundación de Villa Juárez, took the lead in constructing the town market, and returning migrants helped to fund the improvements to the plaza and the church.

Migration provides opportunities for people in Villa Juárez. New migrants rely on the experience of older generations of migrants to identify places to go, jobs to apply for, and skills to acquire. As in many older migrant-sending towns, generations of experience have accrued in Villa Juárez, and remittances are a major part of the local economy. In central Mexico, the rural economy has long relied on migrants to support both those who do not

Between Here and There. Daniel Morales, Oxford University Press. © Oxford University Press 2024.
DOI: 10.1093/oso/9780197612590.003.0001

have access to their own plot of land, and those who do. When individuals or households choose to migrate, they rely on pre-established structures and retrace the experiences of those who have migrated before them. When migrants return with money, goods, and information, they are not only helping their own families but also encouraging others to migrate. In this way, the migration is self-constitutive, with people's actions on both sides of the border creating changes that trigger further migration.

In researching the states' history and spending time in Cerritos, Villa Juárez, Rioverde, Cárdenas, and many smaller towns and villages, it became clear that the region and migration have long been interconnected. The now-defunct railroad station at Cerritos not only carried sulfur and copper ore, corn, and other goods to distant markets but also transported generations of people east to Tampico and north to the United States. Listening to the history of Villa Juárez and its people's migration, I was struck by how similar these stories were to others I had heard across the region. Since the mid-nineteenth century, migrants had come from the northern border states of Sonora, Chihuahua, Coahuila, Nuevo León, and Tamaulipas. However, the large-scale migration that dominated the twentieth century was primarily driven by migration from the central/north-central states of Guanajuato, Michoacán, Jalisco, Aguascalientes, Zacatecas, Durango, and San Luis Potosí. The history of Mexican migration to the United States is a two-way connection that binds villages to the communities in the north.[1]

These close connections between *aqui y alla* ("here and there") do not appear in most Mexican American histories, which focus on the alienation of belonging in the United States. There is a disconnect between the history of migration, the history of Mexican American communities in the United States, and the ways in which people in the past described their own experiences of migration. Much of what has been written about Mexican migration has centered on the role and actions of the US government, especially immigrant policy and border enforcement, showing the ways in which policy has shaped the experiences of migrants and marginalized ethnic communities.[2] Another set of work has focused on how immigrants fared over time in the United States and primarily revolved around questions of adjustment, acculturation, assimilation or lack thereof, and identity. This work has tended to stress the formation of settled communities, labor struggles, and processes of racial identity formation as the migrations of the 1910s led to permanent settlement in the 1920s.[3]

The longstanding pattern of circular migration, especially in the first half of the twentieth century, has gotten far less attention. Although cyclical migration patterns and Mexican villages' dependency on remittances in the late twentieth century have been examined, this model was established decades earlier.[4] This book revisits the era of the first mass migration, between 1910 and 1940—that is, from the Mexican Revolution to World War II. It reconsiders Mexican American community formation within the broader context of ongoing circular migration, both between the United States and Mexico and within the United States. The latter dynamic has been least recognized or understood. Permanently settled migrants were in the minority; most were constantly on the move. They trekked around the country following work in agriculture, mining, and industry. They voted with their feet to resist local vagrancy laws and labor agents who tried to control them. They organized mutual aid organizations and unions. And they sought to return to their hometowns in Mexico. Circular migration and settlement were not successive phases, but always concurrent and dynamically related. This can be best seen by going full circle, starting and ending with communities in Mexico.

These continual links to Mexico offer a new perspective on assimilation, political identity, and organizing in the migrant community. By expanding the field of analysis across national borders, this book captures the ways that transnational practices and ties shaped communities in both countries. People and communities engaged in a common currency of exchange—experience, information, organizing, and ideologies—that linked them across time and space. Migrants rarely challenged conceptions of community centered in the nation-state; the politics of both Mexico and the United States made that impossible. For these migrants, transnational migration did not mean transcending the state but finding ways to stay connected even when they were apart. Most migrants' daily lives were rooted in one state or another, but their communities, politics, culture, norms, and family expectations took the form they did as a result of transnational currents.

This book builds its claims about circular, regional, and local migration networks and patterns on new data from two census cohort studies—a national study and a local case study in Chicago. Using the US Census, Mexican Census, and border and city records, it traces Mexican migration patterns from 1910 to 1940 of 2,500 families. It is the only study of individual and family migration patterns across the first three decades of mass migration between Mexico and the United States. (See the Appendix for details.)

This quantitative material underscores several important patterns. First, circular migration was more extensive than scholars have recognized. More than 50% of Mexican migrants who had arrived in the years before 1920 went back to Mexico at some point before 1930. This trend was strongest in the Midwest and California, regions that received the bulk of their migrants from central Mexico. Interstate migration was just as common an experience as international migration for migrants in this era. Mexicans circulated not only within regional circuits but also across regions and industries. For example, it was common for an agricultural worker in Texas to become a beet worker in Michigan or a factory worker in California. Most Mexican migrants who went to urban centers such as Los Angeles, San Antonio, or Chicago between 1910 and 1930 left within ten years.

There were multiple types of migration, with local and regional circuits overlapping national and transnational circuits across the United States and back to central Mexico. This migration was not unidirectional, and many people did not live in any location for very long. Primarily migratory laborers, they moved in alignment with employment opportunities. A large proportion of them, more than half, circulated back into Mexico regularly or semiregularly. Many crossed the border as seasonal agricultural laborers, a significant proportion of whom followed regional migratory circuits: cotton from east Texas to Oklahoma, vegetable harvests up and down the Rio Grande, beet harvests from Colorado to Michigan, and fruit and vegetable crops from the Imperial Valley to the San Joaquin Valley of California. Medium and large cities acted as hubs of migration as networks guided people into and out of them, following the major railroad routes and industries. Circular migration, both within the United States and between the two countries, was both regular and highly irregular. There were some established seasonal circuits, but a lot of this movement was haphazard. Migrants might express their intentions to go back every year, but such regularity was often the exception rather than the norm.

Second, physical and economic mobility was highly dependent on where Mexicans fit within the larger migrant economy. Whether individuals or families settled down or migrated, whether they began to identify as Mexican American or not, were choices framed by their employment and community. Seasonal unemployment was structurally built into many of these jobs, hence the migratory life. Most people migrated back to Mexico or within regional circuits. Moving to other jobs was one of the few means by which they could improve their wages and working conditions. Due to agricultural

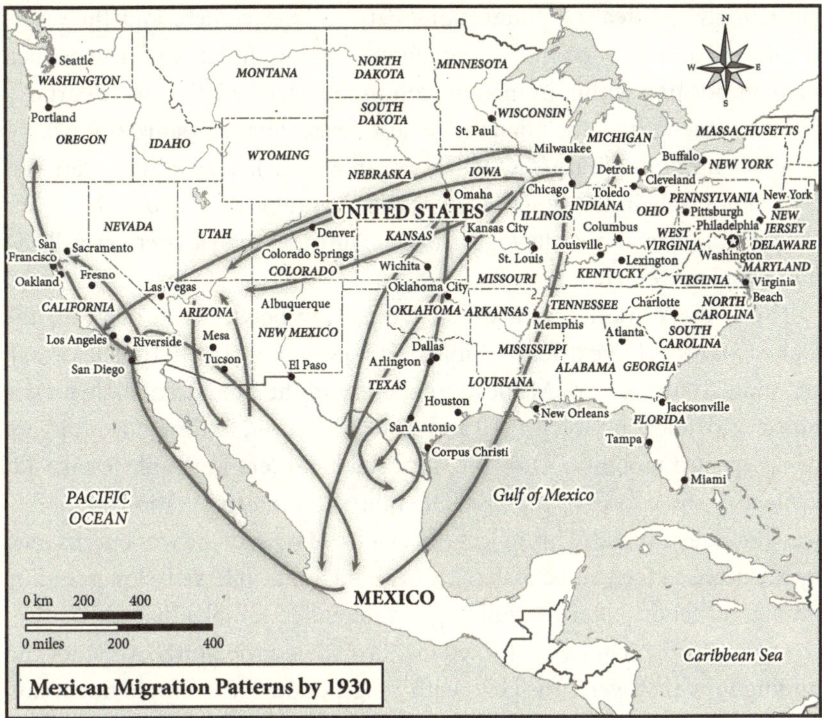

Figure I.1 Regional and local migration circuits overlapped with national and transnational routes throughout the 1920s. Most of the new migration was driven by people from central Mexico.

picking cycles, many were precluded from settling even if they wanted to. Their trajectories varied, however. Some could and did become more settled over time, bringing their families from Mexico to the United States, but most Mexican migrants did not have the stability needed to do so and relocated without their loved ones according to the particular needs of the industries that employed them.

The two major exceptions to this pattern were tenant farmers and the stable "middle class." Farmers and their children had little economic or spatial mobility given the exploitive cotton contracts into which they were locked in the farm economy of Texas. The small but critical middle class in Mexican communities was also stationary. Their settlement was made possible by the migratory majority, and vice versa. They were the brokers who formed the core of ethnic Mexican neighborhoods, especially the civic life of these places, but they also acted as critical nodes in migrant networks, particularly by creating connections between newcomers and their new employers and locations. Their economic stability in large part depended on their position within immigrant communities, where they were part of a key constituency that included small businesses, church organizations, labor unions, and *mutualistas* (mutual aid organizations). This middle class was critical not only in the functioning of the migrant economy but also in the spread of information, ideologies, and organizations that later crystallized into social movements.

Third, the workings of a migrant economy between Mexico and the United States led to extremely limited socioeconomic mobility. The overall economic status of both Mexican migrants and their children made no significant advances between 1910 and 1940. Moreover, settling down did not bring upward mobility.[5] Only the most stable settlers were able to take advantage of some form of economic mobility, and intergenerational mobility was likewise minimal. This reflects the nature of most of the work performed by Mexicans in the United States. Mexican migrants followed a longstanding immigrant labor pattern of holding a different set of jobs than the native-born workforce.[6] They were locked into low-wage agricultural, railroad, and mining jobs that were unstable, with long periods of unemployment and strong barriers to upward mobility. Both the structures of the industries and the dynamics on the ground led employers to use Mexican migrants as the base labor of the American West.

The structural patterns that shape migration today were created during these decades before World War II. In 1900, fewer than 3,000 people officially migrated from Mexico to the United States, but by 1920, tens of thousands were traveling in both directions every year. Following the conquest and annexation of the Southwest by the United States in the mid-nineteenth century, the industrialization of northern Mexico and the American West uprooted millions of people. Many were displaced within Mexico, some migrated, and many more joined the revolution. The Mexican Revolution drove migration from central Mexico on a scale never before seen. Some 500,000 migrants traveled north, the bulk of them into Texas. Whereas young men from *haciendas* and mines had previously dominated the migrant flow, this stream carried families and people from every economic class. The revolution coincided with an economic boom in the American Southwest.

American companies imported the industrial working class, mainly from Europe and increasingly from Asia and Latin America. Anti-immigration restrictions passed in 1917 when the United States entered World War

I ended the influx of European workers. Concurrently, the US Secretary of Labor created a series of exceptions to immigration restrictions (notably the ban on foreign contract labor). Under this program, 72,000 Mexican workers crossed into the United States over a three-year period. After the war, the 1921 Immigration Act and the landmark 1924 Johnson-Reed Immigration Act severely restricted migration from Europe and Asia, ending an era of those regions as major sources of labor even as it exempted the countries of the western hemisphere, especially Mexico, from numerical quotas.

Through the 1920s, the US economy and demand for labor continued to grow. In the American West, capitalists depended on non-whites and immigrants for the railroad, mining, and agricultural industries. They sought to create a de-politized and racialized labor force that lacked the protections of white settlers/citizens. In this, they were aided by immigration laws that kept these workers in increasing legal precarity, the establishment of the Border Patrol in 1924, and the criminalization of undocumented entry in 1929, as well as by state laws. Seen as "others," "birds of passage," and criminals, these migrants were easy targets for expulsion in the repatriations of the 1930s. With the start of the Bracero Program in 1942, the US government replaced unregulated migration with regulated labor, contracted and imported under its control.

In Mexico, public discourse and the government increasingly turned against migration. The 1917 Constitution limited migration to those who had labor contracts, and President Álvaro Obregon devoted resources to repatriating those in the north and to creating colonies (free agricultural land to those who were willing to relocate, clear, and work the claim), a position held by every Mexican president through Cárdenas. With the 1926 Migration Law, the government went further, creating a migration police force to regulate and stop uncontrolled migration. During that decade, however, the Cristero War, an armed conflict between the Mexican government and Catholic rebels that raged from 1926 to 1929, drove tens of thousands from their homes and encouraged local governments to promote migration as an alternative to land redistribution. As a result, hundreds of thousands of Mexicans continued to migrate. By 1930, nearly one million Mexican-born people lived in the United States. The Great Depression put official policy to the test as returning migrants created a series of crises over land redistribution. In other words, on both sides of the border, the state acted to control migrants, shaping their lives through law, policing, and violence.

Why did people migrate? I asked people in Mexico and the United States why they had gone north, expecting to hear stories of broken dreams. Migrants needed to raise enough money to make the journey, survive obstacles on the road that ranged from bribes to violence, and face the extremely dangerous and increasingly difficult task of crossing the border. They were often exploited and discriminated against once in the United States. Why would anyone assume these risks? Many of those I interviewed in San Luis Potosí and Guanajuato migrated during the Bracero Program era and had family members who had made the journey around the revolution. When I asked if they knew about their relatives' motivations, they frequently described their ancestors' choice to migrate as a necessity but also an opportunity.

Migrants and family members of migrants from before the Bracero Program told stories that highlighted common themes: the Mexican Revolution, railroads, Cristeros, mining, cotton, and sugar beets. But nearly all of them also had a destination in mind and knew someone in the United States. They described how their families came to join uncles, cousins, brothers, and fathers in communities like Miami, El Monte, San Antonio, and Chicago. In studying the places where migration became deeply ingrained in the local culture, it was possible to see the paths created by early migrants. Mass migration on the ground looks like many micro migrations between communities, networks, and families in both sending and receiving places. As migrants went north, they sent back information, and when they returned, they brought back experience. This experience, combined with money raised from others in the community, made it easier for others to go north. These networks of people and information helped migrants mitigate and navigate the risks of migrating. This set of reinforcing logics also made up the political economy of migration, which affected migrant-sending areas as much as it affected Mexican American communities.

People left their homes in search of jobs or to escape violence, but how they did it, where they went, and which places they returned to were highly dependent on their particular positions within the larger economy. Railroad workers were the most mobile and the least likely to stay in a job for long. Cotton and beet workers also moved regularly. Regional migratory circuits developed in California, Texas, Arizona, and the Midwest, but these regional circuits regularly overlapped to a large extent with workers moving from region to region and from industry to industry. Migration could not have functioned without recruiters and brokers, who acted as the critical link between new arrivals and older communities and institutions. They helped migrants acquire housing and jobs, redress wrongs, and negotiate a foreign world as much as the migrants' direct links back home did. Just as importantly, Mexican communities in the United States were anchored by a stable minority of skilled workers and owners of small businesses such as grocery stores, pool halls, and boarding houses. This was the middle class—the men and women who made up most *mutualistas*, charity organizations, and civil rights organizations.

By 1930, there were about a million Mexican migrants in the United States, with tens of thousands crossing in both directions every year. Mexican and Mexican American spaces were being created across the West and Midwest, as people settled and created communities. In Mexico, villages and towns were changed by the rise of transnational circular migration. Hundreds of thousands of families were being supported by work in *El Norte*, pushing traditional family structures to change as women took on more public responsibilities. These practices gave rise to a culture of migration that saw going north as a path for young men to support their families and a rural way of life. Circular migration became normalized across both societies, despite the significant efforts both nations undertook to control and end this reality.

Migration met with a range of responses. Scholars and intellectuals in the United States at the time sought to understand and explain Mexican migrants through a European immigrant framework oriented towards settlement and assimilation. Politicians argued about the "Mexican Problem" and quotas. The Mexican government promoted its *México de Afuera*, with the post-revolutionary state as the defender of the people. Mexican American activists in the Southwest generally sought to maintain Mexican culture while working for civil rights. Some radical organizations such as the *Partido Liberal Mexicano* (PLM), Industrial Workers of the World (IWW), and communist unions pushed back against a conception of belonging centered on the nation-state. Union leaders Emma Tenayuca and Luisa Moreno articulated visions of polity for people of the borderlands that did not depend on one state or the other but were based on their labor, common peoplehood, and history. Their transborder visions were violently repressed. In this era, the rise of mass migration forced intellectuals, migrants, and governments to think about Mexican migrants' place in society, but their discourse always lagged practice.[7] In letters and interviews, nearly all migrants saw themselves as primarily "Mexican" even as they built a world of transnational practices that challenged that identity. Most could not conceive of themselves as something else; they were part of the community they had left. However, they did use these frameworks to organize for material change and advocate for a broader conception of "Mexican." Those who returned used an expansive vision of *México de Afuera* to lay claim to citizenship and land in Mexico. Those who stayed in the United States joined efforts to lay claim to better pay, working conditions, and rights from the New Deal state, creating a base for later organizing. Migrants fought for recognition in both societies.

The politics of migration on both sides of the border was the product of reactions to people and the local social structures they created. In the United States, the government responded to migrants' organizing with campaigns of intimidation, violence, and ultimately, repatriation. Meanwhile, the Mexican government responded by discouraging people from migrating and by seeking to control their migration and, later, their return. During the Great Depression, both governments, along with most civic organizations, saw repatriation as the only solution. Those who left to return to Mexico, sometimes dividing their families, pushed the limits of what was possible, joining protests and agrarian movements for land. For their children, adjustment was difficult but possible. Yet even mass land redistribution was not enough to satisfy the demand for better conditions and opportunities. In the 1940s, migrants and communities turned the Bracero Program to their advantage, relying on local networks to operate, creating transnational families, going on strikes, forming unions, defying expectations, and evading the program when needed. To maintain their rural way of life and improve their situation, they had to leave again. Even as both countries saw migrants as problems, as outsiders ineligible for participation in the nation, migrants continued to build transnational lives through the twentieth century.

The title of this book, *Between Here and There—entre aqui y alla*—places the dislocation of people at the center. Millions took part in migration between Mexico and the United States during the first half of the twentieth century. Many stayed and built a new world together; others returned, using their migration to enhance their own lives or those of their family in Mexico; many lived lives in between. Mexicans circulated, worked, and resided in a vast space from central Mexico to the upper reaches of the American Midwest. This space was held together through social networks that expanded the geographic parameters of migration while fostering consistent communication. Building on local and regional work as well as transnational and cross-border scholarship, this book argues that the relationship between economic transformations, US and Mexican domestic policies, and migrants' actions must all be taken into account to understand how migration became a continuing reality.

To showcase the ways that migration to individual places were part of larger national and international processes, this book looks at dynamics on the ground. It explores town networks in San Luis Potosí, remittances in Guanajuato, consuls and newspapers in Texas, and small businesses and personal networks in Chicago. It offers a set of case studies that address different regions, but when seen together present a transnational whole. Each chapter focuses on a different aspect of the political economy of migration, but the dynamics they discuss operated in other regions as well.

Chapters 1 and 2 track the formation of an economy of migrant labor across northern Mexico and the American Southwest as it disrupted older forms of production. This new economy was intensified by the Mexican Revolution, which unleashed further cycles of displacement, refugees, and relocation. Mass migration took off with the pull of industrialization (and its relatively high wages) in northern Mexico and the resulting push of economic and social instability in Mexico. Violence further limited people's choices and drove them to leave home for safety and survival. Two states in the heart of migrant-sending north-central Mexico, Guanajuato and San Luis Potosí, illustrate the preconditions of land alienation, mining industrialization, and railroad construction that fueled migratory patterns. Town-based networks provided the transportation, capital, and information migrants needed to travel north.

The narrative then shifts to the United States, where political and business elites recruited migrants to create a government-subsidized, low-wage, industrial workforce that transformed the American West. Immigrant labor made the mining, cotton, fruits, sugar beets, and railroad industries possible, while urban centers became manufacturing hubs connected to regional and international migration routes. As they were drawn into migrant labor, workers struggled under precarious circumstances without the benefit of legal protections or many avenues for socioeconomic advancement. Chapters 2 and 3 demonstrate how migrants navigated their transnational lives, finding ways to circumvent and resist control at the border and in the interior.

The exodus of 10% of the population caused considerable alarm across Mexican society. As more and more people migrated, they sent back information that enabled others to follow their routes. Circular migration reinforced this dynamic as many returning migrants brought back and shared firsthand knowledge and experience. Chapter 4 focuses on the public sphere and the ways in which the press, bureaucrats, and others reacted to these changes. Migrants, along with local officials, consular officials, and migrant agents, were as influential in shaping events as federal officials were.

The Great Depression created unemployment crises that hit the Mexican communities in the United States hard. Chapters 5 and 6 examine how this impacted San Antonio and Southern California, two places where massive agricultural economies were built on migrant labor. Building on the long history of *México de Afuera*, the Mexican government, *La Prensa*, and nearly every civic organization in Texas supported the return of Mexican citizens and were critical to making repatriation a reality for them. Simultaneously, in Southern California, local officials led the largest repatriation campaign in the country, fueling calls for unionization among Mexican workers.

Chapter 7 shows how in Mexico returning migrants vied for land and resources with those who had stayed behind, increasing the pressure on the government to enact land redistribution. However, land reform did not resolve the structural causes of migration, and in the late 1930s, and especially the 1940s, a second generation from central Mexico moved north across the border as an economic survival strategy. From this point forward, migration was an important component of the rural economy of central Mexico, one that supported rather than competed with rural landholding. By the time World War II accelerated the need for Mexican labor in the United States, migration had become ingrained in the US economy. The Bracero Program formalized and sanctioned the political economy of migration between Mexico and the United States.

Migration between Mexico and the United States continues to be a topic in the headlines daily. The patterns of contemporary migration—the dependence of industrial and agricultural employers on Latin American labor, the locations where people cluster and the trajectories they travel, and Mexico's dependence on remittances to support the rural economy—were all established during the first half of the twentieth century. So too did the "Mexican Problem," the vision of walls and a sealed border, a border patrol that has grown into the largest police force in the United States, and the mass expulsions of people from the polity originate during these decades. At the same time, migrants also established a tradition of challenging companies and governments through daily action, civic organizations, and labor organizing. It has been forgotten that the years 1933 to 1940 witnessed the largest organizing activity among migrant workers before the Chicano movement of the 1960s. The expansive political visions of these Mexicans in the United States continue to reverberate today.

1

Revolution and Migration

The Rise of "Migration Fever" in San Luis Potosí and Guanajuato, 1890–1920

Manuel Pérez, an agricultural laborer from Guanajuato, heard stories: "I became acquainted with a number of boys in my hometown who excited me with the idea of coming to work in the United States." He explained that "since I didn't have the means with which to come, I told those friends that I would meet them here. One of them, however, lent me enough for the ride to Ciudad Juárez, Chihuahua, telling me that we would take an *enganche* [labor contract] in El Paso. I came [to the United States], leaving my wife and my child, who was then about five."[1]

Later, when he arrived in California, he ran into other people from his hometown who gave him advice on not taking railroad work. Perez was just one of dozens who left his town in the 1910s. His account contains many of the constant refrains in migrants' stories: interest sparked by information via friends and families, financing the trip by borrowing from acquaintances, using information from hometown contacts to ease the journey, and leaving behind family, with the intention of sending money back.

The conditions that propelled this mass migration were created by the industrialization of the Mexico-US borderlands and the violence of the Mexican Revolution. However, large-scale structural forces do not explain why one area, but not another, might send many migrants. This chapter examines the interplay of economic forces, revolutionary violence, and the personal choices involved in leaving. It does so by looking at two states in central Mexico: Guanajuato, in the heart of the Bajío valley, and San Luis Potosí, in the less densely populated north-central part of the country. While mass migration was initiated by labor recruiters and later encouraged by revolutionary violence, it grew to such a large scale because interpersonal networks spread information and established durable pathways. These networks are important for migrations everywhere, but to date, no in-depth

Between Here and There. Daniel Morales, Oxford University Press. © Oxford University Press 2024.
DOI: 10.1093/oso/9780197612590.003.0002

studies have illuminated how they were established and reproduced in early twentieth-century Mexico.

Much has been written about the politics and economics underlying mass migration, but far less is known about the migrants themselves. From their perspectives—revealed in letters to family members, in their songs, and in interviews conducted by researchers, government officials, and others—migration looks not like a process controlled by impersonal global and political forces, but rather like a dynamic continuously contested by events on the ground and the actions of people. Migrants' personal networks operated within the larger structural forces of revolutions, government policies, and labor markets; they too constituted elements of the larger structures of migration.

The *Porfiriato* and the Railroads

Porfirio Díaz became president in Mexico City via a coup in 1876, he would go on to rule nearly uninterrupted for more than three decades. The *Porfiriato* pursued a liberal developmentalist agenda; altered the nation's agricultural, mining, and industrial sectors; and intended to reform the economy and society along "scientific" lines. The regime supported the expansion of private land ownership over communal lands, consolidation of land under *hacendados* (plantation owners), and shifting to exportable commodity crops, such as sugar and henequen, rather than crops for local consumption. Across Mexico, land holdings became more concentrated as indigenous villages and independent farmers lost land through privatization, consolidation, and outright theft. In the mining, oil, and railroad industries, Díaz encouraged heavy foreign investment through land and tax concessions, the use of police and soldiers to create favorable labor conditions, and the creation of new settlements for foreigners. His large patronage network enabled various sectors of society to become part of the political system while maintaining their ostensible independence. Those outside this network found a violent peace enforced by federal *Rurales*, the mounted gendarmeries, and a modernized army. Rebellions were put down across the periphery of the Mexican state; in the case of the indigenous Yaqui tribe in Sonora, this resulted in repression and slavery. Díaz sought to keep a balance between British, German, US, and French investments in order to deter foreign interference such as the US and French invasions in the nineteenth century.[2]

Traditionally, foreign trade in Mexico went to Veracruz and overseas markets; railroads changed this equation. Following its victory in the US-Mexico War, the United States annexed the northern half of Mexico. Two groups of US investors vied to build a national railroad network, with large financial subsides and land grants from the government. One group built the *Ferrocarriles Nacionales de México* (Mexican National Railway); going from Mexico City to Nuevo Laredo in south Texas, it passed through San Miguel Allende, San Luis Potosí, Saltillo, and Monterrey, with branch lines through Morelia to Pátzcuaro and El Salto. A second group, which also controlled the Santa Fe railroad in the US Southwest, built the *Ferrocarril Central Mexicano* (Mexican Central Railway). This much larger network ran one main line through the sugar-producing areas of Morelos to Mexico City and another north to Torreón and El Paso, where it connected to the Santa Fe railroad lines to Chicago. The network ran a major branch through the Bajío states

Figure 1.1 The construction of the Mexican Central Railway created the infrastructure that tens of thousands used to migrate to the United States. William Henry Jackson, Mexican Central Railway train at station, Mexico, ca. 1880–1897. Library of Congress Prints and Photographs Division, LC-D418-30155.

of Jalisco, Aguascalientes, Michoacán, and Guanajuato and another branch east to San Luis Potosí, Tampico, and north to Monterrey.[3]

Construction of the railroad projects and the concurrent mining boom would not have been possible without a large labor force. An estimated 40,000 people worked on the construction of the Mexican Central. Most of them were recruited from central Mexico by *enganchadores* (labor contractors), and after their time on the railroad, they searched for work in other industrial centers. There they were joined by hundreds of thousands of peasants who had lost their traditional lands to *haciendas* (plantations). This large-scale internal migration and displacement would not have been possible without American investment and was one of the major preconditions for the subsequent mass migration.[4]

The completion of the *Ferrocarril Nacional de México* and the *Ferrocarril Central Mexicano* in 1888 and 1884, respectively, created the connections necessary for goods and people to travel deep into both nations. The Mexican Central linked to the Southern Pacific Railway and the Topeka and Santa Fe Railway at Ciudad Juárez/El Paso, while the Mexican National ended at Laredo, where it joined up with the Texas-Mexican and the International and Great Northern railway systems. Initially, the railroads boosted the economy. The Mexican gross domestic product (GDP) grew 3.7% a year from 1880 to 1910, while transportation costs fell dramatically and tonnage increased.[5] Internally, the vast new network boosted interstate trade, grew regional centers, and integrated the Mexican state.[6] Over time, the railroads generated social tensions as companies and *hacendados* came to own most of the land around them, leading to many cases of violence and small revolts.[7] Internationally, they tied the Mexican economy to the United States, especially in the Mexican north. With the flow of capital across borders, the increasing movement of goods, use of wage laborers, and growth of migratory labor inside of Mexico, certain sectors of the Mexican workforce were moving towards a common labor market along the borderlands.

San Luis Potosí

The *Porfiriato* in San Luis Potosí is, in many ways, a microcosm of the economic changes that swept over central Mexico. San Luis Potosí lies in the central north of Mexico; the state slopes from the high plains in central/northern Mexico east towards the lowland jungles of the Huasteca. Although

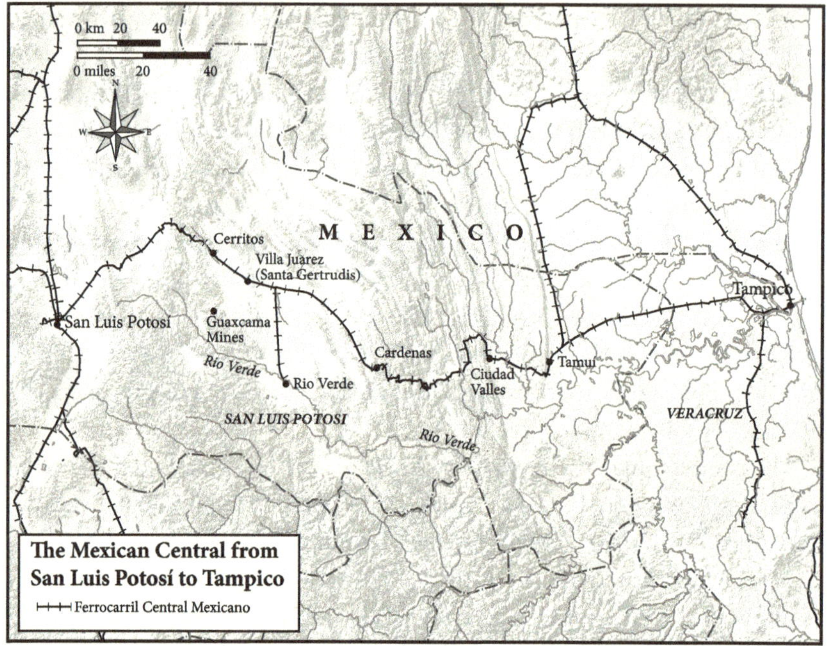

Figure 1.2 The Mexican Central Railway from San Luis Potosí to Tampico.

much less dense than states in the western Bajío, it became a center of migration. With large mining-, railroad-, and plantation-based agricultural sectors, its story illustrates the relationship between economic change, violence, and migration.

In the 1880s, both the Mexican Central and Mexican National railroads ran lines into and out of the city of San Luis Potosí, the state capital, linking the interior of the country to the north and east. While the Mexican National ran a branch line into the mining center of Matehuala, the most significant rail project ran east to the port of Tampico, in the state of Tamaulipas, on the Gulf of Mexico. Construction of the Mexican Central turned out to be much more complicated than most investors thought, requiring twelve years of construction across several mountain passes to cover the distance between Tampico and San Luis Potosí. In addition to the normal concessions of land next to the railroads, the state government levied a special tax from 1878 to 1880 to finance the line. After the railroad was completed in 1890, San Luis Potosí and Tamaulipas experienced growing inequality. In the city of San Luis Potosí itself, economic growth lagged, and a series of railroad strikes

Figure 1.3 Construction of the Mexican Central Railway through the Zona Media from San Luis Potosí to Tampico in 1902. "El Ferrocarril en Rioverde," 1902, Museo Nacional de los Ferrocarriles Mexicanos, México DF.

Figure 1.4 The Mexican National Railway in San Luis Potosí. William Henry Jackson, Mexico National R. R. Station, ca. 1880–1897. Library of Congress Prints and Photographs Division, LC-D401-3973.

in 1908 broke out over wages and the segregation between Mexican and US migrant workers.[8]

The construction of the railroad encouraged the consolidation of land from small holdings into larger ones on an unprecedented scale. *Hacendados* in the center and south of the state took over their surrounding villages. By 1910, an astounding 82% of the population in the state lived within *hacienda* boundaries.[9] In and around Tamazunchale in the state's southeastern Huasteca region, where new *hacendados* took land from indigenous villages, a series of violent disputes continued until the revolution. Many of the valleys in the Huasteca became cattle operations, and large areas were fenced in with barbed wire so that villages could not use the *hacienda* land for foraging, as had been their traditional right. As the number of independent landowners fell, *rancherías* became smaller and less numerous; as *haciendas* grew, large numbers of towns lost common lands they had previously claimed. Twenty-two families came to own a third of the state's land.[10]

The concentration of land into *haciendas*, loss of autonomy by villages, and movement towards income based on wage labor had dramatic effects on the agricultural economy. Production was reoriented towards commercial crops for export and away from subsistence farming. Cotton, sugar, coffee, tobacco, and henequen production rose dramatically. As profits from maize production dropped comparatively, it had to be imported from the United States.[11] Furthermore, the real wages of rural workers and conditions of tenants and sharecroppers deteriorated over time.[12]

Traditionally, silver and gold mining made up the largest sector of the San Luis Potosí economy, but new metals soon came to rival them. From 1890 onwards, the smelting of lead, copper, iron, zinc, and sulfur grew exponentially, with the Guggenheim-owned American Smelting and Refining Company (ASARCO) buying up the previously independent *Companía Metalurgica Mexicana* and, later, the American National Metallurgical Company. The presence of large US-dominated firms in the state tended, over the long term, to spur migration to large urban centers. This was not in the interest of San Luis Potosí *hacendados*, who resented the higher wages that the mining companies paid their workers. In one case, local *hacendados* refused to sell land to US mining officials, who explained in a company report, "The proximity of an industrial center always does serious harm to agricultural concerns, since the latter then never pay the wages offered by the former."[13]

Before the revolution, the relationship between the *hacendados* in the area and the people who worked for them was exploitative. The Zona Media's short rainy season meant that irrigation was needed for the most demanding agricultural production, something that benefited the largest and most capitalized *hacendados* of the region, such as the Hacienda de San Anton Guaxcama, the Laguna de Santo Domingo, and Angostura. Angostura was owned by Antonio Espinosa y Cervantes, one of the richest men of the state. The *hacienda* bordered Santa Gertrudis de la Carbonera (also known as Villa de Carbonera) on two sides to the south. The residents of the town held a grant from colonial decrees to about 1,700 hectares. In 1879, Espinosa y Cervantes claimed about 350 of those hectares as part of Angostura. When the residents of the town brought in a judge and government surveyors who upheld their claim, Espinosa y Cervantes used his connections to have state troops resurvey the land in his favor. The village, like many in the state, was completely enclosed by *haciendas* by 1910.

To the southwest, the Hacienda de San Anton Guaxcama had existed in one form or another since the seventeenth century. The *hacienda* boasted more than a hundred families, its own aqueduct system, a convent, and vast ranch lands. Indeed, the tiny church town of San Gertrudis de la Carbonera seemed more like a satellite of the *hacienda* than the main market town of the area. This imbalance in power between the people of the valley and the state elites had only grown since the establishment of sulfur mines in the mountains above Guaxcama during the late colonial period. However, these mines remained small until the railroad was completed in 1890.

After the Mexican Central completed the branch line linking San Luis Potosí to the Gulf of Mexico, most of the freight of the railroad went through the valley, with passenger and fueling stops at Cerritos Cárdenas and Rioverde, the largest city of the valley. Although most of the agricultural production of the area continued to be sold in local markets, major changes occurred at the mines in the area. Two new mines were established above Cerritos and Guaxcama. By 1910, more than 700 miners worked at the Guaxcama mines. These workers supported several hundred other jobs in the immediate vicinity, especially the nearby town of Buenavista.[14]

Guanajuato

Guanajuato encompasses two very different regions: a mountainous north that is rich in mineral ores and the Bajío valley in the south. Historically one of the regions in Mexico where capitalist production most shaped society, Guanajuato saw greater economic growth than neighboring San Luis Potosí.[15] The state experienced a silver and gold mining boom when the United States began to purchase large amounts of silver and American companies bought and recapitalized old mines in Mexico.[16]

However, it was the southern part of the state, with its massive agricultural region, that had greater consequences for the history of migration. Located northwest of the central plateau of Mexico, the Bajío basin stretches across five states and constitutes the most productive agricultural region in Mexico. In the Guanajuato Bajío, there was a mixed economy with many small landholders (*rancheros*) but in the years before the revolution, *haciendas* consolidated land from autonomous villages and become more powerful

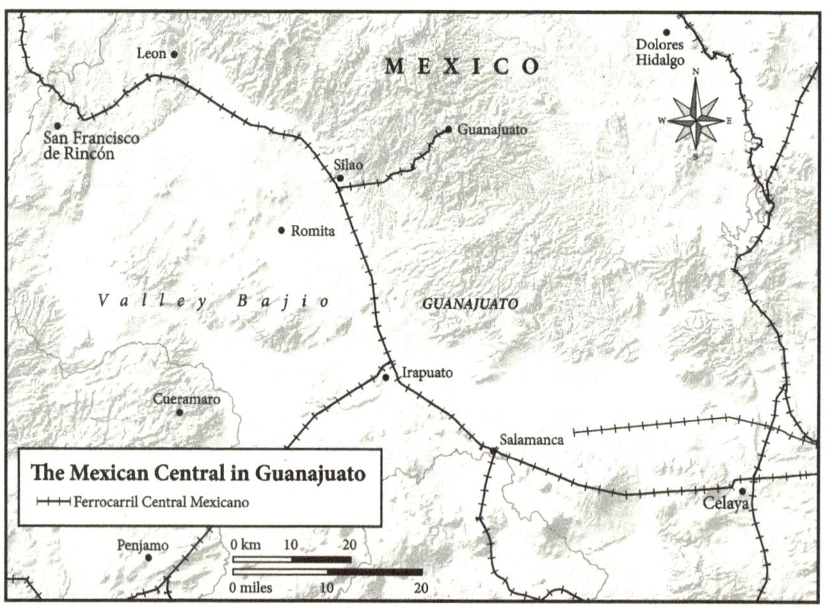

Figure 1.5 The Mexican Central Railway in Guanajuato, from San Francisco de Rincón to Celaya, with Leon, Silao, Guanajuato, Romita, Irapuato, Salamanca, Pénjamo, and other towns shown.

than the numerous independent *rancheros*. Landholdings were smaller than in the central north, mostly because they held a larger percentage of highly fertile lands. The result was strong profits even in years when the production of maize decreased.[17]

The cities of Celaya and San Francisco de Rincón were situated at different ends of the state of Guanajuato but shared several traits. Eventually, hundreds of men, almost all of whom who worked in agriculture, would leave these towns to work in the United States. The state capital of Guanajuato at the center of the mining economy had traditionally been the center of economic activity. The arrival of the railroads changed this; by 1900, León, Silao, and other agricultural projection hubs had become the centers of population growth.[18] Celaya's economy, like that of many cities in the area, was agricultural. Located near the eastern end of the Bajío basin, it was surrounded by some of the country's richest agricultural land. A center of trade and agricultural production since the colonial period, it also became a manufacturing center. Because the Mexican Central and Mexican National railroads converged at Celaya, it was an important junction for the movement of goods. In addition to a railyard, the city had telegraph operations, warehouses, and oil- and food-processing factories as well as distilleries and an electrical generation plant.

San Francisco de Rincón had no mining or manufacturing economy. The first city linking Guanajuato with the mountainous Altos de Jalisco, it was critical market town for farmers from the Altos and home to a large agricultural economy and several major *haciendas*. In 1884, a line of the Mexican Central established a station linking it to the rest the country. As cities in the region grew, they began to pull migrants in from the surrounding countryside. By 1907, San Francisco de Rincón had developed into a small industrial center teeming with small businesses, especially hat-making. The earliest recorded migrant from the town was Gumercindo Ramírez, who was probably one of many who joined the railroads in those years. By 1910, there were newspaper reports of groups of men leaving the town to work for the railroads and the fields of Texas.[19] The towns of San Francisco de Rincón and Celaya became centers of migration activity as citizens moved out from them to other parts of Mexico. While the people who migrated from San Luis Potosí often came from mining or railroad backgrounds, those who migrated from Guanajuato came primarily from agricultural backgrounds.

Haciendas and *El Norte*

In 1906, Jose Encarnacion Impina wrote to Luis Toranzo, the owner of the Cerro Prieto Hacienda southeast of Rioverde, San Luis Potosí, "I am thinking of selling all my *haciendas*, not because they are not profitable or cause me any losses, but I already hear the approaching steps of the commune. You cannot imagine how the countryside is here in San Luis . . . it is like a desert, and the people are departing in droves for the north."[20] Though clearly an exaggeration, Impina's letter reveals the mindset of landowners in the state. No large-scale violence had broken out, but small acts of violence caused fear among *hacendados* and spurred migration by workers. In the countryside, *hacendados* came to see their control of local labor under threat from mining companies, railroads, migration north, and violent revolution.

As large-scale mining and export-oriented agriculture expanded, people in central and northern Mexico increasingly became unemployed or wage laborers rather than subsistence farmers. When market prices dropped, greater numbers were reduced to poverty than ever before. This new relationship between labor, land, and capital also threatened traditional hierarchies, as *hacendados* suddenly found themselves competing for workers. Migration tended to come from areas that were undergoing capitalist transformation, or at least adjacent to it, mainly from small towns a few days walk from rail stations. This caused large-scale internal migration within Mexico as this transformation unfolded. When news of even higher wages across the border started to circulate, employers also found themselves competing against jobs in *El Norte*. Wages in Texas and California were four to nine times larger than those available in Guanajuato, Jalisco, and Michoacán.[21] Some *hacendados*, especially in the north, embraced these changes, recruiting workers from central Mexico and rivaling Laguna operations by offering higher wages and by providing schools, healthcare, and other services.[22] Others fought against these changes to maintain traditional patron/peon relationships. Although Article 11 of the 1857 Constitution had established the right to enter and leave the country, various tactics had been used to keep workers on the land, and *hacendados* increasingly turned to more forceful methods.[23]

Amado Delgado, a *jefe político* (political machine boss) in Guanajuato, resolved to stop migration, which he saw as labor theft. In 1910, he forcibly removed *peones* (farm laborers) from trains and put recruiters in jail. But even this did not prevent the exodus of workers, large numbers of whom bought tickets to another part of Mexico before buying tickets to the United States. The *jefe*'s efforts were recorded by Frank Stone, a Bureau of Immigration official, who traveled through Mexico to assess the sources of migration to the United States. In his journeys to the migrant-sending states of Chihuahua, Aguascalientes, Guanajuato, Jalisco, and Michoacán, he found that the workers who were leaving were mostly from the *haciendas*, especially those that grew staple crops. In these states, local governments had started to take a variety of approaches to migration. Some states losing population to other parts of Mexico passed laws prohibiting the contracting of laborers outside of their state. In the Laguna district of Durango, *hacendados* routinely complained that migration to the United States caused losses during the cotton chopping and picking seasons. Over the five years before 1910, they raised wages from 25 cents a day to 62½ cents a day. The *hacendados* he spoke with "attribute[ed] the necessity for increasing the wages to the migration of the *peones* to the United States; as the men returning from the United States every year instilled dissatisfaction among the *peones* remaining on the *haciendas*, and those who had once been in the United States soon become unmanageable and of little use." As a result, Stone wrote, "*Hacendados* themselves [were] doing everything in their power to discourage the migration of *peones*."[24] In another part of the country, the US consul was told by angry landowners that "a *hacendado* from Vera Cruz was asked by his laborers for a night school. He was pleased with their interest and provided a teacher. After about three months about twenty-five [out] of thirty of his best laborers left for the United States. They had wanted to be able to pass the literacy test." In Zamora, Michoacán, the *jefe político* claimed that 2,000 people left per year, and he responded by jailing and arresting migrants coming through the town.[25]

Wages in the mining areas of Coahuila and Zacatecas were also rising in order to keep workers from going to Arizona's mines. When a migrant returned, he might give "a glowing account of the conditions obtained here; the result of which is that when he leaves for the United States, he is accompanied by one of more of his neighbors, each member of the family contributing a small share to sending one of its younger members."[26] Overall, as people left in large numbers, agricultural wages in some migrant areas rose to compete with wages on Mexican railroads, which were in turn being forced up by the prospect of US railroad work. US government officials, *jefes políticos*, *hacendados*, and Mexican government officials lacked reliable information about this new migration and disagreed about its causes and how to bring it under control. They did, however, agree on its undesirability.

Migrants were coming from areas where capitalist development was dispossessing people of land, inequities were growing, and work was increasingly precarious. To escape this, they increasingly migrated to northern Mexico and eventually followed this economic logic to its ultimate conclusion: *El Norte*. One man from Guanajuato left after learning of others from his *hacienda* who had gone to Kansas and St. Louis. Along with some friends, he followed their path, eventually reaching Chicago.[27] Migrants often borrowed money to finance their trips. DeGregorio Vázquez, an illiterate man from Ojos de Agua, Guanajuato, was a waiter until 1907, when his friends told him about opportunities for work and even lent him money for the journey. He contracted himself out (*engancho*) and worked on railroads in Arizona before becoming a foreman and moving to California with his wife. By 1927, he had become a landholder and sent for his sisters. Nevertheless, he still hoped to return to Mexico.[28] This economic logic unnerved many of the *hacendados*, who had overturned traditional relationships and created an agricultural proletariat only to see many of them leave. Even worse, the patience of the vast majority who had stayed was wearing thin.

The Mexican Revolution

Starting as a political challenge to President Porfirio Díaz's re-election by liberal Francisco Madero, the Mexican Revolution became a social revolution with multiple warring factions that lasted for the better part of the 1910s. The revolution was, in many ways, a reaction to the Porfirian-led transformation of the economy. The loss of land by indigenous and rural communities, along with the concentration of wealth by powerful landowning families and foreign-dominated companies, created social tensions. Industrialization led to an export/resource-dependent economy in which foreign companies benefitted most from productivity increases. By 1910, the United States, Britain, and Germany controlled most of the mining, railroad, and industrial capacity of the country.[29] American owners controlled 130 million acres, the bulk of which was held by only 160 individuals or corporations.[30] More importantly, economic growth stalled, exposing the structural limits of this development model. Rural agricultural wages fell 17% and industrial wages by half in a decade.[31] A series of incidents, including uprisings and revolts in the northern borderlands, and urban strikes undermined Porfirian legitimacy.[32]

Not until the political crisis triggered by the 1910 election did a large-scale revolt break out. Madero's campaign against Diaz's re-election inspired people beyond his urban liberal base, including villagers, indigenous communities, *hacienda* workers, and *serrano* (highland) people of the Mexican frontiers, all of whom had recently lost their traditional autonomy to the new economy. Rural rebellions erupted out from Morelos to Sonora and continued after Madero became president. Soon afterwards, Madero was killed in a coup, and conservative general Victoriano Huerta installed himself as president, sparking a new wave of rebellions across the country. After Huerta was defeated, revolutionaries turned against each other as two broad coalitions under the Conventionalist and Constitutionalist banners fought across the country, nearly a million people died between 1910 and 1920. Even after Venustiano Carranza and the secular liberal Constitutionalists won control of Mexico City and instituted a new constitution in 1917, disorder and violence continued into the 1920s.[33]

Along the US-Mexico borderlands, there was significant overlap between migrants and those who joined the *Partido Liberal Mexicano* (PLM) and Villista movements. While the PLM had only a small role in the revolution, its widespread network was influential in the north. Brothers Enrique Flores and Ricardo Flores Magón founded the PLM in 1905 against Diaz but were forced into exile in the United States. From there, they published the newspaper, *Regeneración*, established local chapters across the US Southwest, and launched cross-border strikes and short-lived revolts until they were arrested and prosecuted by the US government.[34] Francisco Villa's movement meanwhile had significant appeal to those who lived in northern Mexico, especially cross-border railroad and mining workers.[35] There were so many returning migrants in the Villista movement, and in the interview record, that anthropologist Manuel Gamio came to believe returning migrants had helped spread discontent and revolutionary ideas in northern Mexico, stemming from their contact with industrialization and their comparisons of their own country with the United States.[36] From the early 1910s until at least the mid-1920s, the borderlands remained the place from which various factions launched revolts.

Revolution and Migration in San Luis Potosí and Guanajuato

It did not take long for the revolution to reach San Luis Potosí. Within days of Madero's uprising, villages in the Huasteca, including Tamazunchale, revolted, usually against local *hacendados* and government officials. Despite government efforts to quell the unrest, over the course of a few months much of the rest of the state joined the revolt. While in the Huasteca region the revolution was primarily comprised of indigenous villagers who had lost their lands to *haciendas*, in the rest of the state it was Hispanicized *hacienda* workers living in enclosed villages who revolted. In Ciudad de Maiz, the Cedillo brothers began to unite groups of *rancheros* and *hacienda* workers under their banner.[37]

The railroad from San Luis to Tampico became a frequent target of various factions, with control of towns changing hands with relative regularity. At one point, the state government resorted to train inspections of men going to work in the United States, imprisoning or conscripting into the army those without written contracts.[38] Wilbert L. Bonney, local US Consul in San Luis Potosí, wrote a series of reports to the State Department on revolutionary activity. On September 22, 1912, he summarized the general working conditions, arguing that the revolution was economic rather than political in nature and that the violence was aimed at local oppressors. He viewed migration as an escape valve and wrote that laborers, having few options, "have resorted to other means to accomplish their objective. These means are as follows: 1) Labor Strikes 2) Emigration to the United States 3) Enlistment in the army [and] 4) Joining the lawless bands of marauders," the latter referring to rebel groups of *rancheros* that had formed throughout the state.[39]

Cerritos in particular became a strategic point for anyone trying to control the railroad and the east-west road to the city of San Luis Potosí that passed through the town. During the worst of the fighting, the town was almost abandoned, with several thousand men leaving the area. The same was true in the rest of the valley. In a span of just four months, twenty-four *haciendas* were attacked.[40] The owner of Angostura was executed by the Cedillos. Rebels under the Vaquista banner laid siege to Rioverde, the largest city in the valley. Over the next six years, the city was a frequent target. When *hacendados* tried to use violence to enforce the old paternalistic order, their victories proved Pyrrhic, with losses of efficiency, workers demanding higher wages, or worse, people leaving to join the rebels or to head north. *Hacienda* workers proved particularly supportive of rebels.[41]

The mines in the region were not spared. While miners were not very revolutionary in general, in San Luis Potosí there is evidence of miners joining the revolution to press their village land claims.[42] Mines were susceptible to work stoppages, which sent laborers off to seek jobs elsewhere. In March of 1912, the mines of Guaxcama closed, throwing 700 men out of work. Some joined the revolt; some migrated. The Hacienda de San Anton Guaxcama was destroyed, and workers forced the owning family to divide the land.[43] This launched a long legal dispute over ownership of the *hacienda* that did not end until 1938.[44] Out of work and located near the Mexican Central railroad, men soon began migrating to northern Mexico and the United States. Cerritos, in particular, was an origin point of railroad and mining workers in the late 1910s and early 1920s. In San Luis Potosí, the revolution was primarily a local affair, with a guerrilla war waged between different bands, a weak state, and *hacendados* until the Cedillos took control of the state. In subsequent years, factions continued to fight, bandits roamed, and the rail lines were cut.

In Guanajuato, the more stable social relations of the Bajío meant that, at first, fewer people were willing to take the risk of open rebellion. Although there were economic inequalities and social tensions in the Bajío, its large population of freeholding *rancheros*, weaker village structure, and longstanding *haciendas* mitigated revolts.[45] This is not to say there was no violence in San Francisco de Rincón and Celaya, which experienced a significant, widespread banditry and personal violence.[46] In both cities, middle-class residents attempted short-lived revolts, and people rioted against the *Porfiriato* and food shortages. Despite this, the countryside did not join the cause until the outside war reached the area.[47] The state was a strategic target for all sides in the conflict because of its railroad hubs. In the spring of 1915, full-scale war came to the state as Constitutionalists and Conventionalists fought a series of battles along the Bajío basin. Around the same time, José Inés García Chávez led a revolt that cause widespread violence and brought down much of the *hacienda* economy.[48]

It is not surprising that Celaya and its surrounding areas saw emigration as a result of the revolution. It did not become a ghost town like Cerritos in San Luis Potosí, but thousands of people left the surrounding countryside for the United States. These were primarily agricultural workers and people from small villages rather than miners or railroad workers. San Francisco de

Rincón was relatively unscathed by the major period of fighting and, instead, suffered its most violent upheaval with the Cristero War (1926–1929). The war in the Bajío started when the anti-clerical President Plutarco Elías Calles sought to enforce the anti-Catholic provisions of the 1917 revolutionary constitution. The Church declared a boycott on religious services, and its supporters armed for war. The conflict became a guerilla war of attrition on both sides, with the government using revolutionary veterans from across the country against local Cristero militias. Landowners small and large generally supported the Church, while the pro-land-redistribution *agraristas* supported the government.

Migrating from the Revolution

Destitution drove large numbers out of the country. Rudy Hernández's parents came from the central-north state of Zacatecas in 1916. As he described his hometown, "it was very ugly; there was no food or [place] to live. There were fires . . . destroying houses. Everything was chaos, no order." They travelled by train into Texas and eventually settled in California.[49] Trini Gamez's parents and grandmother, Guadalupe Álvarez Sánchez, shared similar stories with her about losing everything in the revolution. The family crossed into Texas and became migrant farm workers in the cotton fields.[50] Locario Lopez from Zamora, Michoacán, explained his decision: "I had to leave because the revolution was very difficult . . . We had formally all been in the United States, and we had gone back to Mexico to stay permanently, but when I could not make a living, I left my wife and children and came to the United States."[51] The displacement of hundreds of thousands of people across Mexico was one of the major legacies of the revolution. Not everyone faced these challenges alone, but regardless, the revolution forced refugees to rebuild in the most difficult of circumstances.

Jesus Gonzalez was a shop owner in Guadalajara when his shop was ransacked by Villista troops and he was conscripted. He fled, taking a train from Torreón to Ciudad Juárez. He crossed into the United States and worked as a track laborer along the Santa Fe railroad in California, Kansas, Oklahoma, and Texas. He eventually became a miner in Miami, Arizona.[52] His journey was not unique. The revolution brought large numbers of middle-class Mexicans north of the border. Many had fought in the revolution for one faction or another. While Luciano Herrera was a Marxist and generally supported the Mexican Revolution, he was also a landowner and had no predisposition to fight. After his friend became an officer in the Constitutionalists army and pressured him into joining, he escaped to Juárez, where he worked for the railroad; eventually, he went to Los Angeles and sent back money to his wife and daughters.[53] Jesus Frano was a colonel in the Mexican Army until the Constitutionalists won, at which point he left with his family for the United States and eventually organized a *Cruz Azul* (a locally organized medical association) branch and several fraternal organizations.[54]

When asked by an interviewer why he left, Severino Medina answered, "because there were a lot of bandits, there was no government, they would arrive here, beat you with a carbine . . . they would take everything." By then, the Medina family had already survived eight years of instability and fighting against the Federal government, but this was too much for a family with a baby. So, in 1918, he decided to leave. He worked with an *enganchista* to clandestinely cross the border and found a job in San Antonio. He then sent for his wife and child, who came by train. They settled in Texas, where he became a store owner.[55]

Like many others, José Rocha was displaced by the revolution. He traveled across Mexico looking for work before coming home to Leon, Guanajuato. There, he found that his brothers had returned; "they told me about all the things they had seen in the United States . . . I then decided to come to the United States." He crossed into El Paso, where he took a labor contract on a railroad. He disliked the work and soon left, crossing the border a few more times before he married and brought his family to California. where he started a small business. He described his motivations as a search for adventure and a search for better pay than what he could make in Leon as a musician.[56]

Manuel Santa Cruz was a business owner in Chihuahua until the revolution-induced economic depression, after which he made his way to Davenport, Iowa. There, he worked in a steel foundry before coming to own several pool halls in Chicago.[57] After he was conscripted by revolutionaries who protested his uncle's pro-Díaz newspaper, F. Huerta left Mexico and worked as a printer and on the railroads. He used his savings to send for his mother and sister, who promptly started a boarding house. The family acted as an economic unit wherein the women ran a small business while the man worked for the railroad.[58]

The revolution prompted the migration of numerous writers and ex-politicians. Some were supporters of the *Porfiriato*, while others belonged to factions that lost out in the ensuing power struggle. Although they did not consider themselves "migrants," they went on to play a key role as exiled elites in Mexican communities in the United States. San Antonio emerged as the hub of exile activity; there, the Spanish-language press provided an opportunity. Rómulo Munguía, an editor for *El Dario*, an opposition newspaper before the revolution, left for Texas and joined the staff at *La Prensa*.[59] Jose Lanides González was a mine owner and *alcalde* (mayor) of Mapimi Durango before the revolution in 1911. He started several newspapers and eventually became the administrator of *La Prensa* in San Antonio.[60] Pedro de la Lama came from a well-connected military family. His liberal newspaper in Veracruz was able to get away with critiques of the government because of his connection to Aureliano Urrutia, then Secretary of Government under Huerta. However, he was eventually jailed and left for San Antonio, where he became the editor of *La Justicia*.[61] Jose M. Ramírez M. entered the family business. His father edited the daily paper in Guayamas, Sonora, but the family left during the revolution and settled in Tucson. By 1927, the younger Ramírez was the owner of various printing presses used by newspapers in the city.[62] These men were among the many educated elites who came in this decade and greatly expanded the scope of Spanish-language media north of the border.[63]

The Business of Migration

The violence, economic devastation, and general instability in towns and villages continued long after the primary political struggle for power ended. While some parts of the economy shut down during the armed phase of the revolution, the long-term impact was far more devastating. By 1917–1918, unemployment and destitution had shot up, even as political stability was returning. The return of passenger trains gave people a way out, however, and this can be seen in migration trends. Official migration decreased at the beginning of the revolution, but by 1915, more migrants were on the move than before the war.[64] States in northern Mexico increased in population during the 1910s due to an influx from central Mexico. However, the north-central plain states of Durango, Zacatecas, and San Luis Potosí all lost between 20% and 30% of their pre-war populations.[65] From 1911 to 1917, at least half a million people legally emigrated from Mexico to the United States.[66]

In the short term, the revolution caused a series of refugee crises along the border. In 1910–1911 and again in 1913, violence drove refugees into US border towns as different factions vied for control of Mexico's border towns. The US government held refugees in large outdoor pens. Eventually, many of them were released into the country and went on to settle permanently in the United States. The first reports of migration restarting came as early as 1913, when hundreds of railroad workers arrived in El Paso after much of the mining industry shut down.[67]

In the long term, the revolution encouraged a growing business of migration. In northern Mexico, businesses in places like Ciudad Juárez and Laredo had emerged before the revolution to help people cross. These included boarding houses, ferries across the Rio Grande, coyotes (smugglers), and labor contractors. These people were called "coyotes" along the borderlands, a name that would stick in the popular imagination of both countries. Investigator Luis Felipe Recinos reported on large networks of labor contractors in Ciudad Juárez, most of which were recruiting in the open. People used coyotes not only to cross the border undetected but also to get false passports and even to obtain documents to cross legally. Not much separated the work of labor contractors and smugglers. Many were part of groups or "gangs" that offered various services.[68] In Juárez, dozens of boarding houses sprung up "offering, not only food and lodging, but effective assistance in crossing the border." Inspectors were concerned with the large number of ferries operating over the border as well as "physicians professing ability to remove the signs of disease," who offered to help people pass medical inspections at crossing points.[69] In Nogales, Sonora, there were reports of local officials taking kickbacks from labor contractors, recruiting people for American companies, prompting a protest to the new Obregon government.[70] Obregon tried to stop the use of *enganchadores* along the border, but this failed when it became clear the federal Mexican border officials were working with them to facilitate the cross-border traffic.[71] Labor contractors, often associated with railroad companies, traveled the routes between central Mexico and the border to recruit workers. It was common for *enganchadores* to stand on train platforms exhorting people to go to the United States.[72] With the growth of migration in the late 1910s, these networks grew into sophisticated operations and expanded into the Mexican interior.

A large industry dedicated to border crossing developed in Torreón, turning it into the primary railroad hub for migrants leaving the Bajío. Some of these businesses and agencies were sponsored by the railroad industry and included *enganchadores*, houses, and places to get the necessary paperwork. Their activities ranged from handing out labor contractor cards from recruiters advertising their agencies to much more complex systems. Especially along railroad routes, entire networks of people, businesses, and organizations built an infrastructure to provide money, guidance, and housing along the way. Investigator Recinos reported seeing in Torreón migrants who arrived in small groups of four to ten people from the same or nearby village and who sought out a coyote or *enganchador* to cross together.[73] The city newspaper *El Siglo* ran an exposé on what it called "La Banda," a group of men that ran a migration operation based in Torreón. La Banda apparently bribed enough officials that agents of the *Departamento de Migración* did not know who they could trust.[74]

In February of 1918, a group of about fifty men were questioned at Pedrito, San Luis Potosí, as they were embarking on trains to the United States. They told authorities they had been recruited by an American *enganchista*, provided documents, and no government authority had tried to stop them.[75] They did not seem particularly concerned about the laws. Such scenes occurred across the region. *Enganchadores* and coyotes were critical facilitators of this process, bringing information, capital, and transportation together.[76]

World War I

American entry into World War I in 1917 brought increased demand for labor at the same time that Congress passed an Immigration Act significantly limiting migration. Based on eugenic assumptions, the Act instituted a literacy test; raised fees; banned migration for a plethora of health, moral, and political reasons; and severely cut migration from Asia. Combined with wartime conditions, the law cut off the bulk of migration from Europe. Across the US Southwest, employers objected to the 1917 restrictions and warned of the prospect of wartime shortages. In response, the Secretary of Labor agreed to temporarily suspend the law for Mexicans, as well as on contract labor. What started as a series of exemptions quickly became an organized program for the recruitment of Mexican workers across the agricultural, mining, and railroad industries. The exemptions did not end until 1921. As a result, Mexicans moved beyond the borderlands and deep into the nation's interior. Between 1917 and 1920, migration from central Mexico ballooned, peaking at 80,000 legal entrants and between 20,000 and 50,000 more who entered as "non-statistical migrants," as Mexicans who stayed in the United States for less than six months were not counted in official statistics. In theory, the latter came for short visits, but significant numbers came to work.

In recalling that period, Mexican migrants tended not to mention the various laws or the efforts of border authorities, but instead to focus on how the social climate around them affected their own decision-making. As one migrant describing San Antonio put it, "You should have seen it in 1918 to 1919. There were many more Mexicans than whites. With the need for *braceros mexicanos*, they came over the border as fast as they could. They came by train, by stage, auto, and wagons. Many came on foot."[77] Aguilera, from Monterrey, described a similar phenomenon: "When I first began to hear very much about the United States some seven or eight years ago, it seems that most of those whom I knew were coming to the United States were coming to study, and when they went back, they told the others of the opportunities that there were in the United States for work."[78] A beet picker in Texas who came in 1920 exemplified how far word could travel: "We came from Michoacán . . . We heard about the sugar beets. I had heard about beets and cotton in Michoacán."[79]

Another remembered, "The first time I came to the United States was in the war time. In 1918. I went to work in October in the vicinity of San Antonio picking cotton. In those days, the wages for picking cotton were good. They paid $3 a quintal. Then, after that, things slowed down, and I went back to Mexico in 1920." Across Texas, wages paid for labor, from clearing lands to picking cotton, shot up.[80] Still another remembered, "I left Mexico in early 1918. That was during the war. Things were very quiet down there then. I was in the United States—labor was scarce, and wages were good, so I came up here. They paid $3.50 for a quintal of cotton."[81] Sr. Caribales, a fellow migrant and boarding house owner, remembered, "The companies here needed help. They sent *enganchistas* to the large Mexican centers in this country and to the border. After that, it was not necessary. The tide [had turned], and they came by themselves."[82]

People trusted the word of those they knew when making the decision to migrate. Serafin Sánchez described his thinking: "During the revolutions of Madero and Zapata, I wrote down to my relatives when they sought a place to go, so they came here from the interior of Mexico."[83] Another man from Zacatecas explained, "On the way, we met a family at Colonia Juárez who had some people who had relatives in the Pecos Valley in the United States. They had received letters from them saying how good business was in the United States and the high wages after the war."[84] Despite the hardship, they eventually found railroad jobs on the Santa Fe Railway. They "heard that things were good in Illinois" and made their way there.

The Mexican government developed a contradictory policy toward emigration. At points during the revolution, President Carranza encouraged the disaffected to migrate. Yet he had also decreed migrants had to have passports to leave the country, more as a symbol than reflecting any practical ability the government had to enforce such a law.[85] The new constitution passed in 1917 included a clause intended to protect and control Mexican migrants going to the United States. Article 123, Section 16, required emigrants to have contracts with employers before leaving. The *Departamento de Migración* assisted those who desired to leave, and Carranza even offered railroad passage to the border to those who wished to join the new US wartime exemptions program.[86] The program aligned with the federal government's preference that migrants have contracts, be enlisted, have passage paid for, and have pay held back in savings until they returned to Mexico. Not everyone agreed. Various states reported labor shortages due to emigration, putting the federal government on the defensive in the press. Politicians across northern Mexico reported a "exodus" in the fields as workers went north.[87] Most local and state governments opposed the program. The governors of Jalisco and Tamaulipas objected, while the governor of Sonora threatened to place a head tax on emigrants.[88] Mexican consuls reported that, though they worked with companies and contractors, state authorities in Chihuahua blocked their efforts, and officials in Sonora prevented miners from leaving.[89]

With the rise of Álvaro Obregón to the presidency of Mexico in 1920, the federal government shifted its stance. Responding to criticism in the press and the rise of US deportations, it began to issue circulars warning of the dangers of migration and spreading stories of abuses.[90] When a major postwar recession hit in 1921, the exceptions program came to an end. Suddenly, tens of thousands of migrants were left in destitute conditions.[91] Obregón personally managed the response, expanding the number of consuls in the United States and sending money to pay for food, shelter, and return tickets to repatriate Mexican migrants. An estimated 150,000 were repatriated, and approximately half received assistance from the Mexican government. The government started to make plans for the creation of agricultural colonies for returnees, but funding ran out, and no colonies were ever established. Still, even as the program sought to bring people back, more were preparing to go the other direction.[92]

In the early 1920s, the Mexican government and most elite opinion came to see migration as a problem to be controlled, if not stopped. During the 1920–1921 recession, a government official described the return of migrants as a "sorrowful caravan that arrives day after day to our borders, like a prodigal son in search of a home."[93] The press and the government saw migrants as victims of *enganchadores*, coyotes, and American exploitation and sought to counter the information that was leading so many to leave. However, these early efforts were severely limited. Not until 1926 did Mexico pass a *Ley de Migración* (Migration Law) and establish a police force within the *Departamento de Migración* to undertake a larger effort.[94] As information spread throughout central Mexico, there was increasing disagreement in the public sphere about whether the stories told by returning Mexicans and recruiters were myth or fact.

Debating Migration

Aureliana Aguilera described how he went back and forth from his home in Morelia to Detroit. "I first came to the United States in 1918. I went back in 1920 and returned in 1921, went back again in 1924 and returned in 1925, and have just gotten back the first of this year from another trip. It is such a short way that one can easily return. The fare to Laredo from Detroit is about fifty-six dollars, and from there to my town it is about twenty-six *pesos*."[95] Despite the lack of support from both governments and the obstacles placed in migrants' paths, the early 1920s saw a normalization of circular migration. Most labor migrants were men, the majority of whom left their families at home. Usually, they did not bring their families north until they had spent years working. Most used migration as a strategy to improve their economic positions in Mexico and saw their stays in the United States as temporary.

Sam Ramírez's circular movement began when he became a migrant within Mexico. "When my parents died in 1912, I went from my town in Michoacán to Mexico City. In 1917, I had heard about the United States, so I came. I went to work on the Pennsylvania Railroad and then returned to Mexico, but I returned to the United States and went to California. Then

I returned to Mexico. [Then] I came to Gary, Indiana."[96] Circular migration could even become a near-annual affair for some. Talking to migrants going back to Mexico on a train, inspector W. C. Nester noted, "One man said he had returned to Mexico every year since 1917, i.e. for eleven years."[97]

Corridos (ballads) sung in central Mexico and passed from person to person expressed working-class hopes and fears.[98] While most sang about lost love, famous outlaws, and revolutionary exploits, recounting brave men who stood up to Huerta or the Texas Rangers, a few of these oral stories reflected on the experience of migration. One *corrido* sung by Cecilo Chávez outside Union Station in Los Angeles went like this:[99]

We're on our way
Arriving at the city of Leon,
Admiring it, I stayed
To see its lights.

On arriving in Aguascalientes
With pleasure and care,
I haven't fixed my passport
For lack of money.

Then I passed Zacatecas,
Paying a lot of attention.
In the passenger train,
My heart was broken.

We arrived at the station
That is called Fresnillo,
Where every Mexican
Visits the Miraculous Child.

Well, very near Fresnillo,
You can see the forested hills
Where you can find
That Christ Child of Silver.

St. Nino of Fresnillo,
Thou hast favor,
Christ Child of Silver,
Grant me that I may come back.

The train is leaving
To get to Torreón,
Christ Child of Fresnillo,
give me your blessing.

On our way to Chihuahua,
Well, from here, I say goodbye,
Farewell, my beloved country!
Farewell, all my friends!

Now, with this goodbye
From my Mexican homeland,
I have come to Ciudad Juárez,
Oh! Virgin of Guadalupe!

This *corrido* captures the route that many people took, from Guanajuato up to Torreón to Ciudad Juárez and El Paso on the Mexican Central railroad. It also illustrates the decisions people made as they weighed the risks of migration, whether or not to secure passports and legal entry, and the spiritual nature of the journey.

In this ballad, a man from Guanajuato sings about his state as he leaves; there is a strong ambivalence about going north, about abandoning his home and family. The singer asks for blessings before leaving and tells his audience that he left because he was unable to make a living and had no choice.[100]

I'm sad and regretful
To suffer and to suffer,
Mother of mine, Guadalupe,
I ask you that I may return.

Mother Mexico is my country,
Where, Mexican, I was born.
Give your blessing
With your mighty hand.

I'm going to the US
To be able to support myself
Goodbye, my beloved country,
You are in my heart!

Well, I am not at fault
That I abandoned so my land.
It is the fault of poverty
That we live in misery.

Well, I'm on the road,
And I left from Salvatierra,
I pray, Mother of Light,
That I may return to my land.

We're going to Celaya
With resolution.
Bye bye, Mother of mine,
Immaculate Conception!

We're arriving at Irapuato
On our way to Silao.
Mother of Loretito,
Let me return to your side!

We arrive at Salmaca;
Goodbye, San Pascual.
Give me your blessing,
My Father of Mercy!

Goodbye, Guanajuato beautiful,
My state where I was born.
I'm going to the United States,
Far, far away from you.

The following ballad, composed around the 1920s, written down in 1930 by researchers in Texas, and performed by Manuel Esquivel in the 1970s, captures some of the contradictions in going to *El Norte*.[101]

What do you say, Darling?
Let's go up North.
I have arranged everything already,
I have the passport,
The consulate gave it to me so that we
may cross.

How beautiful it is to love!
How lovely it is to love!
To take delight among pretty flowers
You know well, my love,

That I can't forget you,
My little sweetheart.
We'll leave together
On the train that goes to the border.

You'll ride in my arms,
Mistress of my heart,
Even though your mother is opposed.

The north is lovely, I'll never forget it,
Because you can make money,
I'm a Mexican that adores his
homeland
And, for me, that comes first.

Let's go up north, cradle of the
northerner,
With you at my side,
Let's go up north, Land of dreams,
Cry of the repatriated.

This ballad is also tragic: a man who has been north before singing to his beloved to join him in journeying north again, where the two lovers can be free of her mother. Unlike many migrants in his era, this man already has papers and seems to know the path. He justifies his decision to leave Mexico by telling his audience how much money can be earned. He sees migration as an opportunity to leave his station in life, calling *El Norte* the land of dreams. Yet he is singing as a repatriated person, someone who has been forced to return to Mexico, his dreams shattered. The dream is an illusion. Traveling thousands of miles in order to find work meant leaving family and home behind. It was a calculated risk.

This dual position—migration as opportunity, migration as exile—appears repeatedly in migrants' accounts. They were not mutually exclusive. Rather, they capture the deep ambivalence many felt about the inherent contradictions in migrating. While some sought to leave villages, free themselves from traditional hierarchies, and look for adventure, migration was traumatic for those who left because of instability or poverty. Few thought of themselves as abandoning their families, or Mexico, as they took pains to reassure those left behind. But large numbers of those left behind did feel abandoned and feared the effects of the temptations of the migrant life on their men.

In towns and villages across central Mexico, the pull of circular migration was increasingly hard to ignore. Pedro Macias, a farmer in his native town in Pénjamo, Guanajuato, came in 1921 after "the boys of the town talked about the United States and this thing and that" to the point that he was convinced to go. He became a railroad worker, and in 1923, he went back home and told his own stories.[102] This could have cumulative effects on certain villages, where half the men had left by the 1920s.[103] People looked to make sense of the large migration diaspora, as the reality and practices of transnational migration did not lend themselves to existing categories of belonging. In Mexico, most government officials, writers, and elites saw migration as a mistake, something that needed to be stopped, with increasing force if necessary. Migrants themselves, however, continued to see themselves as completely Mexican and migration as morally defensible and necessary.

Migration Fever

The unprecedented scale of migration alarmed not just the federal and state governments but the Catholic Church. In 1920, José Francisco Orozco y Jiménez, the Archbishop of Guadalajara, wrote a letter in which he urged priests to "defer in a prudent, yet strong manner, the faithful from the *migration fever* that appears to have overtaken all Mexicans, making them understand that the lack of work that practically forces workers from other parts of the county to migrate does not exist in the archdiocese."[104] He declared a "holy crusade" against migration to save the nation and save souls from the corrupting influence of the Protestant America. Migrants risked losing themselves, their religion, their culture, and their patriotism while working for a country that had exploited Mexico.[105] From then on, it was the official policy of the Church to discourage migration. These efforts, like those of the Mexican government, were not very successful. By the mid-1920s, migration had become one of the most popular responses to ongoing economic disruptions, violence, and insecurity.

Something peculiar happened in the village of Santa Gertrudis de la Carbonera, San Luis Potosí, in 1923. Antonio Baron returned to his family after several years away. This was not in itself an unusual event; dozens of men had left in the previous ten years to work in other places in Mexico. However, Baron was coming from the United States, he told stories of the north, and in the years after his return, his family members joined him on his trips north. It is likely that others had gone before, but people in the town remembered his success as spurring others to go.[106] Larger towns in the valley, like Cerritos and Rioverde, several miles away, had long histories with mining, railroads, and migration, but Santa Gertrudis de la Carbonera, a day's walk from the rail stop at Cerritos, hadn't been part of this pattern. He was one of the first in a long history of migration to initiate a long history of migration. In Guanajuato, both Celaya and San Francisco de Rincón had, by 1920, developed into sending regions where hundreds of people had gone based on town-centered networks.

By the early 1920s, migration reached 100,000 people a year (both documented and undocumented).[107] Although Mexican migrants from this period are sometimes seen as leaving feudal peasantry to encounter modern capitalism, many were coming from areas of Mexico where government-sponsored industrialization and foreign investment had already profoundly changed the landscape.[108] In regions where migration became a part of life, several patterns are clear. Migration could not have occurred without the economic transformation of central and northern Mexico, high population growth, and loss of both autonomy and a stable agrarian society, which turned millions of people into landless peasants forced to work in the market. This transformation was underwritten by the transnational flow of vast amounts of US capital. As land was lost and railways, factories, and mines were built, people in central Mexico turned to migration, internal and by extension external. Migrants provided the labor that made the industrialization of northern Mexico possible. This was a double-edged sword for both capitalists and workers alike, however, as people followed the logic of the new economy across the border. The collapse of the *hacienda* system and the widespread violence during and after the revolution displaced hundreds of thousands of Mexicans and fueled migration transnationally. This helped turn a largely labor migration of young men into a mass migration of families and various social classes.

In general, migration came from areas where the economy was being rapidly transformed around export commodities. There, harsh local conditions, decreased standards of living, and access to transportation combined to encourage people to leave. Yet economic and land dispossession only partially explain why certain areas witnessed large amounts of migration: other parts of Mexico had similar socioeconomic profiles but did not send numerous migrants north. Even within regions, there was great variation. While mass migration is an international phenomenon, it's deeply rooted in local conditions. In some villages, almost half of the men of working age emigrated, while other places were hardly affected by the "migration fever." Likewise, some towns without a nearby railroad connection saw significant migration as residents traveled to rail hubs.[109] Moreover, the migrants were not the poorest of their communities: a larger percentage spoke only Spanish than the Mexican population as a whole, but many were from small *ranchero* families or were *hacienda* laborers (though rarely *peones acasillados*, workers dependent on the *hacienda*) and some were skilled workers. In other words, they had some social and economic capital to make the journey.

A combination of economic disruption, violence, and interpersonal networks was needed to start a chain of migrations. Within this process, organizations, brokers, and the public sphere helped structure the migratory system. Upon closer inspection, it is clear "migration fever" emerged from personal interactions within towns and villages. People reduced the inherent risks by relying upon those they could trust, especially family members, as they traveled in groups and utilized distant connections. This web of interpersonal relationships and associations linked people across space and time, lowering the uncertainty and cost of travel. These information links spread "migration fever." Word of mouth, letters, recruiters, posters, and radio ads encouraged people to extend their trust to others and facilitated journeys across thousands of miles.

People quit their jobs and *haciendas*; took loans from friends, family members, and *patrones*; and traveled north in groups, in families, and as individuals. They went with those they knew, with contractors, and with strangers. They rode on trains and automobiles, stayed in boarding houses, and bought food and provisions at the border and places beyond. They relied upon brokers, coyotes, and officials who looked the other way. They did not stop moving when they arrived but continued to migrate between employers, states, and regions. Many of them eventually returned to Mexico and related stories of their journeys. Through all these actions, they created durable patterns of circular migration that spread across both nations.

Despite the hardships Mexicans faced and would continue to face in the late 1920s and 1930s, for many migration to the United States offered the promise of a better life. Mexicans left home for a multitude of reasons, but through their individual and family choices, migrants took part in the creation of something new, for better and worse.

2

Navigating the Borderlands

Migrants in the Mining and Cotton Regions of Arizona and Texas, 1900–1925

From the pre-colonial period to the late nineteenth century, the borderlands between Mexico and the United States, whether inhabited by Spanish, Comanche, French, Confederates, or Americans, remained largely beyond the control of distant nation-states. This situation changed in the years before the Mexican Revolution when new settlers profoundly changed the physical, economic, and social patterns of the region, and the borderlands became the center of a growing cross-border economy. After the US-Mexico War forced the surrender of much of northern Mexico to the United States, regional economies developed on both sides of the border. This chapter examines how developments in the nineteenth-century and early twentieth-century cotton and mining industries led to the creation of transnational migration routes. As the US government and corporate partners sought control over this space and labor migration, migrants strategized to navigate the situation on their own terms.

Despite the myth of the US West as an open region that could fulfill the democratic dreams of independent families, small landholders, and free labor, industrial capitalism shaped society here more heavily than anywhere else in the country.[1] Colonists and industrialists worked with officials to wrest the land from Native American and *Tejano*/Mexican American populations, reshaping the economy around large-scale agribusiness and mining. Using a combination of migrant Mexican, American, European, and Asian labor, the cotton and mining industries radically changed the social and natural landscape on a transnational scale.

As anti-immigrant sentiment rose, efforts by the US and Mexican governments to create a real and enforceable national boundary crystalized into a system that sought to police the movement of people across the border. This, combined with the growing Jim Crow system of segregation, created

Between Here and There. Daniel Morales, Oxford University Press. © Oxford University Press 2024.
DOI: 10.1093/oso/9780197612590.003.0003

separate legal, educational, and social spaces in Texas and Arizona and was enforced by violence. Meanwhile, mining corporations and agribusiness aimed to create a large, docile, deportable, and politically powerless workforce, mostly comprised of minorities and/or immigrants. Capitalists used their authority to shape state laws in Arizona and Texas as well as federal immigration policy, notably the World War I contract labor program; the 1917, 1921, and 1924 Immigration Acts; and the Immigration and Border Patrol bureaucracy. Despite their efforts, governments, corporations, and landowners were never able to achieve complete hegemony. Workers' actions forced these powers time and again to assert greater control, including the use of widespread violence between 1915 and 1921.

A transnational and borderland, rather than a local or frontier, perspective highlights the connections that allowed people to not only survive but to organize.[2] Through their actions, Mexicans created an infrastructure of brokers and associational networks that sustained their communities and guided them as they made their way through both states. As families developed strategies for navigating immigration controls, they pushed back on those who sought to control their movement and labor in small and large ways.[3] They relied upon the continual flow of information to find jobs and to keep moving. While organizing and strikes were not the most common forms of resistance, they were not rare either. The same system of circular migration and flow of information that tied communities together facilitated the spread of labor organizing across the borderlands.

During the 1910s, many migrants participated in revolutionary activities and joined in radical calls for change. While US writers at the time (and since) thought of the Mexican migrants arriving in the United States as preindustrial peasants, these workers left areas with long traditions of union and political organizing as well as revolutionary activity, and they drew upon that experience when they crossed the border.[4] Although labor unions thought of migrants as outsiders, less committed, and perhaps scabs who might cross union lines, worker mobility could subvert corporate power. The movement of people across the region aided the spread of the *Partido Liberal Mexicano* (PLM) and the Industrial Workers of the World (IWW). It also allowed radical networks to form and operate on both sides of the border and made revolts, as well as strikes at Cananea, Bisbee, and many other places, possible.[5]

By looking at the migratory circuits that transformed the US-Mexico borderlands, this chapter highlights common processes of displacement, family strategies, labor recruitment, state enforcement, capitalist logics, and migrant agency in Arizona and Texas. To illustrate the overlapping and interconnected circuits of people and information that drove migration, it adopts a macro view of events that took place in disparate locations. As migrants passed El Paso, the largest entry point on US-Mexico border, they encountered the state in the form of the Bureau of Immigration. From there, they migrated outwards, to the mining regions, the railroads, and the cotton fields.

Tens of thousands of migrants and their families worked in the mining and cotton borderlands. They interacted with myriad social actors—politicians, immigration bureaucrats, growers, companies, labor agents, brokers, and various other intermediaries—with whom they continuously renegotiated the conditions of their migration. In doing so, they used the weapons available to them, small acts such as quitting jobs and leaving and larger ones such as labor organizing across the border. Eventually, migration patterns shifted as people left agricultural and mining jobs and increasingly went to work in cities and the interior.

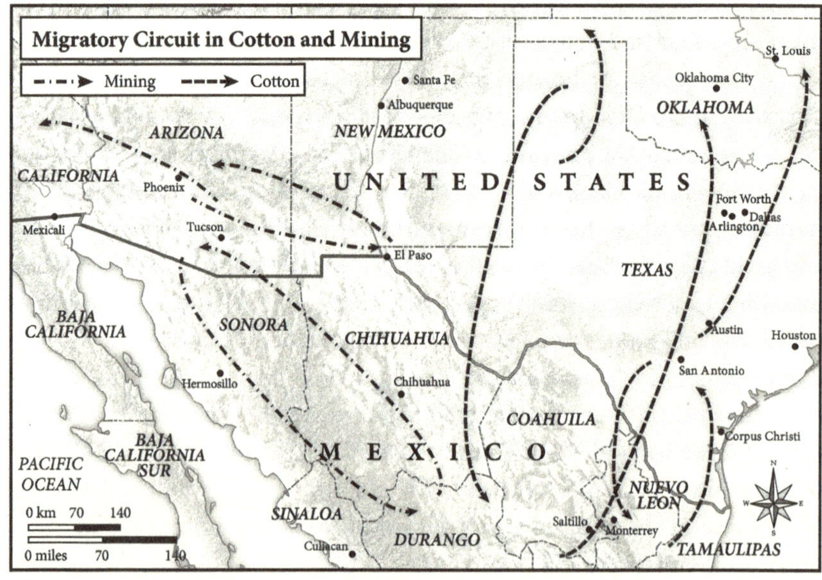

Figure 2.1 The migratory circuit in cotton and mining.

Northern Mexico

The world of mining has always required migratory labor in Mexico. During the 1880s and 1890s, lead, zinc, antimuonium, mercury, coal, and most importantly, copper grew in importance alongside the traditional metals of silver and gold as drivers of the economy. Cities like Monterrey, Ciudad Chihuahua, Torreón, and Juárez transformed into large industrial centers with the arrival of the railroads to serve factories and smelters built by British, German, and American investors.[6] The largest single copper mine was at Cananea, where the Cananea Consolidated Copper Company (CCCC), owned by William Cornell Greene, maintained tight control.[7] The Kansas City Smelting and Refining Company operated mines in the Sierra Mojada from which it shipped ore to its smelter in El Paso, Texas, via the Mexican National Railway.[8] The Montana-based, Rockefeller-controlled Amalgamated Copper Company purchased many of the remaining independent copper companies in Mexico.[9] Elsewhere, the Phelps Dodge Corporation had mines at Moctezuma from which it shipped ore to its smelters in Bisbee, Arizona. Over time, much of the mining industry in Mexico came to operate as an extension of the US industry.

The single largest employer in the industry, the American Smelting and Refining Company (ASARCO), consolidated varied Guggenheim interests into a single company that spanned northern Mexico and the US West. In addition to its US holdings, ASARCO operated mines and smelters in San Luis Potosí, Aguascalientes, Guanajuato, Durango, Chihuahua, Oaxaca, and other places. In Monterrey, it built the largest smelter in Latin America, the Gran Fundación Nacional Mexicana. Operating on both sides of the border, its mines, foundries, and factories were linked to each other and to distant markets by rail. Overall, tens of thousands of people labored in the mines, smelters, and railroads of northern Mexico; few were local. ASARCO's Mexican employees came from the central highlands, creating a large body of wage-earners accustomed to migrating for jobs.

Mexico's industrial revolution was powered by coal, which was needed to construct and maintain the railway system. The northern state of Coahuila became the country's center of coal production. Like the copper industry, it was dominated by large international firms, the largest being ASARCO. However, the Madero family controlled various mines and smelters that remained independent of the Guggenheims, including their own smelter at Monterrey. With their higher wages, the mines became a draw for workers from central Mexico. The Unión Minera Mexicana flourished for a time during the revolution but was dissolved after the government put down strikes through force.[10]

Located just 25 miles from the US border, the Cananea mining district in Sonora was in many ways an extension of the mining networks of Arizona. The CCCC shipped tons of copper from its mines north via rail.[11] Tensions rose between managers and the Mexican workforce of 5,300, especially over the higher pay and better conditions enjoyed by the company's 2,200 American workers. Mexican and Yaqui indigenous workers lived in poor conditions in makeshift camps, whereas the Americans lived in a modern company town. Large numbers of Chinese migrants also lived at Cananea to work in the mines and small businesses.

Práxedis Guerrero, a PLM guerilla leader, joined union organizers in Arizona and then founded several "Club Liberals" to spread the message on both sides of the border. Their work led to a failed raid into Sonora in 1906 and a large PLM presence at Cananea.[12] When the company announced that workers would be paid by piecework, Mexican workers walked out. On June 1, 1906, several Americans who worked for the company fired shots into a crowd of 3,000, killing several people. In the ensuing violence, people were killed on both sides. William Greene requested reinforcements. The governor of Sonora called up a posse of 275 men from Arizona, mostly Arizona Rangers, who along with a contingent of *Rurales* led by Emil Kosterlitzky violently crushed the strike.

US authorities and the Mexican government worked together to arrest the PLM leadership on both sides of the border, including Ricardo Flores Magón in 1907. The PLM in turn led a wave of small uprisings in 1908.[13] To many Mexicans, these events illustrated the Porfirian government's prioritizing of American industrial interests over those of Mexican workers. Protests erupted in some parts the country, and the slogan "Mexico for the Mexicans" became popular.[14] In Cananea, some who had walked on the picket lines joined revolutionary forces after 1910, while more left the city and migrated north to mines. In 1911, workers from Arizona and Sonora combined to organize another short-lived strike at Cananea. Throughout these strikes and union efforts, workers circulated between the mines and the other major growth industry in northern Mexico, cotton.

The cotton migratory circuit in the borderlands was the culmination of a century-long expansion, using free and unfree labor.[15] American colonists seeking to expand slavery westward started cotton plantations in Mexican Texas during the 1820s. They came into conflict with the Mexican government in the Texas-Mexican war, in which Mexico lost control of Texas; Mexico subsequently lost the rest of its north in the Mexican-American War (1846–1848). During the US. Civil War, cotton was exported from Matamoros, and this encouraged the growth of a domestic cotton industry in Mexico, which picked up during the 1880s with the arrival of rail transport.

In Laguna, a region with abundant fertile land, the arrival of the railroad, irrigation, large-scale commercial agriculture, and migrant workers created a cotton boom. Its population increased from 20,000 people in 1890 to almost 200,000 in 1910. Torreón grew from 200 people in 1890 to 43,000 by 1910. Drawing water from the river Nazas, the *haciendas* grew cotton and guayule.[16] Across the region, small landowners and traditional villages were pushed out, replaced with landless migrant workers. While the wages they earned were higher than those of other agricultural *haciendas*, they were still low. Upwards of 50,000 seasonal workers came to the region to pick for a few weeks. These cotton workers subsequently participated in circular migration routes.

In the 1920s, Catarino Lermo remembered the migration of workers from the Laguna to Texas: "The Mexicans used to walk to cotton picking or ride the burros. Many of them stayed and grubbed land. Some returned to Mexico every year. They went as far as Guadalupe and Austin and the Sabine River and returned."[17] The Laguna region developed a symbiotic relationship with the cotton industry of its northern neighbor, Texas, turning it into both a destination and a sending region for migrants. Cotton in Laguna matured several weeks earlier than in Texas, its season lasting from August to October. By late September, growers had to contend with a population of 30,000 pickers who left the fields for better wages in Texas. Laguna growers' efforts to prevent workers from departing before the picking was finished were for the most part unsuccessful. The region offered wages sufficient enough to attract people but not high enough to keep them.[18]

In Sonora and Arizona, the Yaqui, who had lived in the region for thousands of years, were displaced by these changes. While some communities embraced change, others rebelled against Porfirio Díaz. In the 1890s, the federal government defeated them in a scorched-earth campaign that cost hundreds of lives. Afterward, 15,000 people were deported into forced labor in the Yucatán, and others were dispersed to work on local *haciendas*. Displaced Yaqui fled north across the border to seek safety, establishing communities at Tucson and Yuma, Arizona. Across northern Mexico, displaced Yaqui went to work

Figure 2.2 In Sonora, Mexico, Yaqui Indians, enlisted in the Mexican Army, being transported by boxcars. Frank and Frances Carpenter Collection, Library of Congress Prints and Photographs Division, LC-USZ62-116979.

in the mining towns of the region including Cananea, the *haciendas* of the Laguna, and railroads across northern Mexico. The Mexican Central Railway hired thousands, separating them into Yaqui labor gangs. The Santa Fe Railway followed this pattern with separate Yaqui section labor gangs across the US Southwest. The Yaqui became the largest Mexican indigenous group participating in circular migration specifically as indigenous migrants. In these cross-border spaces, large numbers of Yaqui joined the PLM and IWW, and large numbers later joined the Mexican Revolution.[19] Their struggle for labor part of their ongoing struggle for land.[20]

Overall, the expansion of the Porfirian economy in the north led to the growth of industries that relied on wage labor, migrants from other parts of the country, and links to US markets while destabilizing agrarian communities. Some northern families, like the Terrazas of Chihuahua and the Maderos of Coahuila, grew increasingly powerful by vertically integrating agricultural and industrial operations, but the arrival of markets had a detrimental effect on *rancheros*, villages, and indigenous communities. Workers flocked to mining operations and *haciendas*, as well as left in droves.

Figure 2.3 An indigenous section gang at work on the tracks in the Atchison, Topeka, and Santa Fe Railway yards. Jack Delano, Needles, California, 1943. Library of Congress Prints and Photographs Division, LC-USW3- 021392-E.

One mine in Chihuahua estimated it lost 8,000 workers a year to mines in the United States.[21] In Sonora, employers complained that 80% of their workers from central Mexico had migrated to the United States.[22] In other words, these operations acted as a steppingstone for workers.

Cotton and Mining in the US Southwest

Picking cotton under the desert sun was some of the hardest work imaginable. Workers—men, women and children—got up at 5:00 a.m. and reported to the fields well before sunrise. Groups of pickers moved up two rows at a time, crouching down as they worked to free the cotton from the plant and avoid the razor-sharp bristles that covered it. Their hands became calloused from continual cuts. Pickers worked in hundred-degree heat from sunrise to sunset with maybe one break and little in the way of water, supplies, or housing. They worked as fast as they could, as they were paid by the weight of their bags, each bag weighing up to 100 pounds. An experienced picker might produce up to 300 pounds in a day. Most averaged half that and took home just a dollar a day for their efforts. The poor labor conditions ruined bodies and shortened life spans, as consular reports of the dead show. Yet year after year, Mexicans from central and northern Mexico joined with *Tejanos*/Mexican Americans in a great labor migration circuit that started in the Laguna region of Mexico and moved north through Arizona and Texas before families headed back or moved on other types of work. Few made the entire journey; instead, people joined and left at various points along the circuit. Journalist and scholar Carey McWilliams describes an "initial vanguard of about 25,000 Mexican migratory workers. As the army marches through the Robstown–Corpus Christi area, and additional 25,000 recruits join the procession. By the time the army has reached central Texas, it has probably grown to about 250,000 to 300,000 workers. Recruits join the army, follow it through a county or two, and then drop out, to be replaced with new families from the next county."[23]

Cotton made up the largest circuit in the migration between Mexico and the United States, but before cotton could boom in the US Southwest, the people and land needed to be transformed. After the Treaty of Guadalupe Hidalgo was signed, roughly 75,000 Mexicans became US citizens; excluded from this figure were 150,000 indigenous people, who were subjected to military raids and forced labor. Mass waves of white settlers arrived, many of recent European origin. Natives were forced into reservations, while Mexican Americans were subjected to disenfranchisement and rendered outsiders on their own lands.[24] The Reclamation Act of 1902 provided federal funds for western states to irrigate, dam, and control rivers to create new farmland. The irrigation of the lower Rio Grande Valley enabled the expansion of cultivation, and the cotton crop of Texas more than doubled.

The economy of Texas had traditionally been built on ranches, obtained through the dispossession of *Tejano*-owned lands following the Texas War of Independence. The arrival of irrigation intensified these trends. As ranches gave way to plantations, property values rose, wages fell, and thousands of

(a)

(b)

Figure 2.4a and b Cotton picking in South Texas. Dorothea Lange, 1936. Library of Congress Prints and Photographs Division, LC-USF34- 009810-E & LC-USF34- 009828-E.

small *Tejano* farmers were forced to sell their land due to the boom-and-bust cycles of cotton prices.[25] A large number of these former landowners became tenant and sharecropping farmers, especially in the cotton-growing region. Paul Ortis's family migrated from Mexico to Gonzalez County and became sharecroppers, which meant that the family only kept half of what they grew. Paul and his siblings worked in the cotton fields from childhood, and he became the primary caretaker at a young age when his father was drafted into service in World War I.[26] Like their African American and white Anglo counterparts, *Tejano* and Mexican families were trapped in a cycle of debt to growers who supplied equipment and capital. Increasingly they were replaced by new migrant farm workers from Mexico.[27]

Texas' history of social, racial, and economic stratification meant that farmers had few avenues to improve their situation. The 1920 and 1930 census figures provide some details about the trajectories of Mexican tenants (and sharecroppers) vis-à-vis migrant farm workers. Almost a fifth of the total 1930 sample, representing 195 individuals, were tenant farmers in Texas.[28] Unlike other agricultural workers, almost all of them were living in the same place in 1930 as in 1920. If they did move, it was within the same city or county. They also showed the lowest occupational mobility of any group. The same was true of their children. Most of the second generation were also agricultural workers, and some also become tenant farmers. Compared with agricultural laborers, most of whom were living somewhere other than where they had been ten years earlier. In other words, tenants stayed even when their economic prospects were not good.

By the 1910s, 50,000 Mexicans came every year into Texas, and between 50% and 75% of them returned to Mexico every year.[29] Cotton growers depended on a large infrastructure to supply workers. Individual growers hired labor recruiters and farmers' associations to hire and transport workers from El Paso and Laredo (though many routinely recruited in Mexico proper against the law). From the cities, the pickers would be brought by trains or trucks into the fields. Recruiting involved promises of pay, transportation, and return passage, though actual follow-through varied greatly from employer to employer. Workers were charged the costs of their own recruitment, including housing, food, and rail costs. Contracts could be arranged well in advance of the trip, or at the spot of recruitment, or be avoided altogether.[30] Whole families, including children, were part of the labor contracts, as growers believed families were less likely to quit than men hired individually. This meant there were significant numbers of children in the fields.[31] Women usually traveled the cotton circuit as part of large families, but some did migrate as *solas* (single migrants). Women worked in the fields but additionally took on the bulk of household and childcare labor. Large numbers of migrants worked in groups, as part of crews with a single *mayordomo* (foreman). Crews could include nuclear families, extended relatives, people from the same village, or friends made along the circuit. The *mayordomo* would negotiate for the group and find new jobs. Cotton-picking wages could be as low as 75 cents a day and up to two dollars a day at the peak of harvest. For the most part, workers remained around a dollar a day in the 1910s and a dollar and fifty cents a day through most of the 1920s.

In Arizona, the completion of the Roosevelt Dam in 1911, along with the Reclamation Act, led to a cotton boom across the state. Growers did not need to directly recruit Mexican workers; *enganchero*s or *padrones* (labor bosses common among ethnic immigrants) did it for them. By the end of the decade, over 30,000 Mexican migrants worked in the Arizona cotton fields, making about a dollar and a half a day. However, because of the irregular nature of work in these industries, people circulated between the mines, cotton, and railroads.[32] Growers only needed to hire workers at the peak of the harvest and had no need to employ and pay them year-around. Families had to migrate from job to job in order to survive.

To get copper to market, railroads were built across Arizona, New Mexico, and northern Mexico, which increased the ability of Mexicans on both sides to seek work in these new mines. The Southern Pacific railroad arrived in 1878, connecting Arizona to California, New Mexico, Texas, and beyond. In the 1890s, the Phelps Dodge Corporation built railroads across Arizona to connect to El Paso. In New Mexico, the arrival of the railroad revived old ways of life: as sheep and cattle herding grew, so too did the output of the ancient Santa Rita copper mine while spurring an exodus into neighboring regions.[33] The availability of raw copper from Mexico made it advantageous for ARSCO to build its smelter in El Paso. The mostly Mexican workforce in the company town, called Smeltertown, came from both sides of the border.[34] Independently owned mining operations began to consolidate as Phelps Dodge bought mines in the border area, including those in Sonora, Mexico, and Bisbee, Arizona.[35] The large mine at Jerome, Arizona, remained independent under the United Verde Copper Company. By the early twentieth century, Arizona was dominated by several large copper companies that together produced half of the country's copper output. Companies used their power to carve out local fiefdoms where they could exercise political control over their own company towns.[36]

American railroads were as hungry for fuel as Mexican ones. In the Rio Grande Valley, the coal industry was driven by dozens of small, undercapitalized firms. In Texas, coal companies sent *enganchadores* into Mexico to recruit mine workers, creating a coal migratory circuit. The Mireles family, for example, was recruited from Matehuala, San Luis Potosí, to Rockdale, Texas. José Angel Mireles was married to Amada García, a woman from Coahuila, who also migrated using those circuits. José Angel told an interviewer that, after a while, people came on their own accord after hearing about the jobs in Rockdale mines, making *enganchadores* less essential. Wages in Texas mines averaged $1.75 to $4.00 a day.[37]

Mining towns in the Southwest attracted migrants from as far away as Europe and China, as well as Mexicans from both sides of the border. But workers were compensated as groups, and the most prestigious and highest paying jobs weren't open to all. Most mines operated on a dual-wage system that paid one wage for "white" workers of $2.50 to $4.00 a day and another, lower "Mexican" wage of around $1.50 a day. Citizenship was irrelevant; US-born Mexican Americans were paid the lower wage.[38] Yet even at this rate, Mexican workers were earning far higher wages than back home.

In Jerome, Arizona, the Mexican population grew from a handful to several thousand, and smaller Mexican camps popped up across Yavapai County. Most of these migrants worked for the United Verde Mining Company, which owned several copper mines and a smelter in Jerome; the company openly recruited Mexican miners, drawing workers from Aguascalientes.[39] The town boasted dozens of Mexican associations, stores, and boarding houses. Mexicans lived separately from whites. Jerome's large population of men, mostly in boarding houses or as boarders with families, was similar to other mining towns. Households usually included additional relatives, friends, and renters.[40] Education was also segregated. Migrants organized and gained consular support to create a separate Spanish-language elementary school with funds from the Mexican government.[41]

Miners began to go back and forth between northern Mexico and the US Southwest.[42] Pedro Silva grew up along the border, mined coal in Arizona and Texas for many years, and also worked in cotton before going to Kansas City. There, he became an alcohol smuggler before returning home to Chihuahua and retiring on a ranch he built in Zaragoza.[43] Teresa de Guerrero from Hermosillo, Sonora, came with her husband, lived in Bisbee during the strike, and then moved to Tucson, where she ran the local *Cruz Azul* medical association for the Mexican community. After several years, she and her husband moved back to Sonora.[44] By 1910, Arizona's population had grown to 204,000, of whom 71,000 were Mexican migrants. While outnumbered by the migration of European migrants to the state, Mexicans were the primary labor force for the state's largest industries. They comprised 60% of Arizona's mine workers, more than half of its railroad workers, and the bulk of its migrant farm workers.

The Bureau of Immigration Investigates Labor Recruitment

Traditionally, El Paso del Norte (renamed Ciudad Juárez in 1888), one of the largest cities in northern Mexico, was the gateway to the frontier. The convergence of the railroads changed the dynamic and led to spectacular growth on the US side. The Mexican Central railroad ended at Ciudad Juárez, where it linked to the Southern Pacific Railway and the Atchison, Topeka, and Santa Fe Railway. Juárez/El Paso became the major hub of migration routes. There, workers signed contracts that sent them west to the mining regions or California, northeast to cotton in Texas and Oklahoma, north to sugar beets and steel in the Midwest, or to railroad jobs in all these areas. An estimated 1.5 million people crossed the border in El Paso between 1880 and 1930, an unknown but large number of whom were repeating circular migrants.[45] It is estimated that a fifth of the daily traffic across the border were people who worked in El Paso and lived in Juárez. More troubling for officials were the agents who took contract workers into the interior.[46] The city's economy was also tied to the mining borderlands through its copper smelters. As a hub of migration, El Paso became the center of efforts to control the movement of labor.

Created in 1903 under the Department of Commerce and Labor to staff "inland ports," the Bureau of Immigration initially had only sixty agents to patrol the thousands of miles of border between the United States and Mexico.[47] These agents lacked the ability to establish much jurisdiction beyond their border stations. The bureau's weak presence matched Mexicans' peripheral status in US immigration policy, which prioritized restricting Asian and European migration.[48] Immigration officials viewed Mexicans as the "natural" peasants of the Southwest and had relatively little interest in their movements.[49] Border inspectors routinely allowed Mexicans to pass without question, sometimes not even looking up from their newspapers. The expansion of ferry services across the Rio Grande concerned the inspector general of El Paso only when he received reports that Europeans and Chinese were disguising themselves as Mexicans in order to cross the border.[50] The 1903 law gave officials the authority to deport people who entered without inspection; in the border region, agents primarily resorted to "voluntary departure" of Mexicans rather than formal legal deportation and didn't keep records of those they sent back.[51]

Bureau of Immigration agent Frank Stone's 1910 investigation found a large migration from central Mexico to the major mines in Mexico that often preceded people crossing the border to work in the mines of Arizona and New Mexico. While he suspected people were violating the contract law, Stone could not find evidence for it. Instead, he found that numerous migrants were going to the United States after hearing about the availability of jobs.[52] He concluded, "[Among] the largest employers of labor in the Southwest the claim is unanimous . . . that the Mexican common laborer is a necessity in the development of this section of the United States."[53] The Bureau began a large investigation of labor agent activities that focused on several companies in El Paso. One prominent subject of investigation was John Sullivan of the Atchison, Topeka, and Santa Fe Railway, who lured workers to US jobs by promising food, accommodation, and tickets on Mexican railroads to the border. Another target was Ramon González, who sent business cards to Juárez in search of labor recruits.[54] The investigations revealed the role of small independent agents, such as Rámon González and Zarate & Avina, and recruiting by large companies like the Holmes Supply Company, the Hamlin Supply Company, and the L. H. Manning Company (which supplied the Southern Pacific), which all held contracts from companies to send workers to various regions.

Enganchadores linked migrants and employers across vast geographic spaces and provided the things migrants needed. For example, Rámon González, who grew up in El Paso, was fluent in both Spanish and English and became the city's first Mexican police officer. He used that position to build a business in labor contracting. Working with city authorities, he would arrest people for "vagrancy" and force them into his contracts. He owned several boarding houses in El Paso and Juárez, salons, and even a brothel. He developed such good relationships with governments on both sides of the border, including consulates, that the person in charge of the migrant registry in Juárez sent workers directly to him or Zarate & Avina.[55] In his many years of business, he primarily contracted for the Santa Fe system going to the Midwest but also offered smaller contracts for mining and sugar beet companies, such as the Colorado Iron and Fuel Company. Like other immigrant brokers, his business was essential to the functioning of the dynamic transnational labor market. These transnational networks made his business possible but also brought him government scrutiny.[56]

The labor contracting companies fought off competition from independent Mexican labor agents. Holmes, Hamlin, and other companies tried to form a single monopoly. They purposely excluded González and Zarate & Avina, who subsequently formed a rival company. After much lobbying, the Holmes and Hamlin companies gained the support of Supervising Inspector Frank W. Berkshire, who saw the competition as contributing to uncontrolled migration and lawbreaking. Officials believed that labor agents were the primary cause of Mexican migration and that, if they could be controlled, so too could the flow of bodies. Labor agents were in fact encouraging people to come outside legal channels, sometimes working with coyotes.[57] The result was the "Mexican Agreements," whereby the Bureau of Immigration would work with official contracting companies to eliminate individual labor agents and replace them with salaried company employees. Effectively, the government would control the arrival of workers in accordance with US company needs. Migrants would be forced to sign up for one of the companies and could not choose which one. What Inspector Berkshire saw as progress, however, others saw as a flagrant violation of US law since the government would be working to bring in contract workers. González and Zarate & Avina sued and appealed to the Commissioner of Migration, arguing that this agreement violated the rights of free labor. The Commerce Department started an investigation that, after a year, reversed the decision and rebuked Berkshire. While this specific effort to bring migration under government direction failed, it laid the groundwork for the World War I labor exemptions.[58]

Migrants were not passive in their interactions with labor agents and bureau inspectors. They used labor scarcity to negotiate the best terms from prospective employers. One official described the scene outside its offices once migrants were released: "There, agents representing the railroads and the ranches would make speeches about the delightful quarters, good pay, and fine food they would have if they went to work for their company. When the promising was over, the agents would shout, 'This way for the Santa Fe,' 'this way for the South Pacific,' and so on, the men following the agent they thought offered the best or most benefits."[59] Labor recruiters found themselves competing for labor as migrants held out for better wages and benefits.

Supervising Inspector Berkshire, who heavily influenced the enforcement of immigration policy, was confident that Mexicans did not pose a threat to white labor and instead focused on Asian immigration.[60] Based in El Paso, he came to believe labor agents played a small role compared with the word-of-mouth rumors of well-paid US jobs. Berkshire wrote, "Mexico is a natural source of labor supply for the southwest, and therefore the movement of laborers across the border is, for the most part, a natural one. Such laborers have been passing back and forth over the border for years, and in the great majority of cases the only apparent inducement to migrate is a knowledge that work at better wages than prevail in Mexico can be found here."[61] He believed the vast majority of Mexicans undertook US jobs for a few months a year. Commissioner General Anthony Caminetti agreed with this approach, seeking to exempt Mexican migrant workers from most of the restrictive legislation of the era and even pulling back enforcement at border towns.[62] Officials throughout the Bureau believed migration was temporary, advantageous to the local economic development of the US Southwest, and were not interested in ending it.

Ultimately, the labor agent's primary role was in presenting options to those who had never gone north before, those without personal connections. Brokers facilitated migration and introduced Mexicans to new industries and cities, especially those far from the border. Efforts by labor agents and the Bureau of Immigration to control the flow of migration came up short. Berkshire had to admit that migration would not cease if the labor recruiters went away. Although labor agents certainly played a role in facilitating migration and in determining which companies hired Mexicans in large numbers, once workers arrived they became increasingly difficult to control. González and his peers had very little power over their workers, who constantly quit, deserted, and sought better conditions. Once the brokers made the initial connection to jobs, migrants had little use for them.[63] Labor agents were only one step in the infrastructure of migration. In fact, many migrants left Mexico only after hearing from family or friends who had already made the journey.[64]

Migrant Families at the Board of Special Inquiry

When Victor Zamorano crossed the border in 1917 with seven relatives, mostly women and children, he knew what to say. He explained that he was a miner and lived with his brothers and sisters in Arizona. He had gone down to Mexico to get cousins and other relatives who wanted to come north to work. They gave testimony that there was no work for their respective professions in Sonora. When asked why his relatives did not stay and work in Mexico, he answered, "Because they wanted to come up with us to Winkleman, because all the rest of the family are up there." When asked what they would do, he answered, "Fidel is going to work up there." The inspector asked if there was a lot of work, and Victor answered yes. The inspector, fishing for a violation, then asked if there was a specific place he was going to work. Without hesitating, Victor said, "Everywhere. There is lots of work all over, in the concentrator, in the mines, and everywhere." He also said the women, Josefa and Adela, were "willing to get out and work, to do housework or anything they can get to do." He said they were seamstresses and that there was plenty of such work in Arizona. When the inspector asked his cousin Fidel about work in Mexico, Fidel answered, "There has been no work over there. You can't earn wages down there now." Victor and Fidel both insisted that the nephew, 12-year-old Miguel, would go to school and would not work. With these questions answered and no violations found, the family was legally admitted.[65]

When Bureau of Immigration officials encountered a non-nuclear family or suspected someone of violating immigration law, they referred the cases to the Board of Special Inquiry for further investigation. These cases feature the people affected speaking in their own words. However, these are not unfiltered accounts. Like the Zamorano family, migrants were incentivized to tell stories that fit established legal avenues for entry. Records show that migrants were aware of the major legal pitfalls, were conscious of how their words would be used, and learned to navigate the system to their advantage. Their cases also illustrate the ways in which extended family networks were themselves a survival strategy.

Women, children, and extended family members were usually going north to join relatives who were already working and living in the country. They were also more likely to seek legal entry rather than take the risks of crossing outside the law, but they faced several procedural hurdles. The Alien Contract Labor Law of 1885 made it illegal for migrants to have a job lined up on arrival, the 1907 Immigration Act enlarged the categories of people excluded from immigrating, and the 1917 Immigration Act added a literacy requirement, imposed an eighteen-dollar head tax, and greatly expanded the definition of those excluded, such as those brought for immoral purposes. Extended families had to assure inspectors they were not "Liable to be a Public Charge," they would be able to support themselves through paid work, and at the same time, that they didn't already have a specific job. Migrant documents and testimony were shaped in anticipation of the questions. A. J. Milliken, Inspector in Charge at the Santa Fe Bridge in El Paso, complained about the difficulty of proving immigration violations in such cases: "Most of the Mexicans will tell of work they're going to and show the letter of a friend or relative. They will say they have work, not realizing they are giving testimony of contract labor, but their letters don't show it."[66]

Trinidad Orrellana found herself before the Board when she brought her young sisters with her to join her brother. Her family had migrated from Mexico City to northern Mexico before her brother went to work for the mines in Arizona. When he sent for her, she tried to cross with the rest of their siblings.[67] Women and children were brought to questioning if they arrived outside of nuclear families, usually with a grandparent, siblings, or aunt/uncle. Among the women who arrived at the Arizona and El Paso stations, the majority were going to join relatives. From the thousands of extant files, a few examples suffice to show how family ties and the performance of gender norms framed the experience of migrants. Micaela Quintero appeared before the Board while moving from Cananea to Douglas, Arizona, in 1917. She had worked for the CCCC in Cananea and was going to join her aunt.[68] When Juana Mendoza appeared before the Board, she had been living with her grandparents in Cananea for several years. She told the inspector that she didn't work and her father sent money from Bisbee, where he made $3.40 per day at the Copper Queen mine. She and her brother, she said, were going to join their parents in Arizona.[69]

The Bureau spent a lot of effort launching investigations of Chinese, European, and Mexican women, seeking to find and exclude prostitutes, and laws sought to place Mexican women and children within clearly defined hierarchies.[70] The Bureau's efforts to enforce gender norms extended into personal sexual activity. Women who were not under the supervision of their parents or husband came under immediate suspicion, especially if they were supporting themselves or had children out of wedlock. Some Mexican couples who had already been married by the church were married officially at border towns before crossing in order to avoid these suspicions, though this didn't prevent inspectors' questions. Men could also come under investigation for "moral turpitude" if they were suspected

Figure 2.5 Mexicans entering the United States. US immigration station, El Paso, Texas. Dorothea Lange, 1938. Library of Congress Prints and Photographs Division, LC-USF34- 018215-E.

of being homosexual or didn't strictly meet expectations of outward masculinity.[71]

Children posed a particular problem for Bureau inspectors. American immigration law only recognized nuclear families and, after 1907, children unaccompanied by their parents were considered an "excluded class," so they were admitted only at the discretion of inspectors.[72] This conception of family was in tension with the Mexican *compadrazgo* (godparent) system, in which it was routine for large extended families to live together and for godparents, grandparents, aunts and uncles, older siblings, or cousins to raise children, especially if the parents had migrated or died. Sometimes this also meant children were raised as servants in a wealthier household. The

Revolution led to tens of thousands of adult deaths, leaving children to be raised outside of nuclear families on a substantial scale. As they migrated, families expanded *compadrazgo* across borders as a strategy of survival.

As the volume of transnational families increased, family networks encouraged the further migration of relatives. Large numbers of children went north to join relatives after the deaths of their parents. This was the case for Catalina and Guadalupe Lopez, sisters who were traveling from Cananea to an Arizona mining camp named Tintown; for Dolores Morales, who came north to reunite with her two brothers, miners in Tucson, after their parents died; and for Rosas Quijada, who lost her father, a miner in Cananea, and was going to live with family friends and work as a domestic servant.[73] Again and again, relatives insisted that children would not undertake paid work, and that the family had enough resources to send them to school. The practice of children crossing borders, extending families across space, was becoming normalized.

Estimates vary, but somewhere between a quarter and a third of the migrants from Mexico during the 1910s and 1920s were younger than eighteen. In El Paso, the school census in 1915 revealed that there were 9,141 Mexican/*Tejano* children out of a total ethnic Mexican population of 32,724, nearly a third of the total.[74] Bureau inspectors were responding to contradictory impulses in American society when they inquired into whether young migrants would work and go to school. Anti-child labor laws and compulsory education laws were starting to be passed by states in response to changing middle-class conceptions of childhood that envisioned children less as labor and more as vulnerable treasures to protect. This conception did not extend to non-white children, however; every state included exceptions for agricultural workers where most of the African American and Mexican workforce was concentrated. Girls also were still expected to do the bulk of household labor, which was not considered "work" by government officials. Cities in Texas passed education laws but had no intention of providing it for Mexican children. When informed of the number of Mexican children that would enter local schools, El Paso balked at the expense of compulsory attendance. Mexican children were expected to work, not go to school.[75]

The experience of the Mendoza family was typical. Feliciano Mendoza and his wife migrated to Arizona, where he became a skilled miner earning five dollars a day. When he purchased a small piece of land, he decided to settle the rest of his relatives with him there. Thus, Feliciano's mother, Felicita, and a large group of cousins appeared before the Board in February 1919. The family assured the Board that the younger ones would go to school rather than work. Like others, Feliciano assured the board that he had enough money to care for his family, that the older family members would work, that there were few jobs available in Mexico for their skills, and that they could easily find work in Arizona, though not in any specific place.[76] The unlikely preciseness of the migrants' responses does not necessarily mean they were lying to the authorities. Migration was primarily a family affair, with relatives helping other relatives and acquaintances to cross the border and establish themselves.

In most Board of Inquiry cases, migrants had a destination and job in mind, relying on extended family networks for information. Many did have specific job offers. While they remained a minority, a significant number of women and children crossed the border. Most school-aged migrants probably ended up working for wages.[77] Yet their responses to questions had to fit an acceptable narrative to pass inspection. Once on the other side, wives and daughters of farm workers and miners practiced additional survival strategies. They kept gardens, created mutual associations, and worked to create multiple family revenue streams.[78] Young women often worked, sometimes as domestic servants in the wealthier white sections of town.[79] It was not uncommon for every member to work as part of a transnational family. Migration was difficult, which is why circuits of information—in the forms of brokers, relatives, newspapers, and *mutualistas* (self-help mutual organizations) that sprouted across the region—were critical to the success of extended families.

Information Networks and Brokers in Texas

Cities were places where railroads, labor agents, institutions, word of mouth, and the public sphere collided. Mexican communities shared informal and institutional information that was essential for people navigating their new homes. As these organizations lowered the difficulties of migrating, they linked communities across vast spaces to one another. Farm workers and miners were not isolated from this. Across the region, migrants interacted with long-settled *Tejanos*/Mexican Americans, and older migrants with new.

In addition to El Paso, San Antonio and Laredo were also home to labor agencies that recruited across the region and pushed to the limits of the law. San Antonio in particular became a major recruitment hub, with 20,000 leaving the city for cotton fields in the Midwest every year. *Enganchadores* and workers looking for jobs concentrated around Milam Park, the major plaza on the West Side, along with labor activists and preachers. Aside from the largest labor agencies, most recruiters were not tied to any particular employer. Some were operated by Mexicans and *Tejanos*. The parents of Francisco Guerra were such middlemen: his father was an *enganchador* who contracted Mexicans in the border areas, and his mother owned a grocery store that sold goods to these workers.[80] Not all labor contractors in San Antonio, as elsewhere, were reputable. A man named Campa, for example, charged both companies and his workers fees for his services.[81] Labor contractors routinely gave loans to workers to help them make the journey but could be exploitative, charging exorbitant fees and high interest rates. Others developed loyal followings and good reputations in the community; the same was true of employers.

In addition to networks of people, far-flung communities of migrants were connected by the Spanish-language press, especially San Antonio's *La Prensa*. People would gather in groups to hear one person read the newspaper aloud and then pass it on to others. Papers traveled out of the city via the Santa Fe railroad and other routes. As one labor agent explained, "Many in the railroad camps subscribed; it was typical that twelve papers would be delivered to a camp of twenty-five. About twenty percent of the Mexicans take *La Prensa* in railroad camps."[82] One Mexican who worked on the Santa Fe recounted, "We get *La Prensa* here and when I finish reading it I pass it to someone else."[83]

In addition to its coverage of events in Mexico, perhaps the newspapers' most important section was its classified advertisements that regularly listed hundreds of jobs in agriculture, railroads, and other industries.[84] They included urban work as well as rural employment, and jobs for men as for women. In fact, job openings for women made up more than half of the advertisements, perhaps because men tended to be recruited by large employers. Mexican businesses, boarding houses, and service providers advertised in the newspaper too.[85] Take these, for example, from January 1920:

> "needed, 50 men to clear land, $10 per acre, $1.50 per bush"
> "many workers needed, good pay, permanent work, housing included, go to Portland Cement company in Dallas"
> "needed, 500 Mexicans to clear woods in La Vernia Texas, 25 miles east of San Antonio. 8000 acres of short woods, the price is $1.50 per bush. Do not

delay, come to Lavernia and ask for El Pazon, which is on the ranch of H.B. Holmes. The land is pure; the cut is Oak and Black Jack C.M. POSE (EL Pazon) who never denies a favor to an honest and hardworking Mexican"
"needed, women to wash, sow, and iron by hand and machine"
"needed, women to work in cigarette factory. Come to Fink Cigar Factory"
"rooms for rent, clean"
"furnished rooms in well run house"

The Mexican consulate promoted certain employers in the newspaper. The Michigan Sugar Company was among those seeking laborers for beet work and offered transportation to Michigan and back in October.[86] The consulate endorsed their efforts, along with those of other companies. Labor agencies advertised their abilities to get work for people. "Star Employment Co, *puede proporcionar a usted trabajadores y empleos!*" and similar headlines ran next to ads for consumer products. The same was true of money-sending services. Mayo's Money Exchange related a story of hard-working migrants who tried to save on remittances, only to lose the whole amount to theft. They told migrants that they could be trusted with their hard-earned money. The Los Angeles Mercantile Co. described themselves to readers as trusted by experienced migrants and promised to send money back home faster and more securely than competitors.[87]

Ads also matched workers to new types of work and to people, as did local stores, pool halls, and bars. *Mutualistas* and church organizations were formed to help those in need. A lot of their expenses went to providing food and medical assistance to the poor and repatriating the injured or destitute. Much of their off-the-books work was informal assistance in the form of information, such as jobs where they wouldn't be exploited, affordable places to live, and shops that didn't overcharge. Most boarding house owners, small business owners, and numerous supervisors were *Tejanos* and settled Mexicans. Living and working in the same spaces, these settled Mexican Americans gave practical aid to new migrants and made them part of the community.

Official channels existed too. Both national governments had agencies that spread information among workers. The consulates circulated bulletins explaining workers' rights and held meetings throughout the countryside to address workers' concerns. Even US government agencies spread information about workers' rights.[88] The consulate and organizations like the Mexican Protective League also acted as brokers, linking migrants with work in agriculture. However, migrants saw consulates as serving the interest of businesses more than advocating for their co-ethnics. This suspicion was not helped by the divisions in the migrant community during and after the Mexican Revolution.

Revolution in Northern Mexico

The revolution caused much of the Mexican mining economy to grind to a halt, setting people in motion. In Baja California, the PLM organized a short-lived revolt led by Cananea strike leader José María Leyva. In Sonora, the Yaqui indigenous people revolted. Different factions fought on different sides of the conflict, while others raided *haciendas* and lands owned by American companies in what had once been Yaqui territory. American companies put enormous pressure on every faction to protect US property, and most did so despite hysteria in US media about property confiscation. In 1913, ASARCO shut down all its mining and smelting operations in Mexico, forcing out 7,000 workers. Sonora depended almost entirely on Cananea's mines for its tax revenue, yet workers there turned increasingly radical. When the PLM and IWW took control of the Cananea mines, Phelps Dodge responded by cutting power. Plutarco Elías Calles, who was now in charge of the state, attempted to take over the mines or convince company officials to accept the union, but his efforts failed. Calles appeased company officials by rolling back labor reforms and offering train rides to Arizona for any worker who wanted to leave Cananea. Within a month, 16,000 people had crossed into Arizona.[89] In Coahuila, coal mines were abandoned, workers fled into Texas, and production plummeted until Carranza's forces took direct control, but production only slowly came back.[90]

Across the borderlands, the revolution drove migration. At various points, waves of people arrived at border towns, some driven away by violence and others by food shortages in Sonora and Chihuahua.[91] Jesus Luis Acuña, an indigenous Sonoran, left the seminary and became a mason in Cananea. In 1923, he moved to Tucson, where he started his own construction business.[92] He is one example of how workers used their skills acquired in Mexico to remake their lives in the United States. Conrado Martinez from Parral, Chihuahua, came with his father to work in the cotton fields and then railroads. Afterward, he went to Arizona and became a miner.[93] Daniel Aguilar grew up in Chihuahua as a miner before becoming a store owner there. His wife, Maria, from Durango, was a well-educated teacher. When the revolution broke out, Daniel joined the Villista army, and after his side lost, he fled to Miami, Arizona. There, he worked as a miner while Maria became involved in the *Cruz Azul*.[94] The Aguilar family was one of thousands who made a similar choice.

The cotton economy experienced a similar flight. The Laguna region seethed with discontent. Many migrant cotton workers had returned steeped in PLM ideas, and several revolts occurred in the years before 1910.[95] Once the revolution got underway, the estates were attacked by villagers who had lost lands to the *haciendas*. They were often joined by *hacienda* workers and raids from Villistas. By 1912, the Laguna plantation economy was shattered.[96] Before the revolution, most cotton workers migrated seasonally to the Texas cotton fields, but now, these numbers swelled as more families joined.

Organizing and Revolt in the Fields

The existence of Mexican communities on both sides of the border, the relatively open nature of the border, and the growth of information networks combined to allow radical organizations to flourish. The transient nature of workers in the borderlands made the spread of the PLM possible. When the PLM's leadership fled Mexico, it remade itself as a revolutionary exile organization. The party's syndicalist-anarchist message found a receptive audience in the borderlands.[97] The party's program "offered workers a national minimum wage, an eight-hour day, and a six-day week, and it vowed to eliminate the dual-wage system, end child labor, and abolish the rapacious company stores. For rural workers and indigenous people, the PLM promised to resurrect *ejidos* [communal landholding]."[98] PLM members prepared for revolution while organizing locally for better labor conditions.

The PLM built on longstanding Mexican, Anglo, European, and African American organizing traditions in Texas. While there had been previous efforts to organize tenant cotton farmers across racial lines, union leaders encountered serious obstacles of racial distrust and an inability by union organizers to see the new Mexican migrant farm workers as subjects of organization.[99] As a result, Mexican organizers resorted to working within organizations like the Socialist Party's Renters' Union and the IWW. Numerous Mexicans and *Tejanos* came into agricultural unions through their associations with the PLM.[100] Land League and the Socialist Party organizers, José Angel Hernández, F. A. Hernández, and Lázaro Gutiérrez de Lara, organized large numbers of Mexicans inside of ethnic local organizations. *La Unión de Sembradores Mexicanos, La Sociedad Beneficienca de Agicultores Mexicanos*, and *La Unión de Agricultores Mexicanos* sought to organize Mexican farm workers in the fields during the 1910s and 1920s. In the town of Seguín, tenants and migrant workers joined the Socialist Party local to protest tenant contracts and set a minimum wage.[101] Gutiérrez de Lara personally made many of these links possible, organizing strikes at Cananea, Coahuila coal fields, and the Arizona mines, in addition to the cotton fields of both countries.[102]

The most successful effort to organize Mexican farm workers was that of *La Arupación*, which was affiliated with the PLM. Making use of nationalist rhetoric, *La Arupación* organized more than twenty locals in support of tenant and worker rights but fell into decline due to economic recession and infighting. These short-lived efforts represented real cooperation between the tenant farmers and the new migratory laborers arriving in large numbers. Many of these *Tejano* tenants, landowners, and workers had previous experience organizing during the late nineteenth century. While most white Anglo tenants saw Mexicans as threats, these radical organizations sought to build cross-racial or cross-national alliances.[103] Their efforts came to an end as the PLM was suppressed in both countries and large numbers of organizers in Texas were arrested.[104]

The Mexican Revolution, PLM ideals, and the stifling social environment of Texas produced the most violent revolt against US rule in the twentieth century. The revolt was deeply tied to the changes in land ownership, especially the loss of ranching and farming lands by *Tejanos* in South Texas.[105] By 1915, many *Tejanos* and Mexicans were regularly meeting to discuss PLM revolutionary ideas, and some had experience fighting in Mexico. Revolutionaries issued the *Plan de San Diego*, which called for the secession of Arizona, New Mexico, California, and Texas. They also called for a unification of oppressed people, including protections and lands for Native Americans and African Americans. Aniceto Pizaña, a South Texas rancher and PLM activist, became one of the principal leaders of the revolt. Along the Rio Grande Valley, Mexican *sediciosos*, as they were called, raided farms and took vengeance on those who had wronged them. A large group of raiders attacked the King Ranch flying a flag with the slogan *igualidad e independencia* (equality and independence), mirroring the PLM's *tierra y libertad* (land and freedom). They used guerrilla tactics, moved in small groups, and crossed the border for protection.

The state's response was brutal. Hundreds of Texas Rangers and local police mobilized, in addition to US Army cavalry regiments. While unsuccessful at catching raiders, they terrorized the people of southern Texas with mass arrests in *Tejano* communities. Across the state, radical organizations were shut down and leaders jailed. Agents at times shot indiscriminately at Mexican men whom they encountered. Yet the raids continued despite the violence unleashed on South Texas communities. Raiders found shelter across the border in Mexico, where Constitutionalist forces were sympathetic. Not until the revolutionary situation in Mexico settled down, the US government recognized the Carranza government, and the Mexican government stopped giving *sediciosos* haven did the raids end in late 1915. Across the state, between 500 and 3,000 Mexicans and *Tejanos* were killed through vigilante violence, and thousands were displaced from their homes. Thus ended the last effort to resist American possession of the Southwest through force.[106]

The IWW and PLM in Arizona

In 1906, Fernando Velarde joined the IWW. He went on to found several branches in Arizona and published a Spanish-language IWW newspaper, *La Unión Industrial*, before joining the Mexican Revolution.[107] He participated in the PLM invasion of Baja California and afterward settled in California, where he continued to work as a labor organizer and published newspapers calling for worker solidarity. Velarde was one of many PLM and IWW organizers who successfully built on earlier *mutualista* traditions and social networks among Mexican migrants.[108] Networks of solidarity among Mexican miners, especially among PLM members, contributed to the spread of the IWW in the Southwest. Nationally, the IWW saw itself as the vanguard for a redistribution of property and an egalitarian anarchist society, but on the ground, it organized its locals by ethnicity, relying on ethnic solidarity to function.

At Ray, Arizona, home to an ASARCO mine and a major migrant destination by the 1910s, Mexican miners in 1914, attempted to strike to end dual wages, only to be attacked by white mobs that shut down their efforts.[109] The next year, amid fears of unrest along the border, Mexican PLM supporters discussed joining the prospective uprising laid out in the *Plan de San Diego* but decided against it. Instead, workers struck against the dual-wage system and won a wage increase. Mining company officials sought to link the strike to revolutionary violence in Mexico, saying they were protecting the nation by standing against the strike.[110]

Showdowns moved to other nearby Southwest mining towns. At Bisbee, the white trade union won higher wages that were set to align with the price of copper. In response, the workers at the mostly Mexican Miami camp struck and won similar concessions. After that, workers at Morenci began to organize for the same wage scale. They formed Club Cosmopolita, a *mutualista* that quickly became a labor union. Many of the Mexican union leaders had PLM connections, which is not surprising given the overlapping nature of unions, *mutualistas*, and the organization. The fledging union was able to secure a settlement after several months.[111] In total, seventeen mining strikes occurred in 1916.

With the rise of anti-immigrant hostility that accompanied the US entry into World War I, communists as well as socialists and union organizers were labeled "un-American." Company owners fed the fear of the IWW as a dangerous radical organization that would undermine the American war effort.[112] In 1917, the Jerome Miners' Union began a strike, demanding the end of the dual-wage system. IWW organizers were often labeled as outside agitators and even traitors; to avoid this, the Mexican workers sought to keep the IWW from getting involved in the strike. Although most Mexican workers were not IWW members, some were, and this gave the company the excuse it needed to break up the union. A large vigilante mob led by the local police rounded up more than 2,500 miners, mostly Mexicans. They deported 250 of them, a violation of the workers' legal rights. This set the precedent for a much larger deportation one week later.

In Bisbee, the largest mining district in the state, the IWW-affiliated Bisbee Miners Union managed to unite the large multicultural workforce.[113] Mexicans made up only 13% of the workforce but comprised close to half of the workers on the picket lines. The IWW built on earlier organizations, not only the union, a Western Federation of Miners affiliate, but also the PLM, which had one of its largest organizations in the borderlands at Bisbee. Many of the workers had come from Cananea after it shut down, and the "Magonistas" (a colloquial reference the PLM) were referred to as the "Mexican IWW." Workers described the strike as a fight for the American standard of living and against slavery.[114]

The company worked with the sheriff to form a posse of 2,200 armed men to put down the strike. Going door to door across the city, they rounded up every striking worker they could find. Two men were killed and around 2,000 people

Figure 2.6 A strike by a multiracial coalition under the Industrial Workers of the World in the mining borderlands ended in mass arrests and deportations from the community. Bisbee deportation of IWWs, July 12, 1917. Arizona Historical Society, Pictures-Places-Bisbee-Bisbee Deportation, #43182.

were arrested; 1,186 men were placed in train boxcars and deported. They were carried 180 miles to the New Mexican desert, where they were put in outdoor pens in Columbus, New Mexico. Ninety percent of those arrested were immigrants, with Mexicans making up the largest ethnic block.[115] At least 174 Mexican families were separated by the deportations. Afterward, city charities offered women and families left behind one-way tickets out of town.[116]

In the months following the Bisbee deportations, companies used state-supported violence to break unions across the state. At Morenci, police arrested 250 Mexican workers who they feared might incite violence. The strikes continued, and after several altercations with scabs, dozens of workers were arrested and one killed, Gregorio Zorillo. Eventually, workers gave up and migrated. One group sent a letter to President Wilson requesting repatriation to Mexico.[117] The Mexican government did not take kindly to the return of former strikers. When participating miners arrived in Sonora, state authorities arrested them and sought to deport them from the state.[118] Both governments saw radicalized workers as dangerous.

In Texas, where the mining industry had constricted, a series of strikes had led to unionization under the United Mine Workers of America (UMWA), including widespread incorporation of the Mexican workforce.[119] At the beginning of World War I, the union had struck agreements for higher wages. In 1920, workers struck again for increased wages, while coal companies sought to break the UMWA and introduce the open shop. UMWA membership in coal plummeted from 450,000 to 150,000, and workers were forced to take lower and lower wages. The loss of these high-paying union jobs produced a mass exodus of Mexican workers. By 1925, only 748 remained in the state, and companies shut down the mines. Most of the remaining Mexican mine workers were repatriated to Mexico by the union in 1926 and 1927.[120]

Back in Arizona, Phelps Dodge used the drop in prices, during the postwar recession, to lower wages and purge union members. Attempts to reorganize Mexican labor by the Pan-American Federation of Labor came to naught.[121] The company offered workers passage to the agriculture fields and worked with the consulates to repatriate the rest to Mexico. As one Mexican worker described it, "Many took passage to California. Others went to New Mexico and Colorado. And others, who preferred, went to Mexico. Free because the company gave them [tickets] to wherever they wanted to go."[122] Widespread violence ended efforts to organize Mexican workers in the mines and the fields, forcing workers to turn elsewhere.

In 1921, as employment plummeted, Mexicans became the first to lose their jobs. Mexican consulates worked with employers to repatriate unemployed workers. In Morenci, 1,800 who had survived a decade of turmoil were put on trains to Mexico. This deportation by the company was done in cooperation with the consulate and promoted as a charity for the families.[123] Former mining organizers continued their work in other states, while others returned to Mexico and took part in strikes there.[124] The decline in mining came at a time when cotton production was growing, however, and miners who had previously worked in agriculture ended up joining an exodus to the fields. In the Salt River Valley, more than 200,000 acres were put into production. Between 1918 and 1921, the Arizona Cotton Growers Association recruited more than 30,000 Mexican workers to work the harvests, including workers from a new Mexican labor program.

The First Bracero Program in Texas

When US entry into World War I caused labor shortages, agribusiness, railroad, and mining companies lobbied for an exemption from immigration laws so that they could hire and contract Mexican migrants to meet wartime production needs.[125] In response, Secretary of Labor William Wilson and Bureau of Immigration Commissioner General Anthony Caminetti created a temporary program that exempted Mexicans from the literacy test and the contract law, allowing companies to import workers directly and to pay their fees. While the exemption initially covered only agricultural workers, by 1918 it was expanded to include railroad, mining, and other industries. Over 73,000 Mexicans participated in the program between 1917 and 1921.[126]

The wartime economy led to a large increase in migration, most of it outside the contract program. Government statistics highlight the volume of arrivals. In 1916, 17,198 legal immigrants entered the United States, and another 83,700 came without paying the head tax or taking the literacy test. In 1917, 16,438 legally migrated, and 123,000 came without going through the requirements. In 1918, 17,602 came legally, with 69,000 avoiding the requirements.[127] But because gaining entry through the program was so difficult, it is estimated that twice as many people simply walked across the border to find jobs on the other side.[128]

This first Mexican bracero program was riddled with problems of controlling labor. To understand this program, it is important to understand the perspectives of those who ran the US Bureau of Immigration. El Paso's Supervising Inspector Berkshire was not alone in seeing Mexicans as "birds of passage" who posed no long-term threat to the American working man. US Secretary of Labor Wilson argued that it was preferable to have Mexican laborers since they had always returned home and the alternative was permanent immigrants from Asia.[129] However, the program's structure made it difficult for the Bureau to control. Companies applied to the Bureau for contract workers, and the Bureau registered those workers. Workers were given registration cards. Companies withheld twenty-five cents a day from workers' wages, to be paid at the end of the contract. However, companies for the most part did their own hiring, frequently working through private agencies, and they often did not inform the Bureau about who they were hiring or what they were paying. It soon became apparent that the Bureau had little sway over employers or migrants.[130] Ultimately, most workers circumvented the process altogether, spurring the growth of undocumented labor.[131]

Numerous workers preferred to stay after their contracts ended to find work in other places before returning home. There was more demand for Mexican labor than the Bureau was willing to supply, and for workers, the wages were worth skipping a contract and losing the money that had been withheld and guaranteed return transportation to the border. Letters about laborers leaving the fields came from cotton farmers and railroads almost as soon as the program began.[132] Mexican workers in a few cases acted against bad employers, seeking redress; in most cases, workers simply left bad situations. As reports of desertion and abuse flooded the Bureau, the agency responded by working with consuls and law enforcement. After consuls started to file reports of abuse in the fields, a conciliation committee recommended a series of improvements in conditions.[133] Mexican workers pressed the Bureau on the holding of wages, and after the summer of 1918, the policy was abolished.[134] The Bureau estimated the overall desertion rate at around 30%.[135]

In 1929, a Mexican labor agent named Herrera summarized his experience of the World War I labor contract program:

> I used to try to get cotton pickers in Laredo, but now all they have got in their heads is Chicago or Detroit. They won't stop in Texas for a $10 job. I did pay passports for Mexicans in Nuevo Laredo but they left after a day even when they were paid 2½ cents a pound for cotton picking. We used to take their shoes and hats and put them in another house but they got away from us anyways in 1919, and we used to guard each door for the house they slept in on the big farm. We used to put their wives separate from the husbands, but the men left the wives to come north.[136]

After trying to control his cotton workers for a few more years, the labor agent joined his former workers and went to Chicago himself.

Employers realized that there was little or no penalty for hiring outside the formal contract system. Railroads were used to hiring workers who were off-season from the fields, and vice versa. Yet no mechanism existed for migrants to switch employers.[137] Companies got around the program's inflexibility by simply luring workers with better wages. Employers left out of the program, especially in mining and manufacturing, looked to railroad and agricultural workers as a source of labor. Competition took place even within the same industry as beet growers in the Midwest openly recruited cotton workers from Texas.[138] All employers who followed contracting rules could do was denounce other firms for committing fraud.

At a farmers' meeting, Texas growers raged against the "practice of 'labor theft' by farmers who offered enough of a premium to lure away the hands his neighbors had spent time and money importing. 'I had rather a man would come into my corn crib in the night and steal my corn than to have them bid my pickers away from me' he said amid applause." Others in the meeting wanted to ask attorneys to "investigate the feasibility and constitutionality of a law providing for the infliction of a proper penalty upon any person who shall by persuasion or otherwise induce contract labor to desert its employment, or to accept employment from such person during the term of such contract." Another attendee repeated the rumors that certain labor agents were stealing away workers by the thousands each day.[139] Ironically, the purpose of the meeting was to collude on a daily wage of $1.50 so that employers would not compete against each other. These growers seemed not to realize that such wage fixing was as much to blame for the exodus as anything else.

Efforts were certainly made to enforce contracts. Texas local police arrested workers who tried to leave before their contract was out.[140] The Bureau of Immigration brought several men to the Special Board of Inquiry under "Liable to be a Public Charge" allegations of leaving their employer or for staying past the end of their contracts. In all of the cases, the men were deported. Lorenzo Martinez's deportation meant leaving behind a family he had brought to the United States (his wife and child ended up leaving to join him in Mexico).[141] For the most part, however, the Bureau lacked the resources to pursue those who abandoned their contracts. By the summer of 1918, Berkshire estimated that Mexican migration through El Paso would reach 100,000 the following year, which turned out to be correct.[142] However, desertion was not a major problem, he argued, as Mexicans returned naturally to Mexico.[143] If migration could not be stopped, it was best to know who was coming by keeping the program going, he believed.[144]

While growers and industrialists sought to use the state to control labor, Mexican migrants used the wartime exemptions as an opportunity to force a rise in wages and enter industries and regions from which they had previously been excluded. In doing so, they forced local renegotiations over how these exemptions played, used their initial jobs as steppingstones to other work, and made the program unworkable. Ultimately, the program facilitated the spread of Mexican migration across a wider geographic region, establishing *colonias* (neighborhoods) in areas where they had not been present before, especially the Midwest. As the country entered a postwar recession, tens of thousands of Mexican migrants found themselves suddenly out of work. The program was abruptly ended in 1921. The Bureau let existing contracts expire and did not verify if workers left the country; they just assumed that they would.

Restriction Migration

When Congress severely limited immigration in 1924, the law excluded countries in the western hemisphere. Although Mexican migration was left unrestricted, most could not afford the entry fees or pass the required literacy test.[145] The creation of a sealed border came to be seen as the natural outgrowth of these laws as nativists focused their attention on the Mexican migration. In response, the Bureau of Immigration began to put up fencing along the border and created a series of new procedures that targeted Mexican migrants. At El Paso, a typhus outbreak in 1916 led the US Public Health Service to establish medical inspections at the border. Those seen as respectable were allowed to pass, while those seen as workers were forced to strip, doused with kerosene and vinegar, and had their clothes and luggage fumigated. Soon, this process was applied not just to border crossers but to the Mexican community living in El Paso. People in jails and hospitals were brought to the border for forced baths. Eleven died when the kerosene caught fire. Dozens of houses in Mexican neighborhoods were fumigated and burned down when officials expanded the quarantine to all Mexicans. Groups of women who lived along the border, led by Carmela Torres, rioted.[146]

As Mexican migration became the focal point of the national immigration debate, an effort to pass a bill restricting legal migration from Mexico was led by Congressmen John C. Box, Albert Johnson, and William Harris. Agribusiness opposed any legislation that might possibly damage its labor supply, and the Hoover administration feared diplomatic repercussions with Mexico. However, the State Department was able to defeat the effort in Congress only by establishing an unofficial quota that drastically reduced the number of visas issued, cutting off legal avenues for migration.[147] In a toughening of the Immigration Act in 1929, Congress made unlawful entry a criminal misdemeanor.[148] Those arriving after 1921 without proper documents risked deportation. These changes created the perception of Mexicans as "illegal" regardless of their immigration status and justified their deportations.[149] The increased scrutiny did not stop people from coming, however. Mexicans continued to enter through a variety of methods, from official immigration to going back and forth every few months to claim non-statistical status or simply walking across where there was no border station.

The biggest threat to the growers' source of labor was not Congress but the continual movement of migrants out of those jobs. The Texas State

Legislature passed new laws, ostensibly to improve public safety and to keep people from scamming workers but in reality aimed at controlling workers. The first of these laws, passed during World War I, intended to send workers to farms with labor shortages and bypass labor agencies established the Bureau of Labor Statistics, which conducted surveys prior to a picking season and then directed workers to the job openings in conjunction with the Federal Farm Labor Service. Surveys, not surprisingly, showed the greatest need for harvesting jobs and attempted to steer migrants to those employers. The second of these laws targeted independent labor agents in an attempt to end competition with the state's program. The Emigrant Labor Agency Law forbade agents from recruiting those who already had employment and restricted recruitment locations. All agents had to be registered in the state and pay a $500 bond, plus a bond of several thousand dollars for every county they recruited workers from. This effectively made most recruiting illegal, as only the recruiters for the largest railroads, such as the Santa Fe, paid the bond.

The Texas State Legislature restricted the outward flow of labor from the state. The state employment agency and Interstate Commerce Commission were increasingly alarmed by reports of truckers and others transporting farm workers to beet fields in the north.[150] The legislature passed the Motor Bus Law, restricting the use of personal vehicles to families of the owner and making it illegal to operate a bus or transportation business without a state license. In practice, Texas Rangers stopped and arrested groups of Mexicans as they traveled out of the state. The Mexican Consul at San Antonio, Enrique Santibañez, received numerous complaints about invasive stops, but his inquiries were brushed off. Consulates attempted to provide migrants with a defense by issuing papers to car owners certifying that they were migrating to Mexico or other places.[151] Texan authorities stood by their legislation as justified.

Mexicans regarded transportation, especially automobiles, as a key to greater mobility and a better life. Augustine Martinez fondly remembered going north. He had gone to the United States as a child with his parents and extended family and spent his childhood in the cotton fields. "We were poor," his father told him; "in those days you picked cotton for ten cents." And then his dad saw a big flyer circulated in Texas, "BIG MONEY BIG MONEY! . . . so here we go, let's go. 18–19 dollars an acre, that was sugar beets. . . . we landed in North Dakota, it was cold." They settled in St. Paul, Minnesota, and "then my brother got a city job and my dad started working for the railroad and we moved again. And then he started to work more. By that time we had a little bit more, even a car!"[152]

Employers, however, viewed automobiles as a threat to their control of labor. L. A. Ethridge saw them as undermining his control: "All the miners have cars, some have two or three, but very few save. The singles (men) won't stay."[153] Louis Baily believed that "if the Mexicans have their own transportation they leave to move too much."[154] P. Butts explained that "some pick and then go back. Some pick a week and move on. The Mexicans own cars that is one thing that causes trouble. They are independent and always wanting something better."[155] Mr. Wilkinson, an agricultural agent in Texas, warned, "But if he [a Mexican worker] gets too much cash at the end of the year he may buy a car and quit."[156]

These Texas laws built on a long history of local and state efforts to create a racialized, unfree workforce.[157] It was a common practice for Texas authorities to attach arrested Mexicans to private employers. In 1923, police arrested a group of eight Mexicans waiting on an employment agency on vagrancy charges and coerced them to work on a road construction project.[158] Growers sought to end free labor by making it impossible to change employers. "What we must have is a fix or four months' agricultural passports with a $1 fee." Asked if this did not amount to a peonage system, this grower answered, apparently without irony, "Peonage? But agriculture offers a man work in a variety of trades, driving a tractor and other things. It isn't peonage in the true sense. The penalty for running off would be denial of permission to return to the United States if he violated his passport."[159] Other growers attempted to keep their labor by hiring their own men to force Mexican workers to stay.[160] By the end of the decade, however, growers had a new federal authority to contend with in dealing with migrant workers, the Border Patrol.

Created in 1924, the Border Patrol developed a complicated relationship with growers, sometimes working with them to raid when workers organized, but at other times carrying out raids at peak season. The patrol deported 12,000 Mexican migrants in 1927 and many more in the years leading up to the Great Depression.[161] Whether raids were hostile or friendly to growers depended on the time of year. Growers most objected to them in the summer and early autumn, when it was peak harvest season. This was also the time when most organizing activity took place, however, and in these cases, growers responded by turning to local police, the Texas Rangers, or the Border Patrol. After the harvest, few objected to raids. One grower,

Mr. Stillwell, retaliated against workers who quit by calling the Border Patrol, explaining, "[We] have a lot of Mexicans without papers but we cooperate with the immigration officers and don't let them get away. We rounded up a hundred and fifty who were leaving once."[162] As the Border Patrol only had 400 men along the entire 2,000-mile southern border, it could never hope to stop or even reduce overall migration.[163] The Border Patrol came to rely on agency discretion, deporting some people while legalizing other migrant workers in response to local grower and political demands.[164] Its practice was geared not towards permanently deporting Mexicans from South Texas so much as controlling the free movement of labor.[165]

Workers in the Fields

Across the cotton borderlands, growers sought a landless, rootless, politically excluded, and deportable but stable workforce. Yet they also wanted a workforce that would return year after year. While agricultural interests could usually gain the support of local, state, and federal governments, their power was not hegemonic. Mexicans used their status as workers to make claims against employers and government. Though their everyday actions, they showed they could use institutions, information, and available resources to negotiate their socioeconomic conditions. If need be, they could go elsewhere. And by the mid-1920s, Mexicans were leaving Texas fields and moving on to industries in other states.

While large numbers of migrants participated in direct actions like strikes, the costs of such actions were too high for most. Instead, workers relied on small, everyday forms of resistance. Many Mexican workers along the borderlands and in Texas were organized into crews, made up of men who knew each other and would choose one person to lead them. This person would negotiate for the rest, and the whole crew could walk off the job if their conditions were not met. While not labor unions, crews were a critical component of labor strategy.[166] Day to day, they took actions such as work stoppages, slowdowns, and weighing down the bags with heavy objects.

Workers could and did press for better conditions, stage wildcat strikes, or simply walk away when their demands were not met. One grower complained that Mexicans "will all sit down in the field, and not work if they hear somebody is paying a couple of cents more."[167] Another said, "The Mexicans always strike. Every Monday morning, they want to know if they aren't going

Figure 2.7 Cotton weighing near Brownsville, Texas. Dorothea Lange, 1936. Library of Congress Prints and Photographs Division, LC-USF34-009785-E.

to raise their price. They have anarchists-agitators who go around and tell them what price to pick for. . . . They are highly sensitive and will leave you if you show you are dissatisfied. They will leave without a dime, and with no place to go."[168] Workers went on wildcat strikes to raise their wages when they held the advantage. Farmers, unable to comprehend the idea of assertive workers, resorted to essentialized race-based explanations for this behavior. But the workers' behavior was logical: employers needed labor during picking season.

Whether workers or growers held the advantage in the fields was highly dependent on the state of the harvest. Workers knew growers didn't want

Figure 2.8 Housing for cotton pickers, South Texas. Dorothea Lange, 1936. Library of Congress Prints and Photographs Division, LC-USF34-009807-E.

crops to rot in the fields, which meant the summer and early fall were the most optimal times to press for higher wages or better conditions, strike, or leave. The most common response was simply to leave. In one case at the Coleman-Fulton Pasture Company, the Mexican workforce walked off the job when refused a fifteen-cent increase in the picking rate. The superintendent recounted, "They said if we didn't pay them they would go where they could get it, and my man told them to go, and they went."[169] Few workers were willing to accept the diminishing wages when they began to hear about alternatives. However, most workers waited until after the harvest was over and their contracts had ended rather than risk not being paid.

The exodus of Mexican workers from the cotton fields occurred in parallel with other mass migrations. Millions of African Americans left the exploitative conditions of the South.[170] American-born *Tejanos* too were following the same networks; by 1930, they made up a significant percentage of the "Mexicans" in the Midwest.[171] Texas cotton growers, like their counterparts else in the South, generally blamed migration on unscrupulous agents and dishonest competitors, unwilling to believe that workers had their own agency and felt no loyalty to employers, and sometimes on workers' greed or pretension. Many families left by suddenly sneaking away during the night, lest the grower use unpaid debt as an excuse to call authorities to stop them. Workers saw unpaid debts as a way to retaliate against unscrupulous employers and their company store monopolies.

One Mexican merchant explained the paranoia of growers. "You can't go and talk to the laborers here without asking a foreman. You have to get permission. They fear that the Mexicans coming in will steal their pickers."[172] After speaking with various farmers about their strategies to keep Mexicans on the land, economist Paul Taylor came to believe that "the primary purpose of maintaining Mexican share-croppers on halves [where they paid half of their crop to the landowner] is to immobilize them so that ample labor will be on hand though the year and a large nucleus to start the picking season."[173] This strategy did not work as well with migrant farm workers.

Sr. Másquez, who was working on Byrd Ranch in Texas in 1928, compared the work to other jobs he had held. "Went to Colombia Sugar Beets at Mt. Pleasant, Michigan. [I] like Michigan. They treat you equal there, but not here."[174] Texas came to be seen as a bad place to work by those who had left, even if like Másquez they had returned.[175] Another Mexican in Chicago recalled, "I worked in Texas for a while and there the Texans were bad. I have seen many people treat Mexicans bad, but they are the worst of all. . . . I left Texas because it was hard life there and came to Chicago."[176] Migrants pointed to low pay as a reason for going north, but they also sought out places where they were treated more fairly and where their children could go to school. A Mexican man from Michoacán, who traveled across the beet fields in the north before coming back to Texas, concluded, "Texas is not like the other states. At Bermuda, [Texas], they told us we could not go to the American school, but that we could go to Carrizo. . . . I would like to keep my brothers in school."[177] For him, an opportunity to send family members to school was critical.

Alvaro Ruís, a Mexican who was also a labor contractor in Texas, explained, "The Mexicans who go to the interior of the United States talk about what they get. They say they make $5 a day, like at the rubber factory in Akron, Ohio. They say the American people give them better trade and *refrescos* [food for breaks] but no distinction."[178] Another worker explained his journey from cotton to rail work as an issue of pay: "I left Mexico in 1919 when there was good work in Texas . . . I went north to Detroit in hopes things would be better. Then to Pittsburgh, but they were worse. In 1923 I came to Chicago and worked for the steel mills. I like the work there, it pays well."[179] Not only did the Midwest offer better pay, but migrants felt they were free from direct discrimination.

A man who had previously migrated back in forth between Mexico and Texas explained why he left the cycle: "I headed for the cotton fields but now they were only paying 60 cents a *quinta*. So I decided to come north. There was an *enganchista* in Fort Worth that signed me up. I came to work for the Inland Steel Company [in Indiana]. I arrived here early in 1923. The Mexicans were not many then. More came later in the year and they have been coming ever since. Now they come direct from Mexico, friends send for them."[180] His pattern was similar to that of many who came to the Midwest: recruitment by an agent of a specific company, followed by establishing new links that would make it easier for other migrants to come years later without agents.

Circular Migration from Mexico

By the late 1920s, two overlapping migrant circuits into Texas had emerged. One operated from northern Mexico and the other from central Mexico. Those using the former continued to primarily circulate into Texas, while those using the latter went in large numbers to new destinations. The dramatic growth of Mexican migration into California and the Midwest meant that Texas' share declined from 60% to a little less than half by the 1930 census. This figure included both new migrants and those who had experience working and living in Texas.

The census study shows that a little more than half of Mexican migrants nationally returned within ten years, a figure consistent with reports on the ground.[181] Between 1926 and 1932, 49% of all migrants going back to Mexico came from Texas; of the rest, the majority came from neighboring Southwestern states. Eighty percent of Mexicans in Texas in 1930 were from the border states Nuevo León, Coahuila, Tamaulipas, and Chihuahua. In the rest of the United States, the majority of those returning came from the western and central plain states of Michoacán, Jalisco, Guanajuato, San Luis Potosí, and Aguascalientes. Only 13% of those returning from Texas came from the central states.[182] Demographically, those in the Midwest were also younger, were more often male, and sent more remittances per person than those from Texas.[183] Those who stayed in Texas were older, had larger families, sent back fewer remittances, and migrated for shorter periods of time.[184] This makes sense given the close proximity of Texas and the nature of the cotton migration circuit. Tens of thousands of people could come for the few months of the picking season and then return home.

Migrants from the central Bajío states of Mexico were significantly more likely to return to Mexico than those from border states.[185] However, the majority of workers in the Midwest had previously worked in Texas. This implies that people from central Mexico were dissatisfied with their opportunities in Texas. Migrants from central Mexico had to travel hundreds of miles to reach the border, and so were more likely to use labor agents, coyotes, and other brokers. But this also made it more likely that they would migrate further into the interior. They were not tied to a particular destination and were more willing to listen to those who suggested they keep going north. Given that they were disproportionately young men (though not necessarily single), in contrast to migrants from northern Mexico, they were more willing to take risks. They also sent both a higher percentage of their income to Mexico, as sending money became a form of participation in family life.[186]

Felix and María de la Cruz Gonzalez fled La Barca, Jalisco, during the Mexican Revolution. They crossed the border at El Paso and went to Arizona. There, Felix became a miner in Miami and María gave birth to two daughters, Lupe and Mariana. Felix joined the IWW and participated in several unsuccessful strikes. Because of his involvement with the IWW, he had to leave the area after several years. He worked on the Santa Fe railroad in the mid-1920s, and the family relocated to Santa Ana, California.[187] Like large numbers of families in this era, they moved within the economy of migrant labor. Seeking refuge from violence and economic chaos, they came into the world of mining and cotton in the borderlands. In making decisions, people worked together as families, crossing the border as part of larger strategies. Many families had members working in mining, rail, and picking while keeping a foot in subsistence agriculture, traditional trades, and related small businesses. They used movement itself as a strategy, finding ways around obstacles in their path: using brokers or walking away from them and jobs, working as family groups or in groups of acquaintances, and bringing families across the border by telling the Bureau of Immigration what it wanted to hear.

Migrants did not work in isolation, nor did they have uniform patterns and motivations. They lived in a land being remade through an ongoing project to disenfranchise and economically isolate Mexicans and Mexican Americans. Many *Tejanos* not only lost land but had to turn to migratory labor themselves. They were aided in their migration by labor agents who worked for large companies but were sometimes Mexican American themselves. These brokers acted as intermediaries, flourishing in the cross-border economy of border towns. These *enganchadores* and their influence became a major source of contention. They served as a critical link between employers and employees, introducing migrants to new firms, locations, and industries. Yet their control of labor was very limited and quickly lost as migrants learned how to navigate the world of employment themselves. They used the spread of information, written and spoken, in newspapers, letters, bulletins, and word of mouth to find jobs and organize when they could.

Cross-border networks proved fertile ground for the spread of organizing activity. The PLM was successful among a mobile, marginalized population outside of the traditional confines of trade unions. Bringing together a transnational network of organizers inspired by a broad international movement, the PLM flourished in the borderlands due to its dual interest in political revolution and practical goals. The PLM lived alongside *mutualistas* that could turn into ad hoc unions at a moment's notice. Resistance to exploitation was widespread, and workers could and did strike constantly, often before they were organized into recognizable unions. It was not a surprise that former PLM members formed the core of *Sedicioso*, or IWW support, in so many places. Mexican workers, a supposedly docile population, organized to such an extent that the state turned to mass arrests, deportations, and widespread violence to end their efforts. Companies argued that the migrants' organizing was un-American, a communist conspiracy, and seditious in a time of war. The state's use of violence shows the extent to which it wished to turn migrants into workers without rights, not real "Americans" deserving of equal citizenship. This crusade defeated organizing efforts among Mexican workers for most of the next decade.

Migrant strategies were always framed by and in reaction to the dominance of corporations and the state, the policies they created, and their use of force.[188] Leaving and participating in daily acts of resistance was not an effective substitute for the organizing that would have built more power within American society. When presented with the possibility of settling into secure if low-paying jobs, most Mexican migrants chose to build families, institutions, and large communities, especially in urban centers. This was not a possibility for the majority, who labored in a political economy built around migrant labor, which was held up by a matrix of federal and state laws. Yet they were not passive victims either. Exploitive conditions in cotton, mining, and railroads led to a massive turnover rate among Mexican men and women. Few were willing to stay trapped in the same cycle year after year, and their search for alternatives resulted in a major shift in the location of Mexicans in the United States, the locations sending migrants, and the locations of industries they worked in.

3

Into the North

Railroads, Sugar Beets, and Steel in the Spread of Mexican Migration to the Midwest, 1910–1930

> I went to Pueblo, Colorado, during the First World War. And when it ended jobs were scarce. My father and brother worked in a steel mill. Their jobs ended and we moved to Mexico City. But we liked the United States, so we saved up for four years and moved here. We moved to San Antonio where we met a beet contractor. Then we moved to Iowa. Coming from San Antonio where it was hot, we were wearing summer clothes. We arrived in April, and it was snowing. We the youngest ones in the family, were children. We were really young, but we did all the work.[1]

This migrant's story of circulating between Mexico and places in the United States as his family moved between industries was not unusual by the late 1920s. He was part of the first generation of Mexicans that moved into the Midwest.

By 1930, there were between 60,000 and 100,000 Mexican migrants in the Midwest, more than 20,000 in Chicago alone.[2] This chapter follows the spread of Mexican migration out from the borderlands and into this region, particularly to Chicago. Migrations that began as a response to recruitment in the railroad, sugar beet, and steel industries, especially during World War I, became self-perpetuating as Mexicans established new *colonias* and organizations that formed nodes in interconnected regional circuits. The wartime Bracero Program increased the hiring of Mexican migrant workers in places beyond the borderlands. The further they migrated north, the higher the pay they could earn. Tens of thousands signed up every year to work for the railroad and the sugar beet industries on contracts of a few months. However, as they moved north, they became away of the lower pay and limited

Between Here and There. Daniel Morales, Oxford University Press. © Oxford University Press 2024.
DOI: 10.1093/oso/9780197612590.003.0004

opportunities in these jobs compared to the steadier work in meat packing, steel, and automobiles.

As they escaped the racial prejudice and segregation that marked life in Texas, Mexican migrants moved into spaces where social and class structures were fluid and a place for Mexicans on the racial hierarchy had not yet solidified. For the most part, they settled among European immigrants rather than African Americans. Lured by recruiters with promises of high pay, they also found themselves used as strikebreakers, working the worst jobs the industrial economy had to offer, for low pay and with few opportunities for advancement. Even so, they built dozens of *colonias* across the region, founding a web of organizations, churches, and businesses that turned them into vibrant communities. And companies came to depend on their labor well beyond the original reason for their hire.

These communities were part of a system of towns tied to larger, regional hubs like Chicago, San Antonio, and Detroit that supplied the rural areas with workers for sugar beets or rail work. By 1930, tens of thousands were circulating every year through these interconnected hubs that reached into Mexico. Most of the industries that hired Mexicans in this region wanted temporary labor for a few months, not permanent workers or permanent communities. A census study of Chicago shows that less than 7% of the Mexican migrants who lived there in 1920 settled permanently there. The larger national study shows a similar trend across the Midwest. Those who did settle were disproportionately skilled, had families, or belonged to the middle class, such as those working in steel or automobiles and who owned boarding houses, pool halls, grocery stores, and other small businesses. This core kept the larger *colonia* functioning. As a result, the communities proved lasting, even if most of their residents did not permanently settle there.

Rather than being successive processes, through the period from 1900 to 1930 circular migration and permanent settlement were mutually constituting and reinforcing. Migrants were constantly moving back and forth in the United States and back to Mexico, but many were also settling, even as they intended to return to Mexico. To maintain the sense of space and scale of this migration, this chapter toggles between transnational and national trends and developments on the ground in a few locations. Looking at specific locations illustrates factors such as individual hiring decisions, recruiting, and hometown and kinship networks could and did have long-term consequences. The chapter begins by examining one company, the

Santa Fe Railway, before moving on to mining and sugar beets in Colorado. It then surveys the Midwest hubs of Kansas City, St. Paul/Minneapolis, and Detroit before shifting to the industrial center of Chicago. As the railroad, sugar beet, and steel industries grew on the backs of Mexican labor, these workers created new migration patterns, new communities, and new social realities, changing the Midwest.

The Santa Fe Railway and the Railroad Industry

Founded in 1859, the Atchison, Topeka, and Santa Fe Railway was the largest railroad system in the American West. Starting in the 1880s, the Santa Fe began to use "Mexican" labor in its New Mexico division to replace Chinese workers. From the 1870s to the 1900s, this mostly meant the recruitment and hiring of Hispanic or *Tejano* workers from New Mexico and Texas to work in the Southwest. Large numbers of indigenous Pueblo, Yaqui, Navaho, Apache, Sioux also worked for the Santa Fe or the Southern Pacific. A 1910 report praised their Yaqui workers while noting their tensions with Mexican migrants.[3] In 1905, the company began to use Mexican workers outside the borderlands, hiring 3,000 migrant workers from Mexico. This was less than a third of their total force of section laborers, but the change was already underway. With wages that averaged from $1.00 to $1.25 a day for unskilled section labor, the pay on the northern side was twice that on the southern side.[4] By 1915, Mexicans comprised more than 11,000 workers, two-thirds of the company's labor force, and in 1927, Mexicans comprised 13,000, almost 90% of track labor positions. By 1928, the railroad's Los Angeles division had no workers other than "Mexicans," a label that included both migrants and Mexican Americans.[5]

Throughout this period, the primary way of recruiting and contracting Mexicans was through the labor agencies located at railroad hubs: El Paso, San Antonio, Laredo, Los Angeles, St. Louis, Chicago, and Kansas City. Agencies provided stationery and cards for workers returning to Mexico to help them recruit and offered to pay for transportation to and from the place of employment, to pay for food and lodging on the way to the worksite, and to arrange a contract with an agreed-upon wage. Actual follow-through varied greatly. Some agencies routinely reneged on their promises, and larger ones often forced workers to use credit at company stores and live in company housing. The Holmes Supply Company, for example, supplied workers

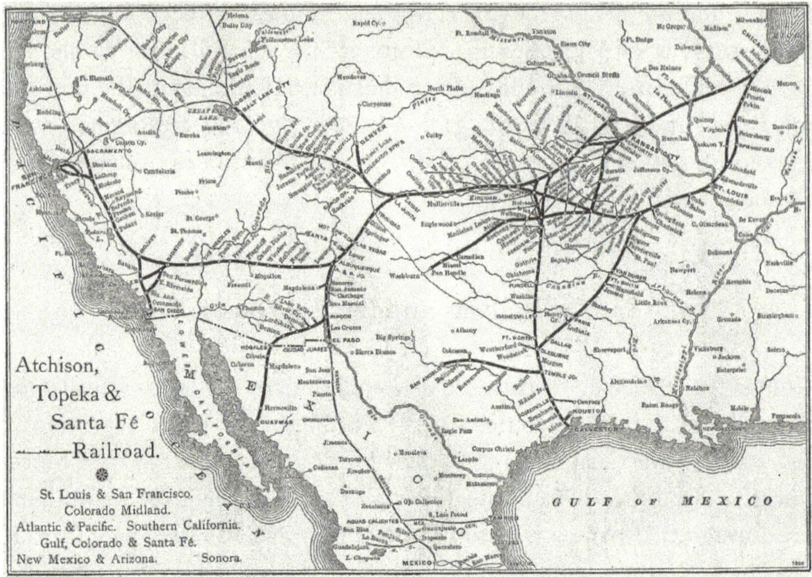

Figure 3.1 Santa Fe railroad map with lines and connections to Mexico. Grain Commission Merchants, Atchison, Topeka, & Santa Fe Railway, 1891. Grain Dealers and Shippers Gazetteer, Chamber of Commerce, Minneapolis, Minnesota, 1891.

for the Santa Fe and ran dozens of stores, labor camps, recruiting centers, and even a clinic in Los Angeles.

Each of the major labor agencies supplied several thousand Mexican workers a year to railroad companies, with the bulk of the hiring occurring in the spring and very little during November, December, and January. Looking at two agencies, the Holmes Supply Company and the Hamlin Supply Company, both of which hired for the Atchison, Topeka, and Santa Fe Railway, demonstrates a pattern of agencies initially acting as drivers of migration at the border but subsequently losing control of workers. Thereafter, they came to depend on Mexicans who arrived by themselves in order to fill their labor contracts. The Hamlin Company shipped between 4,000 and 7,000 workers a year from El Paso between 1913 and 1920, with almost all of them recruited from Mexico, hitting a peak in 1916. From 1920 until 1929, the annual number fell to less than 3,000 and was often below 2,000.[6] In 1926, the Hamlin Supply Company even began to ship workers from Chicago to the borderland states. The Holmes Company showed a similar trend, recruiting about 9,000 workers in 1923 but less than 3,000 by the end of the decade.[7] The Zarate & Avina Company also suffered a general decline, while the L. H. Manning Company had no discernible pattern in its yearly fluctuations.[8] This decline is partially explained by a drop in overall employment as the railroad industry consolidated in the 1920s. However, the agencies decline was much steeper, and Mexican employment remained steady.

As Mexican migrants spread across the railroad industry, they encountered a physically difficult and deeply hierarchical workplace. Long hours in all types of weather were expected, including working outdoors in upper Midwest winters and in the desert sun in the Southwest. This labor entailed a high injury rate; workers were routinely injured and lost fingers and toes. Railroad work caused the highest number of fatalities that Mexican consulates dealt with. While more stable than beet or cotton work, the railroad section labor was seasonal in nature, with large drops in employment from October to February. More importantly, migrants were kept out of the most desirable jobs. The industry was divided between unionized "skilled" and non-unionized "unskilled" occupations. American Federation of Labor (AFL)-affiliated unions controlled access to positions for engineers, conductors, firemen, and trainmen. Mexicans worked as "common" laborers doing track maintenance, track building, and repairs. These non-union jobs were traditionally worked by immigrant men, who could be used when needed and laid off when not.[9]

Much more common than union organizing was spontaneous strikes. Flash strikes could save a person's job and lead to better pay or better conditions at a particular worksite, but they rarely produced lasting changes. In 1903, Mexican interurban rail workers in Los Angeles formed *La Union Federal Mexicana* and struck for better conditions against the Pacific Electric. In Colorado and New Mexico, *Tejanos* tried to organize under the mutual aid organization *La Sociedad Mutualista Ignacio Zaragoza*, but both efforts were defeated after a protracted conflict. In 1905, 300 workers struck against the Santa Fe because they had not been paid. In 1908, hundreds of workers in California struck against the Santa Fe, and company officials only defeated their efforts by deporting them to El Paso. In Indiana, Mexican trackmen went on strike for better pay in 1916 and subsequently for better working conditions. Railroad mutual organizations could press for greater change and often turned themselves into organizing vehicles. The *Asociación Mutua de Trabajadores Unidoes*, for example, led a railroad strike of Santa

Fe workers in San Bernardino in 1918, demanding higher pay and an eight-hour workday.[10]

The AFL did not make a major attempt to unionize Mexican workers. Railroad unions had clauses that excluded non-citizens, and few Mexican migrants were willing to naturalize. This, along with a general hostility towards unskilled workers and non-whites, meant that Mexicans were not represented by any major railroad unions until large numbers joined the Brotherhood of Maintenance of Way Employees in the late 1920s. Instead, workers asserted themselves on a day-to-day level. They could work together to slow down the pace of the work, pretend to work, feign ignorance, speak Spanish so that their conversations would not be understood, or argue with foremen. When these tactics did not work, they did not hesitate to quit. One group of Mexicans quit when an American foreman tried to stop them from smoking during their breaks. F. Huerta, a Mexican migrant who settled in Indiana Harbor (in East Chicago), remembered a time when he and his friends quit together to protest the firing of a well-liked foreman: "The Mexicans liked the foreman and struck unless he should be returned. The rail-master tried to get the men out of the cars, but they asked for their checks before they would get out. So, he gave us our time."[11]

Mr. Williams of the Baltimore and Ohio (B&O) Railroad expressed his frustration at being unable to control Mexicans, at least through force: "The Mexicans are OK or not, depending upon the foreman. If he speaks politely to them and knows how to handle them, he can get a lot of work out of them. If he tries to drive them with a pick-handle he can't get much."[12] Mr. Pratt of the Chicago, Burlington and Quincy (CB&Q) Railroad agreed: "Mexicans' labor is better if it is handled right. You can't cuss the Mexican out or call them down in front of the others or they may quit and take the whole gang with them."[13] Another company manager mentioned the tendency of Mexicans to quit together if they disliked their working conditions: "If the Mexicans don't like the food, foreman, wages, or the job, they just walk away."[14]

Railroad workers worked in small gangs that stuck together, typically managed by a foreman who was assigned by the company. Most foremen were white and segregation kept most Mexicans from being promoted to foreman, though some were by the 1920s. A group of friends, perhaps led by one member, could travel together, sharing resources and working for different railroads. Section gangs were almost entirely made of men, usually single. But some women, such as Nellie Quinn, worked for the railroads and earned wages alongside their husbands.[15]

Boxcar camps were built across the industrial landscape, wherever railroads went. As housing for massive temporary workforces, these camps were not intended to be permanent housing. They usually had wood floors, poor ventilation, and a hole in the roof for a wood stove. Solo men usually slept in company housing like bunkhouses, but they rarely stayed for more than a few years, preferring to live in boxcar camps they built themselves. There, they could live rent-free with their families and cook their own Mexican food.[16] These rolling camps, like their agricultural counterparts, became centers of community life and could be transported wherever the company needed workers.

More permanent camps in cities provided more services and had enough boxcars to assign one per family, whereas in remote areas, up to four families would have to share a boxcar. Large numbers of women lived in these camps, doing unpaid "household" labor to maintain the workforce. While formal work such as taking in laundry, having paid boarders, and cleaning houses did occur, most women participated in the informal economy, including trading tasks, bartering, raising animals, or tending gardens. In these crowded camps, people could share resources, cooking, childcare, and maintenance with other families. As the camps became Mexicanized spaces, their residents could find Mexican food and operate in Spanish. Those working in urban spaces could opt to board with families outside the camps. As one worker put it, "You can buy good Mexican things from stores you know and have your choice for a nice meal. It is always best on the [railroad] section, if you are near town, to board with a family of Mexicans you know even if you have to talk. That solves your troubles and you always eat well with them. There are always some around, it is easy to find them."[17] Camps were marked by environmental risks, however. Near rail yards, moving trains, and roundhouses, the chances of injury or death from trains was high, and chemicals and soot from the railroad rained down.[18]

Santa Fe officials noticed the tendency of migrants to use networks: "They invariably travel in pairs, trios or groups, consisting of relatives, neighbors or compadres."[19] Interpersonal connections drove much of the hiring in the railroad industry. Over time, families learned to avoid camps operated by labor contractors where they would be paid in scrip, which fueled cycles of debt. It soon became clear that there were better places to work. Railroads provided passes for workers to return to El Paso at the end of their season. Some workers used them this way, to establish circular migration patterns and support a family in Mexico. Investigator George Edson found that

"Mexican workers sell their transportation passes to other men going to Mexico on a visit. They cross the border under an assumed name, and later re-enter under their own name."[20] Able to travel thousands of miles at low cost with such passes, workers used the railroad for their own needs, including traveling to take up other jobs.

Throughout the 1910s, railroads had the second-highest turnover rate of any industry. Recruiter W. H. Talbot reported a loss of 40% of his Mexican workers, despite pay being about 30% higher than in agriculture.[21] Desertion had already become a problem by the 1910s. Railroads attempted to control and retain their workers through coercion. Benito Rodriguez, a Mexican and a labor agent, remembered, "We used to lose as high as fifty percent of our shipments. We used to lose especially experienced miners to the Arizona copper mines, and the coal mines. We used to lose nearly half of our shipments to California agriculture." As a result, the railroads "used to lock the doors on the trains and have a piece of lumber screwed on the outside of the windows . . . Now they lock the doors in the parts of the country where [the workers] may jump off."[22] Labor agencies were very concerned about the large numbers of Mexicans who left for mining, lumber, and beets. The desertion rate was over 80% for the Pennsylvania Railroad, while the Southern

Figure 3.2 Railroad companies recruited in Spanish-language newspapers such as this ad in *El Cosmopolita* in Kansas City, 1917.

Pacific created a "permanent order at El Paso for about fifty Mexicans per week, as that is the number which experience has shown to be deserting in that time."[23] Railroads became conduits for other labor markets.

When World War I began, the Wilson administration nationalized the railroad industry. Railroads appealed to the federal government for wartime exemptions from the 1917 Immigration Act and Alien Contract Act of 1885, arguing that they experienced major shortages as maintenance-of-way workers were drafted or left for better-paying work. From 1918 to 1921, they experienced many of the same issues with retention as the agriculture program. Mr. Fink, Assistant Treasurer of the Santa Fe Railway, complained that "the beet sugar companies raise hell with our track force in the spring. They send oily-tongued fellows down the line who promise our men everything and they pick them off right and left." Mr. Goeldner, an assistant to the general manager of the railroad, agreed. He worked with the government to ensure that workers only stayed for six months and tried to keep Mexican nationals west of Kansas, as he had "experience with those that come from Mexico and want to use our road for getting transportation to the beet fields or the steel mills of Illinois or Michigan." He praised the workers who came back to the Santa Fe after returning to El Paso and Mexico annually; some of his employees had made the migratory circuit for as many as twelve years. They formed the core of the railroads' workforce. As for beet recruiters, "We get them on trespassing on our property. We land a few of them every season, throw them off the property or in jail."[24]

By 1928, internal documents from the Santa Fe Railway showed that the Holmes Supply Company estimated yearly turnover at 150% to 200%, "but for publication, it conservatively estimates it at 'over 100%.'" This same report showed that the vast majority of those who left went to other places in the United States, while a significant minority went back to Mexico.[25] Mexican workers commonly took up jobs outside of the borderlands in places that lay along the railroad lines. Some railroads, such as the Santa Fe, encouraged this dispersion, while others sought to stop it. J. R. Silva, an employment agent based in El Paso who for years had sent workers to cotton fields and railroad companies, received a request in 1908 from the American Beet Sugar Company for 100 workers. Ten years later, he was sending 1,000 families every year to the company's fields in Colorado.[26] After struggling with labor retention for years, in 1925 the CB&Q Railroad made an arrangement whereby the Great Western Sugar Company agreed to provide Mexican families with money and housing for the winter while the CB&Q provided the men with winter track labor in Kansas City and then returned them to the beet fields in the spring. This arrangement proved advantageous to both companies.[27] Railroads eventually came to see turnover as a regular part of their relationship with workers and other industries.

Mining and Beets in Colorado

Sr. Barron, president of the *Comisión Honorifica* in Pueblo, Colorado, explained the back and forth between railroads, mines, and beets this way: "Most of the Mexicans here are from central Mexico. Some of them have mined in the metal mines of central Mexico and Chihuahua. Some learned mining in the US, a few go to the beets and to the track when mining is slack. Most of the Mexicans, however, stay in the mines even during the summer when the season is slack. Some miners come to the mines by way of beet and track work."[28] Sugar beet companies moved to a policy of recruiting family labor, and temporary labor camps became semipermanent communities as more Mexicans came to live in these places year-round. These labor camps were tied through money and goods to the hometowns of the workers, be they from Chihuahua or New Mexico.

The largest concentration of *Hispanos* (Mexican Americans whose ancestors predate US annexation) was around Pueblo, but the industrialization of the region brought waves of migrants and settlers. The arrival of the coal mines and sugar beets in Colorado drew large numbers of US-born *Hispanos* into the migrant labor economy alongside the newer arrivals. Fifteen sugar refineries were created within a few years in southern Colorado, attracting Mexican migrants from the railroads and mines.[29] As the transnational borderlands economy that linked northern Mexico and the US Southwest reached into Colorado, it extended into copper mining and sugar beets. Alongside *Hispanos* and Mexican immigrants who migrated from Arizona and New Mexico came workers of Native, Anglo, European, and Asian origins.

Labor conditions were poor. Coal miners were paid piecemeal, and scales were not always unbiased. In 1913, miners averaged around $300 a year, or $2 a day, low by industrial standards but twice what farm labor paid. Despite Mexicans receiving the least desirable and lowest-paid jobs, mines in Colorado paid better than those in Arizona and more than railroad or beet work. Families supplemented this income through small-scale farming and providing services to other workers, such as taking in boarders. Coal towns were company towns, where the land, the housing, and the local institutions were all owned and controlled by the mines.[30] Such control over all aspects of life and the low pay drove workers to organize.

Because mining companies hired Mexican and Eastern European immigrants to break local strikes, there was a widespread belief among white workers that Mexicans could not be unionized. At the Rock Mountain Mines in Boulder, union organizing began in 1910 and persisted through a series of strikes that lasted until 1922, when the union was broken by the state militia. Mexican migrants came to work at the company in increasing numbers, from 1,618 workers in 1918 to 3,218 in 1922. At the nearby Fredrick Mine, the number of Mexicans increased to 2,891 miners and 380 loaders and cutters. Mexicans made up 47% of union members at the start of the 1922 strike.[31] However, other Mexican miners were used as strikebreakers.[32]

While union members worried about Mexicans becoming strikebreakers despite their strong union participation, owners worried about them joining unions. Mr. Watson, the supervisor of the Ideal Mine, where Mexicans made up more than 80% of the total workforce, stated:

> The Mexican is a natural joiner and this is the source of the hold of the IWW [Industrial Workers of the World]. We had four Mexican lodges here when there were only about 150 Mexican miners. Many of the same Mexicans attended lodge meetings four nights a week. They all wore big badges and some of them merely said "*miembro.*" The IWW say to the Mexicans, "This was originally Mexican country. The capitalists came in and enslave[d] the Mexicans and you are not working for them."[33]

In Colorado, no employer loomed as large as the Rockefeller-owned Colorado Fuel and Iron Company. This steel company owned the largest coal mine in the state at Pueblo. The workers at Colorado Fuel and Iron came from thirty-two countries and spoke twenty-seven languages. Up to a quarter were Mexican, and these Mexicans were about evenly split between migrants from Mexico and US-born *Hispanos*. Despite the sheer variety of workers and the challenges of finding common ground, communities organized. In 1913, the United Mine Workers of America built a multiethnic coalition and launched a strike. The company responded by evicting workers, forcing thousands of families to live in makeshift camps, the largest at Ludlow.[34] The governor brought in the National Guard, and on April 20th, they, along with company men, began to shoot into the Ludlow camp. Several people were killed by the shooting and twenty people more from the subsequent fire, twenty of them children. Over the next few days, workers engaged the National Guard in skirmishes across southern Colorado that took many more lives. The violence only ended when Woodrow Wilson sent in the federal army to restore order. In total, it is estimated that between 69 and 200 people died, making this the deadliest conflict between capital and labor in American history.[35]

In subsequent years, migration into Colorado was reshaped by the spectacular growth of sugar beets. Before the twentieth century, the United States got its sugar primarily from sugar cane plantations in the Caribbean or Hawaii, but the imposition of high tariffs led to the creation of a domestic industry that by the mid-1920s was cultivating from 1.2 to 2.0 million tons (2,000 lbs. each) per year.[36] The sugar beet industry argued that sugar cane was a tainted commodity, made by unfree labor in colonial empires. [37] The tariff, along with irrigation projects, ensured that the industry went from a tiny experimental source of sugar to the primary source in the country. Vast fields began to open from Michigan to Washington State. As more and more farmers switched to growing beets, they began to hire labor outside of their families. First, they used European migrants, but eventually, they turned to Mexican labor. Farmers owned the land and signed contracts with large refining companies that controlled the factories, storage facilities, seeds, equipment, and credit farmers needed.[38]

What really made the industry's growth possible was migrant labor. Founded in 1901, the year it built its first sugar mill in Loveland, Colorado, the Great Western Sugar Company became the largest refiner in the region. Unofficially, with its contracts and control of rail transportation, its power over its farmers was absolute. Great Western Sugar, not the farmers, did the recruiting and hiring for seasonal contracts. The company initially hired US-born *Hispanos*; by 1920, half of those recruited came from Mexico. The company set the prices of the sugar and the wages paid to the workers. Along with the Utah Sugar Company, the American Sugar Refining Company, and the Holly Sugar Company, Great Western dominated sugar beet growing in the West. By 1909, the beet sugar industry was employing 26,000 Mexican workers a year, rising to 40,000 in the 1910s and 1920s. Migrant Mexican labor did not come to work fields that already existed. Rather, the land was transformed into beet fields *because* of the availability of migrant labor and railroad transportation.

During the key harvest season in October, growers wanted a large, temporary, and migratory workforce. Additionally, they needed large labor forces for thinning, blocking, and hoeing, physically demanding tasks that involved stooping. Each acre of beets needed about 120 hours of work per season, a situation companies tried to address by having the migrants themselves take responsibility for the beets by subcontracting land. As company official R. H. Cottrell explained, "It is necessary to bring in transient workers. Usually, a substantial part of the cost of recruitment and transportation is borne by the company. The company's office in this activity is only that of agency to secure farm help for employment by beet-growing farmers."[39]

As the World War I program recruited for the beet industry, tens of thousands of Mexicans went into the Upper West and Midwest. This greatly interrupted the village-based regional circuits of migration in New Mexico and southern Colorado and integrated local workers with the larger circuits from Mexico.[40] Like the railroad companies, beet companies sought to ensure a mobile and temporary labor supply, assuring the public that Mexicans would not stay and create new communities. Encouraging workers in other industries to skip on contracts, sugar beet companies advertised through newspapers and radio across the Southwest and even into Mexico. They not only promised higher pay but better treatment and respect than they received in Texas.[41] One Michigan beet grower who advertised on radio stations near the border provoked an investigation by the Bureau of Immigration.[42] A recruiter from the Spreckels Sugar Company "raided Carranza's army in Mexico and brought back with him for sugar-beet work 1,400 soldiers," causing a small crisis at the border.[43] Recruiters traversed the borderlands to sign workers for yearly contracts. Great Western alone spent $360,000 a year on recruitment.[44]

Growers sought to control workers with contracts, low wages, and debit. Robert Barr, a farm manager, explained why he sought to keep his workers in debt: "The farmers need cheap labor, and the Mexicans furnish it. The families are more stable than the solos. The solos drift out in mid-season or else they don't appear for work at all." In response to the question of what effect advances had on the Mexicans, he replied, "A family in debt and without money can't move."[45] Fred Holmes, superintendent of the Holly Sugar Company, explained that "the Mexicans drift away from beets. About 20 to 25 percent of them leave [in a season]. The solos don't remain very well. We provide quarters and advance groceries in order to get the Mexicans to remain."[46]

(a)

(b)

Figure 3.3a and b Mexican beet workers and the shacks they lived in, Colorado. Lewis Wickes Hines, July 1915. Location: Rocky Ford [vicinity], Colorado, 1915. National Child Labor Committee collection, Library of Congress, Prints and Photographs Division, LOT 7475, v. 1, no. 3935 & LOT 7475, v. 1, no. 3934.

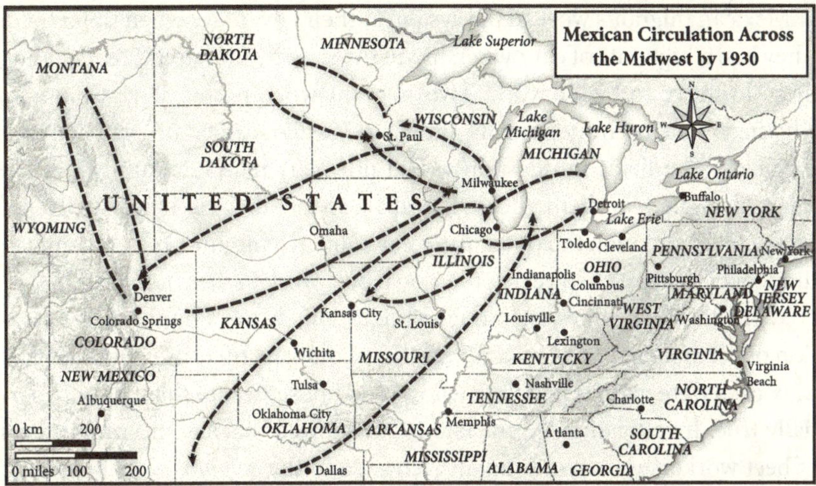

Figure 3.4 Map of Mexican circulation across the Midwest by 1930.

While sugar beet companies used labor camps and temporary pickers for harvest, beets demanded months of labor. In response, the Holly Sugar Company of Colorado Springs created a system of poorly built, wood-constructed labor camps with twenty apartments to a building, which accommodated a hundred people. The company didn't charge rent and provided coal for the winter to encourage people to stay.[47] Over time, sugar beet growers moved to tenant contracts and family recruiting. In a 1924 census of beet farmers in the Mexican colony of Greeley, only five land contracts were for single males; the other forty were for families that ranged from two to nine field hands (the company only counted people capable to picking beets). Most had between twenty-five and forty-five acres of land, the average being about thirty-two acres. These statistics were similar across all the counties in the region.[48] The industry encouraged the use of child labor and fought the 1916 Child Labor Act, which it concealed by signing contracts with the heads of families.

Workers countered where they could, taking advances and leaving. This exasperated farmers: "Now the farmer may tell the Mexican what's wrong, and the Mexican says '*no sabe*' or threatens to leave. The farmer may have advanced him money and would lose it if he left, but the Mexicans are the only viable labor supply and we have got to have them."[49] Another farmer complained, "First they [Mexicans] worked by the sack. Then they wanted a contract by the acre. The rascals struck for their own rates. They will quit a job if they don't like the treatment."[50]

Mexican migrants worked the system to their advantage when they could. They had a high rate of car ownership in the state by the late 1920s, enabling them to move to better work. Two migrant workers in Eaton, Colorado, who had come up from Arizona and New Mexico teamed up on a contract for fields. The fields in question would normally require a family, but the migrants signed for them fifteen days apart so that they could work together on one field and then the other and clear $300 in a month. One of them had thought of this after two years of seasonal beet work in the Eaton area.[51]

While the companies encouraged migration, farmers opposed the creation of permanent Mexican communities. Company officials countered that Mexicans were natural migrants who would not settle, but this was only partially true. Investigations in the late 1920s showed that significant numbers of beet workers were wintering in Denver, and the *colonias* were becoming permanent. Large sugar beet companies generally wanted workers to stay; Great Western went so far as offer free homes to families that stayed in the *colonias* it built. These *colonias* became new centers of life, with churches, *mutualistas*, and links to each other and the larger region.[52]

Pueblo was home to the largest and most established Mexican community in the state. Families with generations of roots in the region were joined by new migrants from New Mexico and Mexico. The city was home to a Spanish-language newspaper, a consulate, a *Comisión Honorifica*, a *Cruz Azul*, *La Sociedad Mutualista Ignacio Zaragoza*, and other *mutualistas*. The Catholic Church was active in the Mexican community. It established several organizations, including the fraternal organization the Knights of Columbus, which became heavily involved in outreach to migrant farm workers and created the Mexican Welfare Committee of Colorado.

Run by Thomas F. Mahony, the Mexican Welfare Committee of Colorado started primarily as a charitable organization, helping people with funds, job leads, and places to live, but it eventually began working on policy issues. The committee became the first to investigate systematically the working and living conditions in the beet fields. Investigators found that most Mexican families earned about $400 a season in the beet fields, though often less than $300; this income was not enough to last them through the off-season.[53] The committee also found that at the average price of $21 to $25 per acre, a single man could only earn $250 a year, which meant that women and children had to work in the fields for a family to survive. Children began to work in beets as young as 8 or 9 years of age and had mortality rates several times higher than those of Colorado as a whole. Most migrant children did not go to school, and those who did almost always missed school during the beet harvest and could be absent for half of the school year.[54]

In the absence of any significant unions in the fields, the Welfare Committee took on the task of representing workers before growers and advocating for better contracts in 1919. The committee negotiated with the Mountain State Beet Growers Association but did not make much progress. The major companies tended to collude on the prevailing wages at the beginning of the season, a practice that was both illegal and widespread. While the moderate Welfare Committee always denied IWW presence in the fields and called it a scare tactic, its leaders were concerned about the appeal of communist organizations among workers. Mahony warned both Catholics and the AFL about their own failures and the need to do something about the situation in the fields.[55] Around this time, the AFL began an organizing effort led by Clemente Idar, hoping to counter the growth of radical unions. Idar's efforts were limited by the unwillingness of the main office to help and the disinclination of Mexicans to become naturalized citizens.[56]

In 1928, the Welfare Committee publicly defended Mexican field workers against efforts to create quotas for Mexicans as had been done for other immigrants in the 1924 Johnson Reed Act. It argued that, in Colorado, "18,000 Spanish and Mexican hands were employed in fieldwork. They cared for 110,000 acres of beets, about two-thirds of the state crop." The report was among the first to show that Mexican labor not only helped the beet industry but expanded the entire economy. "Instead of depriving other laborers for work, the Mexican and other Spanish-speaking beet workers make possible the employment of thousands of other workers, skilled and unskilled, during and following the sugar manufacturing campaigns each year."[57]

Mexicans in the sugar beet fields of Colorado worked together to represent their interests. Organizations in Pueblo and Denver sought aid for the unemployed, repatriation for those who wanted to return to Mexico, and fought against child labor in the fields. In the sugar beet towns of Greely and Johnson, they organized against segregation in shops and won. Building on union efforts in the coal mines in 1927, the IWW began a campaign to organize the sugar beet fields. Led by Lauro Valdez, workers in Greeley created their own campaign, growing this union to fourteen locals. Another campaign by the AFL led to the creation of the Beet Worker Association in 1929. These efforts were accelerated by the Great Depression. The United Front Committee organized a statewide beet workers strike in 1932 and gathered in Denver to create the United Cannery, Agricultural, Packing, and Allied

Workers of America (UCAPAWA). The unions pressed for higher wages and the end of child labor in the wake of the Jones-Costigan Act in 1934 and Sugar Acts in 1937 that set a minimum wage for beet work.[58]

Many of the same forces were at play in the sugar beet fields around Saginaw, Michigan, as scholar Kathleen Mapes has found. By the late 1920s, Mexican migrants made up 75% of that state's beet workers. Mexican workers for the Michigan Sugar Company refused to work when they found out part of their wages were being withheld until the end of the season, forcing the company's hand. The same company reported more than a third of its workforce left before the end of the contracts.[59] In the late 1920s, workers organized a series of lawsuits and investigations against beet growers in the state for cheating them out of wages, overcharging for groceries, and refusing to make final settlement.[60] In the late 1930s, they organized a series of strikes under the Agricultural Workers Union, seeking fair wages and the end of child labor.[61]

Across the Midwest, it is estimated that more than 90% of those who had just arrived to work in the sugar beet field stayed after a year, half of those moving on to cities, but only 35% returned to Texas.[62] Despite their attempts to build a proletariat in the fields, few Mexicans desired to stay in the North, especially during the winters. Instead, many used each job as a springboard to another type of work, especially in urban areas and the steel industry, before returning to Mexico with what they had earned.

Across the Midwest

When Domingo Lopez and his father migrated to the United States, they joined a steady stream out of their hometown of Silao, Guanajuato. Workers from Silao had been leaving for years to work for the railroad, including his uncle, who they were joining in Topeka, Kansas. Domingo and his father settled into *La Yarda*, a boxcar *colonia*, or *barrio*. They found a city full of people from Silao.[63] Migration more often than not looked like this, as micro connections between towns and businesses guided people from one Mexican village or region to a US "daughter" community. *La Yarda* became one of the largest Mexican communities in Kansas and a starting point for families to move into other parts of Topeka and industrial employment.

Juan Martinez grew up in poverty in Durango but heard from others who had been north that things were better in the United States, so he and his brother left. Over the next few years, the siblings worked on railroads and then beets from El Paso to Nebraska to Kansas City. After a while, Juan returned to El Paso, where he married and became a steelworker.[64] His experiences exemplified common migration circuits that developed between El Paso and the Midwest, but also between urban centers in the Midwest and back to Mexico. *Colonias* in places such as Topeka, Kansas City, St. Paul, Milwaukee, St. Louis, Chicago, Saginaw, Detroit, and as far east as Bethlehem, Pennsylvania, were parts of webs connecting to smaller towns and Mexican villages.

The people recruited by the railroad and beet industries were primarily migrants from Mexico, but they included large numbers of US-born *Hispanos* from New Mexico and *Tejanos* from Texas. As one recruiter put it, "We get solos from Fort Worth, Kansas City, Buffalo, and El Paso. Those from Texas are usually cotton pickers. The New Mexico ranchers are all right. We get railroad and cotton workers and pool hall floaters. Many do their buying in sterling [silver from mines] and may winter there."[65] After the start of the Depression in 1930, the migration north to work in railroads and beets became a primarily *Tejano* phenomenon. *Tejanos* generally traveled in large, extended family units by truck under a single independent recruiter, rather than the large numbers of small families traveling by train recruited by large companies.[66]

By the mid-1920s, the Mexican communities in the Midwest were large enough that railroad and sugar beet companies no longer needed to recruit from the border. The American Beet Sugar Company got about half its Mexican workforce from New Mexico and other parts of Colorado, as well as about 1,800 families a year from other parts of the country. The Michigan Sugar Company shipped about 2,000 workers a year into the state, while the Holly Sugar Company of Colorado also recruited about 1,800 families.[67] Employers were aware of these changes. Phill Dale of the Eaton Sugar Company wrote, "We used to bring up Mexicans from New Mexico, meeting them at El Paso. Now we don't have to go so far south. There is plenty of labor now."[68] Back in El Paso, J. R. Silva, a Mexican labor contractor, wrote that "[Midwestern labor agencies] are shipping Mexicans to the railroads out of Chicago, Kansas City and Los Angeles now and fewer out of here."[69]

Benito Rodriguez, a Mexican recruiter, noted: "After a year or two [migrant workers] sent for their families but if they returned home they took their families with them. They used to return [to the railroad] more than they do now."[70] The Santa Fe was not alone in encouraging the settlement of families and the establishment of permanent communities. The Illinois Central began to send passes for families as well in an attempt to create a more settled population of Mexicans in Chicago.[71] The B&O Railroad took advantage of the fact that other railroads were bringing Mexicans; their Chicago yards operation hired hundreds of migrants.[72]

The Campa family was part of this trend. Perfecto Campa left Irapuato, Guanajuato, in 1913, following his twin brother, who had gotten a job for the Santa Fe in Kansas. After working for a few years, he was joined by his wife Benita in 1916. They lived in "*el ranchito*," a Santa Fe railroad camp in Florence, Kansas, where most of the Mexicans lived. There, they tended a garden to augment his earnings and raised four children, including Diego. Diego remembered that Florence was strictly segregated, even including the Catholic Church, and that his sister had been held back a year in school because she spoke Spanish. As a young man during the Depression, he dropped out of school and went to work for the railroad. Eventually, the family moved to Newton, Kansas, a city with a larger Mexican community.[73] Joe Jaime's parents traveled across the border from Aguascalientes. "My uncle Rosario Garcia, I don't know if you would call him a sponsor, but he made it so we could come up." Rosario helped them obtain work at Railway Ice Co., and the family lived in what Joe described as a "army like barracks" in Argentine, a neighborhood in Kansas City.[74] The trajectories of these two families are illustrative of how some railroad workers became settled, especially those arriving as families.

Kansas City's Mexican community became one of the largest in the Midwest. The Santa Fe was the largest employer of Mexican migrants but was complemented by other railroads and the meat-packing industry. As early as 1903, there were reports of Mexican railroad workers living in the boxcar communities between the tracks. The railroad encouraged workers to stay in the city over the winter and work in the cities so that it would be easier to hire them back the following year. The Mexican Revolution brought large numbers of families and middle-class migrants to male-dominated neighborhoods.[75]

The neighborhood of Argentine in particular became a major destination for people from the town of Tangancícuaro, Michoacán, and the surrounding countryside. Historian Judith Laird found that "Tangas" helped each other find housing and jobs, and after a few years, they would send for family members. As one person put it, "We try to come here to get together . . . not to be with strange people."[76] They helped each other move up the occupation ladder so that Tangas came to predominate in the railroad shops. Back in Michoacán, women were taking charge of day-to-day household affairs after men left, and goods and remittances were sent from the United States, stimulating the local economy and further migration. Another major cluster of migrants from Guanajuato helped each other and, over time, were disproportionately represented in the railroad warehouse.[77]

Argentine was joined by new Mexican neighborhoods in Rosedale, Frisco, Turkey Bottom, Armourdale (a major meat-packing center), and the Westside. Over time, boxcar camps began to take on a more permanent character, and the Santa Fe began to replace wood shacks with small brick houses. The Westside became the largest of the six neighborhoods. The communities boasted two Lady of Guadalupe churches; a few Protestant churches; business districts on 23rd, 24th, and 25th Streets that included pool halls, groceries, restaurants, and boarding houses; and a major Spanish-language newspaper, *El Cosmopolita*. More settlement meant more women and families, and the first US-raised generation of children. By the late 1920s, Mexicans were increasingly segregated, most notably in local schools. Kansas City had no pre-existing Mexican community, so new migrants instead settled in Eastern European neighborhoods and lived among them for decades before slowly becoming the dominant group. This differed from the Southwest, which had a much clearer dividing line between white and "Mexican."[78]

Kansas City and St. Louis emerged in the 1920s as important nodes for migratory labor and key centers for railroad worker recruitment. From my census cohort study data, about a dozen Mexican families from the sample lived in the Kansas City area in 1920, but only two of them remained in the city in the 1930 census. This signals the high rate at which families were moving out of these communities, as well as the stable, skilled workers who stayed. Scholars Valerie Mendoza and Judith Laird found a similar trajectory in their studies; long-time residents were those who had secured stable employment, were small business owners, or had become white-collar workers. They were the backbone of community organizations, the *Comisiónes Honorificas*, *Cruz Azul*, *mutualistas*, and Mexican consulates in these places.[79] *Comisiónes Honorificas*, located in at least twelve Kansas cities in the late 1920s, pressured the Mexican consulate in Kansas City to become involved in cases of railroad and sugar beet workers not only in Kansas, but also in Nebraska and the far north.[80]

Mexican communities popped up wherever railroad, sugar beet, or packing work was available. Sugar beets led to the creation of permanent *colonias* in Lincoln and Omaha, Nebraska. Railroads led to communities in Des Moines, Sioux City, Mason City, Fort Madison, Valley Junction, Davenport, Bettendorf, Moline, and Rock Island, Iowa. Mexican boxcar communities in the upper Midwest were often invisible to local communities, located on the edge of cities or in small towns.[81] Milwaukee had the largest concentration of Wisconsin's Mexicans, who worked in beets and various industrial fields. Midwestern Mexican *colonias* were less stable than their Southwest counterparts, however, as they had no established US-born community or as many middle-class or professional migrants.[82] *Colonias* were overwhelmingly male in the 1910s and well into the 1920s, and many of these men lived in boarding houses. Most were without families and moved between jobs.

Sugar beets created the Mexican community in the Twin Cities. The American Beet Sugar Company built a series of *colonias* in Minnesota. From there, Mexicans left for nearby cities. In St. Paul/Minneapolis, the Mexican community was mostly on the West Side in two neighborhoods where European immigrants lived. Meat packing helped to stabilize the Mexican community, offering steady, year-round employment. The West Side had a settlement house, Neighborhood House, which was modeled on Hull House and sought to assist and promote assimilation in the immigrant community. There were also various organizations, including the *La Sociedad Mutua Benéfica Recreativa Anahuac* that aided people in emergencies. *La Sociedad* had a women's auxiliary that sponsored festivals and events to preserve culture. These contributed to the feel of an urban village, though constant turnover meant that many organizations were not stable. About 600 lived in the city and hundreds more circulated between it and the beet fields. In total, an estimated 110,000 Mexicans lived in the Great Lakes region by 1930.[83]

Studies of Michigan show the same patterns.[84] Starting in 1915, Michigan beet companies began using recruiters and special railway cars to bring Mexican workers from Texas fields. By 1927, there were over 40,000 Mexicans working in Michigan, mostly around Saginaw but also in the northern part of the state; in just five years, they went from 33% to 75% of the sugar beet workforce. Companies turned to family labor; one study in 1924 found that 52% of sugar beet field workers were less than 15 years of age.[85] After the 1920–1921 recession, Mexicans very quickly started leaving the fields and going into industrial employment, especially in the winter. While some left because of the bad conditions, others never went to the fields at all. As one person put it, "We were friends. [The men I met on the train] already knew

Detroit, so I went to Detroit with them, preferring to work there than in the fields."[86] Migrant workers began using cars to move from field to field and back to Mexico, where they could sell the cars at a profit.[87] Detroit and the beet fields in Michigan acted as a single system, feeding workers to each other in regional labor circuits. This was true of the Midwest as a whole, where urban enclaves were supported by migratory agricultural workers.

Detroit was home to the second-largest Midwestern Mexican community, the bulk of whom worked in automobile factories. Fifteen thousand Mexicans lived in Detroit by 1928, with 4,000 working for the Ford Motor Company and another 200 attending its engineering school. The high employee turnover rate meant that, after some years, most jobs were obtained through networks rather than company outreach. These workers supported thousands of related industrial jobs. Javier Tovar, a prominent Mexican in Detroit, explained how the community grew:

> The high wages at Ford's attract the Mexicans as well as others. Some Mexican from a small country community in Mexico writes home and says that he is getting six dollars [a] day up here and that each American dollar is worth two Mexican *pesos*, and since the majority of the people cannot read, the word is passed from mouth to mouth, becoming more exaggerated as it goes, until some get to thinking that money can be shoveled up in the streets here, and there is a wholesale movement up here.[88]

Thousands of men and women worked in dozens of factories across the city beyond the auto industry. By 1930, the city had a significant middle class, a Lady of Guadalupe church, a Baptist church, consular office, and web of *mutualistas*.[89]

Transnational Circulation

When Francisco Mares ran away from his hometown with a girl against the wishes of her family, he turned to his friends. They helped them go to New Mexico, where he worked on the *traque* (railroad) and *betabel* (sugar beets) before returning to Mexico. Francisco returned with a few friends to El Paso but lost money before going to Miami and then to Globe, Arizona.[90] Mares's experiences were typical of village and kinship networks that guided people from one destination to another. As one Mexican worker told an interviewer,

"It is not five years ago since I left San Luis Potosí for the US. I had an uncle who lived in the city of Pueblo, and I directed myself there. As soon as I got to Texas, I had to work so it was the track for me. Since then, I have worked from the south to Illinois and in Ohio and Michigan just lately."[91]

Antonio Herrera continued circulating until he finally brought his family to Chicago. "I first came [to] the US in 1916. Then I was in Laredo, Texas, where I worked on a farm. I went back to Mexico during the war and worked in an oil refinery. . . . In 1920 I came to this country again and worked in the steel mills at Joliet. From there I went to work on the railroads in Kansas. I worked around Topeka for a while. In 1924 I went to Mexico and brought my family."[92] By the 1920s, Herrera was just one in a steady stream of people who migrated not only across the Midwest and the United States but also back to Mexico with regularity. One man went back and forth between central Mexico and Kansas City six times between 1910 and 1929, working for the Santa Fe, picking cotton, and taking industrial jobs.[93]

Ernesto Rodriguez, from Zacatecas, traveled the rails and worked in Los Angeles, Portland, Salt Lake City, and Nevada before settling in Pocatello, Idaho. There, he worked as a barber for the local Mexican community. Most Mexicans in Pocatella had come as strikebreakers at the local steel mill, but numerous stayed after the strike ended. Rodriguez also worked as a broker, dispatching workers to potato, sugar beet, and pea harvests across the Upper West. During this time, he joined the local barbers' union. Eventually, he decided to return to Mexico and moved to Lagos de Moreno, where he became involved in the land redistribution movement.[94]

Financial need drove migrants to pursue these circular migrations. Jesus Gonzalez traveled from Jalisco to El Paso to California and then to Kansas, Oklahoma, and Texas along the railroads before returning to Mexico for several years. But the lack of work drove him north.[95] Dan Rios, from Zacatecas, migrated between Mexico, El Paso, and California before working the beet fields in the Midwest. He told investigators that he was planning to return to Mexico and had sent $900 back in remittances.[96]

Francisco Carpio, who had created the *Cruz Azul* in Pueblo, reflected on the migration from Mexico to Colorado and back: "The Mexicans are low in seniority because they are unstable; therefore, they are laid off first. The Mexicans come to steel from the beets or railroads. The Mexicans like the work in sugar beets pretty well, but it does not last enough." Carpio acknowledged that saving enough to stay in Mexico was difficult, so many stayed in the economy of migratory labor by circumstance rather than choice: "We expect to go back after the season, but we don't have money to go. Then we are not satisfied when we go back to Mexico so we return to the United States . . . if there were a big boom in Mexico the Mexicans would go back."[97]

The Windy City

All rails led to Chicago; it was the western terminus of most eastern railroads and the eastern terminus of every western one. The premier city of the Midwest, it drew on the resources of the West, transportation, markets, and the environment to create economies of scale that allowed it to become the primary destination and source of goods across a vast region.[98] With two million residents in the early twentieth century, Chicago was at the center of a web of industrial Midwestern cities. When Mexican migrants began to arrive in large numbers in 1917, it was as an extension of these industries.

South of downtown, Chicago is split by a web of railroad tracks and several large rail yards. These rail yards were home to the Illinois Central, Santa Fe, Union Pacific, Burlington and Quincy, Rock Island, and smaller railroad companies. Rail yards were also home to large boxcar camps; not officially neighborhoods, they were still home to much of the city's workforce, especially of Mexican migrants. As early as 1910, the Santa Fe had a few workers in the Chicago branch, though it was not until after 1915 that they began to be hired in large numbers. As the use of Mexican labor by Chicago rail yard companies spread, it became common for labor agents to send workers to the Midwest, and from there, these workers would be sent north. In addition to the Santa Fe, the Rock Island and Union Pacific Railway shipped Mexican workers directly to Chicago. In 1916, several railroads brought hundreds of Mexican workers to the Near West Side of Chicago and nearby boxcar camps. By 1920, Mexicans had become a major presence on the railroads and were expanding to railroads that had never recruited them. The adoption of Mexican workers was uneven in Chicago. They dominated the large transcontinental railroads, comprising most of these companies' workers, while smaller, regional railroads were slower to adopt Mexican migrant labor. Of maintenance and repair workers for the Burlington Railway, 80% were Mexican, but just 4% for the Terre Haute Railway.[99]

At the south end of the city, three neighborhoods became centers of Mexican migration after 1917. The area around Lake Calumet was home to the largest concentration of steel factories in the United States, in addition containing every other type of industrial activity. The industry was dominated by a few conglomerates, including US Steel, which owned a massive plant, South Works, and several others in the area. South Chicago became the main neighborhood for the US Steel plant; it was mostly Eastern European, especially Polish. A few miles away, across the state line, was East Chicago, home to its own constellation of steel factories. The largest of these was Inland Steel, in the neighborhood of Indiana Harbor. Farther east was Gary, Indiana, which continued the trend with several large US Steel and independent steel factories. While US Steel hired more Mexicans than any other steel company, it did so in several factories across the Midwest. Inland Steel hired them at Indiana Harbor and at South Chicago, making the Indiana Harbor neighborhood the densest concentration of Mexicans in the Midwest.

Jose Diaz and his wife, Maria Garcia, followed the railroad to various places, including Kansas City, where their first son was born in 1918. Jose continued to look for better work, taking the growing family to South Chicago in the early 1920s and then the Near West Side and settling in the

Figure 3.5 The workforce at Inland Steel drew from around the world; over 53% of East Chicago's population was foreign born. Watch drawing at blast furnace at Inland Steel on May 3, 1920. Image courtesy of the Calumet Regional Archives of Indiana University Northwest.

Back of the Yards, where he worked at McCormick Place. His early death in 1927 sent his eldest son, Joseph, to work in meat packing for Armour.[100] Likewise, the Naria family lived in various boxcar communities across the upper Midwest, working for the Santa Fe until they settled in Chicago.[101]

Chicago was the center of recruitment and transportation of workers to the sugar beet industry. Just east of downtown, on the wrong side of the Chicago River, was a dense neighborhood of tightly packed housing and small to medium factories. The area didn't have a dominant employer or ethnic group; rather, people from a dozen ethnicities lived in close proximity, leading to a high density of national Catholic churches. At the center of the neighborhood was Hull House, the immigrant settlement house built by Jane Adams to assist immigrants with the skills they would need in their new home. There, dozens of labor agencies lined Canal Street as the Near West Side, which became the winter home for thousands of beet workers every year.

The Mexican population was enmeshed in back-to-back incidents in 1919 that rocked race relations in the city. In July, a race riot broke out after a teenager floated across an invisible line that divided a segregated beach and was killed. Soon, white mobs, mostly from the working-class European immigrant neighborhoods, began to attack African Americans en masse. Homes and businesses belonging to African Americans were targeted, leaving hundreds homeless, thirty-eight people dead, and hundreds wounded, including two Mexicans who were mistaken as African American.[102] Then, in September, tens of thousands of steel workers went on strike for the right to unionize. The strike was a disaster for the Amalgamated Association of Iron, Steel, and Tin Workers and the AFL. Companies used violence in suppressing the strike, often with the help of state governments, and by January 1920, most of the strikers had given in. A large part of the defeat can be attributed to employers exploiting divisions along ethnic and racial lines.[103]

Steel companies sent agents to the South and Southwest with the express purpose of hiring African Americans and Mexicans in order to break the strike and foment racial tensions. Over the course of the five-month strike, 30,000 African Americans and about 10,000 Mexicans were recruited into the industry. Agents of the major steel companies promised workers free transportation, a signing bonus, as much as four to five dollars a day, and room and board on company grounds. Companies distributed fliers on railroad lines as workers were heading north to work for the railroad companies or the beet fields.[104] The heavy recruitment effort in steel ended after the strike but picked up again amidst other strikes. Though some African

Americans and Mexicans refused to cross union lines, striking workers saw these workers of color as undermining their efforts and excluded them from future organizing efforts. Although numerous steel factories let go of their African American workers after the strikes, they kept hiring Mexicans. In South Chicago, companies explicitly hired Mexicans over African Americans to avoid tensions with European workers.[105] The strikes had introduced thousands of Mexican workers to South Chicago, Indiana Harbor in East Chicago, and Gary, Indiana. By 1925, there were about 10,000 Mexican steel workers in the Midwest, roughly half of whom were in Chicago, comprising 14% of the industry's workforce.[106]

In 1922, railroad workers went on the largest railroad strike since the Pullman Strike of 1894. In response to the post-war recession, the railroad industry imposed large wage cuts that targeted the railway repair and maintenance workers, including Mexicans in the Southwest, rather than the unionized jobs of the Brotherhood members. Seven different unions that mostly represented unskilled workers went on strike. This involved 400,000 workers, including 100,000 in Chicago. While Mexican and African American workers joined the strike in the South and Southwest, the industry also recruited them as strikebreakers in Chicago and gave them company housing. Large-scale violence and an injunction from the federal government broke the efforts, and the strike was defeated. Over the long term, the strike brought increased hiring of Mexican and African American workers in the Midwest.

Likewise, Mexicans gained entry into Chicago's meat-packing jobs during the war, but they came in large numbers in 1921, when packing house companies sought to break a strike. They came to the area around Union Stock Yard, where Armour, Swift, Morris, Hammond, and Wilson had centralized the nation's meat packing. The area lacked paved streets, sewers, garbage pick-up, electricity, and other city services. Its migrant residents were overcrowded into its poorly built buildings, their working and living conditions immortalized in Upton Sinclair's *The Jungle*. The neighborhood's commercial heart was at 47th and Ashland, while much of its mutual aid activities took place at the University of Chicago Settlement House.

And so, each industry had corresponding neighborhoods—the Near West Side for beets and small manufacturers, Back of the Yards for meat packing, and South Chicago for steel—in addition to boxcar camps (railroads) where large Mexican neighborhoods formed. However, *colonias* were not only *barrios*, isolated neighborhoods of concentrated urban poverty, but connected people throughout the region. Chicago itself had satellite cities—East Chicago, Gary, Joliet, Aurora, Waukegan, and Elgin, each with their own Mexican communities.

Chicago in 1920

My census cohort study of Mexicans living in Chicago in 1920 shows how these demographic trends looked in a single locality. The sample comprised 521 randomly selected male heads of household, who made up the main population studied, and their families, for a total of 931 individuals.[107] This sample group was followed through the 1930 census. To complement the sample population and compare it with other groups, US Census tract data were also used. These data underscore Mexicans' residential location vis-à-vis those major ethnic groups in the city.[108]

The big three industries (railroads, meat packing, and steel) show up on the 1920 census as the main employers of Mexicans in Chicago (Table 3.1). These industries made up a little less than half of all the industries where Mexicans were working during the 1920s but influenced the migrant economy in ways disproportionate to their numbers. These industries' hiring and importation of Mexican migrant workers led to the establishment of Mexican neighborhoods around them. Companies offered entry

Table 3.1 Largest Industries Employing Mexican Migrants in Chicago, 1920

Railroads	122	Telephone/Electric	7
Stock Yards	60	Office	7
Steel Mills	28	Private Employer	6
Meat Packing	20	Candy Industry	5
Hotel	18	Church	5
Factory	15	"Rand House"	5
Auto Industry	13	Unknown Industry	24
Restaurant	11	Other Industry	95
Education/City	11	Other	60
Music/Theater	9	Total	521

Source: Data from the 1920 census, available at Heritage Quest: http://www.heritagequestonline.com/prod/genealogy/index

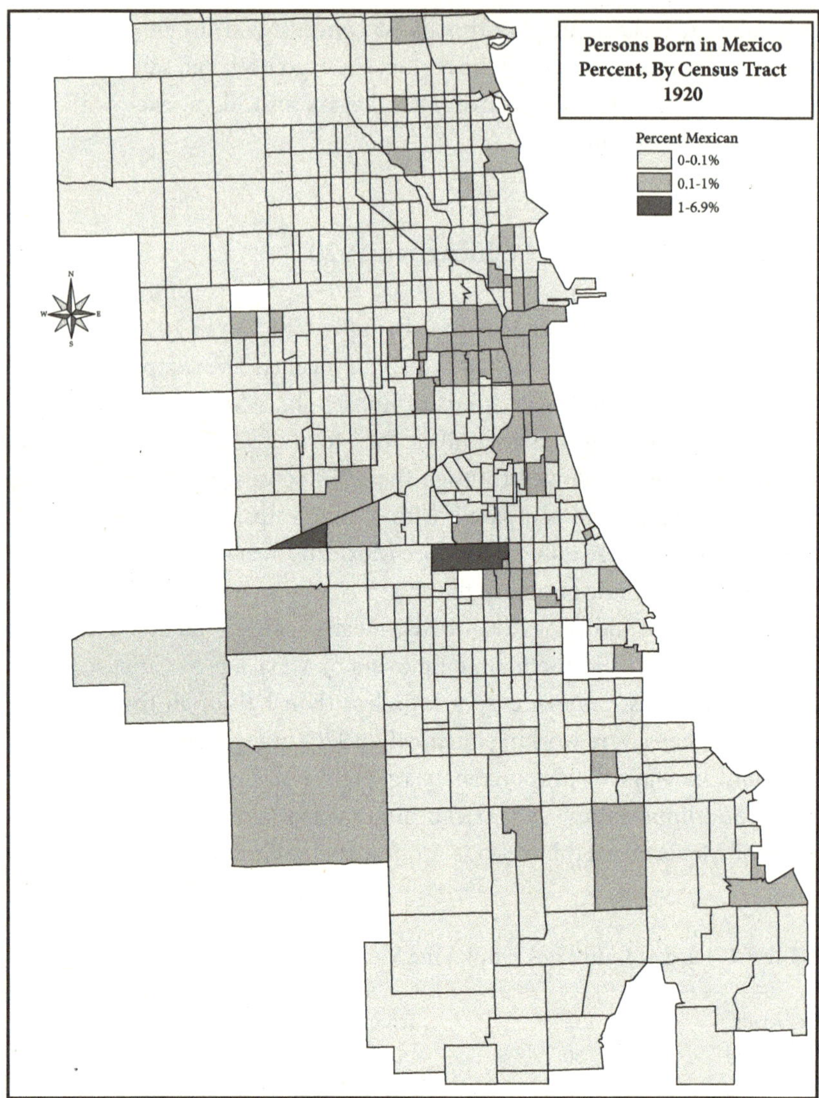

Figure 3.6 Chicago 1920, Mexicans as a percentage of the population in neighborhoods. Information from the University of Wisconsin Census Track Data for 1920.

work for new migrants, paid them more than employees of other industries, and the worker's wages supported many other types of johns in the surrounding neighborhoods. The big three industries were followed in importance by the hotel and auto industries. Railroads hired more than twice the number of Mexican workers as the next largest industry and acted as a gateway industry.[109] The benefits of free transport and cheap housing made the industry especially attractive to single young men. A large number of Mexicans were observed living in boxcars alongside other railroad workers.[110]

Labor and migration studies usually divide workers into five general categories: unskilled, semiskilled, skilled, white-collar, and professional (Table 3.2). Not surprisingly, the largest group in the sample were unskilled workers (56%), followed by semiskilled (14%) and skilled (14%); together, these blue-collar workers made up about 84% of the Mexicans working in Chicago.[111] More importantly, most migrants had spent time in other places in the United States before coming to Chicago, with even unskilled workers averaging 4.4 years since their first entry into the country. Unskilled workers, on average, had spent less than half as much time in the country as skilled workers. The Mexican migrant population in 1920 was dominated by young, unskilled workers brought over by industries to secure a labor force during a time of labor tensions.

The average Mexican migrant in 1920 was 23 years and 9 months old, had arrived sometime after 1915, and was unmarried. European migrants were generally older, with 40.5% coming before 1900 and 45.4% between 1900 and 1913.[112] Compared to the rest of Chicago and the national census study, the Mexican sample population was male, single, and young, generally in their twenties and early thirties. Many counted as single in the census likely had wives in Mexico. There were three men to every woman in the Mexican community, compared to 1.15 among European immigrants.[113] Over half of the census sample consisted of single men, and a Mexican

Table 3.2 Skill Type Compared to Other Factors in the Mexican Sample Population, 1920

	Unskilled	Semiskilled	Skilled	White Collar	Professional
Total Size (n)	292	75	74	35	17
Average Age (years)	29.6	28.0	31.2	29.2	30.4
Family Size (n)	1.96	1.93	2.2	2.3	2.2
Time in United States (years)	4.4	7	9.4	8	10.25

Source: Data from the 1920 census, available at Heritage Quest: http://www.heritagequestonline.com/prod/genealogy/index

Table 3.3 Marriage Rates in Chicago Among Various Groups, 1920 (population over 15 years)

	Native White	European Immigrant	African American	Mexican
Marriage Rate	58%	70%	59%	34%–47%

Source: Burgess and Newcomb, *Census Data of the City of Chicago 1920.*

woman older than 15 years was twice as likely to be married as a man of the same age.[114] European migrant marriage rates were almost twice as high (Table 3.3).

A substantial population lived in railroad boxcars along the south branch of the Chicago River and west of South Chicago. South Chicago had the largest boxcar community in the Midwest. While most of the Mexicans who lived in these train cars were single, some families also lived in them.[115] Boxcars lacked adequate heating, ventilation, or sewage disposal systems. While some people lived in boxcar camps for years, adding extensions, porches, and chicken coops, most moved into other housing as soon as they could afford to.

For the most part, Mexican families in Chicago during the 1920s lived in the dense neighborhoods near the largest employers. A large number lived in *casas de asistencia* (boarding houses) and with families that took in boarders. Young boarders tended to live together.[116] While accounting for only a third of the households, families doubled the size of the sample. The average family had three individuals—a father, a mother, and a young child—although some households had upwards of ten. The largest clusters of migrants tended to live in the Near West Side, in the Back of the Yards, and in South Chicago. Families tended to rent or own housing rather than live with other families or boarders.

Indiana Harbor and South Chicago

As one migrant described his journey to Chicago, "I had just come from Mexico in 1923 when I heard from a friend of mine about the good work there is in Chicago. He had a brother who had gone from Aguascalientes in Mexico directly to work for the Inland Steel Mills. I came in the early fall and went to the plant for work the day after I got here."[117] His story was common by the 1920s. Inland Steel had become one of the nation's largest hirers of Mexicans, attracting employers to Indiana Harbor and the neighboring South Chicago. By 1930, there were 5,343 Mexicans in Indiana Harbor, comprising 10% of the city. The *colonia*, just outside the Chicago city limits, had the largest concentration of Mexicans in the Midwest. The South Chicago neighborhood was nearly as large, at 4,300. Farther south, 3,486 lived in Gary.[118] This company and its neighborhood reveal much about how the migrant economy worked.

During the 1919 steel strike, Inland Steel aggressively recruited Mexicans; it transported 150 and housed them on-site in bunkhouses. After the strike, it laid off most of those workers, but in 1923, it hired 3,600 Mexicans. Its Mexican workforce numbered well over 2,000 through the decade. By the late 1920s, Mexicans made up the largest demographic group in a workforce that included many European immigrants, some American-born whites, and a few African Americans. Inland had more Mexicans on its payroll than any manufacturing company at a single location, including Ford. George Edson estimated that, in total, the company's Mexican workforce alone sent back $1,000,000 a year in remittances, or nearly one-fifth of total US remittances to Mexico.[119]

While Inland Steel heavily recruited during strikes, Mexicans came on their own as word of industry wages spread through workers returning to Mexico from the Southwest.[120] Francisco Martinez heard about steel while working in Kansas for the railroad, and he brought his wife and children to Indiana Harbor, working first for a cement plant and then for Inland Steel.[121] As one man who had migrated during the revolution put it, "I found no work [in El Paso], but a friend brought me to Indiana Harbor where I went to work in Inland Steel."[122] Another worker said simply, "I came to Indiana Harbor seven months ago. I came from Kansas City. There they told me the work was very good here and paid well."[123] The steel factories assigned numbers to workers to keep track of payroll, as they had trouble keeping track of names. Mexican workers began to use this to their advantage, renting their numbers when they went back to Mexico or selling them to newcomers.[124]

Inland Steel continued to have thousands of Mexicans on its rolls even as high turnover meant that very few stayed for more than a few years. Despite the company's high pay, the Mexican workforce had a turnover rate of 88% a year, which is much higher than that of the white or African American workers but about half the turnover rate of the railroads.[125] Most of the Mexicans at Inland were from the central Bajío states and had "leap-frogged" the borderlands to the Midwest via employment in industries in between.[126] Most had worked in other places before coming; only 25% had come directly from Mexico.[127]

Most workers circulated back and forth between work at Inland and other places. Luis Franco had worked in Texas agriculture before moving to the railroads, and then was recruited into Inland Steel.[128] Serafín García's family had worked in Texas before working in the sugar beet fields. They stayed in South Chicago at the urging of friends, who told them they would be closer to the sugar beet fields of Michigan and Ohio in the spring. Eventually, they settled permanently in town.[129] One man migrated back and forth between El Paso and New Mexico before going to Pueblo, and from there to Indiana Harbor, making use of the skills he had learned as a steel worker in Pueblo.[130] By the late 1920s, nearly all of the Inland workforce was made up of migrants who had come north after 1923. Nearby, other steel companies began to replicate this pattern.[131] Migrants encouraged others to join them. For example, Patrico Granado helped his friends get a job at US Steel in South Chicago, encouraged them to come, gave them financial assistance and temporary lodging, and introduced people to the neighborhood.[132]

Mexicans began to warn each other about sugar beet recruiters. One circular read, "A poor Mexican crosses the border and signs the papers that the *enganchista* gives him. He cannot read English and does not know what he is signing. He is told that he will be shipped to where he wants, given free room and board and fare back to Mexico. They think that they are going to work near Chicago and land some place in Iowa. It is for that reason of the many tricks and deceptions that the people who are coming up from Mexico are on the lookout for the *enganchistas* of the *betabel*."[133] This circular by the *Obreros Catolicos* encouraged migrants to take industrial work, to set their own course.

Indiana Harbor shows how the patterns identified in the Chicago census study operated on the ground. While the number of Mexican workers at Inland declined over the 1920s and the company closed its on-site housing, the Mexican community around the factory continued to grow until the Great Depression. Sr. Buitron, like many in the neighborhood, never worked for Inland Steel and instead moved to take a job at a cement plant at Indiana Harbor.[134] Companies around Inland began to hire Mexicans in large numbers, making the *colonia* an important node of the regional migrant economy. Rev. Galindo in Indiana Harbor described the changes: "In

1924 most of the Mexicans were singles. Now they are mostly families. They colony is growing. Some come direct from Mexico; others come from other parts of the United States. They are going and coming all the time. They tire of one kind of work and look for better work."[135] Indiana Harbor was quickly becoming a permanent community. Small businesses and civic organizations catered to residents. *Los Obreros de San José*, the largest *mutualista* in the community, raised money to build the Lady of Guadalupe church in 1927, sponsored events, and published the Spanish-language newspaper *El Amigo del Hogar*, while the Cuauhtémoc *mutualista* aided those in need.

In South Chicago, along 89th and 93rd Streets, Mexican boarding houses, pool halls, grocery stores, drug stores, and restaurants supported those working at nearby US Steel, Illinois Steel Mill, Wisconsin Steel, and Youngstown Sheet and Tube. Francisco Huerta and his sisters opened their boarding house and Spanish-language newspaper there. Sr. Galindo owned a Mexican drug store that also sold newspapers and books from Mexico City. In 1923, a Lady of Guadalupe church opened, soon followed by several Protestant churches. The neighborhood became home to several *mutualistas*, church organizations, and the Masonic society *Obreros Libres Mexicanos*. Small businesses boomed. Helena Svalina catered to Mexican migrants in her shop and boarding house, as did Eugene Navarro. Both rented to single male workers. Meanwhile, Mercedes Rios, an English speaking *Tejana*, became a social worker, advocate, and officer in the local *Cruz Azul*. She acted as a broker in the community, connecting people to government services, credit, and jobs.[136] One Mexican from Aguascalientes described how "more and more families came in the neighborhood [and] more and more of the men went out to live with them. I went out to live with a family from Torreón. They had been friends of my father and were very friendly to me. The first pool hall that I remember that was run by a Mexican was on 89th Street in South Chicago."[137] Forty-three percent of Mexican families had boarders, compared to 42% for African Americans and 17% for foreign-born whites. The neighborhood was further divided by the micro-migrations that had created it. Some blocks were dominated by people from Techaluta, Jalisco, or the indigenous Yaqui community, while other blocks were dominated by those from Zacatecas, Michoacán, or Durango.[138]

Before long, Indiana Harbor/South Chicago became regular stops on migratory circuits moving Mexicans into and out of the city. Workers in California or Colorado who were later interviewed frequently mentioned "Indiana Harbor" or "Inland Steel" as one of their former places of residence, along with Kansas City, Detroit, and other Midwestern locations.[139] As important as this part of the migrant economy was, it also limited opportunities. These jobs were in many ways better than agriculture, yet they also often locked workers in the worst parts of the industrial economy. Mexicans couldn't join unions in the steel plants, were segregated in the plants, and infrequently moved into skilled positions.[140]

Migrant Sample by 1930

Fred Gomez was born in Texas in 1923 to a mother from Jalisco and a father from San Luis Potosí who had come up during the revolution. The family migrated to Texas, Oklahoma, and Nebraska before coming to Chicago. There, his father worked as a barber and tailor in the Near West Side, serving a mainly Mexican clientele. His job stability allowed the family to put down roots, send their children to public school, and attend masses at St. Francis of Assisi, one of the few churches with Spanish services at the time.[141] Home to 2,500 Mexicans, the Near West Side was the central hub of Mexican Chicago, home to the small Mexican middle class and the largest institutions, including the consulate, Spanish-language newspapers, and Hull House. A study in the late 1920s counted forty-four Mexican businesses and another two dozen in the Brighton Park area a few blocks south.

The 1930 census counted 20,000 Mexicans in Cook County, Chicago was home to several Spanish-language newspapers, including *México* (renamed *El Nacional*), *El Heraldo Juvenil*, and *Correo Mexicano*. It was also home to various mutual aid societies, including *Mutualista Benito Juárez*, *Mutualista Ignacio Zaragoza*, and *Frente Popular*. Banks started to advertise and offer services to Mexicans sending money back home. The Italian State Bank had a "Spanish" department that catered to Mexicans sending money to Mexico. Mexicans also used the US Post Office, the South Chicago Savings Bank, Union State Bank, and Calumet National Bank to send remittances. The Atlas Exchange Bank, which placed ads in Spanish-language newspapers, had 550 accounts by Mexicans and sent seventy to eighty remittances a week, ranging from a few dollars to hundreds.[142] Mexicans were bring hired by every type of employer. Marshall Field Mattress Factory, among other companies, didn't have to recruit, as one researcher was told, "If he wants another worker, he tells some Mexican there, and the employee always produces next day some brother or cousin or sister who wants a job."[143]

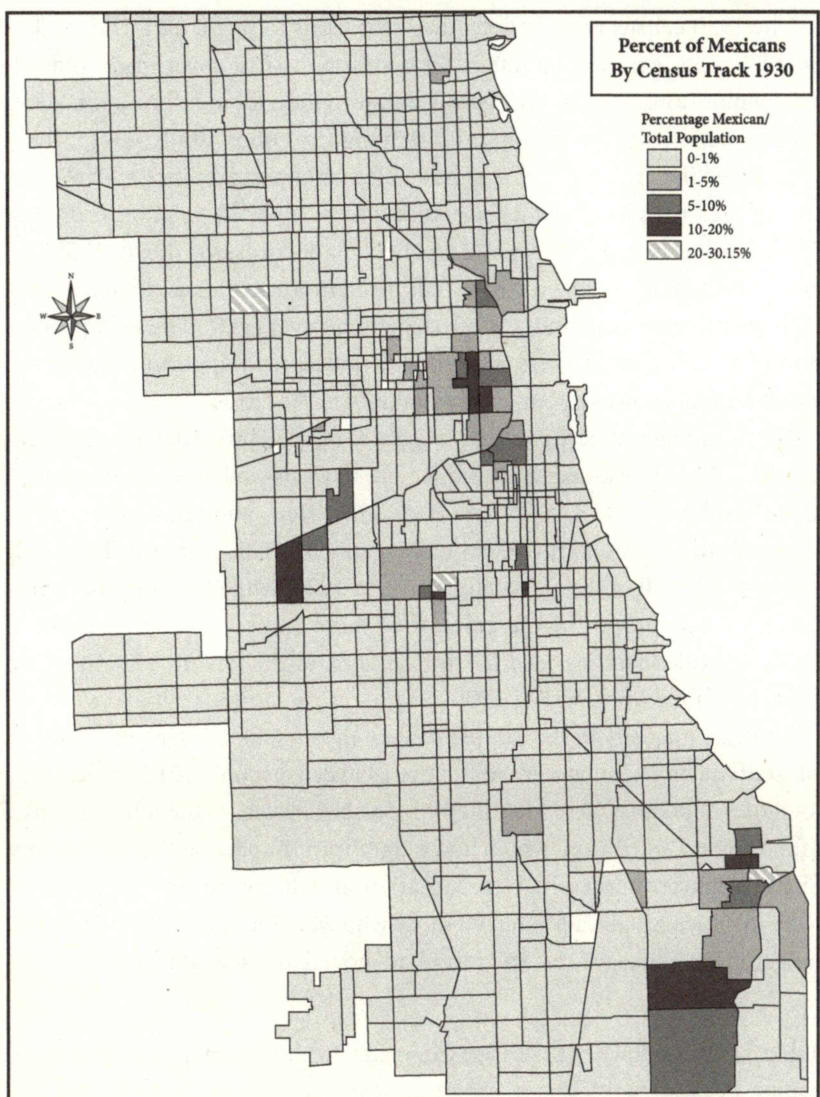

Figure 3.7 By 1930, the Mexican communities in Chicago had grown in the Near West, Back of the Yards, and the Lake Calumet area. Mexicans in the Near West Side had also spilled over from Italian neighborhoods into African American neighborhoods. Information from the University of Wisconsin Census Track Data for 1930.

The 1930 census is an undercount, as it tends to be for all working-class people, and Mexican migrants had reasons to distrust government officials asking questions. Even so, the census can provide a lot of information about general patterns in the community. Among the cohort study group, those who stayed in Chicago had the most stable and largest families, at an average size of 5.23 people. Unskilled workers moved with the migrant economy, while small business owners and teachers tended to settle down.[144] Skilled and professional workers were the oldest and most experienced groups, both with over twenty years in the United States on average.[145] The high proportion of white-collar workers is not due to widespread opportunities for upward mobility, however, but to their stability in the city.

Mexican migrant occupational categories in 1930 broke down as 39% unskilled, 15% semiskilled, 17% skilled, 19% white-collar, 9% professional, and 2% other (Table 3.4). The meat-packing, steel, and railroad industries were still the big three in 1930, but by a much smaller margin. They only accounted for 30 of the 101 males found in 1920, while teachers and artists make up a disproportionate amount of those individuals found again in 1930. Unskilled laborers had fallen from 42% of the total in 1920 to a little over 30% of the workforce by 1930.

The vast majority of the sample did not live in Chicago ten years later.[146] Most of the households were not in the 1930 census; only 101 families, for a total of 270 people, were identified.[147] The census was taken after the onset of the Great Depression, which had a significant impact on the community. Single men were hardest hit by repatriation, and they were the most likely not to be in Chicago a decade later. Of those who were found, about half were no longer in the Chicago area, and most had moved to places as far as California

Table 3.4 Breakdown of Skill Type Compared to Other Factors in the Mexican Sample Population, 1930

	Unskilled	Semiskilled	Skilled	White Collar	Professional
Total Size (n)	39	15	17	19	9
Average Age (years)	36.6	36.58	46	35.3	43.3
Family Size (n)	5.16	4	3.78	3.93	3.83
Time in United States (years)	16.24	17	22.58	18.7	26.2

Source: Data from the 1930 census, available at Heritage Quest: http://www.heritagequestonline.com/prod/genealogy/index

and Texas. Even with the fairly biased sample group that was found in 1930, several trends are apparent. Families were disproportionably represented among those who stayed. Most migrants no longer lived in Chicago, though some families still lived in the Midwest a decade later.

The study shows how the community in Chicago grew even as the bulk of workers continued a migratory livelihood. In 1917, the Mexican population was negligible. By 1920, it was 1,141 people, and by 1930, it was 20,000.[148] The community consisted of a combination of people who were arriving, departing, and staying. This rate varied year by year based on the economy, events in Mexico, and US policies. The rate likely dropped after the 1924 Immigration Act, as the difficulty of migrating increased. For Chicago, the ten-year rate for settlement was 7%; the unusually high 93% attrition rate includes 30% to 45% who left within a year, and another 25% within two years. Chicago, like other large urban centers, had a growing community of permanently settled migrants, even as the majority of new arrivals departed relatively quickly. Eventually, the settled population would grow large enough that it would exceed the size of the migratory population, even as the underlying dynamic stayed the same.

By 1930 a small but significant second generation of men and women had entered the workforce. For the most part, they followed their parents into the same occupational categories. Children of highly skilled blue-collar workers were the only exemption, displaying wide mobility. The constant turnover of workers, seen in the census sample and in the Chicago study, meant that few workers stayed more than a few years at a single location, and they didn't move up the economic ladder.

While there were no legal restrictions like those in Texas and California, Mexicans faced significant hurdles to integration.[149] Mexicans were not a majority in any of the neighborhoods they lived in, and they never made up more than a third of the residents of the new West Side, Back of the Yard, and South Chicago. Mexicans were usually charged higher prices for apartments than their European neighbors, to which they responded by creating multifamily households; 43% of Mexican households took in boarders.[150] In South Chicago, Mexicans, like African Americans, were relegated to the worst blocks closest to polluting factories and to the worst buildings.[151] They were viewed by their neighbors as competition for jobs and kept in the lowest-paying positions at most factories. As a result, migrants in Chicago tended to reject the assimilationist logic pushed by settlement houses and social workers, and to instead forge a positive Mexican identity based on post-revolutionary nationalism as promoted by Mexican civic institutions in the city. In effect, they became Mexican once in Chicago.[152]

Mexican Chicago was an ongoing process in the 1920s.[153] The everyday practices of ongoing migration, looking for work, sending remittances, cultural affinities, and family ties back home were a major part of migrants' experience in this era. The census data revealed the extent to which Chicago was just one place among various that migrants lived in. The results were very similar to the national study, but the city and its young community showed even more heavily the migratory nature of most Mexicans' lives. From 1917 to 1920, several thousand Mexicans arrived in the city to work in several industries. Railroads, along with sugar beets, provided a gateway into meat-packing, steel, and other industrial jobs. The bulk were first-generation young men following kinship networks into the city and hoping to make money and return to Mexico. The area's Mexican population was heavily dependent on the cycles of these industries; when the Great Depression began, most of those who didn't already have families there left.

The Great Depression

The Great Depression was a pivotal period for Mexicans across the Midwest. In Detroit, the community was devastated by the repatriations of the 1930s. Created by Diego Rivera (who supported return), the *La Liga de Obreros y Campesinos* worked with state and local officials and the consulate to send Mexicans home. The International Labor Defense of the Communist Party offered the only opposition in Detroit but was overshadowed by the consulate and pro-repatriation organizations. Four thousand were repatriated from Detroit, leaving a community only one-fifth its former size.[154] In East Chicago and Gary, Indiana, the American Legion and local governments organized a series of forced repatriations. In Indiana Harbor in East Chicago, 1,800 people were repatriated, half of the entire community, and 1,500 were sent away from Gary, including US-born children.[155]

There was no organized repatriation campaign in Chicago proper. As a result, its communities did not see the wholesale departures that characterized other places in the Midwest. The city's Immigrants Protective League successfully opposed forced repatriation but did help coordinate voluntary repatriation with the Mexican consulate. During the period, some *mutualistas* and the Spanish-language press pushed back against anti-Mexican rhetoric and pressured the consulate to resist deportation efforts. In Chicago, Vice-Consul Adolfo Dominguez, who worked *Departamento de Protección*[156] cases, became such a thorn in the side of local judges and police that Judge Thomas Green, a vocal anti-Mexican judge, had him jailed for contempt of court. Dominguez had pressed for the arrest of white residents that had attacked several Mexican children during a race riot in South Chicago in 1931. Green was forced to release him when the State Department noted the vice-consul's diplomatic immunity.[157] Even without being forced to leave the country, about 40% of the Mexicans in the city repatriated due to widespread unemployment.[158] They were denied relief and Works Progress Administration jobs, and they faced police harassment. Some, like their counterparts in other parts of the country, saw return as inevitable and took advantage of the opportunity for subsidized return and perhaps land.

Those families that did manage to permanently settle in the United States had to work long, hard hours to make even the smallest headway, but they did find some success over time. Yet for the majority, settlement was elusive, especially during the Depression. The communities in South Chicago and East Chicago were smaller but more stable after the Depression, with fewer single men, more families, and the presence of a second generation. In 1936, Mexicans in South Chicago joined the Steelworkers Organizing Committee (SWOC) to unionize the steel industry; a year later, workers at Inland in Indiana Harbor organized.[159] In joining these Popular Front union movements during the late 1930s, the oppositional Mexican identity in reaction to discrimination gave way to a US-based identity among those who stayed. The web of social organizations that grew in the 1930s allowed leaders to rise and the community to press for civil rights in the post-World War II period.[160]

The Pull of the Migrant Economy

Places like Chicago, Detroit, San Antonio, Los Angeles, San Luis Potosí, Celaya, and San Francisco de Rincón never existed in isolation. As anchors of regional migration circuits, these were nodes where smaller circuits connected to larger transnational ones. They drew and sent migrants to certain industries while sending large numbers of migrants from one to another. The same was also true of small towns, villages, rural areas, and countless locales on both sides of the border. Far more people moved among the industries that banded spaces far apart than ever stayed in only one place. The migrant economy's structural conditions, created by government policies and capitalist growth, were dependent on migratory labor but were shaped and co-dependent on the decisions made by individuals within communities. A variety of push factors (hard rural life, violence, and hunger) and pull factors) jobs, social and economic freedoms, family, and opportunity) have always been the contradictory impulses that drive people to leave home. Whether seasonal, annual, or decade-long stays, workers lived transnational existences that spanned these spaces.

One persistent theme in the writings and interviews left by migrants of this era was the belief that they were going to return to Mexico one day, even as they built more and more transnational practices. Rev. Galindo, of Indiana Harbor, described the pull Mexico held: "The Mexicans don't want to buy property because they are expecting to return to Mexico sooner or later; so they say, why buy? Many go back to Mexico but most of them return to the United States. They don't want to be [US] citizens. The countries are close; it is only two or three days to Mexico, and if they went back they would be strangers in their own country."[161] José S. Rodriguez saw his work at Illinois Steel and in South Chicago as temporary; he informed researchers he was planning to return to Mexico as soon as possible.[162] Jesse Perez told researchers that "returning to Mexico is much simpler than returning to Europe," and that discrimination made Mexicans reluctant to become citizens. This attitude was encouraged by the Mexican elite. In 1928, presidential candidate José Vasconcelos came to Chicago's Hull House to address the *mutualista Ignacio Zaragoza*. In his speech, he compared migrants in Chicago to Israelites in Egypt, facing discrimination and suffering in a foreign land, and urged them to return to Mexico. Several months later, president-elect Pascual Ortiz Rubio visited as well, promoting efforts to encourage return.[163] After two decades of mass migration, the role of migration in Mexican society had become a major political issue.

4

Entre Familia y Patria

The Paths of Migration in Central Mexico, 1920–1930

But let them give us jobs
And pay us decent wages;
Not one Mexican then
Will go to foreign lands.[1]

When the Mexican Revolution broke out in 1910, Daniel Aguilar was a small business owner in Chihuahua. He joined General Francisco Villa's forces and participated in various battles before Villa put Aguilar's business past to use and sent him on missions to the United States to procure weapons. After the war, Aguilar resettled in Chihuahua and opened a cantina. By 1923, his business began to struggle. As he contemplated his future, Aguilar struck up a conservation with the man who supplied his alcohol. This man told him that he had worked as a miner in the United States and that the pay was good in Miami, Arizona. Aguilar knew and trusted this man, and took his advice. He set out for Arizona and got a job at the same mine.[2] Never once did he think about the laws against migration in either the United States or Mexico.

Aguilar's story is not unique. Encounters like his could spur new migrations. A returned migrant might tell another person about their experience north of the border while they rode together on a train, or a villager might see a migrant returning with money and strike up a conversation. These connections, encounters, and networks of people collectively created a new economy and culture of migration.[3]

Though migrating in the 1920s was not easy or routine, it was increasingly common. Repeat migration was not characterized by a single type of experience; rather, it was a range of actions people took in response to their situations. Circular migration could be a regular occurrence, seasonal or annual. It could also be irregular, with people returning only after several years

Between Here and There. Daniel Morales, Oxford University Press. © Oxford University Press 2024.
DOI: 10.1093/oso/9780197612590.003.0005

in the United States, triggered by death, deportation, or search for a spouse. Whether a particular person made further trips north, or even moved north permanently, was highly dependent on location, industry, and family circumstances. While most Mexican migrants in the United States planned to return to Mexico at some point, large numbers stayed for years. At least 40% did not return until the Great Depression. However, the majority of the census sample population was no longer located in the United States ten years later, mostly because they had gone back to Mexico. Such circular migrants played a critical part in the migrant economy. Through them, town-based interpersonal networks functioned and allowed others with less social and economic capital to go north. As a result, migration in the 1920s involved more women, children, and families than had been the case ten years earlier.[4]

Building on nationalist rhetoric that saw Mexico as the rightful place for Mexicans, the Mexican government undertook an unprecedented effort at migration law enforcement during these years. After the passage of the *Ley de Migración* of 1926, toughened in 1930, the Mexican government issued directives discouraging migration and sent agents to stop it. However, migrants mostly brushed aside these efforts to control their movement. As more people participated in the migrant economy, many widely profited from it, and a range of local actors came to see migration as a solution for unrest.

Throughout the decade, it is estimated that up to 100,000 people crossed the border each year, legally and otherwise.[5] Looking closely at this traffic makes clear there was no separation in migrants' minds between economic, political, and cultural factors. Insecurity, in the form of violence, local politics, and local culture, shapes people's decisions. The violence of the Mexican Revolution and the subsequent Cristero War are inseparable from the other causes of migration from central Mexico. Migration was intertwined with the political circumstances that shaped all aspects of Mexican society. Once underway, mass migration began to change Mexican society. As people left and others came back, the resulting information and capital changed conditions on the ground and created pathways for others to follow. This new economy made it easier to move but also tied families and towns into continuous patterns of migration in order to maintain economic stability. Migration evolved from something that a few men did to something in which many participated; even those left behind were active participants. Migration eased the pressure for political and land reform in migrant-sending areas, at least in the 1920s. A new culture of migration began to grow and augment these networks, even as across society people were suspicious of those who went north.

Salvaconductos in Guanajuato and Aguascalientes

The nature of migration changed between 1910 and 1930 as it became embedded in localities. The scale of this shift is evident in the paperwork, particularly *salvaconductos*, passes issued by municipal governments that people submitted when they sought to go north from Guanajuato, in the migrant-sending Bajío, and Aguascalientes in the mining central/north. The paperwork from these areas shows the extent to which people were relying on local networks.

In the last week of May 1929, Ramon Torres set out from San Francisco del Rincón and asked for a pass to go north. He was 36, married, and employed in Mexico, but he had his sights set on Texas. With him were two relatives: Ramon Torres, who was 20, and Moises Torres, 27. They joined a group that included J. Encarnacion Hernandez, 25; Margarito Alcala, 25; Elias Segura, 37; and Pedro Segura, 23. Three of the seven were married. They worked in Mexico as *jornaleros* (laborers) and did not have job offers in hand. Migrating without a job offer was technically a violation of Mexican immigration law. Torres had possibly been to the United States before. Regardless, he and his companions knew that many others had made similar trips before, and that some did so on a regular basis.[6]

Lists of *salvaconductos* provide a snapshot of the era's migrants. While the statistics forwarded to governors were supposed to include all people who received certificates from municipal presidents, listing important information like migrants' names, ages, civil status, accompanying family members, whether they had jobs in Mexico, whether they had job offers in the United States, occupations, and places of origin, such information was only recorded intermittently. Some places recorded only names; others simply noted how many people got papers. The intervals between these reports being sent depended on the individual office or governor. However, enough reports contained sufficient information to give a sense of the patterns of migration from Guanajuato. An examination of two groups of reports from the state, one from July to August 1929 and another from December 1929 to January 1930, shows how migration was structured before the Depression.[7] Some 218 men requested documents from local officials. About 80% of these men

Table 4.1 Employment Status of Migrants from Guanajuato, June–August 1929 and December–February 1929–1930

	Job in Mexico?	Offer of Job in US?
Yes	117	12
No	51	163
No Answer	50	43

Source: Data from *Departamento de Estadísticas de Migración, Departamento de Migración.*

were migrating without their families, though some were accompanied by as many as five family members. Some women were counted among these family groups going north. Though most of the men in the reports were traveling alone, nearly half were married and likely saw going north as a way to support their families left behind.

Although having a direct job offer was against US immigration law, some men were willing to admit to Mexican officials that they had positions lined up (Table 4.1). Offers likely indicated that this was not the first time they were migrating, since these trips were unlikely without direct connections to an employer.[8] Although unemployment certainly influenced people's decisions to leave the country, more than two-thirds of migrants held a job in Mexico when they decided to go north. For them, the opportunity to earn higher wages was compelling. It was not the poorest who left but those above them in the social economic hierarchy, who possessed some skills. The overwhelming majority, however, did not have direct job offers. Of the twelve people in the reports from the four months examined who had such offers, all were traveling with others and were headed to specific destinations. This makes it likely that they were repeat migrants.

Even without specific job offers, people often had very clear ideas of where they were going, often mentioning specific places as deep in the US interior as Ohio and Michigan. Most migrants were heading to Texas (Table 4.2), though often they had specific locations in mind, such as Chapel Hill, Buda, and Artesia Well—none of which was a major destination center for migration. Only five people during the four months examined named the state in general and not a specific city. This suggests that they had enough information and confidence to leave a job and set out for a specific location.

The vast majority of migrants in Guanajuato came from a fairly short list of counties (municipalities), which included Celaya, San Francisco del

Table 4.2 Destination of Migrants from Guanajuato, June–August 1929 and December–February 1929–1930

Texas	56%	West	3%
California	8%	No Fixed Destination	19%
Midwest	14%		

Source: Data from *Departamento de Estadísticas de Migración, Departamento de Migración.*

Rincón, Ciudad Manuel Doblado, Yurira, Uriangato, Salvatierra, Apaseo, Cuerámaro, Dolores Hidalgo, Irapuato, and Tierra Blanca. Only two of these contained large cities; the rest were rural *cabezeras* (municipal county seats) with large farming populations and, importantly, railroad depots. The migrants probably came from villages a few days' walk from the *cabezera.* The patterns in San Francisco del Rincón and Celaya illustrate these patterns on the ground.[9]

By the late 1920s, San Francisco del Rincón had been sending migrants to the United States for more than two decades, and to other parts of Mexico for even longer. During December 1929 to January 1930, several groups of men sought papers. Their average age was 30; the oldest was 57 and the youngest 14. Exactly half were married. Every single one indicated they had a job in Mexico, though only two said they had a job offer in the United States. About two-fifths reported that they were agricultural laborers, another quarter indicated they were urban laborers, and the rest said they were tradesmen. Eighty percent of the people from San Francisco del Rincón indicated Texas as their destination, a much higher percentage than the migrants from Celaya or other towns in Guanajuato.[10] From the specific reports, you can compare migrants' demographics, from which you can see the extent to which people leaving included family and friend groups (Table 4.3).

Table 4.3 Percentages of Migrant Groups from San Francisco del Rincón and Celaya, Guanajuato, that Shared Certain Characteristics

Nuclear Family	34%	Similar Occupation	58%
Relatives	60%	Same Destination	90%
Similar Age	90%		

Source: Data from *Departamento de Estadísticas de Migración, Departamento de Migración.*

Migrants relied on information from others in order to make the journey, decide upon destinations, and acquire jobs.

On December 8, 1929, three men left San Francisco del Rincón. Filomeno Martinez headed north, alongside Martin Martinez, his relative (though their exact relation is unclear). They were both hatmakers and headed for El Paso. With them was Filogonio Gallardo, a laborer who was the same age as Filomeno, 40. These two had probably known each other for some time, and both had migrated before. Considering their ages, they might have previously migrated together. A week later, J. Jesus Alba, a 39-year-old merchant, left for Texas. He was followed a few days later by Anciento Munoz, another older merchant going north. A week after this, another group of three men departed San Francisco del Rincón: Francisco Villaneva, Aurora Pais, and Salvador Rodriguez, ages 23, 19, and 14, respectively. Their connections are unclear, but they went as a group to Arizona.

A month later, a much larger group left Rincón. Consisting of ten people, it included a family and two women, along with several young men between the ages of 16 and 22. With one exception, all headed to Texas. Of this group, several of the young men shared a last name, and the two women were related to each other. None of the others were related. They were likely friends or, perhaps, distant relatives. A week later, another group of ten men, ranging in age from 18 to 42, also left. Of these, two shared the last name Soto, and three shared the last name Chavez. Six were in their mid-20s.

Records from Celaya reinforce the pattern of migrants traveling with those they knew to destinations with which they or others were familiar. At the intersection of several railroads, Celaya was at the heart of Guanajuato. Information from July and August 1929 shows the effect of interpersonal networks in driving migration. Large groups continued to leave through August, almost all of them comprised of men. One of the groups consisted of young men who were unemployed, but unemployed migrants were in the minority. Two-thirds of the men reported having a job in Mexico, and none reported having a job offer. Their average age was 28, like that of the men from Rincón, and just over half of them were single. While a majority were traveling without families, at least ten families traveled north in these two months, a much larger number than came from Rincón. The migrants also came from a much greater range of occupations: about half were agricultural workers, a large group were non-agricultural laborers, and at least six were skilled tradesmen, including a shoemaker, a carpenter, and a mechanic. They also headed to more diverse locations; one-third were on their way to

(a)

(b)

Figure 4.1a and b Palacio Municipal, San Francisco de Rincón, and Calle Marquez. Postcard photographs, ca. 1930. @mfmexicoenfotos.com.

the Midwest, including six to Chicago. The majority that headed to Texas were traveling a significant distance from the border, with thirteen people going to San Antonio, five to San Benito, and three to Houston.

In the first weeks of January 1930, three men from Celaya requested passes to leave the country. They were Valentin Varges; his son, Felipe Varges; and Pedro Estrella, who was probably a friend of the Vargeses. Valentin was nearly 60; the other two were 16 and 25, respectively. The father worked in the fields, and the two young men worked in town learning trades. Only Estrella lacked a job in Mexico when they left. The Vargeses said they were going to St. Louis, probably not the first time for the elder Vargas, and Estrella said his destination was Fort Worth, Texas.

Two weeks later, they were followed by a group of young men, all headed to Texas. The oldest was 32 and the youngest 21. Only one was married, and all were farm workers from the area around Celaya. Of these, three shared the last name Torres, and two more shared their middle last names, indicating they were probably related. Two more were unrelated, but as they were going to the same destination as the others, they were probably well-known to the others. A week after the young men left, a large group that consisted of several families also departed. All but two had occupations in Mexico, and none had a specific offer of work. One family group consisted of three pairs of married men and women; all three men were surnamed Ramirez and were either brothers or cousins. The three men were laborers and headed to Chicago together. Two other families were on their way to San Benito, Texas. Both were fairly young, and though they had different last names, they might have been friends. Several older men were heading to Houston, and two older families were traveling to Detroit. These older men going to Michigan likely had emigrated before. Finally, five different men, three with families, went to San Antonio. Three of them shared the last name Rios and were accompanied by other family members.

Migrating hundreds or thousands of miles for the opportunity to earn higher pay is not a task undertaken without planning and thought. This is likely why so many of the migrants from San Francisco del Rincón and Celaya traveled with people that they knew. Hardly impulsive, risk-taking young men, half of the men who got passes from municipal presidents were already married when they left, and significant numbers were going to places where, in all likelihood, they had gone before.

In the state of Aguascalientes, the number of people granted legal immigration papers dramatically declined in the latter half of 1929, as it did elsewhere in response to US pressure.[11] In Guanajuato, passes were being issued to general migrants while, in Aguascalientes, they tended to be issued to long-time circular migrants who were legally crossing back and forth. This is difficult to confirm as most reports on the issuance of passes and people leaving to the north contained little detailed information. Local officials in Aguascalientes generally did not ask as numerous questions of migrants as did their counterparts in some other places. However, they did ask about wages and employment in more detail than agents in Guanajuato. Migrants used their networks to acquire jobs at specific US firms. The people who got passes in Aguascalientes were older, and almost all of them were repeat migrants. Some seemed intent on migrating permanently, and the majority were likely doing so legally.

Looking at the six months from December 1929 to May 1930, one of the few stretches during which data are available, shows some of the differences in migration compared to the same time period in Guanajuato. In Aguascalientes, seventy Mexicans were reported to the governor as having been issued passes. Eleven of these had families, bringing the total number of migrants to eight-five. As in Guanajuato, the sex ratio was predominantly male (71 to 14) and most men were going by themselves (59 to 11), though there is also a lot of evidence to suggest that people were migrating within social circles and had long experience in doing so.

Thirty-eight reported that they were going to a specific job, and of those, twenty-six reported the exact wages that they were going to earn, some down to the penny. About half of these wages were around two dollars a day, but some migrants reported wages as high as five dollars a day. On average, they anticipated earning $3.14 per day. What accounts for their relatively high wages is that there were few agricultural laborers in the Aguascalientes sample; most were railroad, mining, or factory workers (Table 4.4). About one-fourth of the people who requested passes had families living in the United States. These two facts suggest that most of the men had worked themselves into more skilled professions and had links across the border. This was particularly the case for those going to Arizona mines and foundries. Three different groups specifically mentioned having jobs at the United Verde Copper Company in Jerome, Arizona, their destination, and two mentioned that they already had siblings working there.[12] This suggests that, in certain areas, even people with good jobs in the United States participated in circular migration.

Looking at individual migrants shows how these patterns played out on the local level. The migrants from Aguascalientes went to a more diverse

Table 4.4 Employment in United States of Migrants from Aguascalientes, December 1929–May 1930

Railroad	18	Other Manufacturer	10
Agriculture	5	To Family	18
Mining	4	Student	6
Foundry	3	Tourist	5

Migrants who were students or were traveling to family were not necessarily seeking jobs in the United States. Large numbers did, but for others, rejoining family or going to school was the primary reason they sought a pass.

Source: Data from *Departamento de Estadísticas de Migración, Departamento de Migración.*

set of places than those from Guanajuato, with nearly as many going to California as Texas, some going to Arizona, and others going to western states like Utah, Wyoming, and Montana (Table 4.5). Like the migrants from neighboring towns to the south, they were headed to specific locations, suggesting familiarity with their destinations. Many of the men seemed to know each other. One group, for example, included two people named Nuñez, and another included several people named Gonzalez. It was not uncommon for everyone in such a group to have the same destination. In one case, a group of seven men indicated they were going to San Antonio to work on the railroad, and all reported wages from $2.40 to $4.00 a day. Even though none shared a last name, it is likely that they knew each other. In another case, even though no large groups came at once, a large number of men wrote down Los Angeles as their destination and either the Santa Fe or Union Pacific railroads as their job, usually reporting wages between two and four dollars a day. Networks of information and support likely allowed people from the state to work in those specific firms, diminishing the migrants' need to travel in groups.

Table 4.5 Destination of Migrants from Aguascalientes, December 1929–May 1930

Texas	35%	Far West	12%
California	33%	Midwest	6%
Arizona	14%		

Source: Data from *Departamento de Estadísticas de Migración, Departamento de Migración.*

Even skilled migrants with families in Mexico tended to return to their home country. When they did so, they spread information about their jobs so that others would join them in the same lines of work. The sets of data from Aguascalientes and Guanajuato are not exactly comparable. In Aguascalientes, *salvaconducto* passes were given to those who were migrating legally, while in Guanajuato, it sometimes seemed like anyone who wanted to go north got a pass. Also included in the Aguascalientes numbers were some parents with children going to attend American schools, some tourists, and a handful of women going to join their husbands or relatives. In general, Aguascalientes migrants were more experienced, had more families, and more often than not, had jobs awaiting them.

As the migrants from Guanajuato and Aguascalientes show, young adults had ties that allowed them to leave with others for places that, while unfamiliar to them, were known to someone they knew. In an earlier era, men might have traveled and migrated alone with the help of a labor agent, whereas in the 1920s, almost everyone was traveling with someone else, whether a family member or an acquaintance. Migration was becoming something that happened quite regularly among the men from Guanajuato and Aguascalientes as a way to support their families and secure their futures in Mexico. For these people, migration was both circular and social, an extension of community ties. In 1926, an estimated 25% of migrants already had family in the United States they were going to join.[13] The social spaces where people lived and the ties that linked them had expanded to encompass places thousands of miles away and drew in more and more communities in Mexico.[14]

Information: From Friends, From the Government

Mass migration is not just an economic phenomenon but a political one as well. As American elites relied on imported (and increasingly undocumented) Mexican labor, politicians across Mexico struggled to respond. In the meantime, violence and displacement continued through the 1920s as demands for land redistribution went mostly unmet in the Bajío. The Cristero War that was waged in the migrant-sending states added new waves of refugees. State and local politicians began to encourage emigration even as people were told to stay by the Catholic Church, newspapers, and the Mexican federal government.

Information and literacy became key commodities for potential migrants. People were learning from those around them how to navigate the US immigration system. This could even lead to humorous situations. When Salvador Sotelo left for the United States, he did so with loans from people in his hometown and journeyed with two friends who had already lived there, one of whom boasted about his knowledge of English. So it was a shock to him when they arrived and his friend didn't understand the *enganchadores* at the border. After recovering from his shock, Sotelo journeyed to join his older brother, who had migrated several years before.[15]

In towns and villages across central Mexico, information on how to migrate was not hard to come by. In San Francisco del Rincón, Esaúl González Luna was remembered for his success in America. From the Altos de Jalisco, at 17, he took the train from San Francisco del Rincón to Ciudad Juárez and into Arizona. There, he worked in a mine and became a superintendent. In the 1920s, he returned to Mexico, built a cement house for his family, and married locally. Several years later, he and his wife established a textile business in San Francisco del Rincón that became a large factory. His success encouraged others to leave.[16] This type of example worried some observers, who noted that "the Mexican who returns to old Mexico is called a 'northerner' by his neighbors; he is a hero in his village; he has been everywhere, he has seen everything, he knows everything—what he says is listened to with great respect and carries great influence with his hearers."[17] In villages across the region, returning migrants told their relatives, friends, acquaintances, or even people they had just met about their trips north and how they could follow in their footsteps.

Acquaintance connections were critical in spreading information about migration. While family is thought of as a "strong" link, "weak" links like acquaintances produced more information and opportunities for migration, even though a family member leaving might make a person more likely to leave. Chance encounters with a returned migrant could spur new migrations.[18] The patterns from Guanajuato indicate that for large numbers of people it was easier to find a job in the United States than in Mexico City, as that is where their information networks took them. Studies of the villages, Cherán and Tzintzutzan in Michoacán found that a significant culture of migration had developed by the 1940s, even as people who returned mostly resumed their premigration lifestyle.[19]

The government countered with an information campaign of its own. Governors in migrant-sending states urged the federal government to stop emigration. In response, the *Secretaría de Relaciones Exteriores* (SRE) sent them circulars listing the requirements for legal entry to the United States and telling them to distribute the information.[20] Shortly afterward, the *Departamento de Migración* sent booklets to governors containing information meant to dissuade migrants from heading north and encouraged states to make copies and hold dedicated conferences to educate local officials.[21] It was especially important to "warn municipal presidents to refrain from telling workers that the certificates they issue to them will be enough for them to migrate without difficulties."[22] In Guanajuato, the secretary of the interior responded by saying he would support "conferences in order to combat the migration of Mexican workers and peasants," while not taking meaningful action.[23] These official sources of information carried less weight with residents than word-of-mouth exchanges of information.[24]

Capital

In Chicago, a Mexican migrant from Michoacán who was also a bank employee explained: "I returned with my mother to Mexico to my native village and stayed a year, but we returned to the United States though we had planned to stay in Mexico. In my village about half of the men have come to the United States. Mostly women remain in Mexico. They are supported largely by money sent from the United States. Every day we sent about fifteen or twenty dollars to Mexico through our bank."[25] A similar phenomenon was occurring across central Mexico. Those who went north sent back and returned with capital, in the form of remittances and goods, that families and towns desperately needed.

Looking at the objects migrants brought back provides a sense of the scale of the back-and-forth movement (Table 4.6). Starting in 1926, when the government exempted repatriates from duties on cars, 38% of returning families came back with automobiles. Most of them brought clothing, photographs, animals, and household goods like furniture and kitchen utensils. A significant minority hauled goods that could be used in economic pursuits: tools for their trades, vehicles, machines, or agricultural equipment. Others returned with only the money they had saved, while still others returned with nothing. In general, those who did return with goods prioritized items that eased their work. Such goods could change their owners' stations in life, but they often broke down. Mexican anthropologist Manuel Gamio, writing

Table 4.6 Selected Objects Brought into Mexico by Returning Migrants, 1927

Object	Total Number	Ratio of Object to 100 Returning Migrants	Object	Total Number	Ratio of Object to 100 Returning Migrants
Clothing*	3720	100	Automobiles	793	37.54
Photographs	2706	118.53	Trunks	807	38.19
Chickens	2447	116	Tables	596	28.21
Chairs	2156	112	Stoves	581	27.58
Beds	1745	82.88	Sewing Machines	349	16.57
Kitchen Utensils	1642	78	Tool Sets	289	13.72

*Trunks, suitcases, and bundles.

Source: Permit No. 202, *Secretaría de Relaciones Exteriores*, December 14, 1926, in Gamio, *Mexican Immigration to the United States.*

in the 1930s, found that most of the machines people brought back to the colony of Acambaro, Jalisco, had ceased functioning within a year.[26] Without skilled upkeep, the machines were ill-suited for use in rural Mexico.

By the late 1920s, goods and money were coming back to Mexico at significant rates, but these varied alongside trends in violence and migration. Gamio's data on remittances for two two-month periods in 1926 and 1927 showed the rate at which remittances were being sent back to Mexico during the peak months in late summer versus the slower months of winter. Even in wintertime, those figures were significant. A total of 23,446 money orders were sent through the US Post Office from July to August 1926, and 17,709 were sent from January to February 1927. While California had fewer Mexican migrants than Texas, a much greater proportion of the remittances went from that state to Mexico (8,582 and 6,313 money orders in January and February 1927 respectively). The Midwest also sent a disproportionate amount, led by Illinois (2,923 and 2,107 money orders) and Indiana (1,242 and 837 money orders). While Texas sent fewer remittances as a percentage than California, it was more stable, with less seasonal variation.[27] In total, the amount of money remitted increased from 5 million pesos in 1919 to 16 million pesos just four years later; it remained between 10 and 16 million pesos a year throughout the 1920s.[28] In some years, such as 1927, the amounts sent back were much higher because the Cristero War caused people to send money rather than return to Mexico with money in hand.[29] This translated from five million dollars a year in slow years to eight million dollars in peak years, with the average remittance being forty-eight dollars.

The bulk of remittances went to the heart of migrant-sending central Mexico (Table 4.7). Most of the funds went to the three states that sent the most migrants—Michoacán, Guanajuato, and Jalisco—followed by the smaller states where the migrant economy took root as well as Mexico City. In terms of remittances sent back to Mexico, most of those from Texas went to the border region. California had more remittances from people from northern and central states, while the majority of remittances from the Midwest went to central Mexican states.

Remittances came through both the US Post Office and private banks that catered to migrants. At one bank in the Imperial Valley, 134 people remitted an average of forty dollars each over the course of 1926. First National Bank, also in California, reported a similar amount.[30] In Orange County, California, a bank reported that Mexicans sent back between thirty-three and sixty remittances per month.[31] Meanwhile, in Gary, Indiana, most migrants were sending money back, with 250 to 300 people sending back between twenty and twenty-five dollars, 200 or more sending back around ten dollars, and a handful sending between seventy-five and a hundred dollars a month. Max Gallinatti of the First National Bank of Gary reported that sixty Mexicans remitted money from his bank in sums ranging from ten to thirty dollars and occasionally over forty dollars a month. The post office at Gary reported that it sent "from 10–30 money orders a day for Mexicans, in sums ranging from $10 to $50 and occasionally as high as $100. The business represents a considerable outflow of the money to Mexico, going mostly to the state of Michoacán."[32] In Chicago, various bank clerks reported that

Table 4.7 Largest Destination of Remittances, July–August 1926

Michoacán	4,775	Distrito Federal	1,196
Guanajuato	4,659	Zacatecas	1,140
Jalisco	3,507	Chihuahua	1,046
Nuevo Leon	1,913	Coahuila	903
Durango	1,400	San Luis Potosí	869

Source: Table 8, Money Orders Received, in Gamio, *Mexican Immigration to the United States.*

migrants' remittances were between thirty and thirty-five dollars but could vary from five to a hundred or even, in one case, a few hundred dollars. The amounts were substantial for the era and critical for families in central Mexico.[33]

The growth of migration in the 1920s is a testament to the government's inability to solve structural problems in the Mexican economy after the revolution. In the United States, an agricultural worker could earn six times as much as he usually would doing the same work in central Mexico. The daily mean wage was 1.15 pesos or $0.57 a day, or $17.67 a month vs $2.00 a day in the most basic US picking jobs, and most jobs paid higher still.[34] Within Mexico, industrial production did not return to pre-revolution levels until the end of the 1920s, while agricultural production didn't recover in this time period at all.[35] For agricultural workers in Mexico, going north would, at worst, earn a family about the same amount as staying in Mexico and had the possibility of a much greater return, especially the farther north a person traveled. The amounts could improve their situations but were rarely enough to let someone leave the migrant life.

Remittances were even a driver of migration. Using the resources of their communities to go north, migrants drove an economy based on the circulation of information and remittances. Migrants funded the migration of family members and sent/brought back money and goods. All this lowered the economic and social costs of others following in their wake, creating a self-sustaining cycle. As migration networks spread and involved more families, they became a way to gain much-needed capital, allowing people to build houses, buy land, or counteract the uncertainties of and drops in agricultural production. This was especially true of younger people, who often did not have access to the land or resources to support family. As such, migration functioned as a way to relieve demographic and economic pressures on families.[36] The return of capital to Mexico from migrants changed society. As people turned to migration as the primary means of social mobility, they expanded the migrant economy while changing expectations.

The Cost of Migration on Families

As families became more dependent on migration outside of their home communities, those left behind shouldered enormous pressures and paid a high social cost. Across central Mexico, men often left their wives in the care of in-laws. Fathers left their children, seeing them perhaps once a year. If both parents migrated, their children often grew up in the care of relatives, such as grandparents or an aunt.[37] This culture of migration first began in the 1920s and was accompanied by a growing set of cultural expectations that young men would migrate and subsequently return.

In Chicago, Robert Redfield interviewed a couple who had gone back and forth in 1925, whom he identified as Mrs. and Mr. G. The husband crossed the border and worked in San Antonio and sent money back, but his father-in-law urged him to return to Mexico to take care of his family. After a year, he did. For a year, he tried to make a living in Mexico, but he found himself anxious to leave again. Eventually, he moved to the Midwest and took his wife with him. He told Redfield that he was saving to bring other family members north.[38] Manuel Pérez, a migrant from San Francisco del Rincón, went north, leaving his family behind when his friends told him about the United States. For several years, he remitted money to support his wife and child, once sending about $200. Eventually, he returned and brought them to live in California, though he maintained that he planned to return to Guanajuato as part of an experimental repatriation *colonia* at Acámbaro.[39] While migration could be regular, it was often not; this irregularity was part of the fabric of migratory life. As circumstances changed, intentions and plans changed.

Jesus Gonzales left his small shop in Jalisco because of the revolution and traveled from Kansas to California before becoming a miner. His travels also took him to Torreón and across Chihuahua, but he found it difficult to leave the life of continuous migration and returned to the United States. To him, his time back in Mexico was not of a different nature than his migrant life outside the country. He went wherever the mining work took him.[40] Manuel Lomeli, like many miners, kept his family in Mexico. A migrant who left for Miami, Arizona, when a friend told him of the money he could earn there, Lomeli said he did not plan to settle there. In 1923, after a dispute with a mining engineer, he returned to Torreón, where his family lived. He did not stay very long; within a year, he had returned to the migrant life.[41] Pedro Flores migrated to Miami, Arizona, in the 1910s, becoming a miner there. He also established a boarding house in the town while sending money to his family in Mexico. However, in the late 1920s, he returned to Mexico and became a miner in Sonora. These types of back-and-forth movements were common.[42]

Even when migrants sent remittances to support their families, these could prove insufficient, and the savings were rarely enough to enable permanent settlement.[43] Large numbers of families were supported by regular remittances. Other families were abandoned when breadwinners left. One person in San Ignacio Cerro Gordo explained, "There in the United States, they are riding about in automobiles; here their families are without food to eat, and must eat nopal (cactus pads). Many—perhaps one third—don't write; one man with many children hasn't written for eight months. Two men from San Ignacio have families there, and here, too."[44] This aspect of migration came across in *corridos*, migrant ballads that commonly include stories of homes lost and those left behind. "*La Canción del Interior*," a ballad written in Jalisco in 1932, tells one such story. Here is a selection from the *corrido*:

Of those three coming along,
Which one pleases you most?
That one in the blue dress
Seems to me the best.

Come here, stop chewing,
Don't chew nixtamal[45] now.
We are going to the United States,
Where we will enjoy ourselves.

Hear the train now, Chinita,
Hear what whistles it gives.
Only one favor I ask of you,
That you won't cry over there.

Dearest, I am tired,
And we are scarcely at Torreón.
So that I won't feel tired,
Will you sing me a song?

What a charming song,
I have never heard it before.
Sing me still a prettier one,
And then I will sing to you.

I told the *reenganchista*
That I was coming back,
But that I was not coming alone,
That this time I would bring a
companion.

Don't send me to Texas,
Not to the State of Oklahoma.
They are disagreeable places
Where they hate one who smokes.

But the pay is going to start
So that my sweetheart may spend it.
Half is for her
And half for my family.

Here, don't take advantage,
You enjoy the best there is.
You know that you are married
And under obligation.

Yesterday afternoon I got a letter
That my parents sent me
In which, weeping, they asked
And begged me to come back.

I don't know what to do
In order to go to my country.
I begin to think
That here I leave this woman.

I remember an ungrateful one
Whom, at one time, I loved,
But it has been my price
That I have not loved her since.

Chinita, I charge you
That when you think of me,
Ah, never, never forget
That I was your adorer.

The birds no longer sing,
And the stars give me no light.
The flowers have no scent
Because love is lacking there.

But I was so unfortunate
In loving that woman
That I have sworn by the Eternal
Never to love another.[46]

This song about a repeat migrant who goes north with his girlfriend but has neglected to tell her of his wife and family back in Mexico conveys the dual existence of those regularly moving. Even though his parents beg him to return to his family, he does not want to leave his lover, but in the end, he does and fulfills his family obligations. While this *corrido* seems, at first, like the tale of a brokenhearted bracero, it could also be a cautionary tale for braceros, reminding them of their responsibilities to their loved ones. It was a common experience for communities and families to struggle with expectations when divided by the border and apart for long periods.

Locario Lopez explained how life apart strained his family: "My wife wants me to send for her. Women's work is easier here than in Mexico. My wife didn't want to send me a picture of the children for fear the picture would satisfy my homesickness and I would not want to return to Mexico."[47] Lopez had migrated to provide for his family during the revolution, to keep them in their home, and felt pressure from his wife to return. Similar scenes played out throughout Mexico as people struggled to keep families together and maintain ties during migration. Pictures of the family served as symbolic links and messages about the duty of a father and his place in the family.[48]

The Venegas family used letters and pictures to keep in contact through the 1920s and 1930s. In nearly a hundred letters, Miguel Venegas kept his father, mother, and brother back in Jalisco, Mexico, informed about US life, business prospects, and his wife and children's well-being. His correspondence often included long descriptions of events big and small, intended to make them feel like part of a single unit despite the distance. Letters frequently included pictures of children, Miguel, or his wife and items from their grocery store. Venegas's letters make clear that, like many others, his family thought of themselves as living in exile in the United States until circumstances in Mexico allowed their return. Yet Venegas didn't return until a short visit in 1931. He moved back to his hometown in the 1930s.[49]

(a)

(b)

Figure 4.2a and b The Venegas family communicated through a transnational circuit of letters, postcards, and photographs that kept the family together across Mexico and the United States. Venegas Family History Album, p. 9 & 44. Venegas Family Papers. Department of Archives and Special Collections, William H. Hannon Library, Loyola Marymount University.

Isaac Gallegos Cervantes wrote to his childhood friend Carmen Rodriguez from the United States. He was a second-generation migrant whose father had left a decade earlier. With the help of friends and a loan, he had made his way to Texas, bribing an official to gain entry. He traveled back and forth, using his short stays to try to woo Carmen. She would urge him to stay, but he would leave nonetheless. She gave him a handkerchief to remember her by. For several years, they sent a stream of heartfelt letters, but she rejected him when their correspondence was discovered by her family. Eventually, they confessed their love for each other, and he returned in 1926 to marry her.[50]

José Rocha, a barber from Leon, Guanajuato, who left at the insistence of his brothers, traveled across the United States but got tired of the migrant life. He had savings and decided to go back to Leon. While there, he learned that his brothers had become successful in New York, and as he put it, "I stayed a year in Leon and got tired of being there for I earned very little in the barber trade and anyways I wanted to keep on adventuring so that I started again on the road to the United States."[51] Like others, Rocha found the attractions of migrant life difficult to leave behind, even after he had accumulated the savings that were his original goal.

Agapito Martinez and his family had a similar story. Martinez left Guanajuato during the revolution and worked on railroads and odd jobs in Arizona before going to California and marrying Leonaides Viveros, who had migrated with her family years earlier. Despite a well-paying factory job in Los Angeles, he had always wanted to go back to Mexico. So in 1925, with $2,000 in savings, he moved his family to Abasolo, Guanajuato, a town southwest of Irapuato. His daughter, Ofelia, remembered it as a hard time, but the family tried to make it work. They opened a small store in town, but as relatives and townspeople asked them for loans or took goods on credit, the family business struggled. So in 1927, they decided to go back to the United States. They left all their belongings behind, intending to return to Mexico after a short stint, but never did.[52]

Migrating back and forth created complications such as uncertain work, changing locations, and varying legal status. Some did it for opportunities and adventure, while others because they saw no alternative. Once they embarked, they had to struggle with both their own and their communities' expectations. Many found it difficult, if not impossible, to return and settle down, as the money they had saved was never quite enough or some unforeseen situation would make them decide to cross the border again. Some left intending to permanently settle in the United States; others planned to go for short periods or one more season. These intentions could change over time. Through all this, a set of social expectations grew, in the media, in popular culture, and in the public sphere, helping to produce a culture of migration.

Migration in the Public Sphere

In Mexico City, the post-revolutionary state had to contend with the fact that a tenth of the population lived north of the Rio Bravo (also known as the Rio Grande). Government officials, intellectuals, and public culture debated migration throughout the 1920s. Some argued that it was a betrayal of revolutionary ideals at a time when the country needed its citizens. A counterdiscourse developed that emphasized the benefits of migration; Manuel Gamio, a well-known scholar of the period, argued that migrants learned democratic and capitalistic practices in the north and returned as modern, progressive citizens better able to build the nation. Either way, both sides saw Mexico as the rightful place for the Mexican migrants and rarely noticed the ways circular migration was becoming embedded as a way of life.[53] Gamio believed migrants had a lot to offer Mexico. As he put it:

> In fact, these Mexicans have acquired during their stay in the United States valuable experience in agriculture or industry; they have learned to handle machinery and modern tools; they have discipline and steady habits of work. Moreover, their material and cultural requirements are generally greater than they were when they left Mexico. Having risen in the economic scale, they have been able to better themselves not only as to food, clothing, living quarters, and acquisition of tools and furniture, but they have also abandoned, wholly or partly, fanatical religion; they tend to join together in cooperative or charitable organizations, and they have acquired the habit of reading the newspapers. They frequently have savings in the bank, and perhaps a small house and the lot upon which it stands.[54]

Gamio's primary interest was in Mexico's political and economic development, he saw those who returned as a force that could develop the country along the lines revolutionary elites, liberal and secular, desired. He saw Mexicans who settled in the United States as a troubling trend and advocated for US policies that would discourage permanent settlement. In Mexico, he promoted policies that would ease their return and encouraged the creation of colonies for returnees, where they would be less influenced by the traditional ideas of their home villages.[55] His ideas became much more influential in the 1930s, when the Cárdenas administration took up his recommendations.

Within the government, a group of public intellectuals and bureaucrats wielded outsized influence on the state's official policy. In the short book *La Migración y Protección de Mexicanos en el Extranjero*, Andres Landa y Pina, head of the *Servicio de Migration* department in the *Gobernación* (Interior Government), urged Mexicans to stay home and contribute to Mexico and avoid being discriminated against. The same was true of Giberlo Loyo's book *Emigración de Mexicanos a los Estados Unidos*. Meanwhile, Alfonso Fabila used his account of traveling to Los Angeles, *El Problema de la Emigración de Obreros y Campesinos Mexicanos*, to record widespread discrimination. The writings, which were distributed to consulates, painted migrants as gullible victims of recruiters. Within the SRE, General Consul of San Antonio Enrique Santibañez published a collection of essays in *Excelsior* in Mexico City where he argued that Mexicans probably didn't learn important skills or advance economically in the north, so the Mexican government should discourage migration and encourage repatriation where possible.[56] The government's official view remained solidly anti-emigration, and all sides in elite circles agreed that the return of Mexicans was for the best, even if they could not agree on why. This shaped the public discussions migrants faced upon their return and what they had to respond to when they were writing to their families, singing *corridos*, or writing to officials.

Warning of the difficulties migrants would encounter, newspapers were filled with accounts of broken hopes and the broken bodies of those who had returned, deported or in destitution. Abuses by US officials and cases of discrimination were widely published in the press, taking material from *La Prensa*, *El Continental*, and other papers. The Catholic Church too cautioned parishioners against moving. Bishops issued warnings against migration, and local priests used the pulpits to urge people to stay home. Local priests argued that men lost their morals going north, abandoned their families, and engaged in drinking and other vices. Was migration an opportunity or fool's gold? Unease characterized fiction and newspaper accounts, letters, *corridos*, and personal encounters, about migration and the effects that returning migrants were having on communities. These cultural products illustrated just how pervasive the topic was.

Several *novelas* on the migrant experience were published in the 1920s. The writers, for the most part, longed for a pre-revolutionary Mexico and used their books to show how migration undermined traditional values. Exiled journalist Teodoro Torres, who worked for the newspaper *La Prensa* in the 1910s before eventually going back to Mexico, published *La Patria Perdida* in 1935.[57] In this novel, a Mexican migrant comes to the United States and starts farming in Missouri before going back home, only to find that the Mexico of his youth no longer exists. The peaceful *hacienda* life he envisions is not in Mexico but in the US Midwest.[58] Unlike Torres, Conrado Espinoza saw Mexico as the only option for Mexican migrants. After writing for *La Prensa* and other publications, Espinoza published *El Sol de Texas*, a morality tale about two Mexican migrant families who are morally and materially ruined when they go north. The book contains accounts of widespread discrimination in Texas. Only the family that embraces repatriation back to Mexico has any hope of redemption.[59] Daniel Venegas, who moved to Los Angeles in the 1920s, edited the newspaper *El Malcriado*, wrote plays, and authored a novel about a Mexican migrant, *Las Adventuras de Don Chipote*. This novel is another morality tale about the problems of migration, but it focuses on the ways US culture, specifically jazz age materialism, threatens to corrupt those from Catholic Mexico. Chipote is only saved when he is forced to return to Mexico and to the wife he had abandoned.[60] Rafael Muñoz, who returned to Mexico in 1920 after several years in exile, wrote *El Repatriado* about protagonist Andrés, who loses his way in the United States. Andrés wears suits even in rural Mexico, becomes highly materialistic, and no longer cares about the Mexican Revolution. He is redeemed only in death.[61]

Much like the writings that urged men to return, *corridos* on both sides of the border feature themes of the desirability and morality of migration. Multiple *corridos* from this era address fears of the loss of culture, morals, and Mexican-ness in the United States.[62] In "Platica Entre dos Rancheros," a returning migrant boasts about his success up north.[63]

If you could only see how nice
The United States is;
That is why the Mexicans
Are crazy about it.

You can't imagine how it is
To live like a lawyer,
With a good shirt, good suit,
Good overcoat, and shoes.

. . .
I had nothing more to wish;
I knew the state of Texas,
And there I got as many
As a dozen women.

Some of these were pretty women,
Classy blondes, the kind
Who go through the streets
All dressed in silk.

The migrant then tells of his exploits as a boxer and criticizes those who have stayed behind for their lack of initiative and their devotion to the Church and the Cristero cause.

But you have never left
The ranch, or your parish school;
You still believe in wooden images
And in the divine virgin.

Come, man, unbandage your eyes:
Don't let yourself be exploited
By men who claim to be wise
And who study only to rob.

. . .
And here one believes in miracles
And in blessed souls
And in going to kiss the hand
Of the priests

But believe me, the capitalists
Have blinded us
In order to be able to rob us;
They are a lot of scoundrels.

It isn't that I want to talk
About those rich men,
But you can see for yourself
That they are terrible thieves.

They describe hell to us
And devils with lots of tails,
As well as San Ramon Nonato
And also the immortal soul.

Pay no attention to that, partner;
Don't believe those follies.
They are simple nonsense,
They are simple frauds.

At this point, a man who has not been north intervenes, defends the Catholic Church, takes out a knife, and threatens to kill the returning migrant. The migrant begs for forgiveness in the name of San Antonio, betraying his supposed secularism. The man who had not left forgives him but says those who are coming back are simply loudmouths.

In another *corrido*, the singer addresses criticisms of those who have gone north common in communities and the press. In "Defensa de los Nortenos," the unknown singer defends the migrant's decision. He addresses stereotypes that arrogance is the main driver and instead blames Mexico's structural inequality, which forces migrants to leave in order to provide for their families.[64]

What they say about us
Is nearly all true,
But we left the country
From sheer necessity.

I myself could have told you
That many come back boasting;
That is why the local press
Speaks harshly about them.

But those who are to blame
Are those unkind employers,
Who don't give their people
Enough to buy a jacket.

I'm not criticizing the country,
But I certainly tell you
That many of the laborers
Are naked to their navels.

The peon is always burdened,
Is treated with cruelty;
The rich should like to see his head
Where they see his feet.

They treat him like a slave,
Not like a useful servant,
Who pours out for the rich
His last drop of sweat.

I don't say that in the north
One is going to well off;
Nor because one wears a suit
Is one elected to Congress.

One has to work there,
Hard, in the American fashion,
But one succeeds in earning
More than any of our countrymen.

Let my countryman say
If I am telling a lie,
For it's needless to ask about
What we can clearly see.

Many people have said
That we are not patriotic
Because we go to serve
For those accursed people.

But let them give us jobs
And pay us decent wages;
Not one Mexican then
Will go to foreign lands.

We're anxious to return again
To our adored country,
But what can we do about it
If the country is ruined?

The singer addresses returning migrants, telling them that they should not boast about their status, but he notes that if one works hard, it is possible to earn more in the United States. Although he sings of migrants' love of their country and desire to return, he again leaves for the north and invites fellow compatriots to join him.

Was circular migration a necessity for families in central Mexico? Was it good for men, families, and communities? These questions have no easy answers. Politicians, newspapers, writers, and academics, as well as communities and families, debated the desirability of the pattern of going to *El Norte*. Ambivalence about migration was reflected in interviews in rural communities. When asked about their interest in migrating, most farmers in Jalisco expressed a desire to go, but others were hostile. One man said, "No, I won't wish to go; it is too far. This is *mi tierra*." When pressed about his neighbors, the man responded, "Yes, and they return," though interviewer Paul Taylor thought he was jealous of those who had gone north.[65] While most official culture saw migration as undesirable, there was broad disagreement on whether the fault lay with the migrants and coyotes/*enganchadores* as elites, as newspapers often said, or with structural problems in a society that remained agrarian and where land distribution was deeply unequal.

The Cristero War, Jalisco, and *Agrarismo*

The continual migration back and forth created its own momentum in the town of Arandas, Jalisco. One man who had traveled to the United States in 1913 returned to live in the town, but then went back again before returning in 1929 with two trucks, a material improvement that did not go unnoticed by his neighbors.[66] Another resident explained that migration was caused by opportunity: "The worst work in the United States is better than the best here. The *repatriados* say that treatment is good and wages are good, and there is much machinery."[67] A small rancher supported his family from the United States, going back and forth multiple times from 1910 to 1928, while a ranch laborer went in 1922, returned the same year, went again in 1924 and returned the same year, and went in 1926 and returned again in 1927. Even middle-class residents like W. Rebeling, a local doctor, took out loans to go north.[68] Patterns found in Arandas extended across the region.

Outmigration accelerated with the de la Huerta rebellion and the subsequent Cristero War. Despite not being centers of the Mexican Revolution in the 1910s, the rebellion's heartland was the Bajío region and the Altos of Jalisco.[69] The war became an additional reason to migrate from Guanajuato, Jalisco, and Michoacán, places that were already sending the most migrants north in the 1920s.

Miguel Venegas and his family fled when the government froze the assets of their general store in Zapotlanejo, Jalisco. A member of a major Cristero organization, the Union Popular (*Unión Popular*), Venegas was an active participant in protests against the government, and though he was never part of the armed struggle, his brother Alfonso's involvement as a printer for the *Liga Nacional Defensora de la Libertad Religiosa* made him a target. He went to Jalapa and on to Aguascalientes before deciding to go to the United States. After his family took the train to Ciudad Juárez to meet him, they went on to Los Angeles, where he remained active in Cristero affairs through letters. His brother was killed by government forces during the conflict, and because of the local *cacique* (municipal political chief), Rosario Orozco, Venegas was unable to return until the 1930s. His active correspondence with relatives back home, however, kept his family on both sides of the border in frequent contact.[70]

The level of migration shot up as people sought escape from government forces or from pressure to join the rebellion.[71] One migrant, explaining why he left in 1927, said, "They wanted all the men to fight (for the Cristeros), but I told them, 'you [are] catholic and I am catholic, but I don't want to go and fight like a fool.' My father wouldn't give me the money to go to the States, so I sold two steers from his herd to get the money. Finally, when he saw I was determined to go, he gave me $500 (US) and 200 pesos to get to El Paso."[72] Rafael Orendain was forced to migrate, along with many of his neighbors, as the local economy declined. He eventually came back to Jalisco and joined the Cristero Rebellion, but his side lost.[73] After two brothers, Ezequiel Huerta Gutiérrez and Salvador Huerta Gutiérrez, were executed by federal troops for their role in the resistance, their oldest children had to support their families. One, Salvador Huerta, went to Chicago, and others went to Los Angeles.[74] Among the migrants who fled the Cristeros was Helidoro Barragan, who said, "They wanted money; it was very dangerous. They had already killed José Luis Cháves and raped two young women down by the bridge. When I heard they were looking for me I went into hiding."[75]

The new waves of migrants from these areas did not go unnoticed. Newspapers printed an account of a woman who "reported that 'everyone who can is preparing to leave for the United States' since 'there are families who do not have the necessities of life and who pass entire days without eating.'"[76] In areas with long migration histories, it is not surprising that people turned north to escape the violence of the Cristero War, or that migrants helped advance their side from across the border. Although this support from the diasporic population helped sustain the struggle in the central highlands, it did not change the course of the war.[77]

Mexican states' migration policy during the 1920s was framed by two opposing forces: the United States and local governments. In Guanajuato and Aguascalientes, local governments were supporting migration by issuing *salvaconductos*, but this occurred across the region, in Michoacán, Zacatecas, San Luis Potosí, and Jalisco. At the same time, residents continued to demand land redistribution. One returning migrant in Arandas said that "people are too poor here; all the time they want to fight, and they take all you have in taxes."[78] Money for the journey north was often lent by elites in the town, frequently the same people who complained about labor shortages. They also wrote letters of introduction for migrants that facilitated their moves north. One *ranchero* summed up the situation: "The *hacendados* prefer to let the workers get away so they won't concentrate in pueblos and ask for land. They would [be willing to] loan money to emigrants. The laborers go from the *haciendas* here the same as from elsewhere."[79]

These contradictory motivations influenced the ways that migrants, local governments, and the national government interacted. Political scientist David Fitzgerald has shown that, while the federal government urged local governments to restrict migration, "The municipal government of Aranedas issued hundreds of *salvaconductos* for men, and less frequently their families, seeking work in the United States or other parts of Mexico."[80] During the Cristero Rebellion, "municipal presidents ignored repeated federal instructions to 'make intense propaganda' to dissuade emigration."[81] In Arandas, migration became a safety valve that checked *agrarismo* (armed militias pressing for land redistribution) and reform movements in the 1920s. Local officials often found that allowing residents to migrate away, with the possibility of providing desperately needed remittances, was preferable to risking resistance and violence. As a result, thousands of Catholic Cristeros and their Agrarista opponents left the Altos.[82]

The area of high migration, the Bajío, had a high population density but also some of the most unequal land distribution in the country. Given these characteristics, it is surprising that there weren't even more petitions for land redistribution, especially compared to southern Mexico. Statistical analysis showed that *agrarismo* was particularly weak in localities with high migration rates, as political reform was undercut by mass departures. As political scientist Emily Sellars has found, migrants were disproportionally landless, literate, young men, the very people who were agitating for reform. The long legal bureaucratic process of applying for land could really only be undertaken by literate young men, but they were instead leaving. A community needed a certain number of landless beneficiaries to receive land; officials in fact sometimes cited rates of emigration as grounds for rejecting agrarian petitions.[83] Seeing their neighbors migrate could lower moral and solidarity among those left behind, raising the costs of activism. In turn, the return of migrants in the 1930s sharply increased general pressure for land redistribution.[84]

Seeking Control: *El Departamento de Migración*

When Alvaro Obregon left office, more than half a million of his countrymen were in the United States, despite his efforts at repatriation in 1921. Plutarco Elías Calles, the new president of Mexico, was well aware of the limits of government power, having played a significant role in these repatriation efforts as *Secretario de Gobernación*, and he sought to build a modern bureaucracy and police force to regulate migration. The SRE increased its consular presence in the United States, and the *Ley de Migración* of 1926 established the *Departamento de Migración*, required migrants to register with the government and have identification, limited migration to several exit points, and cracked down on *enganchadores*. The law made emigration through unauthorized points punishable by two years in prison or a fee and levied additional penalties on those who took advantage of migrants. The *Departamento de Migración* undertook the effort to make these laws into reality.

Under US pressure, the *Departamento de Migración* went beyond Mexico's own immigration laws, which banned workers from leaving if they did not have a contract, and began to ban migration by people who did not meet all the requirements for US entry, in particular the head tax and illiteracy provisions. By the late 1920s, Mexican officers enforced emigration law by circulating "propaganda to discourage people from trekking north if they could not qualify for legal entry," positioning themselves "at train depots [where they] questioned arriving migrants and attempted to turn back those unable to comply with US entry requirements" and patrolling "the border to stop Mexican workers from illegally entering the United States."[85]

The Mexican federal government had its own reasons for regulating migration; it was not simply carrying out US interests. The *Departamento de Migración* ran its campaign largely free of US influence and was mostly reacting to pressure from local politicians at border towns and public scandals in the press. Again and again, border politicians petitioned the department to stop the continual flow of migrants from central Mexico. The municipal president of Nuevo Laredo sent numerous letters to the department asking for more agents, investigations, and enforcement against coyotes and labor contractors. Politicians, the SRE, and the agency were also concerned about large-scale deportations leading to large numbers of destitute migrants being dumped in border towns. The *Departamento de Migración* would have to pay to send these migrants back to their hometowns. Considering the abuses and dangers migrants frequently faced, these were not unreasonable concerns.

Much of the department's attention was focused on the smuggling of contraband and people. Migrant smugglers had created ever more complicated border-crossing strategies by the mid-1920s, using cars, boats, and trains. Consuls in the borderlands, *Departamento de Migración* agents at the border, and officials in Mexico City saw *coyotes* as their primary target. In reports expressing the need for agents and railroad passes, they regularly pointed to coyotes as the reason that migration remained uncontrolled.[86] In correspondence, they acknowledged that the new regulatory regime "has provided opportunity for unscrupulous men, usually known by the nickname Coyotes, to make immoral and inhuman traffic cruelly exploiting these braceros."[87] Public circulars called attention to the dangers of coyotes and illegal crossings, and how people became victims to these human traffickers.[88] By framing the issues as one of unscrupulous coyotes, the *Departamento de Migración* and that SRE publicly portrayed themselves trying to protect their countrymen from exploitation rather than stopping migration.

The *Departamento de Migración* took a paternalistic attitude towards migrants, seeing them as victims duped by labor agents, coyotes, fliers, and overly optimistic information. Seeking to curb this, the government created a public counternarrative that told people not to migrate unless they could afford to do so legally, although it failed to acknowledge the difficulty of legal migration for the average person. Migrants had their own tactics dealing with these institutions. The dynamic between local governments, the businesses of migration, brokers, migrants, and federal agencies shows how policy was negotiated as it was enforced.

The Business of Migration

Large-scale legal migration had its own unique economy. People charged for every step of the process, from stays in hotels to photographs and railroad tickets. Migrants were propositioned along the lines leading to the border, paid five to ten dollars to cross with a guide, and rented legal documents for two dollars, much less than the eighteen dollars in fees that it cost to cross legally. Coyotes and labor contractors (*enganchadores*) told people what documents were needed to cross the border and helped them to obtain them. There were usually labor recruiters and companies waiting on the US side as soon as people crossed, blurring the line between legal labor contracting and illegal smuggling. Some coyotes also contracted workers to local Texas farms. Assistance that could help people cross legally could easily turn into a process of deceiving officials. This included helping people pass the literacy exam, even teaching some language classes, renting legal documents, obtaining papers, and helping them pass health inspections.[89]

A whole industry developed in Nuevo Laredo to support migration. In one report, agent José Inez Pérez described arriving migrants being besieged by "drivers of all vehicles, try to bring them to certain accommodations, photographic workshops, where they charge exaggerated amounts for accommodation, meals and photos." Owners of establishments paid high commissions to drivers to lead migrants there. When migrants tried and failed to legally emigrate, "hotel owners offer their services to send telegrams asking for money and help, and they charge double amounts or triple the true cost of telegrams and commission that they are paid. All the lodges and hotels are attended regularly and daily smugglers or 'coyotes,' making proposals to the braceros not to pay the high rates of immigration, and offer them passage across the border by fording the Rio Bravo. The amounts charged for subsequent smuggling, range from ten, twenty and thirty pesos." Pérez didn't make a distinction between smugglers and the businesses that profited from exploiting Mexican migrants.[90]

Yet little could be done to slow or stop the business of migration. The economy was mostly legal, involving small businesses, hotels, doctors, labor agents, corrupt officials, and others who widely profited. The Chamber of

Commerce in Laredo tried to capture this business by printing "daily fliers to be distributed among the working people who arrive for purposes of migration, which is to publicize the address of hotels, guest houses, pictures and outlets for tickets, stating what is charged regularly for passengers to take advantage of such information" and also hiring a crier to call out this information in the streets.[91] The business of migration began to draw the government in.

The line between legal and illegal activity was made blurrier as some officials partnered with those who provided services. Assistance that was normally not allowed could be authorized by local politicians or federal agents. In Nuevo Laredo, one official, Arnuldo de los Santos, was known to work with Candelario Guajardo, a smuggler, labor contractor, and coyote who ran a very profitable business using cars to ferry across the border. Those who bought tickets from Guajardo could expect little government scrutiny.[92] At Saltillo and Torreón, the municipal presidents and other officials were known to look the other way at coyotes who gave them kickbacks.[93] This laxity extended to the *Departamento de Migración*, where agents came to certain agreements with those in the business of migration. Agents could and did issue letters of recommendation to migrants to allow them to move without harassment. At Ciudad Juárez, drivers who helped people cross paid a fee to local officials and migration agents for cards that authorized their traffic as long as they didn't overcharge migrants.[94] In 1926, an investigation found that agent Samuel Lozano even smuggled migrants himself.[95] A bureaucracy with little manpower, low budgets, and even lower pay, corruption gave the *Departamento de Migración* much needed flexibility as it navigated between its official policy of hostility to migration and the reality on the ground. The widely dispersed profits of the business of migration gained it legitimacy among numerous actors, forcing officials to accommodate their interests, including one of the largest industries in the county, the railroad.[96]

The Mexican National Railway, owned by the Mexican government but functionally independent, was much more interested in ticket sales than enforcing regulations. Government officials sought to bring the railroad into the system by having rail agents enforce its policies and, in turn, US immigration law. However, given its strong conflict of interests, the railway proved a poor partner in this endeavor.

The *Departamento de Migración* and its predecessor, the Migration Service, established eleven stations, including ones at Monterrey, Torreón, Guadalajara, and Irapuato. They also established thirty-seven substations, at Matamoros, Nuevo Laredo, Irapuato, Empalme de González, and Saltillo, among other places where they boarded trains and inspected for papers among the migrants heading north. In explaining this policy to President Calles, the *Departamento de Migración* argued that "due to the circumstances that have resulted in a steady increase in the migration of Mexican workers, we must not only check papers at the borders, but at stations and along railways in the interior."[97] Patrolling the interior proved difficult, however, given the department's small budget and staff. On multiple occasions, agents in Matamoros reported that migrants were using cars, often with the help of local coyotes.[98] The inspector at Torreón explained how migrants simply went around inspection stations.[99] Farther east in Matamoros, station head Fernandez Landero described a similar phenomenon in which migrants would go around the *Departamento de Migración* station in Saltillo by getting off trains and boarding again later, by taking a train to San Luis Potosí and Tampico and then north to Texas.[100]

Although agents were meant cooperate with the railroad in limiting migration, the records of their relationship from 1925 to 1935 show that railroad officials were reluctant to cut off their own revenue stream and instead paid lip service to the government. They occasionally distributed memos and circulars within the company saying that people should work with agents and not sell tickets to migrants who lacked all the proper documents. These warnings had little effect on the employees who sold tickets, accepted them, and ran the railway.

The results were not surprising. Migrants continued to arrive at the border from more than thirty destinations in Guanajuato, Jalisco, and Michoacán. A government agent complained that railroad agents at "Matehuala, San Salvador, San Miguel de Allende, and Gòmez Farías continue selling second-class tickets without restriction to points north of Saltillo."[101] Railroad ticket vendors in Mexico City were even telling migrants that they could buy tickets straight to Laredo and arrange their papers to cross there without any problems.[102] This so frustrated agent Manuel Limon Maciel at Ciudad Juárez that he accused the railroad of undermining immigration policy by prioritizing its own interests.[103]

In 1930, the Chief Inspector of Migration sent a report to the President of the National Railways, J. Sanchez Mejorada, requesting that he order ticket agents not to sell tickets to Mexican braceros trying to migrate.[104] Nothing this perennial problem, the inspector claimed that 40% of migrants going north did not fulfill the necessary requirements to emigrate. Only by taking strong measures could they staunch this flow of migrants because "unfortunately in our experience, persuasion has been unsuccessful in dissuading braceros from trying to penetrate stealthily with the help of coyotes who are responsible for the crimes incurred by braceros."[105] Several days later, Mexican President Portes Gil sent a message to Mejorada requesting that agents not sell tickets to migrants unless they had papers showing they had met all requirements to enter the United States.[106] Mejorada told the president that they had already issued a circular that addressed these issues. The circular, distributed to every ticket agent, outlined the dangers migrants faced in making the journey and the dire circumstances that would befall them and force them to return home. A second circular added that ticket agents were to sternly warn potential migrants about the requirements to cross the border and the dangers they faced. These measures fell far short of what the *Departamento de Migración* had requested.[107]

The Mexican National Railway sought to find a balance between ending potential undocumented migration and perfectly legal internal migration. Migrants were a major source of revenue for the passenger trains at a time when northern Mexico was growing economically and continued to draw migrants from central states. It was difficult, if not impossible, for ticket officials to distinguish internal migrants from US-bound ones, especially because large numbers of people started out as domestic migrants before continuing across the border. The flow of migrants who crossed north with all their documents, the flow of retuning migrants, and the flow of internal migrants bound for the mining, cotton, or oil industries could be disrupted by an attempt to cut down on those who might become undocumented in the United States. As a result, the railroad took a pragmatic approach, and didn't ask too many questions.

Migrants and the *Departamento de Migración*

Migrants could and did use the Mexican federal government to achieve their own goals. In states along the US border, regional migration and international migration often overlapped, complicating the department's response. People frequently went to the *Departamento de Migración* in addition to Mexican consuls to report abuses by American officials at the border. This was especially true of residents in the borderlands who were used to going back and forth with ease. They frequently appealed to the *Departamento de*

Migración when US Bureau of Immigration agents acted in ways they saw as unjust.[108] At other points, officials worked with borderland residents and sometimes US employers to issue special permits for workers of certain companies to cross the border.[109] In most cases, however, the department could do little other than start an investigation and publicize the issue in the press.[110]

When agents did enforce the rules, boarding trains and demanding papers from people, they sometimes encountered unexpected resistance. This was especially common near the border, where people were used to traveling without restrictions. Migrants would appeal to local officials, who frequently complained that railroad inspections slowed trains down, made them late, and upset passengers. In one case, José Choren and his father, Cecilio Gutierrez, were stopped by *Departamento de Migración* agents and ordered back to Morleón, Guanajuato. They wrote an angry letter stating that Mr. Gutierrez had already been to the United States, specifically Chicago, three times and asking why they had been turned back and what they needed to avoid being stopped in the future.[111] When R. Castaneda asked the *Departamento de Migración* what papers were required for migration, he was given a list of what he needed to satisfy officials. He was one of thousands in 1926 to solicit such information.[112] The most common correspondence was from people who sought either documents or instructions on how to migrate legally.

Government agencies discouraged undocumented crossings but could actively encourage migration even when it was not policy to do so. Throughout the 1920s, consuls would give Mexican passports to people who had been deported and wanted to legally re-cross into the United States.[113] Consuls could and did issue paperwork ex post facto to those who had avoided Mexican immigration rules in leaving the country.[114] In other cases, it was common to provide documents to help legalize the status of those already in the United States.[115] This type of discretion was common at the SRE, where officials had to deal with the situation in front of them. This meant helping their countrymen's status in the United States, even at the cost of the agency's larger emigration goals.

The *Departamento de Migración*, in a paternalistic guise, also sought to protect the gender and moral norms of the country. For women, migrating north legally was a fraught process. Women who were not directly accompanied by their fathers or husbands needed permission from the department even when they were clearly the main breadwinners or were accompanied by other relatives. For some, this process proved straightforward, but others encountered difficulties. Guadalupe Simental had to explain that she had been abandoned by her husband before she and her daughter would be allowed to join her brothers in Los Angeles.[116] Maria Mora and Serfina García both had to explain that they were going to join relatives in Los Angeles and that their parents were dead.[117] Teodora Torres Ornelas wrote a long letter expressing her dire circumstances in Mexico and her wish to join relatives in Los Angeles.[118] In other cases, women applied in groups, sought permission as students, or had other reasons, but they always had to explain themselves in ways that aligned with traditional gender norms even when they were in fact going north to work.

Jesus Cevallos appealed to the *Departamento de Migración* in 1927 to be allowed to take his young siblings with him to the United States after his previous solo migration in 1929. His case took a while before he was allowed to go with them.[119] Although children in Mexico were expected to work from a young age, especially in rural areas, by the 1920s the post-revolutionary state put more emphasis on getting the children to attend primary schools. Officials were more conscious about keeping minors from participating in labor migration; agents tried to keep people from leaving if children involved might be forced to work. While the *Departamento de Migración* did not have an equivalent to the US Bureau of Immigration's Board of Special Inquiry, it did have to grant permission for minors to cross without their direct guardians. A significant proportion of these cases pertained to students bound for specific schools for Mexicans in the Southwest, illustrating the growing importance of education in cross-border migration by the late 1920s. Others, like Rosario Hernandez Torrez and her mother, were going to join US-based family members in California.[120] These cases point to the fact that, by this time, most were second-wave migrants, joining people who had gone before them, and in many cases, these were not their first crossings.

Mexican federal institutions participated in a variety of contradictory policies that both hindered and promoted emigration. The *Departamento de Migración* was very limited in what it could accomplish and, given the gray area between legal and illegal migration, could be used by people to aid migration. This was most glaring in the cases when the SRE or *Departamento de Migración* gave documents to migrants who had been deported due to incomplete documentation, a practice that their American counterpart, the Bureau of Immigration, also did at times in the 1920s and frequently during the subsequent Bracero era.[121]

The growth of migration, with the tacit support of local officials, elites, and state governments, occurred in direct opposition to the efforts of the Mexican federal government. The Mexican government's attempts to regulate and curtail this activity primarily show how deeply ingrained migratory circuits were becoming by the late 1920s. State immigration bureaucracy was weak, understaffed, and underfunded, making enforcement difficult. As a consequence, federal impediments factored less into migrants' calculations about whether to leave than more immediate and local concerns, such as family, economic need, and insecurity, including armed conflicts. Additionally, transportation and migration businesses further undermined effective enforcement. Various sectors of Mexican society, from the railroads to local governments, supported migration and proved adept at resisting pressure from the federal government.

Focusing on the practices of the Mexican state rather than its words shows the massive disconnect between official restrictive policies and the reality of a state not able to stop migration. Its campaign of enforcement and control along the border and the interior was unsuccessful. Instead, its efforts were meant to respond to a political imperative to act, criticism in the press, and post-revolutionary public pronouncements by various presidents promoting return. It was a performance of control. People found the information provided by returning migrants, whom they knew, more persuasive. Ultimately, Mexican federal government agencies were primarily reacting to the dynamics that guided and drove migration in Mexican society.

In the second half of the 1920s, the Mexican government created a more restrictive migratory regime. The views of the government and elites remained the same—that migration was a tragedy born of the revolution, opportunist labor agents, and coyotes, and that it was best for Mexicans to stay home or return from the United States to rebuild the nation. What had changed was a willingness to build a migration regulatory apparatus, to reduce migration or at least steer it towards legal entry. The government failed to invest in the *Departamento de Migración* to a level of effectiveness and instead relied on propaganda and cooperation with agencies, companies, and local governments, where they faced significant pushback. There is little evidence that all this effort reduced the number of Mexicans migrating, but it did alleviate the most significant abuses (by coyotes, labor agents, or US agents) migrants faced at the border.

People migrated whether they had met all the requirements or not. Looking at how and why they chose to make the journey north starkly illustrates the gap between the policy goals of federal officials, those of local governments, and the desires of migrants themselves. Even after the machinery of enforcement was built, there were far too few agents facing far too many migrants to effectively enforce migration law across the interior of Mexico. Migrants knew the chances of being stopped by *Departamento de Migración* or US Border Patrol agents were low. The national railways, local governments, and businesses had little interest in aiding the government and much more in aiding migrants, who were their customers, constituents, and neighbors. Migrants themselves did not see any of this as wrong, given that officials had accepted their movements for so long. Authorities struggled to respond to migrants' actions at the border and came to accept a certain amount of leeway.

By the end of the 1920s, migration was embedded in the social world of the places migrants came from and part of the sending towns' social structure. People traveled in groups, in families, with acquaintances, and with those who had made the journey before. It is only through the expansion of this social space that migration became not just a temporary jump across the border, as it had been during the late 1910s, but a continuous circuit that, by 1930, supported and encompassed millions across Mexican society. Mexicans built a culture of migration based on the experiences and expectations of family life amidst an overall culture that questioned it. In a number of places, those who may have once objected to migration came to see it as a legitimate way out, from the Cristero War, from an isolated village, or from the general economic stagnation that followed the revolution. And so municipal presidents handed out *salvaconductos*, and elites made small loans to finance the journeys, in order to stave off migrant's greater political demands for land in a deeply unequal agrarian society.

5

Tejas, Afuera de México

Newspapers, the Mexican Government, *Mutualistas*, and Migrants in San Antonio, 1915–1940

In 1939, a group of families "installed themselves in the offices of the Mexican consulate, from where they stated that they would not move until achieving their objective, since—having sold their homes and furniture—they no longer had a roof over their heads."[1] For some, their objective was land in Mexico that the Mexican government had reneged on; others wished to stay in the United States. Similar occupations took place at several consulates across Texas in those months, and the consul at Brownsville, A. Calderon, told *El Universal* that many families felt deceived by the notion "that the homeland had its arms open to receive them at any time."[2] These families were seeking to return to Mexico, ostensibly participating in *México de Afuera*, a general concept that encompassed the belief that Mexicans in the United States should look to Mexico for social and political identity. Yet they could not do so. Their experiences illustrated the limits of the Mexican government's interest in meetings its citizens' demands.[3]

Texas, a state where new immigrants joined both older immigrants and *Tejanos* who had lived there for generations, was home to the largest number of Mexicans in the United States. In San Antonio, home to the largest community, migrants formed webs of social, economic, and political institutions that connected them to each other, American institutions, and back to Mexico. This chapter looks at the formation of Mexican identity based on the nationalist rhetoric of the Mexican Revolution and the institutions that supported it in San Antonio—the *La Prensa* newspaper, the *mutualistas*, and the Mexican consulate—to understand how the ideology of *México de Afuera* worked on the ground. More than simply a conservative ideology, *México de Afuera*, or *Mexicanidad*, enjoyed widespread support because it fit most migrants' worldview. Central to this idea was the belief that people would return to Mexico one day. The Great Depression put this assumption to the test and led nearly every Mexican organization in Texas to support and

Between Here and There. Daniel Morales, Oxford University Press. © Oxford University Press 2024.
DOI: 10.1093/oso/9780197612590.003.0006

organize repatriation. *México de Afuera* ultimately hindered the creation of a forceful defense of Mexican migrants as members of the US polity.

This chapter shows how this ideology mediated the relationship between Mexican migrants and Mexican organizations. As the post-revolutionary Mexican government was in the middle of constructing a nationalist Mexican identity inside of Mexico, the logical next step was to promote nationalism abroad. *México de Afuera* had appeal far beyond its elite base; it was the dominant discourse in Mexican migrant communities until the Great Depression. It enabled working-class Mexicans in the United States to make claims on the post-revolutionary Mexican state and created opportunities for people with few other avenues of redress.[4]

To claim a state and be a citizen has been described by political theorist Hannah Arendt as the right to have rights.[5] If this is the case, then in Texas, Mexicans could only sometimes effectively claim citizenship regardless of their legal status or birthplace. When Mexicans were deprived of wages, injured, discriminated against, or even killed, the local police, Texas Rangers, and local political system did not consistently respond to their claims. In many cases, the state itself was the perpetrator.[6] Mexicans' plight was not covered in the English-language press unless it was to pathologize their poverty. In numerous places, they were excluded from full participation in civic life and forced into segregated public spaces, schools, and institutions, though different standards of inclusion and exclusion were applied depending on the location, person, and situation.

This uneven application of justice created spaces for different methods of organization even as it discouraged most Mexican migrants from seeking formal US citizenship. Organizations such as the Order of Knights of America of San Antonio and the League of United Latin American Citizens (LULAC) argued that Mexicans should look to the United States as their home and organize politically for rights as US citizens. However, most immigrants in this era did not seek to become "American." Before 1930, the largest organizations instead advocated an ideology that stressed their *Mexicanidad*, their unity with the people of Mexico. The three largest promoters of this discourse were Mexican mutual aid societies, the Spanish-language press (especially *La Prensa*), and the Mexican government through the consulates. This rhetoric was adopted by people who used their Mexican citizenship to make claims on the Mexican state from the United States. They put pressure on *La Prensa* and, in turn, the consulate to live up to their rhetoric and respond to the widespread disenfranchisement, discrimination, poverty, and deportation many faced in the 1930s. They also used this rhetoric to claim the right to land upon their return, something large numbers believed would happen.

This chapter focuses on why so many sought to return to Mexico during the Depression and how the Mexican government, through consulates and Mexican organizations, primarily organized repartition in Texas rather than US institutions. Texas disproportionately sent more repatriates to Mexico than California did, making it singularly important to the history of repatriation. Although accounts of repartition tend to argue that US society turned on its Mexican communities, this fails to capture the extent to which Mexican institutions made repatriation a reality and diminishes the rhetoric in the public sphere that heavily promoted return to Mexico.

San Antonio and *Mutualistas* in the 1920s

As one of the central hubs of the Mexican migration system, San Antonio displayed social and political dynamics that were similar to those of other cities with large migrations in this period.[7] Large Mexican enclaves formed under the pressure of increasing segregation that excluded Mexicans from civil society. These communities fostered institutions that ranged widely from conservative to radical, local to national, and that created competing public discourses about Mexicans and their role in American society.

Between 1900 and 1920, the Mexican population of Texas rose from 163,617 to 505,357, about half of whom were Mexican-born and half of whom were US-born *Tejanos*.[8] Located at the center of this was San Antonio, whose Mexican population climbed to 60,000 by 1920, to 80,000 by 1930, and to 103,000 by 1940.[9] The city itself grew from 96,000 in 1910 to 253,854 by 1940.[10] Most Mexicans in the city belonged to the laboring class, either unskilled urban workers or migrant laborers who shifted from urban to agricultural labor as the seasons changed. Urban jobs were concentrated in the sewing, construction, cigar, and garment industries. Employment was irregular for most. Those who fared better were the Mexican American middle class, who enjoyed more regular employment, higher wages, and better access to resources.[11] Along with middle-class *Tejanos*, some newcomers came with skills and worked as white-collar workers, business proprietors, clerks, and writers. Professional and skilled workers constituted 4% of the migrants admitted in 1923, making them a small but powerful group of elites who dominated intellectual and political activity in the city.[12] They included

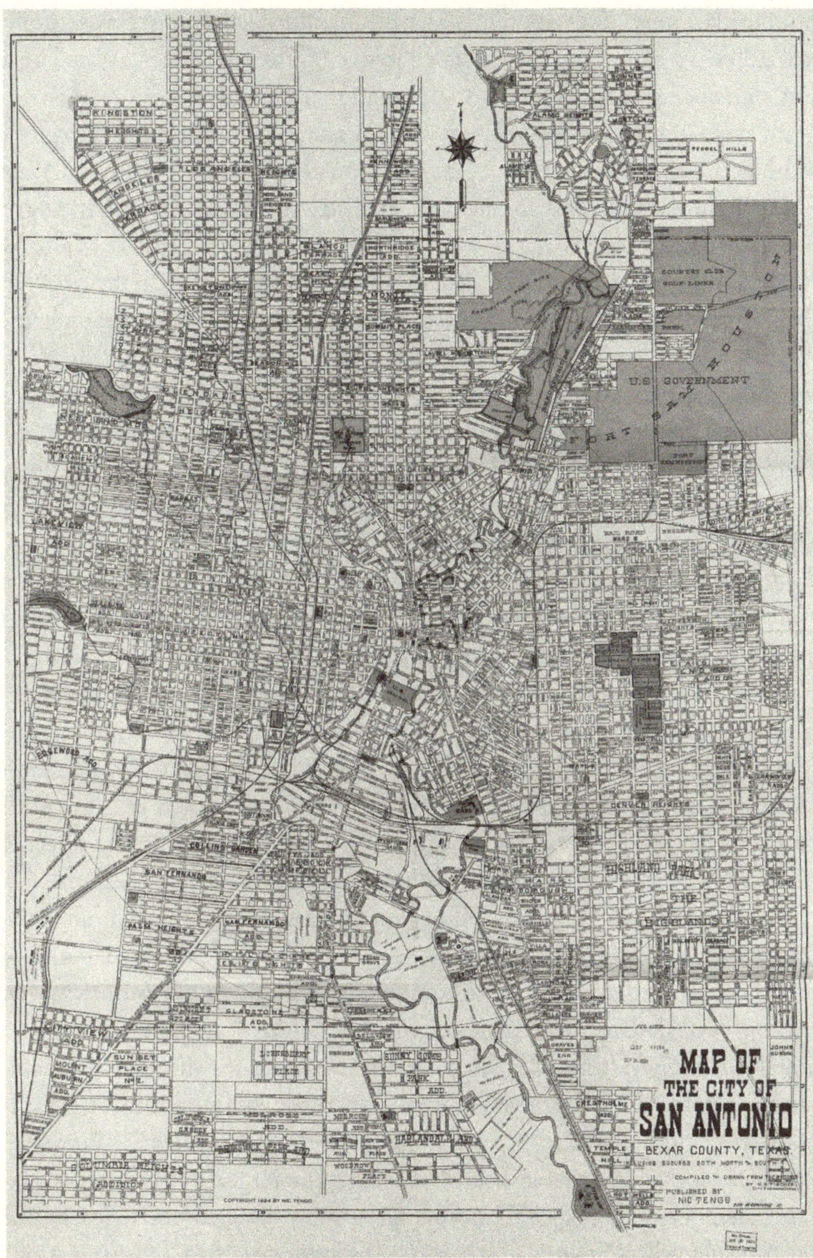

Figure 5.1 Map of the City of San Antonio and suburbs, 1924. San Antonio, Tex. 1924. Map. Library of Congress Geography and Map Division, G4034.S2 1924 .N5.

middle-class men and women, a significant number of upper-class political exiles, and even Catholic bishops in exile from the Cristero War. There was a great deal of residential and occupational mobility, as the average migrant stayed for only a few years, having migrated from agricultural regions at home.[13] Two-thirds of the Mexican population lived on the city's West Side, where overcrowding in the Mexican districts led to high rents and poor housing conditions.[14]

In addition, the city boasted the largest *Tejano* middle class in the country. Even unskilled blue-collar workers earned significantly more if they knew English and had been born in the United States. Large numbers worked in the public sector, military bases, and schools, but they also maintained the businesses that Mexican communities needed, such as grocery stores, tailors, and bakeries. They were the brokers that made the migrant economy function and took the lead in creating civic organizations. It is among these that an American-based orientation began to take hold.[15]

At a time when everyone with origins in Mexico was considered a "Mexican" whether they were US citizens or not, ethnic solidarity offered an avenue for people to organize. *Mutualistas* provided direct services and benefits, sought to preserve Mexican culture, and supported civic engagement.[16] While many *mutualistas* rose out of the direct needs of the community in response to deaths, health emergencies, arrests, school segregation cases, and other major events, other organizations arose as a result of a direct consular intervention. These organizations promoted a strong sense of Mexican identity and community with the homeland, *México de Afuera.*

Mutualistas were part of a web of overlapping institutions that offset the uncertainty of capitalist employment and migration. Texas had many of these, including *La Gran Liga Mexicana*; *La Comité Patriótico Mexicano*; *La Comité de Organización Agrícola*, which focused on agricultural workers; and *La Comité de Beneficencia y Protección Mutual*, which helped with health benefits.[17] Twenty-five organizations made San Antonio their headquarters, including *El Concilio Obrero Mexicano* and *La Sociedad Mutualista Artes Gráficas. La Sociedad de la Unión* was the largest, with over a thousand members. Other groups were built around the Catholic Church, like the *Asociación de San Luis Gonzaga* and *Las Hijas de Maria.*[18] Organizations with a working-class character focused on specific groups or professions, such as masons, shoemakers, and tailors, and fulfilled the immediate needs of their members, who paid a small membership fee and could receive death benefits, disability benefits, or funding for healthcare or other emergencies.[19]

Migrants could use these organizations to obtain work in an unstable economy. In a world without much worker protection, mutual organizations were the primary social safety net of the immigrant working class.[20]

The other major activity of civic organizations was promoting Mexican culture. Spanish-language schools not only provided a practical education, but also instilled a patriotic history of Mexico and civic pride. The societies fostered a collective spirit of solidarity, with members taking part in pledges, statements, and rules that tied them to their ethnic community.[21] They organized a variety of festivities throughout the year: parades and festivals for Mexican Independence Day, *Cinco de Mayo* parades, beauty contests, fundraisers, dances, and public speeches.[22] Others organized around holidays like the festival of the Lady of Guadalupe and promoted Mexican Catholicism. It was in this cultural capacity that *mutualistas* worked most closely with the Mexican consulates. Various *juntas patrióticas* (committees to represent a community), including the *Comisiónes Honorificas*, were created directly by the consulates in dozens of communities to promote a connection to the homeland; the most successful Mexicans in town served on their boards.[23] Their work involved a mixture of patriotic cultural festivities, educational concerns, relief work for Mexicans in need, and later, repatriation drives. Along with other organizations, they formed an infrastructure that sought to keep Mexican migrants' loyalty and identity firmly rooted in Mexico.

Service to the community was another major facet of *mutualista* activity. Several worked with the consulate and *La Prensa* to create Spanish-language schools as alternatives to the segregated public schools.[24] *El Club Cooperativo* created food cooperatives in the area, while the *Brigadas de la Cruz Azul Mexicanas* dealt almost exclusively with medical care, raising money to treat migrants locally or repatriate them to Mexico, and creating several clinics.[25] The *Cruz Azul*'s fundraising and medical care were carried out by women.

Although *mutualistas* were mostly divided by gender and class, this was not always the case. Women served as the organizational backbone of most of the organizations. Although few became top leaders, women typically were allowed to become officers. Carolina Munguía led the *Círculo Cultural Isabel, La Católica*, one of the more influential organizations that promoted an elite vision of Mexican culture.[26] Another divide was class. The bulk of *mutualistas* catered to the stable working class, with few migrant or upper-class members. At the other end of the class spectrum, the *Casino Social* was the primary social club of San Antonio's Mexican elites, and the *Alianza*

Hispano Americana, the largest *mutualista* in the country, was run by these elites. While the Latin Booster Club's members were mostly middle-class, the *Leñadores del Mundo* cut across social classes.[27] American-born, mostly middle-class *Tejanos* had their own organizations, the most important of which joined together to form LULAC in 1929.

Masonic organizations had a long history in the borderlands, participating in the war for Mexican Independence. In the twentieth century, they flourished as centers of critique to Porfirio Díaz and joined different liberal factions of the revolution. In Texas, they promoted a Mexican identity tied to the notion of liberal reason and progress. This included a mission of social and material uplift of the community. They countered stereotypes by changing people's behavior, promoting education and civic participation, and exerting social control through benevolent work.[28] As scholar Gabriella González has described, the identity they promoted "never was a unified entity but rather an imagined community, requiring constant calls for unity through the cultivation of ethnic pride and nationalism."[29] These organizations allowed vast information networks to flourish and often served as incubators for various political movements, newspapers, and unions.

In 1911, organizations from across Texas and the United States gathered at *El Primer Congreso Mexicanista*, organized by Nicasio Idar, his activist family, and *La Crónica* newspaper. The conference sought to bring together organizations for common action under *La Gran Liga Mexicana* and *La Liga Femenil Mexicana*, which was led by women who had been involved in various *mutualistas*.[30] Unfortunately, the gatherings did not lead to a permanent organization. Workplace-based *mutualistas*, including the *Sociedad Mutualista Artes Gráficas* and the *Sociedad Morelos*, organized labor strikes in the 1920s and could turn themselves into unions for those efforts.[31] While this could lead to the formation of a few craft unions, it did not mean successful entry into the larger union movement, as the American Federation of Labor welcomed Mexicans in only limited capacities.

Some of the people who participated in these organizations also advocated for civil rights, especially around policing. *La Liga Pro Mexicana*, for example, proactively pressed for civil rights, defended Mexicans accused of crimes, and partnered with the Mexican consulate on other issues. *La Socieda Protectora de Mexicanos en los Estados Unidos* and *La Liga Portectora Mexicana* provided lawyers to help migrants in need of services. *La Liga Protectora Mexicana* worked with publisher/businessman Francisco Chapa to release Mexicans in jail and won several commutations.[32] The organization ran a regular column in Chapa's newspaper, *El Imparcial de Texas*, that offered legal advice. The *Orden Caballeros de Honor* applied public pressure after the 1911 lynching of Antonio Gómez, while *La Agrupacón Protectora* was formed that year to provide legal protection for the community and worked closely with the consulate on legal cases.[33] It was common for organizations to throw fundraisers for legal defenses, especially if a case became a popular cause in the Spanish-language press.

Organizations took sides in the Mexican Revolution or participated by raising money, smuggling arms, and creating medical brigades. The White Cross, led by women including Leonor Villegas de Magnón and Jovita Idar, tended to the injured along the Texas/Mexico border throughout the war.[34] This brought many of the divides of the revolution across the border and into the ethnic politics of the West Side. While some aided the consulate in spying on potential revolutionaries, others plotted further revolutionary activity. Most organizations banned outright political and religious discussions precisely because of these divisions.[35] Yet the revolution also fostered amongst migrants a political outlook that looked to the homeland and instilled a self-perception as exiles who were awaiting the right movement to return. In 1929, a number of these organizations hosted José Vasconcelos as he made a tour of Texas as part of his presidential campaign in Mexico. In his speeches, he called for a rigorous defense of *La Raza* in the United States. He saw Mexicans in the United States as people with no home and no government to defend them, and he invited them to return to Mexico.[36]

The vast majority of *mutualistas*' work consisted of helping people who were poor, providing care, teaching Spanish, fighting school discrimination, and organizing cultural activities. Their efforts sustained metaphorical and physical links to Mexico while offering practical assistance. Though these institutions did critical work, they were never very stable or secure. Most faced high rates of member turnover, could barely afford to pay benefits during normal times, and faced collapse during the Great Depression. It is perhaps, then, not a surprise that they turned to repatriation in the crisis.

The Spanish-Language Press

Spanish was the lingua franca of the borderlands at the time of the US-Mexican War and remained the primary language and co-official language in some places until the late nineteenth century. Spanish-language papers made this possible.[37] In late nineteenth-century New Mexico, *La Voz del Pueblo*, *El Nuevo Mexicano*, and *El Defensor del Pueblo* were widely distributed and featured writers exiled from Porfirio Díaz's Mexico as well as also local writers and journalists. Countering negative images of Mexicans in print, they created a transnational Spanish-language dialogue that operated on both sides of the border, participated in local politics, and published poetry and literature about everyday life.[38] Writers and publishers participated in a literary world that included the establishment of local libraries. Through these actions, these papers contested the hegemonic discourse of the English-language press and created spaces of resistance for Mexicans.[39] Unfortunately, they were also financially unstable. Of the 136 Spanish-language papers that were published between 1800 and 1900 across the Southwest, 105 ceased publication before 1900.[40]

The Mexican Revolution propelled the transformation of a nascent Spanish-language press in the United States into large enterprises with wide circulations. One of the most significant papers of these years was *Regeneración*, published by the *Partido Liberal Mexicano* (PLM). The newspaper became one of the most radical publications in the country and circulated widely among Mexicans in the borderlands. *Regeneración* was published in San Antonio, then St. Louis, and then Los Angeles. However, after a campaign of pressure by the Mexican and US governments, its editors, Ricardo and Enrique Flores Magón, were arrested in 1917, and the newspaper soon ceased publication.[41]

Between 1900 and 1929, 218 Spanish-language newspapers were founded.[42] Texas surpassed New Mexico as the center of Spanish print culture, with forty-four new newspapers.[43] Other new papers were begun in places with new waves of migration: Chicago, Detroit, Kansas City, and Milwaukee. San Antonio alone was home to half a dozen Spanish-language newspapers, including *El Correro Mexicano*, *El Heraldo*, *El Vacelon*, and *El Imparcial*, and several PLM-affiliated papers, but *La Prensa* became the largest.[44]

La Prensa

Ignacio Lozano, the founder of *La Prensa*, was not new to the world of print. He and his father worked in the business worlds of Monterrey and in the newspapers in Mapimí, Durango, where he wrote for *El Pueblo Libre*. Ignacio studied in Mexico City before his father's death precipitated his migration to the United States.[45] Ignacio and his mother and sisters moved to San Antonio in 1908. At first, he worked for Adolfo Duclós Salinas's *El Noticiero*, but after the death of its founder, he closed that publication and instead became the publisher of Francisco Chapa's *El Imparcial de Texas*. During his time running *El Imparcial*, Lozano opened a Spanish-language bookstore and began to print Spanish titles. Run by his sisters, *La Casa Editorial Lozano* became an important press for Spanish-language literature in the United States.[46]

Lozano founded *La Prensa* in 1913 to cover the revolution, politics, and life on both sides of the border and developed it into the most widely circulated Spanish-language newspaper in the Southwest. Lozano gathered a varied staff, employing many exiled writers and intellectuals, such as Leonides González, Miguel Uranga, René Capistrán Garza, José Vasconcelos, Nemesio García Narango, Querido Moheno, Vito Alessio Robles, and José María Lozano. These writers played a major part in expanding the Spanish-language public sphere in the United States, and Lozano held the presidency of the *Alianza Hispano America*, the largest *mutualista* in the United States.[47]

Dozens of smaller newspapers were published in towns across the Southwest, but it was *La Prensa* that became the voice of the community in this era.[48] It wove together the Mexican diaspora throughout the United States even as, or maybe because, it sought to tie that diaspora to Mexico.

LIBROS EN ESPAÑOL

Compre usted sus libros en español a la Casa Editorial Lozano, 118 N. Santa Rosa Ave., San Antonio, Texas. Es la más barata — —

LA PRENSA

DIARIO POPULAR INDEPENDIENTE

TO ADVERTISERS

We guarantee LA PRENSA has a large circulation than any other Mexican newspaper in the United States. — — — —

AÑO VII. DIRECTOR, Ignacio E. Lozano. San Antonio, Texas, Domingo 7 de Marzo de 1920 Fundado en 1913. Núm. 1852.

LA MISERIA ARROJA DE SU PATRIA A LOS TRABAJADORES MEXICANOS Y EL GOBIERNO SE HA PROPUESTO NO DEJARLOS SALIR

Lo que declaran los emigrados acerca de las causas de su venida a los Estados Unidos

EL PROBLEMA DEL VESTIR

LA HABITACION

Han comenzado ya a impedir el exodo que estamos presenciando desde hace un mes

TAKABATAKE ES ENTREGADO AL FIN

UN CRUCERO JAPONES LO LLEVARA DE SALINA CRUZ A SU PAIS. DONDE LO VAN A JUZGAR

LA EJECUCION DE CIRILO ARENAS

SE RECIBIERON LOS ULTIMOS DETALLES DE COMO FUE FUSILADO EL JEFE REBOLUCIONARIO

UN CICLON AZOTA A MONTERREY

Después de la catástrofe causada por el estallido de la caldera, un vendaval vinó a aumentar el pánico en la Ciudad

MUY PRONTO ESTARA LISTA LA BANDA JUVENIL DE SAN ANTONIO PARA DAR AUDICIONES EN LAS PLAZAS PUBLICAS

LAS PRIMERAS LECCIONES

Figure 5.2 Front page, *La Prensa* (San Antonio, TX), Vol. 3, No. 317, Ed. 1, Wednesday, September 22, 1915.

By the mid-1920s, Los Angeles was the largest area of circulation outside of San Antonio. In 1926, Lozano and a group of journalists relocated there to found *La Opinión*, which is the county's largest Spanish-language newspaper today.[49] Readers turned to *La Prensa* for the latest news on the Mexican Revolution, what industries and places were hiring, and to find missing family members, what was being sold, and what social events were coming.[50]

The newspaper's editorials and coverage were critical of the revolution and the government in Mexico City.[51] As the voice of the exiled elite, the paper was nostalgic about pre-revolutionary traditional society, decried the secularization of Mexican society, promoted a reformed Catholic conservativism, and opposed President Plutarco Calles in the 1920s.[52] The newspaper put its coverage of Mexican politics front and center, minimizing articles on local issues.

Many of the characteristics of *La Prensa*—its focus on Mexico, large literary sections, features on history, work to preserve Mexican cultural identity, and desire to paint the Mexican community in a positive light vis-à-vis the English press—built on the legacy of earlier newspapers. One key goal was to create a real and imagined community around Mexican identity, a community that was both deeply tied to nationalism and that existed outside of the nation itself. Its readers were *México de Afuera*: Mexicans who were outside their home country but still part of the Mexican polity, no less Mexican for being outside the country and maybe even more so because they had to consciously work to preserve their identity. To Ignacio Lozano, Mexican communities in the United States were little Mexicos that could preserve Mexican culture and values and be used to restore and rebuild Mexico when residents returned. To this end, he opposed assimilation into American culture.[53] The newspaper's pages created a space for political debates and dialogue within the Mexican community and with the larger political community. Reading *La Prensa* not only reflected a Mexican orientation but actively made the orientation possible.[54]

Part of the success of *La Prensa* was the fact that a large percentage of the Mexican population in the United States wanted to be part of Mexico. Hence, the newspaper offered an opportunity for "vicarious participation in a Mexican national project."[55] Significant portions were devoted to literature and poetry from famous Mexican writers, such as Martín Luis Guzman, Ruben Darío, and Sor Juana Ines de la Cruz. There were pieces on the history of Mexico by Vito Alessio Robles.[56] People were encouraged to be patriotic, participate in festivals, raise money for compatriots back home, teach their children Spanish, preserve Catholic values, look to the Mexican government rather than the United States for redress, and return home one day.[57] It was critical for readers, then, to be up to date on the latest news from Mexico City so that they could return as soon as conditions improved at home.

The newspaper was also the venue for what historian Nancy Aguirre has called a "Porfirista Femininity," which promoted the practice of Catholicism and supported patriarchy and Eurocentric ideals of fashion, art, education, race, and culture.[58] Beginning in 1918, a section called the *Página para el Hogar* featured fashion, advice, literature, and other writings for women, edited by Beatriz Blanco.[59] The literary section became a forum for Rosario Sansores, Gabriela Mistral, and other female writers. Over the course of the 1920s, the newspaper projected a vision of Mexican women as modern, educated readers, even if they were seen primarily as mothers. They were targeted as consumers, privy to the latest fashion and to 1920s jazz culture with dozens of ads for clothing, jewelry, beauty products, and record players. The writers were also heavily involved in the world of San Antonio and *mutualistas*. Ignacio Lozano's sister Alicia Lozano was part of the *Sociedad de la Beneficiencia Mexicana*, and Blanco was president of the *Club Mexicano de Bellas Artes*.[60]

Businesses in San Antonio advertised to Mexican consumers, projecting a modern community where people could own classic Spanish literature and records of mariachi and jazz music.[61] The newspaper carried the latest news from *mutualistas* and encouraged the formation of chapters of the *Alianza Hispano America* in a San Antonio society section.[62] Beyond the front-page news and opinion pieces, these elements helped to create and sustain the imagined community.[63]

Yet if *México de Afuera* was a transnational vision, one where the Mexican government and the Spanish press would represent Mexican migrants rather than US institutions, it was also a practical response to the situation that migrants faced. Remembering the role of the newspaper in his own life, journalist Rubén Munguía, believed that it was widely read by the working class because of its message of *Mexicanidad*, not despite it. As Mexican workers who had been denied education in Mexico, they could aspire to read and buy the paper in the United States. "These new life conditions and new opportunities led them to think, to choose their destiny, and, despite the biased editorializing and reporting to which they were exposed, they were able to compare the idealized good old days 'that some wanted' with the realities of the life they had left behind." In this way, he says, the newspaper opened up a liberal mindset in its readers despite its traditional conservative goals.[64] The mindset of the elites who produced the newspaper was not fundamentally different from that of most Mexican migrants. Many of the writers had been influential in Mexico and saw themselves as exiles rather than migrants. But most working-class migrants undoubtedly identified as exiles and hoped to be able to return home once the violence had died down or they had saved enough money. Few saw themselves as American. And moving frequently within the migrant economy delayed the creation of a local identity.

Beginning in 1916, the newspaper focused more on conditions in San Antonio. In 1916, *La Prensa* ran a thirteen-part series titled "A Serious and Transcendental Problem: Mexican Children and Schools in the State of Texas." The editorials called attention to the segregation of Mexican children—unlike Italian, Greek, and Japanese children—into separate schools. The newspaper also applauded a principal at Navarro Elementary for addressing the needs of Mexican children and not segregating them. In an example of direct influence, the editors presented arguments to the school board that resulted in the board adopting the paper's recommendations.[65] *La Prensa* also assumed the role of educating its readers, frequently running warnings about conditions faced by migrants, the difficulties of crossing the border, the challenges of getting jobs, and the deportations of those without papers. Articles pointed out the deceitful practices of *enganchadores*.[66]

As *La Prensa*'s imagined community included people in both nations, it began to respond to needs on both sides. In 1919, the newspaper raised money for victims of a hurricane that hit the Texas coast. A year later, it ran a large campaign for flood victims in Veracruz, Mexico, raising $46,535 and building a school there. The following year, it raised $40,000 to build an elementary school in Dolores Hidalgo, Guanajuato.[67] Thus, the newspaper mediated migrants' relationship to their homeland while calling on them to rebuild the nation.

A few years later, the paper ran one of its campaigns for a medical clinic in San Antonio that received donations from across the Southwest and the borderlands.[68] The newspaper organized fiestas in San Antonio. These included the election of a *Reina de la Raza* (Queen of the Race), where the money collected went towards funding the medical clinic on the West Side.[69] *Mutualistas* were rallied across the city to throw fundraisers for the clinic. Even communities in Mexico got involved in the effort; *El Diario de Yucatán* donated $50, while Teodoro Torres wrote articles about San Antonio's Mexican community in the Mexican newspaper *Revista de Revistas* to raise awareness of the poor health conditions and the need for clinics for migrants in the United States.[70] Lozano, along with the consulate, also sponsored a *Biblioteca Mexicana*, a library of 2,000 books in Spanish, including archival collections in the city.[71]

It was through its promotion of *México de Afuera* that the newspaper was most active in local affairs. The English-language press in San Antonio mostly ignored the Mexican community, which left *La Prensa* with the responsibility of portraying the community positively, both to members and to outsiders. Defense of *La Raza* was seen as its duty and drew the newspaper into advocacy for the community. As such, it was common for articles to defend Mexicans as a whole against stereotypes and discrimination when they were criticized in local papers.[72] Newspaper editorials sought to portray the Mexican community in San Antonio as industrious, religious, and law-abiding, contrary to common stereotypes in the English-language press.

The newspaper put pressure on authorities when Mexicans experienced injustices.[73] One issue included an article about three people killed on railroad tracks, and another item highlighted poor working conditions across the country.[74] *La Prensa* pressured the consulate to represent Juan Reyes when the Texas Rangers arrested him for murder with little evidence.[75] The newspaper reported and protested the case of Anastacio Garcia, a railroad worker who was killed by an American foreman. When the foreman was released by the sheriff and judge, the newspaper linked his case to the general discrimination against Mexicans in the state and the English press.[76] In a similar case, where Mexican migrant Refugio Mata was killed by American Pat Stevens, the newspaper advocated for an investigation.[77] The newspaper joined various San Antonio *mutualistas* in trying to save the life of Clemente Apolinar Partida, a mentally disturbed man who was sentenced to death after an all-white jury convicted him of murder.[78] The newspaper also covered the case of José Giner, who was accused of killing an American and who the consulate represented.[79] In another case, the newspaper highlighted the killing of a Mexican by white robbers pretending to be police.[80] In these activities and more, the newspaper acted as both a conduit for information and a link to US politics, the Mexican consulate, and the public sphere.

The Mexican Consulate of San Antonio

After the Mexican Revolution, the Carranza and then Obregon administrations expanded the reach of the *Secretaría de Relaciones Exteriores* (SRE) in the United States, and the number of consulates increased from fifty-one to sixty-two. These administrations recognized that *México de Afuera* could criticize and organize against the state, and the state had to take them seriously. They recognized a need to promote *Mexicanidad* if they were one day to incorporate these migrants back into the body politic of Mexico. For these and other reasons, the Mexican government supported institutions that would foster loyalty and culture abroad and positioned itself as the protector of migrants.[81]

The consulates used a rhetoric of patriotism to promote their vision of what the Mexican community north of the border should be. Perhaps to their surprise, people took them up on their ideas. Providing a forum to access information, jobs, healthcare, and legal and financial help, the consuls made it possible for people to maintain a semblance of institutions and community while far from home. Mexican migrants turned to the consulate for services and information and expected the consuls to take their side in disputes. When this was not the case, they criticized consulates in writing and in the press, using their Mexican citizenship as a source of power.

The *Departamento de Protección*'s work on behalf of migrants—resisting deportations, connecting family members, and dealing with American authorities—made the consulate relevant in migrants' daily lives.[82] The vast majority of the work was non-ideological and put the Mexican government on the same side as migrants.[83] Although the consuls, generally from elite backgrounds, prioritized the Mexican government's interests over those of Mexican nationals living in the United States, they did not ignore their compatriots' concerns.[84] Most of the day-to-day work, especially in the *Departamento de Protección*, was carried out by Mexicans from the local community, including many female employees. One of the most common ways that Mexicans used the consulates was to respond to American authorities, especially with regard to deportations and arrests. Texas had the highest rate of police homicides of Mexicans, and the consulate pressed for investigations, even if few resulted in convictions.[85] When Mexicans were arrested, large numbers turned to the consulate. Workers from the consulate checked on cases and kept track of the prisons holding Mexican nationals so that they could communicate with their family members. Although most Mexicans who were deported did not contest the proceedings and left "voluntarily," those who fought their deportations often went to the consulate for legal assistance.

In addition to providing paperwork, consulates helped migrants gather favorable testimony and legal representation in court through *abogados consultores* (Consular lawyers). A few examples suffice. After her husband died, Petra Moreno had no intention of returning to Mexico and fought an attempt to deport her. She had resorted to public charity and, thus, could be deported as Liable to be a Public Charge; she had had an employer since 1922 and had been in the country continuously since 1920. In another case, Jesus Aguilar came with his family in 1920 under contract during the wartime exemption but decided to stay. They applied for residency but had not heard back when they were arrested for deportation. Aguilar appealed to the consul and received help.[86] During World War I, the consular service worked to free Mexicans who were jailed for not registering for the draft or mistakenly drafted.[87]

Migrants saw themselves as a constituency entitled to representation and the consulate as a source of power that could combat American institutions, be they local farmers or the federal government. When there were immigration raids, the consulate was inundated with requests for help from families, criticism in the press, and general pressure to respond. The same was true when companies laid off large groups of workers or cheated migrants of their wages, or when Mexicans were mistreated by local authorities. Migrants from across Texas appealed to the San Antonio consulate for help. During the 1921 recession, Dallas drew consul Enrique Puig into confrontations with police.[88] During a wildcat strike in 1919, the white owner killed a worker, Jesús Navarrete, sparking a consular campaign for a prosecution.[89] When Mexicans contracted to work for Kink & Monahan's oil fields in Eastland were chased away by angry white residents, including the Ku Klux Klan, they appealed to the consulate and *La Prensa* for help.[90] Similar mob incidents occurred across the state, drawing protests from the consulate and newspapers.[91] Migrants could also organize protests against the city and the consulate when they believed officials had not done enough. In April of 1930, a coalition of groups called for a march of the unemployed in San Antonio to demand work. Leading up to the march, the consul feared that the march would turn against him. Eventually, the event proceeded peacefully. Two thousand people participated, most of them Mexican migrants, although some European migrants and American-born workers joined in the demand for jobs.[92]

Enrique Santibañez, general consul in San Antonio in the late 1920s, worked closely with *mutualistas* to promote patriotism and community formation. His views on immigration were widely published in Mexico, and in 1930, he wrote *Ensayo sobre la Inmigración Mexicana*, an extended essay on the issue of immigration. The essay offered a history of the role of immigration in American society and argued that Mexico should actively engage with its migrants abroad, the way Italy did.[93] Santibañez laid out a picture of an oppressed people who had not developed economically in the United States because of discrimination, educational segregation, and laws that targeted Mexicans regardless of their citizenship status. The laws in Texas against vagrancy and migrant mobility passed in 1929 criminalized the type of normal back-and-forth movement that people were used to, and the Box Bill threatened to exclude Mexicans from legal immigration altogether. In Santibañez's view, most migrants barely made adequate wages, and few saved money or earned enough to make migration worthwhile. He also distrusted Manuel Gamio's assertion that migrants learned useful skills and civics in the United States; he contended that most returned to the same life they led before and that migration didn't help migrants or Mexico. He argued for replacing unrestricted migration with a government-run contract labor program with guaranteed return. He didn't live to see the repatriations, but his ideas influenced the Mexican government's response to the Great Depression and, later, the Bracero Program.[94] Santibañez and other officials were influenced by writers in *La Prensa*, and other newspapers who had earlier called for a bilateral labor program, modeled on those in Europe.[95]

Santibañez, like other consuls, was under constant pressure from the Spanish-language press and from migrants to get involved in labor, political, and immigration disputes. Consulates usually held subscriptions to the major newspapers and regularly sent news articles from *La Prensa* and other Spanish-language papers to Mexico City. *La Prensa*, in particular, was perceived as the voice of the opposition to the government. During the Cristero War, it was barred from Mexico for opposition to President Calles.[96] Yet its prominence also meant that Mexican officials felt they had to respond to it. Mexican officials were particularly worried about items critical of Mexico's government and the consulate's actions.[97] Santibañez sought to curb the influence of *La Prensa* and its critical stance toward both the consulate and the Mexican government. He saw the migrant community as less hostile than the paper but was concerned with the influence of the Catholic Church and other organizations.[98]

The consuls were forced to take up cases when they received public attention. When workers were denied a local school and chapel in McNary, Texas, and had a dollar deducted from their wages, they refused to work and informed *El Continental* and the consulate. As a result of the press coverage, the consulate sent an investigator and intermediary.[99] When Rufugio Lucas, a Mexican, was murdered, *La Prensa* heavily criticized the consul for not doing enough to defend Mexicans against prejudice.[100] In another case, the consulates began to alert the SRE about overcrowding at border cities because of deportations only after *La Prensa* started running articles about the issue.[101] Consuls responded to criticism by writing columns in the newspaper, as when consul Batiza took to *La Prensa* to defend himself against criticism from the local *Comisión Honorifica.*[102]

Consular offices were conduits of information across a transnational community of people. The consulate publicized fraud and abuses by unscrupulous agents. It promoted the US Savings Bank and savings collectives like the *Sociedad de Credito Agricola de la Paz,* organized by the *Comisiónes Honorificas* to send remittances.[103] A significant part of consular work was keeping track of Mexican citizens in the criminal justice system. The consulate kept track of accidents and deaths in the Mexican community and sought compensation from employers, insurance companies, and *mutualistas* while searching for the beneficiaries through newspaper ads.[104] It pressured firms into paying what was due and communicating with families in Mexico. Consuls responded to requests from thousands of people who needed documents to migrate back and forth.[105]

Representation in the Public Sphere

Starting in the 1910s and increasing through the 1920s, representations of Mexicans in the mainstream US media shifted from unthreatening, docile workers to threats to the body politic. They were portrayed as filthy, diseased, and most importantly, criminal. It was against this backdrop that *La Prensa* fought against American justifications of deportation and promoted its own version of return in the early 1930s.

La Prensa and the consulate defended migrants, out of a sense of honor, in the public sphere. Before the Great Depression, *La Prensa* dealt with the latest debates in Congress, such as the 1924 Quota Act, the 1929 Immigration Act, and the proposed Box Bill, to eliminate avenues for legal migration.[106]

The newspaper argued against this legislation while conveying that discrimination and fear of deportation were the real threats.[107] Consul Enrique Santibañez, *La Prensa*, and other Mexican organizations took a careful approach, showing that Mexicans were critical to the economy, that exclusion would insult Latin America, and that migrants were hardworking members of the community.

In a comparison of editorials run in the *San Antonio Light*, the *San Antonio Express*, and *La Prensa*, each paper represented a different position regarding immigration legislation.[108] The *Light* was concerned with the preservation of "American" culture and used eugenic language to support the notion that Mexican aliens were undesirable and to urge mass deportations. The *Express* reflected the views of the growers, bankers, and big business in the city. It portrayed Mexicans as workers but not members of the community. Editorials in *La Prensa*, however, pressed that their work made Mexicans into members of the community. Journalist Alberto Rembao, for example, wrote that it would be "impossible to deport Mexicans en masse, because we are workers who reside here and collaborate with the sweat of our brow and the force of our brainpower to enrich the country that has taken us in."[109]

In response to public pressure, the US Bureau of Immigration and US consulates in Mexico began to curtail avenues to migration; most Mexicans who sought to legally migrate starting in 1929 were denied entry. That year, Congress enacted a law that made undocumented re-entry into the United States a felony, and a campaign to deport Mexicans was soon underway in Texas. As a result, legal migration from Mexico fell dramatically before the onset of mass unemployment.

In late 1928, the Border Patrol began to deport Mexicans on an unprecedented scale. This campaign was focused on the lower Rio Grande Valley. Newspapers gave accounts of raids against agricultural workers, and by early 1929, more than 2,600 were deported from Brownsville, Texas.[110] Despite widespread objections from growers, 15,000 were deported from Texas that year.[111] The following year, the campaign spread to central and western Texas, with thousands being deported.[112] These deportation campaigns continued into 1930 and morphed into repatriation drives as the Depression deepened. The press referred to deportation and repatriation using the same language, illustrating how little the legal differences mattered at the local level.[113] *La Prensa* ran an editorial calling for the legalization of those who were being deported.[114] The Mexican consulate protested these actions to the US government and made public pronouncements on how to fight back against deportation proceedings.[115]

The public ideology of *México de Afuera* drew *La Prensa*, *mutualistas*, and the Mexican government into engagement in US politics in defense of *La Raza*. Yet it also severely limited possible responses to the crisis. For the Mexican government, *México de Afuera* was the extension of the rhetoric of post-revolutionary Mexico into the United States. It provided a framework with which to understand the plight of the migrants to Mexican officials. For Santibañez, it offered a remedy to the displacement the economy of migrant labor had wrought. In this way, it was not fundamentally different than the rhetoric that saw migration as something to be stopped and controlled, or the rhetoric that was constructing a national identity inside of Mexico. This framework led nearly every official who wrote on the topic to call for the return of migrants to Mexico. Every president of Mexico in the 1920s and 1930s publicly supported *México de Afuera* and called on migrants to return. So, when faced with a crisis, they called for citizens to come home.

Crisis in Texas

The Great Depression presented a massive challenge to the Mexican community. In San Antonio in 1933, there were 48,575 persons on relief, 24,313 of them Mexican. Around the country, public opinion turned against Mexicans, including those with US citizenship. Repatriation drives started around the country, led by local and state organizations with cooperation from the Bureau of Immigration. In the years between 1930 and 1934, more than 425,000 people were repatriated to Mexico, at least 40% of them the US-citizen children of Mexican migrants.[116] Of those who returned, about 40% were adult men, 40% were children, and 20% were women. The vast majority (60%) were agricultural workers.[117] This is consistent with the migrant cohort study in the Appendix, where the largest losses of people between 1920 and 1930 were found to be among agricultural workers.[118]

Within the movement to return to Mexico, there was considerable variation in motives and circumstances. They included the formally deported, "voluntarily" returnees under threat of deportation, those threatened by charities and local governments with the withdrawal of aid, those who left because of general fear, and some who saw better opportunities in Mexico.[119]

The number of people departing grew from thousands at the end of the 1930 harvest to tens of thousands in 1931 as organized repatriation accelerated.

The federal deportation campaign continued into the 1930s. In September 1931, *La Prensa* reported that a significant number of the repatriates were American-born children of Mexican migrants, as raids were even carried out in public schools.[120] Although those in the country continuously since 1924 were not subject to removal, many lost their cases anyway. Numerous long-term residents of Texas, including veterans, were deported.[121] *La Prensa* criticized the actions of US officials in this campaign. *El Continental* reported in 1931 that 16,000 Mexicans had been deported through El Paso that year, and a similar number went through Laredo.[122] Even as the pace of formal raids and deportations decreased after 1931, fear continued to sweep through Texas' Mexican population.[123] In the lower Rio Grande Valley, it was reported that thousands of workers had lost their wages as they fled in fear of being forced to return to Mexico. *La Prensa* indicated that many property owners had been forced to sell or abandon their homes.[124]

Over half of Mexicans in the state worked in agriculture. Two-thirds were migrant farm laborers, and another third were tenant farmers. As the price of cotton fell, so did wages. The average wage per 100 pounds picked dropped from $1.33 to only $0.44.[125] As a result, the federal government and the state of Texas passed a series of laws, most prominently the Texas Cotton Acreage Control Law of 1931, to reduce the cotton crop. These laws disproportionately hurt Mexican workers, who filled most of the cotton-related jobs in southern, western, and central Texas.[126] Tenants, sharecroppers, and migrant workers all lost their livelihoods. *La Prensa* reported that these laws were responsible for swelling the number of unemployed. The Agricultural Adjustment Administration in the mid-1930s accelerated this process as more land was taken out of cultivation. Overall, 40% of cotton acreage was taken out of cultivation, including half the cotton fields in western Texas.[127]

As in California and the Midwest, local politicians saw Mexicans as a drain; if they could be rid of them, it was argued, spaces would open up for white families.[128] Yet San Antonio had no welfare department, nothing like the large relief organizations that existed in other places. The city's Unemployment Relief Committee wasn't created until two years into the Depression. Even then, the city spent only fifteen cents per person, a fraction of what Los Angeles spent, and services were often suspended during the early 1930s. Independently, the Catholic Charity Board created programs aimed at Mexicans in 1931, spending $151 million over two years; it was the only agency that spent money. Growers asserted that providing relief would discourage workers from accepting declining wages in cotton. Despite this, editorials in the *San Antonio Express* continued to maintain that Mexicans took government relief. When relief did come, it was from the federal government, but agencies insisted that only citizens could benefit, making most migrants ineligible. When Mexican Americans sought relief, they were often denied despite their citizenship, including 6,700 in San Antonio. Unlike other cities, relief agencies in San Antonio, for the most part, did not organize the repatriation of Mexicans.[129]

More people returned to Mexico from Texas than from any other state. Repatriation from Texas accounted for half of the total and included a much larger proportion of rural farm workers and tenants than repatriation from other states, especially after the collapse in cotton prices and the implementation of laws that kicked people off the land. Despite statewide efforts to remove Mexicans from the employment rolls, growers in the lower Rio Grande Valley kept using migrant labor through the high point of the repatriations and resisted repatriation efforts. The primary points of entrance for repatriate trains were El Paso, Nogales, and Laredo, though Douglas, Arizona, and Brownsville, Texas, were also prominent sites of return.[130]

Exactly how many people were repatriated or deported from the country is contested. The most extensive study of 1930s Mexican repatriation, written by Francisco E. Balderrama and Raymond Rodriguez, argued that the number was over one million, but there is no verifiable record of that many people going back.[131] The vast majority of documentary sources from both sides of the border point to a number between 425,000 and 500,000, depending on the definition and the timeline.[132] This is more than double the number Abraham Hoffman arrived at several decades earlier. Hoffman used the statistics compiled by Paul Taylor, the *Departamento de Migración Mexicano*, and Los Angeles County records to propose an estimate of 415,000 people. Mercedes Carreras de Velasco used Mexican SRE, *Instituto Nacional de Migración*, and Sistema National de Información Estadísticas (MMS) figures to arrive at 311,717 people, though her study only covers the period up to 1933.[133] The most recent estimate, by Fernando Saúl Alanís Encinos, argues that 425,000 people were repatriated between 1929 and 1934.[134]

Because of the circular movement of migrants across the border, a large number of repatriates would have returned to Mexico regardless of repatriation drives. In 1934, Paul Taylor made this argument, calculating 218,000 returns to Mexico right before the Depression and 270,000 departures

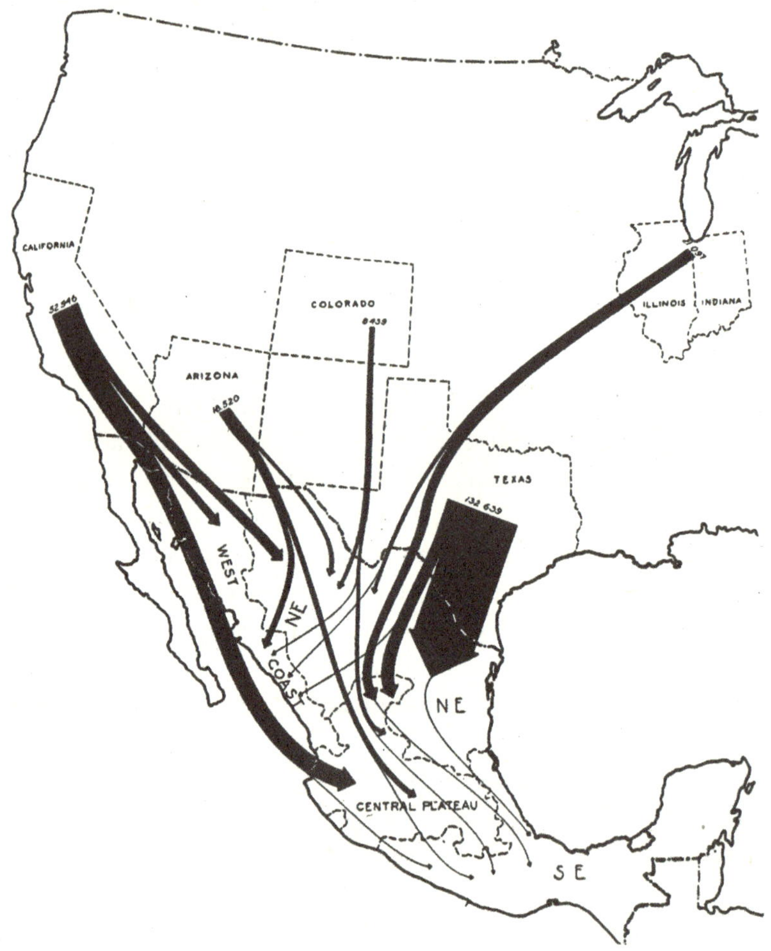

Figure 5.3 Destinations of returning Mexican migrants from the United States to Mexico, 1930–1932. Paul S. Taylor, *Mexican Labor in the United States: Migration Statistics IV.*

during the peak of repatriation, or "hardly 50% greater than the usual repatriation movement of prosperity."[135] More recently, demographers put the number of repatriates at 225,000 over the number that would have gone back to Mexico regardless; many would likely have gone voluntarily as economic conditions deteriorated, with about 40% of the total number being US-born children.[136] What they miss, however, is that repatriation was a highly disruptive event for those involved. While statistically many people were likely to go back to Mexico at some point, it is unclear that any particular person would have gone back during the 1930s, or ever. Although my census study included individuals who were unlikely to settle permanently, they may or may not have chosen to return during the period.[137] Even if a particular person or family might theoretically have returned during later decades, the accelerated return process often involved forced removal, which left migrants unable to bring the savings they would have returned with had they not been forced out in the early 1930s. Therefore, estimates that put the number around 425,000 returnees between 1929 and 1933, about 40% of whom were US-born citizens, seem most accurate.[138] The injustice of the repatriation drives is not about numbers but about the real violence, trauma, and hardship they brought to families and communities.

A Mexican-Led Repatriation

The Great Depression put the words and actions of those who supported *México de Afuera* to the test. The rhetoric provided a framing principle for the repatriation efforts of Mexican communities in the United States and, ultimately, worked to preclude a forceful argument for inclusion in American society. Not only did the Mexican government facilitate the passage of those who wished to return to Mexico, but it also worked with parts of the US government that sought to decrease the presence of Mexicans. Across Mexican civil society, nearly every *mutualista* worked on repatriation efforts. In the city and across Texas, *Comités Pro-Repatriados* and *Comisiónes Honorificas* raised funds and the consulates organized return, with *La Prensa* lauding them on.

The Mexican consulate sought to maintain a delicate balance during the repatriation drives, at it sought to protect some Mexicans who were being forced to leave. It ran a public campaign involving speeches and the distribution of fliers to encourage people to legalize their status if they could do so.[139] In deportation proceedings, those who were legal residents used documents from consuls as evidence of their right to stay. *La Prensa* also printed information about the latest laws and the required papers that people needed to both stay in and leave the country. The newspaper ran an editorial urging those who wanted to remain and those born in the United States to stay to "conserve the spirit of *La Raza*."[140] Rodolfo Uranga in *La Prensa* maintained that many Mexicans who had every legal right to stay were being deported simply because they lacked documentation.[141]

Overall, however, the Mexican consuls encouraged repatriation, working with *mutualistas* and local authorities to return families.[142] They spoke to newspaper and radio reporters about the benefits of going to Mexico.[143] Once large numbers of people began to repatriate, the most important document a migrant could obtain was the certificate of residence. For those who were going back to Mexico, this allowed them to carry personal items duty-free. Requests skyrocketed as the deportation campaign became more heated; about 36,000 people obtained these certificates in Texas in 1929.[144] However, consulates routinely refused to issue them to unaccompanied women, even if they were the primary breadwinners of a family. This prompted numerous women to write to the SRE in protest.[145]

In 1931, the Mexican government created the *Departamento de Repatriación*, which consuls lauded as the Mexican government's way of welcoming home its citizens from abroad. They held meetings in small towns to promote the Mexican government's efforts. When the Mexican government began to pay for the railroad passage for people who wanted (or were forced by circumstances) to return to Mexico, *La Prensa* provided information on how to take advantage of this offer.[146] People wrote a flood of petitions to the government, but funding continuously ran short.[147] A few repatriation projects had been previously planned, targeting middle-class farmers, but these were the exception rather than the norm.[148]

La Prensa's goal was to encourage repatriation, so to this end, it continued to publish articles defending Mexicans' honor and reputations while promoting President Ortiz Rubio's rhetoric for a voluntary Mexican exodus.[149] Publisher Ignacio Lozano had always maintained that Mexicans should return to Mexico to reinvigorate the nation; now, the time had finally come.[150] *La Prensa* optimistically covered attempts to create agricultural colonies in Mexico. In the newspaper, the consulate promoted various government programs that allowed people to return to Mexico, saying it would offer passage and land. *La Prensa*'s writers urged people to return to the homeland to rebuild the nation.[151] At times, this could lead to push back from Mexican authorities, since enthusiasm far outpaced organization.[152] An editorial presented a rosy image of most people returning in the "laurels of victory" rather than in defeat or as public charges. The migrant who returned was "a possessor of a modest fortune, with agricultural tools, household goods, a little Ford car—a 'Fordcit,' and some savings." It said that "re-integration in the homeland will have providential results for Mexico in the present moment in this march for national reconstruction through work."[153]

The consulate was the primary coordinator of repatriation in San Antonio. More than 3,000 left in late 1930, including 125 families moving to a colony in Durango. Eduardo Hernández Cházaro, the new general counsel, arranged for the return of 300 people a few months later, and another group of eighty shortly afterward.[154] By 1931, more repatriates went back in desperate conditions than with ample supplies. Both *La Prensa* and the *Laredo Times* described trains of destitute migrants.[155] The dream of patriotic return and a chance to own land was set against the harsh realities of unemployment and destitution. Only a quarter of repatriates possessed farming equipment.[156]

Across the state, *mutualistas* such as *Comités Pro-Repatriados* and *Comisiónes Honorificas* led the efforts to raise funds, and the consulates organized the logistics of return. In the fall of 1931, 2,700 people were repatriated from the fields of Karnes County, south of San Antonio, when they lost their livelihoods in cotton picking. The Mexican consulate in San Antonio took the lead in organizing this movement out of Karnes, promoting the return as a patriotic endeavor.[157] It worked with the *Comisión Honorifica* to make the arrangements, while *La Prensa* called on the public to help with vehicles and described people returning so impoverished that they migrated on foot. Several organizations, including the *Sociedad Mutualista de Panaderos "Cuauhtemos,"* responded by pledging assistance and raising funds through fiestas and lotteries.[158] Nonetheless, *La Prensa* depicted the departing families as jubilant and confident about the future.[159]

Compare this with US charities and local government. The Bexar County Central Relief Committee was supposed to work with the consuls to pay for the return of the unemployed to Mexico. However, its first repatriation project didn't get off the ground until 1932, and there were few takers for the repatriation funds that were made available. Outside the city, state efforts to force people to Mexico ran into opposition from agricultural interests. Growers insisted that Mexican workers were critical to the cotton and vegetable harvests and stopped state and federal efforts. In the mid-1930s, even after the arrival of New Deal programs, Mexicans (both immigrant and US-born) were shut out of welfare relief and government jobs that were meant for all citizens but mostly went to (Anglo) whites.

In the meantime, Mexicans were returning to a country amid its own depression. The arrival of tens of thousands of people overwhelmed local

Figure 5.4 Mendoza's painting captures the journey of Mexican families to Mexico, framing it as exile. Nora Chapa Mendoza, *Los Repatriados: Exiles from the Promised Land.*

and federal resources. Conditions in border towns were at a crisis point, with thousands of repatriated people stranded without food, clothing, or shelter.[160] Migrants had no clear place to go; in cities, people could not find employment.[161] Various governmental organizations were created to deal with the crisis, but their efforts were inadequate to the volume of need.[162] The colonies represented perhaps the greatest gap between rhetoric and reality. Migrants arrived to find land with nearly no buildings, no roads, no farming equipment, no drinkable water, and very poor soil. Finding these conditions, most people eventually returned to their hometowns.

Over time, as people learned about the realities in Mexico, fewer were willing to repatriate. When it did get a repatriation plan together in the mid-1930s, the Central Relief Committee in San Antonio had a difficult time convincing people to go to Mexico. A few years later, when the consulate sought road workers from Texas to go work in Mexico, almost no one stepped forward.[163] Instead, most repatriation efforts in the next few years focused on workers in cotton-growing areas on the south side of the Rio Bravo, just on the other side of Texas, a region Mexican officials had long wanted to develop.

In the late 1930s, the Cárdenas administration, adopting the position of its predecessors, announced new colonies. Consular reports claimed that thousands would return from the United States if given a chance.[164] While the Mexican government had no intentions of leading a repatriation effort, its goal was to create a viable model colony in case new rounds of expulsions occurred. Unfortunately, this limited aim was not made clear within government. Instead, it was announced that 250,000 hectares on the south side of the Rio Grande were to be set aside for tens of thousands of colonists. García Téllez of the *Secretaría de Gobernación* went to the United States to assess conditions; he wrote that a full repatriation plan would not work, that it would waste money, and that Mexicans would be better off where they were.[165] His warning went unheeded. The consulates were also not given accurate information and soon began to spread a summary of Cárdenas's remarks as a message to the Mexican "colonies" of Texas.[166]

Subsecretary of the SRE Ramón Beteta gave speeches to recruit for a new colony.[167] He contrasted the discrimination and difficult conditions in Texas with the opportunity to own land in Mexico. Beteta sentimentally told his audiences that Mexico and the president invited them to return. He spoke to the "hearts of Mexicans . . . patriotism responded; faith was placed in the homeland."[168] He spoke to massive crowds in San Antonio, Houston, Los Angeles, Chicago, and many small towns in between. In Texas, he told audiences that Mexico would pay for the return not only of Mexican migrants but of all ethnic Mexicans, including Mexican Americans/*Tejanos*, whose citizenship would be recognized without problems.[169] The Mexican government would pay for their return, offer them land in new colonies, irrigate the land, and give them loans to establish new lives. For those who preferred to go to their hometowns, the government would offer transportation home or to *ejidos* (communal land villages) in other states. *La Prensa* ran a series of articles covering Beteta's journey across the state, further drumming up excitement for return to the *patria* (homeland).[170]

People found hope in the message. Beteta reported to the SRE that more than 6,000 people in Texas alone were ready to leave. Numerous people wrote directly to Beteta and President Cárdenas seeking to return in order to obtain land. Jose Guerrero wrote to the president that he was eager for an opportunity to own land; he was referred to the consulate.[171] Pedro de la Cruz and C. Jesus Ramones wrote to Beteta seeking his personal aid in leaving Texas and returning to Mexico, as did June Ernesto Hidalgo.[172] Tirso Valdez explained that he had a son, and while he was a US citizen, he would prefer to be in his homeland if he could work the land.[173] When Reynaldo Osorio asked the president about returning and whether Mexico could use his skills as an electrician, he was referred to Beteta.[174] Jose M. Reyes wrote to Cárdenas seeking repatriation after hearing him on the radio saying that the nation welcomed everyone to the homeland and that there would be land.[175]

Jose Navarro wrote representing thirty families who desired repatriation and were seeking to move all of their belongings, including cars, to Mexico. They had heard that Cárdenas was redistributing lands and wished to be part of the project to rebuild the nation, to "labor on the land and bring forth its fruit."[176] Many more wrote asking to return after hearing about the colonies through the consulates or word of mouth.[177] Migrants were motivated by their own economic difficulties, as well as the lure of free land.

In truth, there was no mass exodus. Many would-be returnees were left out. The government was looking for people with agricultural experience and enough money to pay their own way, something few could do. People believed in the promises of land, and when the government did not deliver, they took action. This is what led to sit-ins in Corpus Christi, Robstown, Brownsville, and other cities. Many felt that they had been duped by the Mexican government. Some refused to go, while others demanded passage and land. In a letter to the SRE, Saldívar Gallegos, the secretary of the Settlers League, a migrant repatriation group, said that people had believed Beteta's promises and many had sold "much of the little" they processed to return to the homeland, which set them even further back.[178] Eventually, a few hundred settlers resettled in *Marzo 18* in Tamaulipas, the last of the repatriation projects.

In Texas, a New Generation

The eclipse of the ideology of *México de Afuera* was the direct result of the repatriation drives and the diminishment of the immigrant community. The consulate fought for the rights of some to stay in the United States and generally advised those with means to remain, but its dominant message was one of return. In the wake of the Great Depression and repatriation drives, a new generation of activists who looked primarily towards the United States articulated a different vision for the future of Mexicans in *El Norte.*

The 1930s saw a marked shift in the population of San Antonio. While cross-border movement never ended, the days of the large-scale migrations of the 1910s and 1920s were over. The repatriation drives resulted in about a third of the community leaving, along with tens of thousands more across Texas. With the departure of tens of thousands of Mexican families to Mexico, those born in the United States made up the majority.[179] Starting with World War I veterans in southern Texas, Mexican American fraternal organizations were constituted across the state and united at a 1929 convention as LULAC. Despite a bilingual first convention, the organization that emerged excluded non-citizens, promoted its American identity, and conducted business in English. During these years, LULAC supported restrictions on further immigration and was strongly anti-communist. It primarily focused on social reform, especially challenging school segregation in San Antonio. LULAC worked with the *Club Democrático* and the League of Loyal Americans to organize the city's Mexican American voters. The mayorship of Democrat Maury Maverick was a catalyst for organizing on the West Side. In the late 1930s, the Catholic Church launched its own efforts, including *La Liga de Agricultores Católicos*, a farmer's union, and more than a dozen church organizations in the city. Local politics began to pit Mexican business owners, the Mexican Chamber of Commerce, and the Mexican consulate against LULAC and reformers, particularly on the issue of urban renewal.[180]

In the 1930s, Mexican Americans across the country actively joined a wave of union organizing. Combining a unionist message with older, radical Mexican traditions, these new organizations launched strikes at the height of the Depression. In 1935, the *Convención Constitutive pro Derechos Mexicanos de Texas* brought together dozens of unions and *mutualistas* to press for political change. In the city, the International Ladies' Garment Workers' Union won strikes at the Shirlee Frock Company, the Texas Infant Company, and the Juvenile Manufacturing Company. The Pecan Shelling Workers' Union, under the leadership of *Tejana* Emma Tenayuca, initiated one of the largest strikes in San Antonio's history in 1938 in response to declining wages. Tenayuca, who had previously been connected to cross-border efforts by the Communist Party and the *Congreso de Trabajadores Mexicanos*, argued in an essay, "The Mexican Question in the Southwest," that Mexicans in the borderlands were tied to the United States, not Mexico, and that their labor gave them a claim to belonging and rights, regardless of citizenship. She pushed for a broad-based Popular Front (in which the anti-capitalist and pro-capitalist left worked together in the 1930s) program of redress for all Mexicans on both sides of the border.[181] The pecan workers joined the socialist- and communist-affiliated United Cannery, Agricultural, Packing, and Allied Workers of America of America (UCAPAWA), but this produced a backlash. The Mexican consulate sought to undermine the communist-led strikes, and most of the city's *mutualistas* were hostile to union efforts as the continual strikes raised fears of the radical left. *La Prensa*, the Catholic

Church, and LULAC also distanced themselves from the UCAPAWA.[182] The pecan workers' strike ended in a temporary negotiated settlement.[183]

New organizations sprang from older traditions, promoting a US-based public sphere. This included new newspapers such as *Sancho Panza* and *El Mutualista*, published by Federico Herrera.[184] *El Pueblo: El Periódico Hispano Americano de Tejas* became an important voice in the region. The Catholic parochial paper *La Voz* changed its name to *La Voz: Periódico de Justicia y Acción Social*. Led by Rómulo Munguía, the newspaper supported the Congress of Industrial Organizations but opposed communists and the union during the pecan shellers' strike.[185] Munguía was from the older Mexicanist tradition but became a transitional figure. He started at *La Prensa* before becoming an independent printer and printing *El Pueblo*, *La Voz de México*, *Vínculos*, and other publications. He created the *mutualista Agrupación de Ciudadanos Mexicanos en el Extranjero*, which continued to support *México de Afuera* well into the 1940s and demand that the Mexican government had a responsibility to protect Mexicans abroad. He also worked to bring Mexican universities to San Antonio. But times were changing, and he supported US-based politics and reform, becoming heavily involved in Democratic Party politics. His wife Carolina as active in political action through *La Estrella*, a Spanish-language radio show.[186] In addition, the English- and Spanish-language paper *El Luchador*, led by lawyer Manuel Carvajal González, pushed for civil rights.[187] *El Defensor*, a newspaper published by Santiago Guzman, more forcefully advocated for Mexicans in the United States than other papers. Guzman supported Mexican American and Anglo coalitions in local government.[188]

Yet *La Prensa* was still the largest Spanish-language newspaper in the 1940s. There was a significant dialogue between the older *La Prensa* and the newer, explicitly Mexican American press in San Antonio. Américo Paredes and his brother-in-law, Oscar del Castillo, then reporters for *El Heraldo de Brownsville*, were heavily influenced by *La Prensa* and its writers.[189] Correspondents from places as far away as New Orleans wrote in the paper, where they reported on events in their respective areas.[190] When workers were promised good wages and conditions in Louisiana and instead found themselves trapped, they wrote to *La Prensa* and the consulates.[191] Most of them were migrants who had lived in Texas before heading east.[192]

Although the influence of the ethnic nationalism of *La Prensa*, the consulates, and *mutualistas* waned as people left and a new generation of US-born Mexican Americans came to the forefront, these civic institutions co-existed with the new generation of writers and activists. Their ideologies were opposite, yet they shared some of the same practical goals. These newspapers and organizations had more in common as voices of large immigrant communities than their politics would first appear, especially in representing the community in the public sphere.[193] *La Prensa* continued to represent the community until it ceased publication 1963, around the time the consulates and older *mutualista* organizations came to be seen as relics by a new generation of Chicano activists. Many would forget a time when their vision of *México de Afuera* enjoyed widespread support.

The Mexican consulate continued to be involved in repatriation, strikes, labor disputes, criminal cases, and other legal matters throughout the 1940s. Yet the repatriation drives marked a shift in which the rhetoric of return met a difficult reality. The public discourse of *México de Afuera* had drawn *La Prensa*, *mutualistas*, and the Mexican government into engagement in US politics in defense of *La Raza*, but also hampered their vision of possibilities in the 1930s. Few saw an alternative to returning to Mexico. They not only worked to organize the repatriation drives but also served as the primary agents in making them a reality. Promoted in the Mexican public sphere in San Antonio and within Mexico, the reality of return, especially to government-sponsored colonies, was mostly disappointing to the hundreds of thousands who made the journey. When President Manuel Ávila Camacho called on all Mexicans to return to rebuild the nation in 1941, few took him up on the offer.[194]

The Spanish-language public sphere that emerged in Texas and was dominated by *México de Afuera* enjoyed widespread support because it fit into the lived experience of most Mexicans in Texas. Most Mexicans thought of themselves as temporary migrants and wished to return home—one day. *México de Afuera* provided a language for migrants to use to interpret their situation. *Mexicanismo*, through the Spanish-language press and the Mexican government, was not the only option available to Mexicans, but it was one of the few that was at least occasionally effective by creating space for people to make appeals based on their Mexican-ness.

It was precisely because migrants were not US citizens that they were able to press the Mexican government and its consulates to act on their behalf. They appealed as Mexican citizens. This may help explain why so few Mexicans were clamoring to become US citizens.[195] Mexican migrants' use of citizenship was strategic and challenged the idea of a single national identity.[196] The consulates intervened to protect Mexican citizens in the United States and insisted that they be treated equally. They showed up in court to represent Mexican citizens. In some cases, they got the US federal government to investigate and reverse local decisions. Only some of these cases were won, yet it was an invaluable strategy for people with few resources.

It is an irony that the most conservative organizations and voices in the Mexican community, and their ideology of *México de Afuera*, could at times become the vehicle of mostly working-class migrant communities. Yet it also made sense to migrants who arrived in the years after the outbreak of the Mexican Revolution. The rhetoric provided a way for Mexicans in the United States to act as transnational citizens of Mexico. They turned to the Mexican government and demanded that it fulfill its rhetoric and defend them in the United States. They wrote extensively to the consulate and the president of Mexico. They asked for, and sometimes demanded, return. They staked their futures on return and pushed back on the Mexican government. They answered the call to participate in the larger national project in their actions, but they called on the *mutualistas*, *La Prensa*, and the Mexican government to do so as well.

6

Caught in the Middle

Migrant Labor in Southern California, 1920–1940

> Now when the apples are ripe the crop tramps come in and pick them. And from there they go on over the ridge and south, and pick the cotton. If we can start the fun in the apples, maybe it will just naturally spread over into the cotton.
>
> —John Steinbeck, *In Dubious Battle* (1936)

These words, spoken by Steinbeck's character Mac, both illuminate and obscure the nature of the agricultural strikes that rocked California in the 1930s. In 1933, strikes that started in the vegetable and fruit fields spread to the cotton fields and beyond, rocking the state's largest industry to its core. Workers took the lead in organizing a vast multiracial coalition that sought to better their conditions. They challenged the largest vested interests in the state. California's political economy was built on the most unequal distribution of land in the entire United States, and the labor on which it depended was imported from the far reaches of the United States' colonial empire. It was in California that the capitalist transformation of the West in the late nineteenth century reached its fullest expression, where capital had the most control over people's lives. New industries arose based on migrant labor, and Los Angeles became the hub of the southern part of the state. Yet it was also here, during the Great Depression, that the most racially diverse workforce in the country turned to radical organizing. Their defeat does not change the fact that, in the wake of the repatriation drives, migrants in the fields challenged the balance of power.

Although Texas was the primary entry point for Mexican migrants in the country, much of the growth in migration was in California, and by 1930, a third of all the Mexicans in the country were living in the state. Even more than in Texas, migrants to California were predominantly from the central Bajío region of Mexico, though they tended to migrate to California after having worked in other states. They moved into long-settled Mexican

Between Here and There. Daniel Morales, Oxford University Press. © Oxford University Press 2024.
DOI: 10.1093/oso/9780197612590.003.0007

American "Californio" communities across the state and quicky dwarfed the US-born population. In Los Angeles, Mexican-born migrants outnumbered US-born Mexican Americans by two to one by 1920; by 1930, the ratio was five to one.[1] From then to the present, Los Angeles has had the largest concentration of Mexicans outside of Mexico City.

This chapter follows the growth of migration across the state, particularly in Southern California, from 1920 until the agricultural strikes of 1933 to 1936. There and throughout the country, society increasingly saw Mexicans as threats, and the "Mexican Problem" became a critical issue in politics. Through the 1920s, the federal government increasingly erected legal and physical barriers to Mexicans' entry. The repatriation drives were particularly intensive in Southern California, yet Mexican workers had built homes, raised children, and created a web of communities across the agricultural landscape that was not limited by a location and state-bound conception of citizenship. They pushed back against those who sought to control their movement, their labor, and their rights. While some sought return, those who stayed behind were more committed to making a life in California. They organized in the 1930s under various banners seeking to improve the conditions under which they labored.

The transformation of agricultural production based on migrant labor was nationwide but especially visible in California, which by 1930 was home to half of the large-scale farms (defined as farms valued over $30,000) in the country. This included 30% of the largest cotton operations, 40% of dairies, 33% of poultry farms, and most importantly, 60% of large fruit and truck farm (vegetable) operations.[2] Following migrant networks, workers came to work on the railroads, where section labor became completely immigrant based, and in the new agricultural fields, where the control of rivers transformed the Southern California deserts and San Joaquin Plains.

Unlike Chapter 5, which focused on why so many saw return to Mexico as the only viable option, this chapter examines those who fought to stay. Even after at least a third of Mexicans left for Mexico nationally, they still made up the majority in the fields.[3] While *México de Afuera* retained significant ideological power, large numbers turned to the radical vision of the Communist Party. Starting with the LA County Berry Strike, the strikes brought significant labor and ideological tensions to the surface, spreading from Southern California to the San Joaquin Valley and the Imperial Valley. Although they took place at the height of anti-Mexican prejudice, they involved cross-racial alliances and involved cooperation between radical and more conventional labor groups. The strikes became a battleground for local and state politics as well as for Franklin Roosevelt's New Deal administration and the post-revolutionary Mexican state. While the particular union was defeated, attempts to organize continued throughout the decade. Only in the late 1930s, after the violent suppression of this radical vision, did the New Deal and the Congress of Industrial Organization (CIO) vision of moderate reform become dominant among Mexican American organizers. The activism of the 1930s was not centered on a particular union, racial group, or ideology, but emerged from the demands of agricultural workers writ large.

California and the West

Industrial capitalism and the federal government shaped life in the West, particularly in California, like no place else. It was in California that the processes of land consolidation, federal subsidies and infrastructure investment, mass agriculture, unequal landscapes, and mass migration reached their apex. There, railroads, mining, cotton, beets, vegetables, and fruit companies came together on one of the world's most productive landscapes. The state also has one of the nation's most varied climates, with several distinct biological regions. The Central Valley, roughly 450 miles long but only about 50 miles wide, was widely believed by boosters to hold enormous potential. Farther south, the Los Angeles, San Gabriel, and Santa Ana rivers fed a large basin and two connected valleys, the San Fernando and San Gabriel. This region became the center of the Southern California economy. To the southeast, the Imperial Valley, sitting below sea level and characterized by extreme heat in the summer, stretched into Mexico and was mostly uninhabited before the twentieth century. Settlers dreamed of diverting the Colorado River into this desert to make a "winter garden." The settler colonial project transforming the West culminated in California.

In the middle of the nineteenth century, several dozen ranching families came to control much of the Central Valley. Then, in the 1870s and 1880s, the invention of refrigerated cars enabled fruit harvested there to be shipped to eastern markets. The irrigation of its farms, the rise of the cannery industry, and the arrival of sugar beets and cotton combined to make the state's crops the most valuable in the country. Maintaining these new industries required a massive agricultural workforce that draw from populations on the edges of citizenship and the nation.

When the US Census declared the closing of the frontier in 1890, many asked what lay ahead for a nation that believed its ideals of individualism, freedom, and opportunity were intimately tied to its expansion into "open" spaces.[4] Native Americans were not citizens and were forced to work under vagrancy laws. They were the primary labor force in California until the middle of the nineteenth century, when they were replaced with Chinese labor after a demographic collapse. The Chinese were denied civil rights, including the rights to become citizens, to acquire property, and to live and work in certain areas. Chinese workers were eventually barred from immigrating at all, first through the Page Act of 1875, then the Chinese Exclusion Act of 1882, and then the Geary Act of 1892, though exemptions remained for merchants and students. In California, the Chinese experienced violence, including the largest mass lynching in the history of the West in Los Angeles in 1871. Manifest Destiny didn't end on the shores of the Pacific Ocean but was transformed into an impulse for empire. By the early 1900s, the United States had taken over Puerto Rico, the Philippines, Hawaii, and several Pacific islands, not to mention occupations of Cuba and various Caribbean and Central American countries. Because colonial subjects lacked citizenship and were considered "US nationals," immigration laws didn't apply to them. Under the *padrone* system, contract workers came from these places as well as Japan, India, Armenia, and Europe. Many workers from the Indian subcontinent were contracted in the Imperial Valley to pick cotton, and they soon became one of the largest groups there. Meanwhile, the Japanese, who had prior experience with these crops, became owners of sugar beet and berry operations. A backlash against the Japanese culminated in the Gentleman's Agreement of 1907, which aimed to prevent further Japanese immigration; the Alien Land Law of 1913, which barred the Japanese from owning farmland; and a complete ban on Asian immigration in the 1924 Immigration Act.[5]

By 1920, 200,000 people labored in California's agricultural industry as migratory workers. They included international migrants but also African Americans and poor whites from the United States. Growers had established a system by which workers were paid differently depending on race, with US-born whites and European immigrants at the top. Companies used migrants as strikebreakers against other migrants, helping to keep wages low and fueling ethnic tensions. Included in this workforce were 30,000 Filipino migrants, who were unable to become citizens but had organized several times into unions, sparking calls for their removal.[6] Growers saw Mexicans as more tractable than others; they could be deported while US nationals could not. By the 1920s, Mexican migrants made the majority of these workers. Various attempts to unionize farm workers of all types under the Industrial Workers of the World (IWW) had been crushed in the 1910s. Growers across the state's industries created farming associations to fight worker organizing and to represent their industries. These associations included central agencies for the employment of workers, which assisted owners and tenants while setting the price of crops and the wages of laborers. Using the language of small, independent family farms, they created an economy reliant on migrant labor.[7]

Southern California

No city in the early twentieth century experienced such rapid growth as Los Angeles. The population of Los Angeles County increased from 100,000 at the end of the nineteenth century to 2.2 million by 1930. This included hundreds of thousands of white settlers/migrants from the American Midwest and South who claimed the land, as well as hundreds of thousands of European migrants and 100,000 Asian immigrants. Nearly 200,000 Mexicans arrived, most from the states of Sonora, Chihuahua, Sinaloa, Zacatecas, Aguascalientes, Michoacán, Jalisco, and Guanajuato.

Los Angeles became a major industrial center, with large garment, oil, automobile, rubber, and shipping industries. The railyards just east and south of downtown provided large numbers of migrants with their first jobs and first homes in the city, in the yards' boxcar camps. Many came to work in the industrial zone surrounding these railyards and in the warehouses and the mining, oil, and construction businesses in adjacent neighborhoods. The city's old core centered around *la placita* (the historic plaza around which the city had grown since colonial times), and next to Chinatown was a largely Mexican neighborhood. The local white elites, viewing the old city as crowded, dirty, diseased, and dangerous, created a new downtown on a hill to the south.[8] Most of the new housing developments in the city or wealthy suburbs had restrictive covenants that kept Mexicans and other people of color from purchasing. Mexicans moved into Boyle Heights, Pico Gardens, Belvedere, and East Los Angeles. The city was only part of the region's rapid growth, which impacted all of Southern California. Los Angeles County developed an integrated regional economy where agriculture and industry sat side by side and gave rise to multiple urban centers.[9] Industries such as oil, automobiles, and textile manufacturing were concentrated in different locations. Following the trail of the Santa Fe and Union Pacific railroads, agricultural production, predominantly fruits and vegetables, became the area's dominant industry. With railroads delivering food to markets, new towns and food-processing plants sprouted up at railroad junctions. Dozens of towns based on this model grew in Los Angeles and Orange Counties in these years, including El Monte, Azusa, Upland, La Verne, Riverside, and Santa Ana. Workers for the industry circulated across the region, which was connected by street car lines reaching from Santa Monica to Riverside.

This landscape was not accidental. In fact, Protestant preachers from the Midwest held it up as an ideal of what a city should be: not a place of poor health, poor homes, and poor people, but a place where all men and women could own a piece of land and experience open space. The goal was to ruralize urban life. It was even said that the city had no slums.[10] In reality, African Americans, Asians, and Mexicans could not buy property in most of Los Angeles or other towns in the county and were segregated into overcrowded rental properties in specific neighborhoods near downtown. In the towns where so many of them worked, they could not even rent housing. Barrios were built outside city limits on land that had no restrictive covenants but also no infrastructure, police, or fire protection. In some places close to the core, such as Belvedere, Mexican Americans owned homes and formed

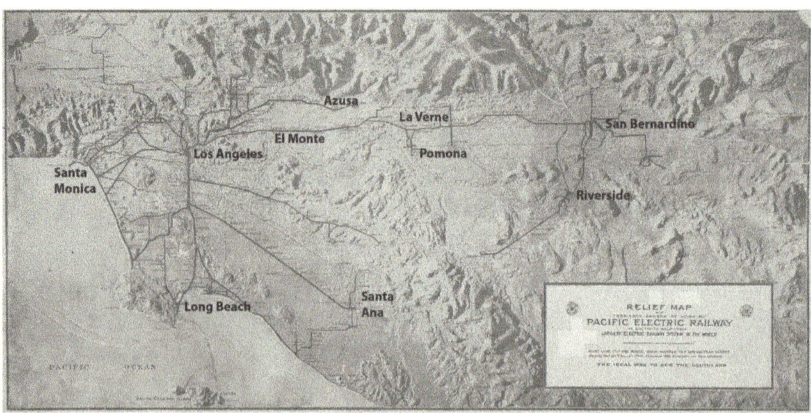

Figure 6.1 Relief map of territory served by the Pacific Electric Railway in Southern California. O. A. Smith, cartographer, ca. 1920. UCLA, Library Special Collections, Charles E. Young Research Library.

a middle class, but in agricultural areas, neighborhoods were more often shanty towns. Not all towns in Southern California were segregated. Citrus towns were company towns where more stable employment led to paternalistic social structures, while cities like Pomona and Boyle Heights were integrated from the beginning.

Los Angeles functioned as both a destination and a hub of migration networks. The hundreds of thousands of jobs available to Mexicans there were mostly unskilled, low paying, and offered few opportunities for advancement. However, they were much better than the jobs available to Mexicans elsewhere, with agricultural laborers averaging $2.50 per day before the Great Depression. Because of the seasonal nature of agricultural labor, tens of thousands of Mexicans migrated up and down the state every year, starting in the Imperial Valley, moving to Los Angeles and Orange Counties, and then journeying north to the San Joaquin Valley. These workers were not isolated from society at large but were instead linked to the migratory and information networks that had brought them from Mexico and across the country.[11] The majority of them did not travel directly from Mexico but came to Los Angeles from other parts of the country, often Texas, the Arizona-New Mexico borderlands, and the Midwest.

Agricultural Migration to the Imperial and San Joaquin Valleys

While Los Angeles County had the largest Mexican population, tens of thousands of people worked in the agricultural fields of the Imperial Valley and the San Joaquin Valley. Using funds from the Reclamation Act of 1902, the Imperial Land Company radically altered the landscape, diverting the Colorado River, laying out a series of towns, recruiting agricultural settlers, and accidentally created a man-made sea when flooding overwhelmed the irrigation system. The companies' holdings extended into Mexico and led to the creation of Mexicali on the border, which became the primary city in the region. What had started as primarily cotton fields turned into vegetable truck farms by the late 1920s.[12] With their proximity to the Mexican border, the growers took advantage of easy access to migratory labor, hiring at low wages and working with law enforcement to end disputes or deport workers when strikes occurred. To the north, California's Central Valley, stretching 400 miles, become a major source of cattle, vegetables, citrus, grapes, nuts, sugar beets, and cotton. From the start, the valley's growth was predicated on capital-intensive agriculture and migrant labor.

Like Mexican workers' travels to other parts of the country, their journeys to California were facilitated by far-reaching transnational networks of jobs, transportation, and information. It was common for Mexican agricultural workers to move via the railways and transition into industrial work.[13] During August, at least 11,500 workers migrated from the Imperial Valley to the San Joaquin Valley, a distance of 550 miles, in caravans of cars. Significant numbers of people went much farther, to the Hood River in Oregon and the Yakima Valley in Washington, sites of apple orchards, or to Colorado and Arizona. Compared with Texas, workers tended to circulate within the region rather than regularly circulate back to Mexico. Most of these workers made between \$350 and \$400 a year. Migration made it difficult for most Mexicans to access government services. Most children were not registered in school since they could not meet residency requirements, and the lack of local residency prevented people from becoming citizens or, even if they were US-born citizens, from claiming aid.[14]

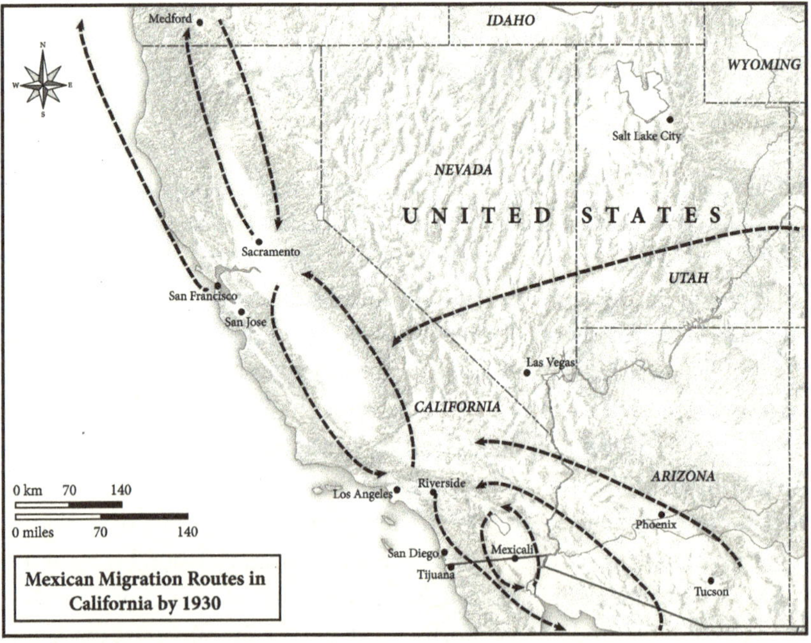

Figure 6.2 Mexican migration routes in California by 1930.

Various types of migration developed based on both the position of an individual and the crops they worked with. A state report on the Imperial Valley found three different types of laborers: those who lived locally; those who followed a particular crop like cotton, hops, corn, or sugar beets; and those who migrated from crop to crop, following the harvest of each crop.[15] Likewise, each crop had its own dynamics: the number of people hired, the difference in labor needs between the off-season and harvest, the length of workers' employment, the technology used, whether there were canning operations in the area, and whether large companies or small tenant farms dominated that crop. The distinction in labor needs between the regular growing season and the harvest was stark and varied greatly from crop to crop. Two hundred acres of asparagus required five men during the off-season but 36 during the harvest; 500 acres of peaches needed 20 men before the harvest and 185 workers, "plus 100 children," during the harvest.[16]

The living conditions of workers in the Imperial Valley and the San Joaquin Valley varied greatly. While some Mexican barrios were permanent parts of towns, numerous were semipermanent, owner-built shanty camps on land rented from private owners. These camps were similar to those in Southern California but smaller and more rural.[17] Other workers made do with even less, building squatters' camps that existed only while they were active at a particular site. The largest farms had their own campgrounds, but many migrant camps sprang up on riverbanks and unused land.[18] Most of these places had dirt roads and lacked electricity, plumbing, and running water. By 1920, large Mexican *colonias* had grown in places like Corcoran and Fresno in the San Joaquin Valley and Brawley and El Centro in the Imperial Valley. As families began to stay at *colonias* on a nearly permanent basis, they developed large settled populations.[19]

Across the agricultural landscape, laborers undertook backbreaking work from sunrise to sunset. They used short hoes that caused back injuries and had little to no access to medical or police services. Because a family could earn much more than a single man, these places were teeming with children. It was normal for children to pick or help with every type of crop. The migratory nature of the work meant that few children went to school, and those who did attended poorly run and poorly funded segregated schools. An estimated 37,000 children were in the fields, out of a total of between 150,000 and 200,000 migratory workers; migrants comprised a whopping 78% of the state's agricultural workers by 1927. Working in the San Joaquin Valley for short stints was more profitable for those who brought more family members

Figure 6.3 Mexican grandmother who migrates with her large family each year from Glendale, Arizona, following crops through California and returns. Santa Clara Valley, California. Dorothea Lange, 1938. Library of Congress Prints and Photographs Division, LC-USF34- 018576-C.

and did not have to purchase food, transportation, or supplies.[20] This meant women in the fields would do double shifts, cooking and cleaning in addition to field work. Writing at the time, Paul Taylor described "the growth of intensive agriculture, highly capitalized, large-scale farming methods, and concentrated ownership, huge payments to farm laborers—[which] together have given us an industrialized agriculture, a system of open-air food factories."[21]

A mobile landscape came into being where a multiracial labor force was pushed into forms of work that offered few opportunities for settlement.[22] Mexicans were not the only farm workers who lived in makeshift conditions. Writing about the Inland Empire, Mary Paike Lee observed, "The Japanese, Chinese, and Mexicans each had their own little settlement outside of town. My first glimpse of what was to be our camp was rows of one-room shacks, with a few water pumps here and there and little sheds for outhouses."[23] Growers racially segregated their workforce by paying different rates, promoting competition between groups that made cross-racial solidarity difficult. White and Japanese workers often occupied a middle position in the fields, serving as skilled workers, tractor drivers, foremen, lease holders, and small tenant farmers.[24] Mexicans and Filipinos frequently saw each other as rivals.[25] Then, in the late 1930s, 300,000 more white migratory farm workers fleeing the Dust Bowl joined the multicultural workforce.

As the *colonias* became more established, Mexican *mutualistas* and institutions developed in small towns and in camps. An infrastructure of businesses and boarding houses arose to support migratory labor. This extended well beyond the cities, with their established middle class, to small towns and camps. People would rent space to others, and families would establish lunch businesses and laundry houses to make a little more money. Groceries were often the center of these *colonias*. Banks too catered to migrants; in the Imperial Valley, the Pacific Trust and Savings Bank specifically tailored pamphlets and bank services for migrant workers sending remittances home.[26] In Santa Ana, the post office reported that the highest remittances were in June, May, and November, while the lowest were in December and October, when few local crops grew.[27] By 1930, hundreds of *colonias* dotted the agricultural landscape, many of which had become permanent communities where people knew each other, and businesses, *mutualistas*, and churches had taken root, even as people continued to migrate for work.

Figure 6.4 All races serve the crops in California. Dorothea Lange, 1935. Library of Congress Prints and Photographs Division, LC-USZ62-137429.

Repatriation in Southern California

The collapse of the US economy in the fall of 1929 led to the end of circular migration from Mexico. Migrants in the United States first felt the effects of the crisis at the end of the 1929 harvest, when tens of thousands were laid off. Mexicans became a scapegoat for the unemployment crisis as a hostile public did not see people of Mexican origin as American, even though many were US citizens. This led to a mass effort to remove Mexicans, with both official and unofficial efforts at deportations often merging.

Secretary of Labor William Doak claimed there were 400,000 undocumented Mexican aliens who could be deported. In response, the Hoover administration carried out raids throughout the nation, deporting thousands and arresting tens of thousands. The California state legislature passed the Alien Labor Act in 1931, making it illegal to hire non-citizens for public works jobs and costing thousands of people their livelihood.[28] In Los Angeles, these efforts were led by the Los Angeles Citizens Committee on Coordination of Unemployment Relief, whose head, C. P. Viesel, claimed there were 20,000 deportable Mexicans in the city.[29] Created to coordinate various entities, the committee held that Mexicans could be induced to return to Mexico through a combination of scare tactics and financial pressure.[30] He encouraged *La Opinión* and other Spanish-language newspapers to run stories that spread fear throughout the community. He also worked with federal agents in their raids and encouraged newspapers to carry stories on the deportation campaign.

Legal deportation ran into limits. On February 26, 1931, agents of the Bureau of Immigration stormed *la placita*, arresting hundreds of people whom they suspected of being in the country illegally. This event caused mass panic in the city's Mexican community and drew a strong response from the Mexican consulate and the Spanish-language newspapers to defend their compatriots. Only a handful of those arrested turned out to be legally deportable, though this also meant that even being US citizens or in the country legally had not protected Mexicans from arrest. Raids throughout Southern California yielded similar results. In El Monte, thirteen people were arrested in one raid, but no one was deportable and several were US-born. An investigation at the Los Angeles County jail found that less than 10% of the Mexicans incarcerated there were deportable. In total, of the thousands who were arrested in the raids, only 230 people were subject to deportation, and 159 more underwent "voluntary departure."[31] Los Angeles County also set up patrols and checkpoints to make sure no new Mexicans entered the county, something they later did to block Okie migrants.

However, organizations could still induce people to repatriate. The Los Angeles County Department of Welfare led the coordination of these efforts. The department falsely argued that Mexicans were disproportionately relying on charity and that sending people to Mexico would result in large savings.[32] It worked with charity organizations across the country as well as the Los Angeles Chamber of Commerce to make repatriation a reality. One common strategy used by these organizations was to offer to pay the cost of return for men and families, targeting those who were unemployed or in need of assistance.[33] The department would present families on relief with tickets back to Mexico and tell them their local aid was being cut off. Threatened families would flee, taking all their belongings in the middle of the night or selling all they had. Families were misled into believing they could re-enter the United States easily, only to find this impossible.[34] Agents were instructed to reject any immigrant who had the "LA County Charities" stamp on their voluntary return card, and in subsequent years, many came without documents to avoid this check.[35]

Most Mexican civic organizations and unions in California opposed continuing migration and supported the repatriation drives of the 1930s. Long-time Mexican Americans and US-residing Mexicans tended to see at migrants as competition, especially during the Great Depression.[36] Ventura Martinez, a grocery storekeeper, exemplified these views, arguing that it would be better for Mexican migrants not to come to the San Joaquin Valley, as they drove down wages for local workers.[37] Similar views were held by Mexican Americans in Southern California, especially when migrants were

Figure 6.5 Relatives and friends wave goodbye to a train carrying 1,500 people being expelled from Los Angeles back to Mexico on August 20, 1931. New York Daily News Archive via Getty Images.

used as strikebreakers. Reformers and the mainstream press in Los Angeles associated the new migrants with poverty, disease, and questionable morals. Some Mexican Americans adopted these views, while others feared that American society would apply these undesirable traits to them, not making a distinction between native-born and migrants.[38]

Coerced repatriation programs blurred with voluntary return.[39] A significant number left under pressure from the Mexican consulate, Mexican *mutualistas*, and the newspaper *La Opinión*, which urged Mexicans to go back and rebuild their country. The *Cooperativo de Repatración* and the *Comité Mexicano de Beneficencia* promoted repatriation and raised funds, as did Los Angeles Consul Rafael de la Colina.[40] Colina worked with repatriation authorities on both the federal and local levels and was in constant communication with the county welfare committee. His cooperation enabled free transportation to Mexico and then into the interior. On several occasions, he personally traveled with county representatives on the repatriation trains from Los Angeles to the border at Nogales or El Paso and then on to Mexico.[41] It was common for the same trains carrying people south to include some who were being deported, some whose returns were funded by the Los Angeles County Department of Welfare, and more whose returns were funded by Mexican pro-return groups. Even though Colina supported sending the poor and destitute back to Mexico, he objected to the scare campaign and the deportation dragnets occurring across the city. He intervened in various deportation cases and assisted with legal representation.[42] *La Opinión* likewise objected to the arrests and singling out of Mexicans and provided information to the Spanish-speaking public on how to avoid being deported.

The roughly 100,000 people who were repatriated from Los Angeles County in the early 1930s represented a third of the region's ethnic Mexican population. Government officials cut off food, denied legal rights, and sent men, women, and children to Mexico with no plan for their care. In the public sphere, the media landscape fed the worst stereotypes of Mexicans, leading to generalized fear. Few in leadership roles in the Spanish-language press, the consulates, and most Mexican organizations stood up for those who wanted their futures to be in the United States.

This loss profoundly affected those who were left behind. Mexican migrants expressed dismay at the options in front of them. *Corridos* from the early 1930s reflect their feelings of betrayal.[43] Once called upon to build the United States, now they were being rounded up. Some sang in support of return to Mexico, rejecting life in America. Others went further, calling for radical action. These include the "Corrido de California" by Bartolo Ortíz, which captures many of the choices migrants faced in the 1930s.[44] The song describes the suffering of the Depression and the circumstances that drove people to repatriate. Yet it also speaks of those who were radicalized by the experience and turned to communism. Ultimately, the narrator sees returning to Mexico as the solution and urges return.

People with pain in my hearing,
I'm going to sing to you
What our people suffer
Because of migration.

Because of the presidents
Of the big companies,
Many people are laid off
Almost every day.

Because of the lack of work
Or cases of indebtedness,
They abandon their homes
To leave the United States.

Since the year of '23
Until the present day,
There was abundance,
But now those times are gone.

In San Francisco and San Diego,
People can't find anything to do.
They have to go to Relief
to get something to eat.

For lack of work
The Mexicans leave,
Going to their free land,
The land where they were born.

Some go with their families
If circumstances allow,
And others are deported
From California to El Paso.

In the cement plants
Or on the construction projects,
People come every day.
It looks like a procession.

In the San Joaquin Valley,
It breaks your heart
To see the poor families
Now migrating.

Some go to San Francisco,
Others to the Imperial Valley,
Sent by the immigration officials
Of the federal government.

Thousands walk the streets,
All of them pale,
Just marking time
In the United States.

Some are communists,
Others speak of war,
Wishing for the fare
To return to their country.

Some migrants worked together to create alternative lives in Mexico. In the midst of a strike in the Imperial Valley in 1930, union president A. Mejía wrote to the President of Mexico asking for repatriation for his workers. After the defeat of the strike, the union created the *Vanguardia de Colònización Proletaria* and sought the lands in Baja California of the Colorado River Land Company, which owned 800,000 acres just south of the border. The organization raised $40,000 dollars and started a mass return. Groups of repatriates and other landless farm workers began to squat on the land and demand repatriation. Rather than see US inclusion as the goal, groups like these saw it as one of a range of possibilities.[45]

Despite the repatriations, most Mexicans stayed in California. Workers and families were still needed in the fields, and agricultural growers went so far as to recruit repatriated workers back during the harvest.[46] With fewer workers available, the balance of power shifted, and workers increasingly turned to labor militancy.

Organizing in the Fields

It was in the shadow of the Great Depression and repatriation from 1933 to 1936 that workers in the field launched the most intense series of organization drives and strikes in California's history. Dozens of strikes led by communist-affiliated unions broke out across the state, from the Imperial Valley to the San Joaquin Valley. John Steinbeck's novels brought national attention to the plight of these farm workers, though they focused attention on the white Okies and erased the Mexican, African American, and Asian participants, who made up the majority. In fact, the strikers were a multiracial coalition of those on the margins of the polity.

With families torn apart and displaced, the demographics of Southern California's Mexican population shifted. Those who were left behind tended to have more steady employment, to have families in the United States, to have lived in the country longer, and to own homes. By 1933, the average length of stay for Mexican migrants in California was over ten years, and half of those who participated in the strikes were citizens.[47] Despite the image of white Okies that dominates memories of this era, they did not arrive en masse until after 1936. The bulk of California's agricultural workers in the early 1930s were Mexicans and Filipinos.[48] These strikes were a continuation of transnational organizing traditions that originated in Mexico, rather than the efforts of particular unions.

Fifty thousand workers went on strike in 1933 alone.[49] Accustomed to seeing Mexicans as victims—as people to be saved, repatriated, or put in their place—the mainstream media could not fathom the idea of activist farm workers and sought to cast blame on communist agitators or an overzealous Mexican consul. But the strikes in the summer of 1933 had much deeper roots. In 1903, the interethnic Japanese Mexican Labor Association led a series of strikes in Oxnard and Ventura County, followed in the 1910s by IWW-led efforts that were defeated at the end of World War I.[50] Many migrants were familiar with organizing activities: some had been present at strikes in New Mexico and Texas in the 1920s, while some had joined radical anarchist organizations. Unionizing was not new, nor were many of the major organizers.

Mexican communities in Southern California blended various ideologies, cultures, and aspirations, with politics ranging from reactionary to anarchist. *Mutualistas* created community providing the basis for political and economic organization. By the early twentieth century, 80,000 people belonged to these civic associations in California. These organizations were forms of social insurance for the working class, paying for funerals and illnesses. Consuls worked with *mutualistas* to celebrate Mexican culture, promote Spanish-language libraries, and establish Spanish-language elementary schools, though no more than ten schools ever existed at once.[51] Los Angeles had enough *mutualistas* that they came together under the *Federación de Sociedades Mexicanas*, which was headquartered in a downtown building along with the consular offices.

In 1928, the *Federación de Sociedades Mexicanas* and the Mexican consulate joined various small unions to create the *Confederación de Uniónes Obreras Mexicanas* (CUOM). Led by Armando Flores, the union included a number of former communists as well as *Partido Liberal Mexicano* (PLM) and IWW members.[52] The union was meant to directly promote the interests of Mexican workers in the United States under a single banner. Culturally, CUOM promoted *México de Afuera*, deployed Mexican nationalist rhetoric, and avoided building alliances with other workers' groups. Consul F. A. Pesquierra explained the strategy of building separate unions as follows: "We desire friendly relations with the American unions, but no direct relations with them; we are too different. We cannot expect Mexicans to get the same wage scale as Americans for a long time. We want to establish relations with the CROM [*Confederación Regional Obrera Mexicana*, Mexico's largest federation of unions]."[53] At the same time, the CUOM pushed to limit new migration nationally. It launched a series of failed organizing drives, and by 1930, it had shrunk to only ten small locals. When the Depression struck, the organization supported repatriation back to Mexico.[54]

Other migrants were part of the radical tradition, having participated in the Mexican Revolution and radical movements in the borderlands. As union organizer Dorothy Ray Healey described, "Mexicans who would come over the border were products of the Mexican Revolution. They were very much influenced by anarchist-syndicalist ideas."[55] In the 1910s, Los Angeles had been the base of support for the exiled anarchist PLM, and Ricardo Flores Magón's *Regeneración* newspaper was based in Los Angeles.[56] Many PLM members were also members of the IWW, forming a network of Mexican organizers in both movements. Workers in the fields were sympathetic to the PLM and its ideals. Guillermo Velarde, who would lead one of the largest unions during the 1930s strikes, was a member of the IWW and the son of PLM organizer and revolutionary Fernando Velarde.

A large number of farm workers had PLM and IWW experience. Pedro Subia, for example, had a long history of mining labor activity in Santa Rosalía, Chihuahua, and had participated in strikes with Abrán Salcido in Morenci, Arizona, and with PLM organizers before going to Los Angeles. José Galván Amaro from Durango, Mexico, had similar experiences. A member of a mining family, he participated in the Mexican Revolution, then migrated to Arizona and Los Angles before becoming a leader in the strikes of 1931 to 1936.[57] The Gonzalez family was forced to move west in the 1920s after strikes in Miami, Arizona. Felix Gonzalez became a railroad worker for the Santa Fe in California, and the family occasionally worked in citrus fruits in Santa Ana, Orange Country.[58] All of these people were part of a wave of mining workers who left Arizona and moved to California in the 1920s in the aftermath of failed strikes. To them, California strikes were the continuation of a long history of migration and labor organizing.

Meanwhile, significant numbers of the rank and file of agricultural operations had previous experience in organizing from their years in the fields, railroads, and mines of the Southwest and maintained regular contact with Mexico. Others had experience in the beet fields of the Midwest or Texas, where everyday forms of resistance—from quitting to wildcat strikes—were common. Some of these workers had participated in Imperial Valley strikes in the 1920s, including the IWW effort in 1922.[59] In 1928, cantaloupe workers formed the *Unión de Trabajadores del Valle Imperial* and went on strike in Brawley. The strike was defeated when growers recruited poor whites and others to work the fields. Two years later, in 1930, 5,000 workers went on strike led by the Trade Union Unity League, the *Asociación Mutúa Mexicana*, and the Agricultural Workers Industrial League (AWIL). The Trade Union

Unity League worked across racial lines, with Filipino, Indian, and white workers joining the effort.[60]

The activities of the agricultural workers took place against a critical set of political events in the United States. After his election in 1932, Franklin Roosevelt declared a New Deal, passing a package of legislation aimed at ending the economic crisis. This included the Agricultural Adjustment Act, which gave growers subsidies to take crops off the market to stabilize prices. Then being passed in Congress, the National Industrial Recovery Act (NIRA), guaranteed the right of workers in industrial employment to unionize and created the National Labor Board to arbitrate disputes. As it was becoming law, organizing exploded across the country, as the American Federation of Labor (AFL) and, later, the CIO acted, and massive general industrial strikes broke out in San Francisco, Los Angeles, and other places. The NIRA being passed would not include agricultural workers, however, which meant that most African American, Mexican, and Asian workers were left out of the New Deal labor protections. Yet most workers were unaware of this and believed that Roosevelt approved of their organizing and union activity and the government would come to their aid against abusive growers.[61]

The AFL did not desire to build a multiethnic industrial coalition, and it supported the repatriation of Mexicans. In explaining why they didn't spend time trying to organize agricultural workers, AFL representative Paul Scharrenburg summed up the union's position to the *New York Times*: "Only fanatics are willing to live in shacks or tents and get their heads broken in the interests of migratory labor."[62] At the same time, concluding that it could not operate effectively within the AFL, the Communist Party began to form separate, independent unions, including organizing farm workers. The party was nearly alone in its attempts to organize African Americans, Mexicans, and Asians in addition to whites. The unions created by the party included the AWIL, which quickly drew people from around the Imperial Valley, where they participated in the strike of 1930. A year later, the union was reconstituted as the Cannery and Agricultural Workers' Industrial Union (CAWIU). Often depicted as a white-Jewish union, the CAWIU had many Mexicans in its ranks and in its leadership in the fields, many of whom were previous or current members of the PLM as well as the IWW and the Communist Party.[63] The overlapping links between radical organizers in these organizations made the 1930s strikes possible.[64] For example, Francisco Media was a Communist Party member and co-founder of the CAWIU, John Díaz worked as an organizer, Frank Samora was secretary of the union, Fred Martínez worked as an organizer in the Imperial Valley, and Angelo Fernando, Tony Poso, John Nava, and Ralph Rodríguez worked in Sunnyvale.[65] In 1933, the party also launched *Lucha Obrera*, a Spanish-language newspaper, to spread its message and to link the party's struggle to the anarchist-radical tradition in Mexico.[66]

In 1933, Mexican workers went on strike in the sugar beet fields from Colorado to Michigan. There were thirty-seven strikes in California that growing season, including 48,000 farm workers. The CAWIU participated in twenty-four of them, involving 33,000 workers, and the Filipino Labor Union led several more.[67] By then, the Mexican government had ended its financial commitment to help returnees; the Los Angeles Chamber of Commerce, which wanted Mexican labor, had stopped supporting repatriation; and repatriations had slowed to a trickle.[68] In the devastation of the 1930s, Mexicans proved particularly receptive to the communist-affiliated unions. This rush of unionizing activity surprised not just white growers but most of the news media, the government, charities, the Mexican consulate, and even unions themselves.

The LA County Berry Strike

The berry strike in Los Angeles County set the pattern for agricultural labor actions throughout the state. Located fifteen miles east of downtown Los Angeles where the San Gabriel River splits in two, El Monte was strategically located to take advantage of the county's agricultural growth. The town called itself the "first American city" in the state, implying it was founded by white colonial settlers from the South and that no one had previously lived there, though in fact indigenous and Mexican populations had lived there for centuries. The city proper was segregated, so non-white farm workers rented private land from farmers and built homes there. Built on riverbanks, these camps often flooded, washing away the homes.

Despite these conditions, by 1930 these camps had become permanent *colonias*, including the Hicks, Hayes, La Mission, Las Flores, Chino, La Granda, and Canta Ranas camps. People came here to work on a new form of large-scale industrial agriculture that relied on irrigation systems, close connections to associated manufacturing, refrigerated railroads to transport produce to faraway markets, and high-volume seasonal wage labor. This is what the founders of El Monte meant when they described the area in promotional literature, as a bountiful "winter garden." Indeed, by the mid-twentieth century, the valley was covered in large farms that produced oranges, lemons, walnuts, apricots, strawberries, and tomatoes; it also contained numerous dairy farms and horse ranches.[69]

Because this work was seasonal, laborers carved out a migratory existence. Pasquala Esparza and her children lived in El Monte with extended family until the work ended, when they would travel annually to the San Joaquin Valley to pick grapes and cotton. As her daughter Jesusita described it, "We didn't work November . . . December . . . January . . . But we used to buy our sack of beans . . . and we'd get our flour . . . so that we could live on those three months we didn't work."[70] Lucy Flores, who grew up outside the camp, told college student Pat Aroz, "Every summer, by August, you'd go into Hicks Camp, and there wouldn't be 50 people in it. Everybody would take off, and go up north, and pick cotton, or pick grapes, and come back. So if you went there in August or September, or whenever the seasons were, it was a ghost town. By October everybody would be back."[71]

The largest camp at El Monte, Hicks Camp, housed 1,000 people permanently year-round and up to 2,000 during the picking season. Mexican workers rented space in shanty camps outside of the city limits. The rent paid for the leveling and the spreading of gravel but not much else. Even the more prosperous Mexicans had to live in the camps because El Monte's racial housing covenants banned non-whites from purchasing homes. Schools and public facilities were segregated in the city.[72] Families living in the camps had to build their own homes, mostly from repurposed boxcars. By 1933, Hicks Camp had been in place for more than a decade, providing a home base to a generation of farm workers. Despite its ramshackle appearance, it was a permanent community with three churches, several grocery stores, restaurants, a walnut factory, and pool halls. Stores were sites of stability. Felix Ramos remembered growing up in his family's grocery store in the neighborhood, which was a center for information for area farm workers.[73] Another store was owned by Ignacio Gutierrez, who had migrated from Guanajuato and worked across the Southwest before marrying another migrant from Guanajuato and moving there.[74]

These camps were just some of the large number of *colonias* in Southern California that housed the region's multicultural labor force. As in other towns in the San Gabriel Valley, the Japanese and Chinese residents were also segregated, and their children attended the same schools as Mexicans, despite their middle-man, small-business role in the area's agricultural economy. The Japanese population of the county had increased to 37,000 people, many of whom were tenant farmers. The Japanese had become lease owners after the 1913 Alien Land Law prohibited them from owning agricultural land. As such, Japanese farmers turned to off-the-books leasing and low-capital truck farming that did not require as much investment in land that was owned by whites. Most were members of the Japanese Growers Association. While farms were mostly owned by proprietors, they tended to grow produce under contract to large national companies, with little flexibility in the price of their crops.

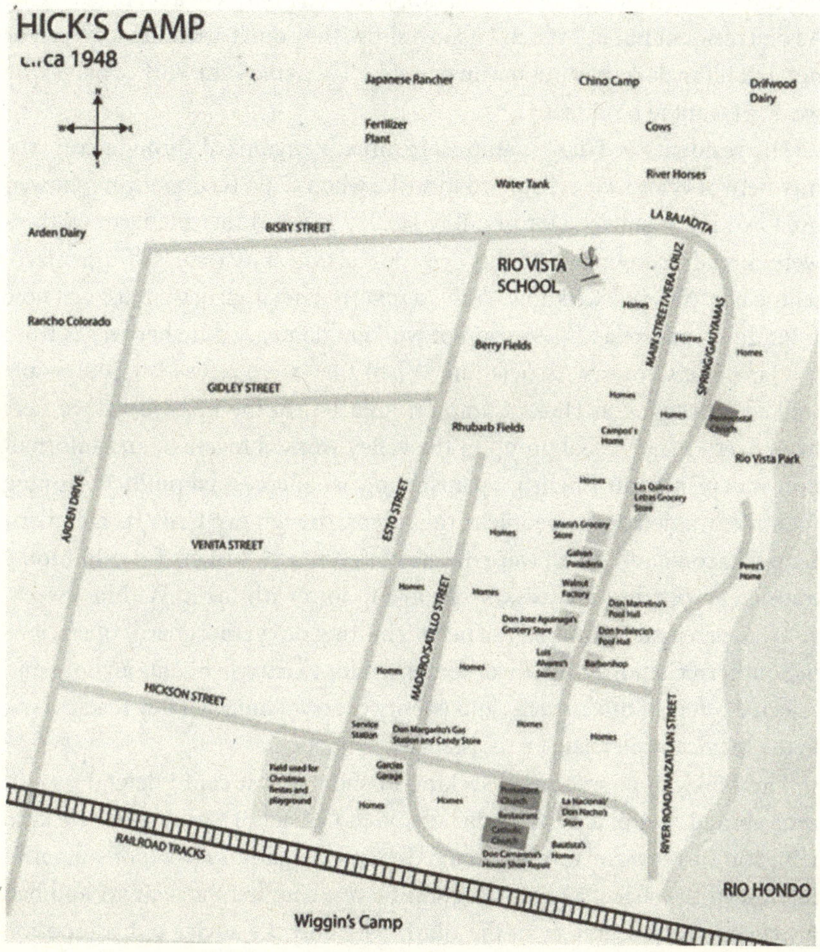

Figure 6.6 Hicks Camp, ca. 1948, based on recollections of families. Courtesy of La Historia Society, El Monte, California.

Conditions in the field deteriorated during the Great Depression. "Our working days were from sunrise to sundown," Richard Pérez remembered. "We would take a half-hour break in the middle of the day to eat. Every day was a working day. Weekends and holidays were unheard of."[75] Employers repeatedly lowered wages to the point that, by the early spring of 1933, workers were earning nine cents an hour. As discontent among berry pickers in the San Gabriel Valley grew, they started to take organized action. The migrant camps around El Monte had been hotbeds of activism since at least the 1910s, when PLM leader Ricardo Flores Magón held events there. Some people in El Monte were still part of the PLM two decades later. Residents in the camps had little use for assimilationist-based politics in a segregated city. As one resident put it, "When I go to a show, they don't ask if I'm a citizen or not, but if I'm dark they put me on one side. The same with work. That is why we don't want to be citizens."[76]

The residents in Hicks Camp were already organized through community networks and were disposed to strike when CAWIU organizers showed up. CAWIU organizer Dorothy Ray Healey recalled that the farm workers were already convinced of the need for action and were self-organized, telling her "Yes, yes, we know, *diablita roja* [red devil-girl], we must act, now calm down and relax."[77] A group of workers demanded higher wages from the Japanese Growers Association. When they were refused, 1,500 people walked off the job at Hicks Camp on June 1st. In the first weeks, workers from every major racial group in the valley worked together, and information was printed in English, Spanish, and Japanese. A committee running the strike was led by the people of the camps, though two CAWIU members, Lino Chacón and J. Ruiz, were on the committee.[78] Strikers from El Monte traveled across the valley asking people to join with them. Within a week, 7,000 people had walked off the fields, shutting down most berry operations in Southern California. The workers asked for twenty-five cents an hour and rejected offers of fifteen cents and twenty cents an hour.[79] They reached out to the Mexican consulate for assistance.

The Mexican government, seeking to show that it could defend its citizens abroad, jumped into the dispute. Vice-Consul of Los Angeles Ricardo Hill, son of Mexican revolutionary General Benjamin Hill, took an active interest in the strike, as did Armando Flores, who led the CUOM and had previously been secretary of the PLM.[80] Against the advice of his superior, Consul Alejandro Martinez, who did not want the Mexican government involved, Hill and Flores joined the strike committee and, at first, worked with the CAWIU and the radical leadership.[81] The Mexican government was primarily interested in getting a quick settlement for the workers, showing its effectiveness, and ensuring that the Mexican nationalists' union, *Obreras Mexicanas*, grew rather than the communist CAWIU.[82]

With direction from Mexico City, the consulate came to a tacit agreement with the police, the Japanese Growers Association, and the Los Angeles Chamber of Commerce to eliminate the communists from the strike. While the strike committee was at a local police station, Hill and Flores called a meeting at Hicks Camp in which they denounced the communist leaders of the strike committee. Hill told workers that if they expelled communists from the ranks, the Mexican government would do everything it could to aid their efforts. Later, the Los Angeles Police Department's Red Squad arrested all the CAWIU leadership and effectively removed them from the strike.[83] The CAWIU wrote leaflets denouncing this action, but this did not change the course of events. A new union was created, the Mexican Farm Labor Union, later known as the *La Confederación de Uniónes de Campesinos y Obreros Mexicanos* (CUCOM). This was a reconstituted CUOM with Armando Flores as president and affiliated with the CROM union in Mexico. Flores reached out to the Roosevelt administration, seeking arbitration under the NIRA. The president did not intervene, but the federal government did provide direct food aid for strikers, a first in American labor history.[84]

Newspapers on both sides of the border covered the strike heavily, making appeals to racial solidarity against the Japanese and for Mexican nationalism. The strike became a popular cause in *La Opinión* and other Spanish-language newspapers. In Mexico, President Abelardo Rodríguez supported the strike, and Foreign Secretary José Manuel Puig Casauranc got US Ambassador Josephus Daniels involved. But it was ex-President Calles who escalated the situation, sending money personally to the strikers and directing government aid—all this despite the strike occurring in another country. The CROM meanwhile organized a nationwide boycott of Japanese goods in Mexico. This put pressure on the Japanese community in Mexico, who experienced a rise in anti-Japanese sentiment and had their businesses threatened.[85]

The Japanese growers in California had their own struggles. Having been kept out of most of the business and power structures of the country, Japanese small business owners relied heavily on vertical networks and associations in order to take out loans, operate their companies, get their products to markets, and sell the products to customers. Japanese growers called on these associations during the strike, raising money and support from the community while lobbying the government and, eventually, the Japanese consulate. To fill their labor needs, at one point Japanese growers invited children to pick berries, and children were let out of school to work. The Los Angeles Chamber of Commerce had reasons to want the strike to end quickly. Most of the landowners had illegal tenant contracts with the Japanese growers, and they did not want attention drawn to these by a prolonged strike. Landowners were also concerned that enthusiasm for unionization could spread to agricultural workers across the county.

The Mexican government sought to dictate terms in messages sent to Washington, DC. In turn, the US Department of Labor's Conciliation and Mediation Service sent E. H. Fitzgerald to mediate the dispute. The sides met on June 26, with Japanese Consul Toshito Satow and S. Fukami of the Growers Association representing the growers and Vice-Consul Hill, Flores, and the strike committee representing the workers. The Los Angeles and El Monte Chambers of Commerce tried to force through an agreement that would raise wages but would not apply to all workers in the region. The workers surprised all of the organizations by rejecting this offer.[86] They demanded union recognition and $1.50 for a nine-hour workday for all workers in the region, and they insisted that any agreement had to include all the strikers. Despite the pressure and the elimination of the communist union from the strike committee, the workers in the field were energized and had no intention of backing down. They had brought in thousands of workers from across Southern California, including non-berry farms, and refused to accept an offer that did not include them as well.[87]

With less competition for jobs following the massive repatriation movement, the strikers knew their labor was needed and pressed that advantage. The President of the Los Angeles Chamber of Commerce regretted that "the loss of 150,000 Mexicans from California in the last three years [had created] a marked shortage of this type of labor."[88] Still believing that they knew their labor force, the Los Angeles Chamber of Commerce recommended that aid be given to strikers, on the idea that "a full-bellied Mexican rarely fights and is more tractable."[89] Federal New Deal officials and local charities gave direct food aid to agricultural strikers. At the same time, local officials were applying heavy pressure on workers and their families to take offers of repatriation to Mexico or offers of passage to the San Joaquin Valley to pick crops there.[90]

Figure 6.7 Manuela Melendez, resident of Hicks Camp. In El Monte, migrant workers organized for better wages, launching a wave of agricultural strikes across California. Melendez Family, Courtesy of La Historia Society, El Monte, California.

While labor camps were thought to be full of migratory networks with shallow roots, by the 1930s Southern California's *colonias* had developed into longstanding communities of families and strong ethnic networks capable of sustaining the extended strike. Both sides used their mutual

Figure 6.8 Earnest Ravago and co-workers. Courtesy of La Historia Society, El Monte, California.

organizations, newspapers, and consulates to raise money and continue the fight. The workers had around 600 active picketers a day, and across the *colonias*, people and organizations provided assistance. The Funeral Society, which normally arranged funerals for the dead, supported the strike by providing food to workers and their families. Women's networks of solidarity kept the efforts going, sharing resources and picketing alongside men. Strawberry picker Zenaida (Saidie) Castro, for example, was an important female leader whose ability to speak English made her particularly valuable within Hicks Camp. The strike committee sent delegates across the country and to Mexico to raise awareness. However, under the CUCOM, their rhetoric turned more nationalist, often pitting Mexicans against Japanese, even as it became less radical in its demands. While the early organizing efforts had included non-Mexicans, they began to leave the effort. At the same time, Guillermo Velarde from the leftist wing of the strike movement became vice president of the CUCOM.[91] Velarde and other union members sympathetic to the CAWIU managed to form an alliance with the communist union on the picket lines even as they were rivals elsewhere.[92]

By July, as the end of the season approached, and no end to the strike was in sight, desperate and hungry workers began to take the charities' offer of passage to the San Joaquin Valley. President Rodríguez of Mexico stepped in to mediate the discussions, while Japanese Consul Satow put heavy pressure on the growers. An offer of $1.50 for a nine-hour day and twenty cents an hour overtime was made, and the workers gave in and accepted. It is unclear if this strike was a victory or a defeat for the workers. Although they won higher wages than before the strike, it was a lower amount than had been offered in the first negotiations. On the other hand, they had gotten a taste of victory, and they knew they could exert pressure for higher wages. Workers had more faith in the CAWIU and the CUCOM, and got experience in organizing a strike. While the CAWIU claimed the strike had been betrayed, *La Opinión* and the consulate claimed it had shown that Mexican unions, with the support of the Mexican government, could take care of their own and achieve victory. This pattern of divided perspectives marked union drives across the state.

Southern California gained a reputation as a hub of labor unrest that would spread as workers migrated to the fields of the San Joaquin Valley. One worker named Garcia, on his way, was quoted as saying, "If there is no strike in the San Joaquin Valley now, there will be when we get there."[93] Growers like Francisco Palomartes knew this and sought to prevent workers from going north. He "did not desire to import any Mexican labor agitation."[94] Another grower, George Clements, thought the Mexicans were "strike mad."[95] Migration was propelling the spread of ideas and coordination among worker networks in California.[96] The Mexican consulates tried to guide the strikes to the more nationalist CUCOM and away from the communist CAWIU in an effort to show they could protect their nationals abroad. However, the labor movement could not be controlled that easily. Workers were frustrated, and many believed that both President Roosevelt and President Calles were on their side. Membership in the CAWIU grew tremendously in subsequent months, as did the ranks of the CUCOM, where Guillermo Velarde replaced Flores as secretary general and took the union in a leftward direction. The LA County Berry Strike was the largest agricultural strike in California's history to that point, but events in the San Joaquin Valley would soon overtake them.

San Joaquin Valley Cotton Strike

Muckraking journalist Carey McWilliams titled his book on the Central Valley's agricultural *Factories in the Field*, and reality matched the provocative title. As in Texas, the region's most important crop was cotton. Although California cotton workers earned more than their Texas counterparts, by 1932 the average wage had dropped to $2.14 a day, and most people earned $300 to $400 a year, well below the poverty line.[97] Encouraged by victories in other strikes across the state, in the late summer cotton workers in the San Joaquin Valley staged the largest strike in state history when 18,000 workers walked off the job.

The CAWIU had gained considerable experience over a few months. In August, it won a brief grape strike at Tangus Ranch in the Central Valley as well as strikes in San Jose and the Oxnard beet fields.[98] Worker committees from the cotton camps approached the organization to deal with the crisis in the cotton fields. While 75% of the workers were Mexican, significant numbers were white Okie migrants, Filipinos and other Asian immigrants, and African Americans. Being a loose organization of work sites, CAWIU's committee included representatives from each major ethnic demographic, though most of the leadership was white. Among the organizers was 16-year-old Dorothy Ray Healey, who would later become a union organizer for the United Cannery, Agricultural, Packing, and Allied Workers of America (UCAPAWA).[99] Bill Hammet and Cecil McKiddy were the main spokesmen for the Okie migrants. Veteran CAWIU organizers Caroline Decker, Pat Chambers, and Pat Callahan were the primary organizers. Caroline Decker, who had nearly been killed while organizing coal miners in Appalachia, was a particularly skilled labor leader and became the public voice of the strike.[100] Among the workers, Lino Sánchez was the primary leader.[101]

Strikers were ejected from their homes by landowners, and as a result, the bulk of the cotton pickers set up camps on public land and land belonging to sympathetic small farmers. Conditions at these camps were poor, with residents lacking basic sanitation, water, and soon, food. The largest of these camps, and the strikers' base, was Camp Corcoran. While people turned to community networks for sustenance and solidarity, county officials and

Figure 6.9 Mexican mother in California. "Sometimes I tell my children that I would like to go to Mexico, but they tell me 'We don't want to go, we belong here.'" Dorothea Lange, 1935. Library of Congress Prints and Photographs Division, LC-USF347- 000825-C-A.

growers sought to isolate the camp and, eventually, clear it. Tensions also existed between camp residents and the city of Corcoran. The school and hospital at Corcoran refused to accept any strikers or their children.[102]

The cotton strike attracted an array of interest groups with their own political priorities. In addition to the Spanish-language press, it was extensively covered by the state's major newspapers and garnered the sympathy of many liberal New Dealers. Carey McWilliams, Paul Taylor, and other writers/observers wrote favorable reports. Dorothea Lange took photos of the strike and labor conditions in the fields; John Steinbeck was creatively inspired to write his novels. When the starving strikers sent Percilla Carlo, a white Okie migrant from the South, to meet with Governor James Rolph, the governor was moved enough to send direct food relief so that the strike could continue.[103] A united front of large agricultural interests, the Republican state establishment, most of the state's newspapers, and local police stood in opposition to the strikers. As during the LA County Berry Strike, Mexican Consul Enrique Bravo sought to negotiate for the Mexican workers and split them from the communist CAWIU, arguing that the consulate could negotiate higher wages. He was continuously rebuffed by workers, and the strike remained in CAWIU's hands.

The strike was a direct assault on the power of farmers, who turned to violence. After the sheriff deputized farmers, a mob converged on the strike headquarters, where 350 men, women, and children had gathered. In the resulting confrontation, Delfino D'Avila, a representative of the Mexican consul, was shot and killed, and then the mob started firing indiscriminately into the crowd. Two more people, Dolores Hernenez and Pedro Subia, were killed and several more shot. This violence brought the federal government into the strike. George Creel, West Coast head of the National Rifle Association, created a commission made up of prominent Californian New Dealers to listen to all sides while the federal government provided direct relief to strikers. The commission settled at seventy-five cents a pound, less than the strikers wanted but more than the growers were willing to give.

Creel and Bravo pressured both sides. Officials withheld food from the strikers, threatened to cut off Agricultural Adjustment Act subsidies to the farmers, and allowed strikebreakers to act. When they threatened to repatriate strikers if they didn't back down, workers responded by saying they had already made plans to return to Mexico.[104] In the meantime, nine infants in the camps died of malnutrition, and an adult, Sabas Aguilas, died after the local hospital refused to treat her. Worn down by violence and lack of food, the strikers accepted seventy-five cents. After the strike, the shooters were acquitted by an all-white jury.[105]

There were at least three dozen strikes in the California fields that year.[106] For the CAWIU, the strategy was to learn where strikes were breaking out and organize the workers into the union after the fact.[107] As Caroline Decker put it, "Nine times out of ten . . . we would learn about these strikes from reading about them in the paper."[108] Pat Chambers agreed: "There would have been strikes anyways. Strikes were breaking out all over. Those strikes would have happened union or no union. It was the historical moment for them."[109] The CAWIU was successful in achieving higher wages in peas, peaches, and cherry fields. Although it achieved such wins in most strikes, it never secured a union contract, a vulnerability that was soon exposed.

The Imperial Valley

The Imperial Valley continued to rely on migrant farm workers through the Great Depression. While most of this workforce was Mexican, it also included Filipinos, Indians, whites, Native Americans, and African Americans. Thousands of workers lived in the *colonias* of Brawley, El Centro, Calipatria, and Calexico on the US-Mexico border. After the failed 1928 strike, another large strike involving 5,000 workers led by the AWIL was quickly repressed in 1930, and by 1933, lettuce workers' wages had fallen to fifteen cents an hour. The anti-communist Mexican consulate sought to organize the workers and avoid a showdown, but most of the Mexican workers wanted higher wages than the consulate was proposing and wildcat strikes began. Lettuce pickers asked the CAWIU to take the lead, and Dorothy Ray Healey, Pat Chambers, and others responded.

The strike quickly grew to involve around 6,000 workers, though the exact number is unknown. Again, separate committees were created for each ethnic group of workers. Joaquín Terrazas, Consul in the Imperial Valley, opposed the CAWIU and worked with growers to create an anti-communist *Asociación Mexicana* union.[110] Escalating from previous strikes, this one involved more organized violence. Anti-communist organizations, farmers' groups, and the American Legion led an effort to have the strike leaders arrested, and a mob beat and ran out of town several American Civil Liberties Union lawyers who came to defend the strikers. A federal intervention by Labor Secretary Frances Perkins and retired Army General Pelham

Glassford failed to settle the strike or end the vigilante violence. The growers defeated the effort, and 2,000 people were evicted from the strike camp by force. A National Labor Relations Board commission later found wholesale disregard for the law among state authorities during the strike.[111] In the aftermath of the Imperial Valley strike, various agricultural organizations joined to create the Associated Farmers. On the surface, this organization coordinated political campaigns to support candidates favorable to landowners, but it also organized farmers to inflict vigilante violence on workers.

Several months later, most of the leadership of the CAWIU was arrested during another strike in Santa Clara, put on trial for criminal syndicalism, and convicted and sent to jail following one of the longest trials in California's history. The anti-communist atmosphere nationwide made it increasingly difficult for Mexican migrants to openly affiliate with the communist CAWIU, and the organization ceased working in the fields. Soon afterward, the Communist Party shifted its activities to existing unions and ended it support for farm workers.[112] Incensed that farm workers had been able to

Figure 6.10 Large-scale agriculture in the Imperial Valley. Gang labor, Mexican and white, from the Southwest. Dorothea Lange, 1939. Library of Congress Prints and Photographs Division, LC-USF34- 019156-C.

get food relief during the strikes, farmers pressured the state and federal governments, and in 1935, the California Relief Administration and Works Progress Administration agreed to drop workers who refused agricultural work.[113] Raising the specter of a foreign communist threat, the Associated Farmers would go on to defeat nearly every union drive in the fields of California in the next few years.[114] In the meantime, farming associations moved away from hiring migrant labor from Mexico and instead recruited from Texas, facilitating the transition to a predominantly US-born Mexican American workforce.

The brutal end of the Imperial Valley strike prompted a renewed effort to return to Mexico. Thousands of workers migrated to the Mexicali Valley in large caravans over the next year. By 1935, the Mexican side reported record crops, while the US Imperial Valley reported a large labor shortage. Lázaro Cárdenas visited Mexicali during his campaign and, upon being elected president, he pressured the Colorado River Land Company to sell their land to farmers. Saturnino Cedillo and other government officials urged these workers to return to Mexico. Repatriates mixed with other landless farmers. Finally, mass armed takeovers and sit-down protests of farmers prompted Cárdenas to seize and redistribute the land in 1937.[115]

New Opportunities, 1936–1940

Even the citrus industry, long seen as a bastion of labor stability, was not immune from the demands of workers. By 1930, citrus had grown into one of California's largest industries, yet few of the citrus towns in Southern California joined in the labor convulsions occurring across the state. This was partly due to the nature of citrus towns and citrus companies, which provided better homes and facilities than other industries. Another was the nature of citrus fruit itself. Citrus provided nearly constant work for eight months of the year, and the work and prices did not vary substantially from year to year. This made it possible for Mexicans to establish permanent homes in barrios in these places, and the profitability of the business allowed employers to offer higher wages than other types of agriculture. In LA and Orange Counties, citrus workers, mostly families, tended to stay in one for location longer periods. Only 17% of citrus workers were non-residents.[116] In the four-month off-season, citrus workers did participate in migratory circuits, but over smaller distances. Most went to the San Joaquin Valley, but they did not transfer any labor organizing after the season. In towns in the San Gabriel Valley and Orange County like Upland, La Verne, Pasadena, and Azusa, significant numbers of Mexicans owned their own homes, something few in the San Joaquin or Imperial Valleys could claim.[117] As a result of these more controlled conditions, which workers compared to *haciendas* in Mexico, most of the citrus-growing workforce did not turn to union organizing.[118]

The industry was not entirely free from strikes, however. In 1936, workers at citrus operations in Orange County near Santa Ana went on strike. Following the shutdown of the CAWIU in 1934, the Mexican nationalist CUCOM became the leading union among agricultural workers. It grew to fifty local unions and 5,000 members as it absorbed former CAWIU members. With Guillermo Velarde at its helm, it had expanded into a multiracial Mexican, Filipino, and white organization that worked with more radicals to organize the fields. A few months prior to the Orange County strike, Velarde and the CUCOM had led the "Backyard Strike" outside Los Angeles—again against Japanese farmers—but had backed down after relentless persecution.[119] In a series of strikes in LA County, the CUCOM had won better wages and even union recognition at some worksites.[120] With this momentum, they moved into the citrus fields. This time, 2,500 workers struck and faced a "state of siege" involving mass arrests.[121] The picket lines became violent as strikers sought to keep scabs from working. Mexican Consul Ricardo Hill pursued a quick, negotiated settlement, but it applied only to Mexican citrus workers. In a statement rejecting the agreement, the union declared, "We will never sign any agreement that ignores the other nationalities and the success of the working class depends on all the workers working together toward the common aim."[122] In response, the Associated Farmers worked with growers, city officials, and local police to defeat the strike through violence. The strike collapsed after Velarde was jailed.[123]

Smaller strikes at sites ranging from dairy farms to fruit orchards erupted during these years, but striking became especially dangerous in the face of the Associated Farmers' violence and anti-communist red baiting. Mexican consulates became involved in labor struggles in order to support Mexican unions that, as in Mexico, would be part of the cooperative governing structure, but they found themselves embattled with communist unions that enjoyed widespread appeal.[124] On the picket lines, moderates and radicals worked together. These strikes were the last large actions in the 1930s that were organized solely along Mexican nationalist lines. In 1937, the CUCOM became a founding member of the United Cannery, Agricultural, Packing, and Allied Workers of America (UCAPAWA).[125] That year, the UCAPAWA, affiliated with the CIO, started organizing in the San Joaquin Valley, and the AFL began organizing significant numbers of factory workers in Los Angeles. The success and growth of the communist-affiliated unions, including the UCAPAWA, forced mainstream American unions to open spaces for minorities in their ranks.[126]

The UCAPAWA brought a new generation of US-born ethnic Mexicans into the labor movement. The destruction of the more radical unions did not end organizing; the consulates did not fade into irrelevance. The Mexican consulate continued to be involved in labor strikes, sought to promote the Mexican government-affiliated *Confederación de Trabajadores Mexicanos del Norte* in the late 1930s, and took a position on issues such as school segregation into the 1940s and 1950s.[127] The bulk of its efforts in the 1940s and 1950s, however, were in support of the new Bracero Program workers rather than long-time migrants.[128] By 1937, the bulk of the Mexicans in California were long-term residents. One study of cannery workers by the California Unemployment Reserves found that the average residency had reached fifteen years.[129] The UCAPAWA was associated with the Communist Party, and between 1938 and 1945, it became the seventh-largest union in the CIO. In California, the union was primarily Mexican and Filipino, was made up of young women, and relied on leaders like Dorothy Ray Healey.[130]

The UCAPAWA managed to succeed where the CAWIU had not, organizing some of the largest fruit canneries in the state and securing relatively high wages for their workers. It was the fastest-growing agricultural union in California's history until large scale violence carried out by the Associated Farmers defeated its field efforts. However, it found fertile ground in stable agricultural towns with large settled populations in cannery operations and food-processing plants. The union organized strikes across the nation in 1938, 1939, and 1940, including the Pecan Shellers Strike in San Antonio, led by Emma Tenayuca. Building on hard-won experience, the union stressed the American-ness of its cross-racial membership while relying on the ethnic social webs in members' networks and communities. Luisa Moreno later expanded these efforts by establishing *El Congreso de Pueblos de Hablan Española* (the Spanish Speaking People's Congress), which drew dozens of Mexican organizations across the country to work on labor and civil rights. Moreno and *El Congreso* argued for Mexican's belonging in the United States based on their labor and long history in the Southwest, encouraging people to become citizens and press for civil rights.

However, even later, more successful labor efforts could not counter the dynamics of the period, especially as the Popular Front gave way to the Red Scare. By the late 1940s, Moreno and five Filipino leaders had been deported, and brutal tactics from the rival Teamsters broke the union's efforts in the 1950s.[131]

In the late 1930s, mainstream unions opened their doors to significant numbers of Mexicans for the first time. In addition to the UCAPAWA, several other AFL- and CIO-affiliated unions organized workers in the factories. In Los Angeles, the International Ladies' Garment Workers' Union organized thousands of men and women in 1933. That year, the workers of Local 96, who were mostly Mexican women, won a dressmakers' strike. In 1937, the CIO-affiliated United Furniture Workers of America incorporated Mexicans into its ranks, as did the Steel Workers Organizing Committee, many members of which later joined the Los Angeles-based Community Service Organization. That same year, while a student at the University of Southern California, Mexican American Bert Corona began his long career in labor and civil rights activism with the CIO and the International Longshoremen's and Warehousemen's Union.[132] The leaders of these organizations built on older Mexicanist forms of organizing. Many had been members of *mutualistas* and other organizations in the 1920s, and they drew on Mexican imagery and the Spanish language as well as American symbols and citizenship-based claims for rights.[133] These unions helped build a Mexican American middle class, one that was urban, no longer migratory, and no longer looking to Mexico. But for migratory workers in the fields, organizing successfully would have to wait until the 1960s.

In the 1940s, agricultural migrants were increasingly replaced by un-free, contract-bound braceros from Mexico; this vision of the political economy of migrant labor did not include Mexicans as possible Americans. Like African Americans, Mexicans and other minorities were mostly left out of the social rights and entitlements ushered in by the New Deal. This was not for lack of trying. Workers in the fields believed they had a right to unionize even as they were left out of the worker legislation of the era. They organized throughout the 1930s to claim the rights that the New Deal espoused for all. John Steinbeck's books, especially *The Grapes of Wrath*, came to define these strikes and the Great Depression in the minds of the American public and earned its writer the Nobel Prize in Literature. However, Steinbeck's works, and Dorothea Lange and Paul S. Taylor's book *An American Exodus*, focused on white Okies rather than the multicultural majority.

The series of strikes discussed in this chapter have typically been examined through the lens of identity, or how US power structures ended the strikes, or how the Mexican government sought to incorporate Mexicans in the United States into its corporatist governing structure. The Los Angeles and San Francisco consulates, under the leadership of Enrique Bravo, F. A. Pesquierra, Armando Flores, and Ricardo Hill, have drawn criticism for their actions during the strikes of the 1930s, especially the LA County Berry Strike of 1933. Bravo took a hard line against the communist CAWIU and orchestrated its ouster from the coalition, a move he defended as pragmatic for reaching a deal but that has been criticized as weakening the strike at a critical juncture. Similar episodes occurred throughout the decade. The consuls repeatedly sided against communist unions and sought to have nationalist unions lead the strikes instead.[134] That said, in light of the considerable violence faced by strikers and Mexicans in particular and the hostility of American and Mexican authorities to communism, migrant workers would likely not have succeeded had they been organized along explicitly communist lines. Connections to the New Deal and Mexican states may have kept the violence from becoming even more extreme or widespread. Over the following decade, the rhetoric disguising workers' exploitation by portraying their actions as a threat to American civilization only escalated.

The 1930s was a transitional time for Mexicans in the United States, as the power of *México de Afuera* declined but did not go away and that of US-based institutions increased.[135] Part of this shift was demographic; more than 40% of the Mexican-born population repatriated to Mexico. In the fields of California, repatriation was the greatest factor in shifting the labor market and the mentality of those who stayed behind. While devastating to those repatriated, it created a new opportunity for those left remaining. They could cripple growers' profits by delaying crops just a few weeks, and the political climate seemed more open to such challenges. Their labor was still needed, and they saw a chance to improve their circumstances. Relying on deeply rooted interconnected communities, migrant workers created new spaces for action in the fields that took even their own organizers by surprise. They sought to survive and maintain agency in the face of increasingly oppressive economic and political structures. While some sought inclusion, others sought a return to Mexico, and still others joined more radical calls for action. These struggles pushed against the prevailing definitions of citizen, acting as transnational citizens while seeing themselves as Mexican.[136]

Agricultural migrant workers made a claim to economic citizenship, seeking to join the New Deal. During the height of the Great Depression, radical unions gave agricultural workers an outlet to organize that responded to their real needs. The vast circulation of these workers across the landscape ensured that their ideas would quickly spread across the region. Shocked by these strikes, the public insisted they had to be the result of outside communist agitators and used this to justify their violent reaction. However, strikers carried these ideas and experiences from their participation in the Mexican Revolution, World War I, the IWW, the PLM, and the Communist Party, as well as decades of cross-border Mexican labor radicalism.[137] Those who participated in strikes did so with a language and vision that had deep historical roots in Mexican communities. All these labor-organizing groups used symbols of a shared Mexican national memory as they made claims to the rights of the American working class. Even after they were defeated, veterans of the 1933 strikes continued to form the nucleus of this period's organized strike activity. Decades later, El Monte activists involved in the Chicano movement of the 1960s would recall these strikes and their parents' pro-union stance as critical to their own activism.[138]

Although the organizing activity among migrant farm workers between 1933 and 1936 happened at the same time as unionizing activity spiked across the United States, it has been omitted from most accounts of this period. Yet this series of strikes, especially the 1933 LA County Berry Strike, showed that it was possible to organize workers in the fields, that workers could be organized across racial lines, and that migrants could take the lead in organizing. By building on the structures that already existed in their communities—networks, local associations, *mutualistas*, newspapers, and Mexican consulates—they proved successful in working with all those who were willing to risk their bodies to organize the fields.

7

El Retorno

Remaking Lives in Mexico, 1930–1942

The family of Mariana Gonzalez faced a difficult choice. They had crossed into the United States during the Mexican Revolution, as was mentioned in Chapter 2, when the father, Felix, became a miner in Miami, Arizona. After the defeat of the unionization movement, Felix had taken a job with the Santa Fe Railway and moved to Santa Ana, California, and then El Monte, where he settled the family.[1] He and his wife, María de la Cruz, by then had two US-born daughters, Guadalupe and Mariana. When the Great Depression hit, Felix, the only wage earner, found himself out of a job. Caught up in the repatriation drives of Southern California, the Gonzalezes received rail passes to Mexico. Felix decided it would be best to return to their hometown in La Barca, Jalisco, where his parents and relatives still lived. However, their daughters did not want to go, especially 16-year-old Guadalupe, who was in a relationship with a man in El Monte.[2] Guadalupe convinced her parents to let her stay, and she married and settled in El Monte.[3]

Eleven-year-old Mariana went with her parents to live in rural Jalisco. Felix had imagined that his family could settle there permanently, but he and María were unable to secure their own land and instead worked as *peones* (farm laborers) on an apricot plantation. After a few years, Felix fell ill and died, leaving María to take care of Mariana. Their lack of resources most likely contributed to Mariana's marriage at a young age to Fermin Morales, an artisan metal worker who made gear for the *charro* (cowboy) market in Jalisco. She gave birth to three children and seemed to have settled down permanently in La Barca. However, she voiced her desire to return to the United States, insisting to anyone who would listen that she was an American and should never have been repatriated to Mexico.[4]

Migrants like Mariana were caught in a bind. A natural-born US citizen, she nevertheless found herself repatriated, a landless farm worker in Jalisco, enmeshed in a community that was suspicious of her poor Spanish and that wanted her to assume the role of a traditional rural Mexican wife. If in the

Between Here and There. Daniel Morales, Oxford University Press. © Oxford University Press 2024.
DOI: 10.1093/oso/9780197612590.003.0008

United States Mexican migrants and Mexican Americans were not seen as truly American, subject to expulsion from the country, the hundreds of thousands of people who migrated back to Mexico challenged ideas of nation and community in Mexican society. The press, intellectuals, and most importantly, successive governments took the position that migrants should return to reconstruct the nation. Although the Mexican government's cooperation and promotion of return made repatriation a reality, government projects faltered when faced with the volume of returnees, and many questioned whether these people hurt rather than helped the nation.[5] Ultimately, government neglect of repatriates' actual needs worsened their suffering. This chapter centers on the actions of migrants like Mariana, who returned to Mexico, spoke to the government, settled in communities, joined agrarian movements, and sought to return to the United States. Their everyday actions created new realities.

Migrants used the government's rhetoric of return to claim entitlement to resources from the government as legitimate citizens deserving of government aid. Between 1930 and 1940, they wrote thousands of letters to the Mexican consulates, the *Secretaría de Relaciones Exteriores* (SRE), the *Departamento de Migración*, and the president of Mexico to advocate for themselves as part of the polity of Mexico, even from the United States. Spurred by this promise and tired of Americans' discrimination, a significant number of migrants believed the claim that Mexican society would welcome them. Their actions illustrated a genuine desire to return to Mexico if they were able to own land.

Faced with dire economic circumstances and receiving little support from the government, the repatriates fell back on the aid of local communities. Returnees' relationships with social and state structures, such as local, state, and federal governments as well as repatriation societies, land-reform organizations, the Catholic Church, and the returnees' own families, shaped their experience of return. With the support of communities, the process of adjustment and resettlement was difficult but not impossible. Hometowns provided structural support for resettlement and reassimilation as well as remigration to the United States in the latter part of the decade. These communities also incorporated them into the ongoing land reform movement in Mexico. However, land reform did not resolve the structural causes of migration, and in the late 1930s and especially the 1940s, a second generation from central Mexico turned to migration as an economic survival strategy. By the 1940s, a mixed agrarian-remittance economy was taking shape that would drive Mexican migration through the Bracero era and beyond.

After repatriates crossed the border from the United States, they continued to move within Mexico.[6] And for some, especially second-generation Mexican Americans, "returning" meant going to the United States rather than to Mexico. Mexican archives about the repatriates are dominated by the records of agricultural colonies, leading to a disproportionate focus on the Mexican government's policies, especially the creation and promotion of settlement colonies.[7] Yet only 5% of returning migrants went to colonies, and possibly as few as 1.25%.[8] Some 15% went to urban centers, and 80% returned rural Mexico.[9]

If state policies and transnational capital created the economy of migration, it was also the result of millions of individual choices made to support families and communities.[10] The same is true of return. The story of Mexican repatriation illustrates the ways in which migrants changed with, adapted to, and endured these events. Their adjustments were not determined by the Mexican government's policies but instead by their families' social capital. Those who went to colonies mostly fared poorly, as few colonies succeeded and people drifted away. In urban centers, those who brought resources, skills, and social capital did well; those who lacked these assets struggled to survive. Most migrants went to their home regions, where they adjusted to rural life to varying degrees. Some married and settled into their region, while others joined ongoing *agraristas* (armed militias made of people who pressured the government for land redistribution). There is significant evidence that Mexican migration continued through the 1930s, especially among the second generation. By the 1940s, an agricultural-migrant economy was beginning to take shape, in which migrating and landholding were not opposed but formed part of the supporting structure of rural life in central Mexico.

The Rhetoric of Return

Post-revolutionary rhetoric in Mexico had condemned migration, and in this vein, public intellectuals, government officials, and successive presidents of Mexico took the Great Depression as an opportunity. Throughout the Mexican public sphere, writers called on the government to sponsor return, especially colonies. In January of 1930, President Pascual Ortiz Rubio visited the United States and gave a widely disseminated speech inviting Mexicans to return home.[11] Unlike US society, which turned a blind eye toward the suffering of migrants and sought to deport them, he announced that Mexico would welcome them with open arms. His call was echoed by other federal leaders in Mexico, the Mexico City press, and the consulates.[12]

Within the government, bureaucrats and high-ranking officials called for action. M. G. Calderon of the SRE argued that the Depression would enable Mexico to gain highly skilled agricultural and industrial workers at no expense who could then cultivate abandoned agricultural lands. Juan José Ríos, *Secretario de Gobernación*, believed there were up to 250,000 workers who would not just contribute to industrial development but could bring culture and civilization. More practically, engineer Javier Sanchez Mejorada, who expanded irrigation projects across Mexico, saw repatriates as the ideal candidates for colonization due to their familiarity with irrigated industrial farming operations.[13] And Andres Ortiz, governor of Chihuahua, believed the expulsion of workers by the US government offered an opportunity to rebuild the economy and put President Ortiz Rubio's call into action.

Partido Liberal Mexicano (PLM) co-founder Enrique Flores Magón turned his attention to the repatriates. The revolutionary had returned to Mexico a few years earlier following a long exile and imprisonment and was appointed subhead of the *Departamento de Migración*. Flores Magón was familiar with the situation of migrants in the United States from his years of PLM efforts. Back in Mexico, during a convention on migration, he contended that returnees would bring more advanced US agricultural techniques and laid out a plan for them to farm unused and abandoned land. Later, he presented President Abelardo Rodríguez with plan for repatriation that proposed a 1% tax on land to help fund the construction of repatriation colonies.[14]

These positions were echoed in the press. Federico Cervantes wrote in *El Universal* that these highly skilled workers would be glad to use their strength and intelligence to build their homeland. Jorge Ferretis reiterated nineteenth-century Mexican ideas about immigration by arguing that most of Mexico's population was passive, mostly native and mestizo, and lacking the desire to improve their lives. He believed Mexicans in the United States were lighter skinned, and so would inject white blood by their return, thereby improving the quality of people in the country. Froylán Manjarrez of *El Nacional* joined in arguing repatriates' racial characteristics would improve the economy and nation.[15]

(a)

THE MEXICAN COMES TO THE LAND OF GREAT TOOLS

(b)

AND TAKES SOME OF THEM BACK HOME WITH HIM

Figure 7.1a and b Diego Rivera depicts return migrants as bearers of knowledge and technology. From *Survey Graphic*, May 1, 1931, p. 173.

Much of the Mexican elite believed in return, but it was Manuel Gamio who set the terms. His studies were disseminated widely, and most in the government came to agree with his views that migrants learned modern technical, cultural, and moral ways outside the country. Diego Rivera, a strong believer in technical progress, created a series of drawings to promote the idea with the caption "The Mexican comes to the Land of Great Tools and Takes some of them back with him." In them, repatriates are depicted bringing back farm machinery to a new post-revolutionary town that had built a school and redistributed lands to *ejidos* (communal land-owning) in 1931, years before most redistribution had taken place. These images accompanied an essay by Gamio promoting colonies.[16]

Organizations Seek Return

While Mexican government officials promoted return as the best option at a time of mass unemployment, this sentiment was much more ambiguous in Mexican barrios across the United States. Some migrants promoted return, but others made it clear they were driven by destitution. Bartolo Ortíz, a popular singer in San Antonio, gave voice to these feelings of longing for home while facing betrayal. In the second half of the song "Corrido de California," he expressed a message common in such songs—the desirability of returning to Mexico rather than stay in a nation that had rejected Mexico's people:

Fly, fly, little dove,
With your hat in your hand,
go and tell Ortiz Rubio
that there go the Mexicans.

Ortiz Rubio promises them
that the Mexicans who leave
will get travel fare
from the border to their homes.

Some go singing,
other unfortunate ones sleep,
thinking of their property
left behind in the United States.

Some are afraid,
and tell their brothers
that if they want to work,
they have to become citizens.

In Mexicali and Nogales
in Piedras Negras and El Paso,
you can see many countrymen
that are going back home.

In the town of San Fernando
It's not something to laugh about,
they blocked off the town
on Ash Wednesday.

They created a great panic,
remember this well,
in the Barrio del Rebote
they rounded up the people.

They asked for passports,
women and children crying,
they took away my father—
God knows when I'll see him.

It's very sad, my friends,
to live under these conditions,
where you have to humiliate yourself,
bowing to foreign ideas.

We must leave this country,
all of us back to our land,
so they won't have a chance
to throw us out.

The one who composed these verses,
left in an airplane,
he wants to stand
on Mexican soil.[17]

The SRE and the *Departamento de Migración* played key roles in the logistics. Consuls kept the Mexican government informed, and they reported to agents at the border and in Mexico City when trains and cars of new arrivals were expected in border towns, the conditions of the passengers, and whether they needed funds.[18] The *Departamento de Migración* coordinated trains back to hometowns and emergency assistance once migrants were back in Mexico.[19] Annual returns grew from 91,972 people in 1930 to 115,705 in 1932, but declined markedly after this as most who were inclined to leave already had.[20]

Civic organizations petitioned the Mexican government for repatriation; these included existing organizations such as the *mutualistas*, unions, *Cruz Azuls*, and groups that were created specifically for return.[21] The *Comisiónes Honorificas* took on the largest role in coordinating repatriation drives.[22] The *Comisión Honorifica* of Pittsburg, California, wrote to the government on behalf of dozens of destitute families there, saying that most of these people had not worked for the previous two years, lived in poor conditions, and wished to return home.[23] A representative of the *Comité Reconstructor* said that dozens of families were ready to move to Mexico and contribute to the nation's progress if only part of their costs could be covered by Mexico. He described these families as suffering because they had refused to become US citizens, but he warned that, if the Mexican government offered no help with repatriation, their children might become American.[24] Concern over children's loyalties was a common refrain in letters.

The *Comisión Honorifica* of Wiley, Colorado, sent letters to President Ortiz Rubio painting a picture of desperation and hunger in Colorado. The commission described eighty families that desired to return because they wanted to die in their homeland, ending with an appeal to *La Raza*.[25] Gustavo del Rio wrote from Lorain, Ohio, representing a small organization there. He told President Ortiz Rubio that his plan could make use of all two million people in *México de Afuera*, where they would add to the nation, and that return would Mexicanize them.[26] Nemesio Peña y Ramo Gòmez asked for help for himself and his fellow Mexican migrants who had been laid off from their jobs in Rockdale, Illinois. He emphasized that, without help, they would have to resort to crime and dishonorable actions to feed their families.[27] He implied that, by helping people repatriate, the Mexican government would maintain not only its own honor but that of all Mexicans in the United States. In writing for his organization *Luz Salaz*, a cotton picker in Mississippi said that he was out of work and could not afford to return to Mexico with his family, and that fifty families in the area faced the same situation. He also bemoaned that his children were becoming Americanized, could not be controlled, and did not help the family. He wanted them to know how to be Mexican. His letter ended a patriotic call for nineteenth-century republican hero, Benito Juarez and "*¡Viva México!*"[28]

Organizations drew on the modernist and patriotic vision that the government advocated in order to promote their own plans to the government. Luis Vera, president of a colony organization, argued that the government should assist members of his group so that they would use their skills to improve the land and help bring modern agriculture to Mexico. Meanwhile, Rosalinoo Araiza, another organizer, highlighted the ways that the people in his group continued being part of the Mexican body politic outside of the country through their devotion to Mexico.[29] With names like the *Comité Pro-Repatriación* and the *Vanguardia de Colonización Proletaria*, colonizers echoed calls to improve the nation.[30] One repatriation group in Los Angeles went so far as to send an agent, L. F. Bustamante, to Mexico City to meet with President Ortiz Rubio on behalf of the *Confederación de Sociales Mexicanas* and the PLM. Bustamante called himself a representative of *México de Afuera*, and promoted repatriation and the establishment of a Spanish-language newspaper in the United States that would encourage the goals of the Mexican Revolution.

Migrant Letters to the Mexican Government

Migrants sought return not just as members of groups but also as individuals, as the flood of letters to the SRE and the *Departamento de Migración* show.[31] These letters demonstrate a genuine desire to return to Mexico in the 1930s, under the right circumstances. In doing so, these migrants were manipulating the forms of the state to their own ends. Their transnational appeals show that they held an expansive view of citizenship, arguing that they were still members of the Mexican polity—*México de Afuera*—no matter where they lived. Tired of daily existences marked by economic desperation and discrimination, they were spurred by the promise of land. Migrants used their communications with the state strategically, making use of a variety of arguments that would elicit a response from the government. Land was critical to repatriates and key to a viable future in Mexico, so many letter writers focused on being able to claim physical space. Some people and groups were already planning to return to Mexico and tried to get the government pay for the journey. In their letters, they used destitution, gender, family, and national identity in their appeals for funds and land.

A significant percentage of the letters were from women. Trinidad Martinez wrote from Nuevo Laredo requesting assistance, emphasizing she was a single mother with daughters.[32] Alvardes de Luz y Ortiz and Juana Ortiz de Lopez—both going to Guanajuato—likewise stressed their status as mothers in asking for funds.[33] María C. Martinez wrote that her husband had become ill in justifying her request for funds to travel from Mexico City to meet him in Chihuahua.[34] Tepoxina Pintado vda. de Ferrer wrote that she was in failing health, could find no work, and wanted to return to Chiapas, her home state, to resume her work as a teacher.[35] Numerous letters used a defense of loyalties as a reason to return. Maria F. Zamarripa wrote President Rodríguez of her difficulties raising two children in the United States, saying that her children were harassed at school for being Mexican and she wanted a better environment for them.[36] Carmen Rivera made a similar appeal for return to her homeland, stating that she and her family were unable to find work because the programs required that she become a US citizen, something she was unwilling to do.[37] Hortensia Vallejo wrote to President Lázaro Cárdenas asking to return to Mexico to find work so that she could support her daughter.[38] Women largely made pleas to the state on behalf of their families and deployed a gendered language of family poverty. They explained why they were deserving of aid and why their husbands could not provide, calling on the president to fill the paternal role and restore women to their homelands and mothers to their children. The SRE approved funding for most of these people.

Migrants were not ashamed to detail their desperate circumstances to the president and government officials. Juan Zamarripa told President Ortiz Rubio that he had been unable to work because of medical problems, which left his wife and children in destitution.[39] Jose G. Saldana sent a handwritten letter to the government asking for repatriation for himself and his family as they had no work and wished to support the country.[40] Apolinar E. Espinosa stressed to President Ortiz Rubio his inability to find work, while Victor V. Gomez expressed a desire to return to his hometown.[41] Ignacio Herrera wrote to President Rodríguez that, having nothing in the United States, he wished to return with his sister and mother to their home in Campeche so that he could be in the land of his birth.[42] Primitivo Rodriguez wrote a series of letters to President Rodríguez, the consulate, and Eduardo Vasconcelos at the SRE describing his state of destitution in Lombard, Illinois.[43] The Mexican government usually reserved what funds did exist for those people in the most desperate circumstances. The *Departamento de Migración* usually ran out of funds in the first half of the year, making it difficult to get help after funds ran out.

In their appeals, migrants highlighted their former service to their nation. Manuel de Valle had left Mexico in 1925 to work in California, had been unable to find work, and had become reliant on charity. He pointed out his military service during the Mexican Revolution.[44] In asking to be repatriated, Marcos Perez reminded President Cárdenas of his service in the revolutionary forces during the war, saying that he had always believed in the nation. Destitute in San Antonio and unable to feed his family, he asked to return.[45] When the government ran low on funds, it usually allocated funds for the return of veterans over other applicants.

Letter writers felt a need to justify their original migrations. When Melchior Sala Hidalgo requested assistance returning, he included a personal letter to former President Calles explaining that he had been "compelled to abandon my people for the plight in which my family and I find ourselves" and that, though he was a descendent of Miguel Hidalgo y Costilla (founding father of Mexico), the necessity of providing for his family necessitated leaving his country.[46] He countered the perception in the public sphere of migration as unpatriotic by emphasizing his duty to his family and the dire choices he had faced. This theme came up again and again in correspondence. Carlos Bastien told the SRE something similar when explaining his request for documents: "I am an enemy of migration, but today I am left without recourse because of my situation."[47] Others shaped their appeal to fit that rhetoric. Mauricio F. Gonzalez wrote of his desire for their homeland after so many years away toiling for nothing.[48] These letters connected their families' well-being to that of the Mexican nation, and their personal responsibilities to that of the state.

Customs exemptions were far easier to get than paid passage, and thousands were issued. Zeferino Ramirez wrote to President Ortiz Rubio that he had been unable to sustain his family for the past three years and simply wanted to return to his hometown with his farming equipment.[49] Aduardo Aragon revealed his family's problems and his desire to return to the homeland and make a new life in Sinaloa in his petition to bring goods, including a weapon for security.[50] Ramon Sierra wanted a similar customs exception when he told President Ortiz Rubio that he and his family wanted to return to reconstruct the Mexican nation through agricultural work.[51] Mariano Moreno sent President Rodríguez his story of hardship and inability to support his family while asking to return with a truck.[52] These letters were forwarded to consulates, who made the arrangements.

Land was a singular motivation for those who sought repatriation to Mexico.[53] Zerino Dominguez told President Ortiz Rubio that thousands of poor Mexicans would return if there was a place for them, particularly if there was land on which to establish themselves.[54] In 1933, forty men repatriating to Rioverde, San Luis Potosí, sought land to cultivate.[55] Adalberto Ojeda wrote President Rodríguez about his desire to return due to his difficult circumstances but also because he had heard about land redistribution and wanted to farm his homeland.[56]

Migrants were not afraid to criticize the government in their letters. When Rodolfo Benavides wrote to President Ortiz Rubio, he protested that the government had invited white investors into the country and given them land while landless Mexicans went with nothing.[57] Martin T. Valles, writing to Ortiz Rubio on behalf of a group of aspiring repatriates called the *Club Libertad y Justicia*, contrasted the efforts made by President Obregon for migrants ten years earlier with the current president's paltry efforts.[58] The Mexican government encouraged people to envision the president as someone who personally cared about their situation, reinforcing a long history of state rule as an extension of personal power.

Newspapers carried stories of the president helping individual citizens in Mexico, Calles promoted his connection to *México de Afuera* through his intervention in the California strikes of 1933, and a significant portion of migrants' letters did spur action from the government. Though only a few resulted in the government paying the full cost of relocation, a large number did result in discounts or other types of assistance, most often certificates of residency or customs exceptions. Perhaps most surprising is that Mexican presidents did read some of the letters and, in a few cases, made comments on the page and forwarded them to government agencies with instructions to do something about petitioners' situations.[59] Despite the low odds of a letter reaching the upper echelons of government, people broadly believed that the president might personally intervene.

If the president saw them as part of the family of the nation, they saw him and the Mexican government as responsible for their return. Explaining to the government exactly why they were deserving of help, migrants explicitly countered public perceptions of the 1920s that they had left their homeland on an unpatriotic fool's errand. They argued that their poverty was not their fault and that the proper role of the president as paterfamilias was to get them home to give them a chance to provide for their families.[60] They argued that their experience in the United States made them perfect candidates for assistance, either because they had learned skills that Mexico needed or because they had left Mexico to support their families who stayed behind and deserved the chance to do the same in their home country. These migrants were mostly unfamiliar with the elites' discussions but were cognizant of public discourse in newspapers and used them to craft their own arguments.

Border Town Crisis

Border towns were particularly hard hit during the Great Depression. Although these towns often received temporary waves of deported and destitute migrants, the economic crisis, especially in 1929 to 1931, took them to an entirely new place. The Mexican federal government didn't have enough funds to move all the returnees to their hometowns. The *Departamento de Migración* estimated that a quarter of returning Mexicans arrived without any resources.[61] Desperate families waited weeks at border towns before being able to arrange transportation south. Tijuana was completely overwhelmed by the number of people returning from California. At Ciudad Juárez, the arrival of thousands of repatriates, half of them destitute, stressed the city's resources to the breaking point. Large numbers of people went homeless, living outside.[62] Various private charity groups were created in border cities in response to the crisis.[63] In Juárez, the city government and chamber of commerce created a charity board, but its funds were almost instantly exhausted. Hungry travelers demanded relief and basic foodstuffs.[64] The head of the *Servicio de Migración* in the city warned that the large numbers of unemployed migrants would worsen the unemployment problem across the nation.[65]

People who found themselves stranded at border towns reached out to the government. Jose Rico, who had gone with his extended family to the United States in 1928 and returned in 1932, stressed that they had returned to the border town of Nogales Sonora on their own to avoid burdening the Mexican government, but that he was unable to find work and wished to return to his hometown.[66] Lúis Gonzales Medina and his family, who had been in the United States for thirteen years, arrived in Juárez without funds. In his letter, he emphasized his illness in explaining why he could not work and needed aid for his family.[67] Men tended to base their letters on the gendered expectation of them as providers, whereas women frequently stressed their destitution and lack of family support. Rose and Maria Castillo, who found themselves stranded at the border, told President Cárdenas that their children were starving.[68] Maria Ramirez wrote to Cárdenas about the death of her brother and her family's struggles to get to Durango.[69] Likewise, Paz Zamarripa and her daughter Socorro Quinero wrote to Cárdenas that they were in a desperate state and pleaded for help.[70] Justa Hernandez, after the death of her husband and her return to Sonora, wrote about the suffering of her children in asking for rail passes to Mexico City.[71] Waves of destitute migrants continued to arrive at border towns throughout the course of the decade, forcing each administration to respond.

Limits of the *Colonias*

The Mexican press condemned America's treatment of Mexicans during the repatriation drives but was also critical of the Mexican government's handling of the crisis.[72] In response, the government publicly announced plans for new agricultural colonies for repatriated Mexicans. These new *colonias* were envisioned as modern, progressive, and model communities. Like the historical *colonias* intended to expand the reach of Spanish imperial civilization centuries earlier, these twentieth-century, post-revolutionary counterparts were seen as a way to redistribute land that had been monopolized, and to symbolize the modern Mexican state.

In 1932, Andrés Landa y Piña, head of the *Departamento de Migración*, established the National Repatriation Committee to oversee repatriation efforts in Mexico. Its executive committee was composed of prominent government ministers. In December, it launched the *Campana Medio Million* to raise half a million *pesos* for the repatriates. A publicity campaign was created to gather contributions from government workers and the general public. States and localities were asked to contribute. A series of fundraisers were held across the country, especially in Guanajuato, Jalisco, Michoacán, Chihuahua, and Nuevo Leon.[73] About 17,000 people, including President Rodríguez, contributed. Yet despite calls for direct relief to migrants, the committee chose to make colonies the primary recipients. The *Unión de Repatriados Mexicanos* was founded to lobby for direct relief to destitute migrants.

The campaign did not live up to expectations. Most of the funds went toward establishing two colonies. The first of these was *El Coloso* in Guerrero, a small colony that lacked funding and government support. The main project was at Pinotepa Nacional in Oaxaca. Other colonies soon failed as well. *El Coloso* was abandoned, and in Acapulco, repatriates abandoned the colony and were transported to Mexico City by then-presidential candidate Lázaro Cárdenas.[74] Some families settled permanently, at the colonies at Rio Salado, La Misa, Bácum in Sonora, and San Luis Colorado, also in Sonora, but they did not flourish.[75] In San Luis Potosí, successive governors publicly invited repatriates to move there and create colonies, but they didn't want to spend any state money on the effort. Several small groups did arrive at various colonies in the state, near Ciudad del Maiz and Rioverde, but the projects did not grow.[76]

Colonies could work if they were combined with large infrastructure projects. The state of Chihuahua invested more funds into colonies than any other state.[77] Home to roughly 1,500 people, the Don Martin Colony was augmented by the creation of the Don Martin Dam.[78] The project worked largely because of its access to water from the Rio Bravo and its proximity to Texas. Antonio Mendez Lomeli, a professor at an agricultural school in Chihuahua when the repatriation started and an advocate of land reform, was put in charge of government efforts to organize *ejidos* near the Don Martin Dam. Lomeli considered repatriates a progressive influence in the villages, where many residents sought to keep the hierarchies and agricultural practices of the past. He saw repatriates as ambitious and less willing to accept the power of local *haciendas*.

Yet he also wrote that at Urepetiro, Michoacán, being able to turn returning capital into commercial ventures was key to success but also extremely difficult. On the road, one family's truck broke down and had to be sold. Families took up short-term work on *haciendas* on their way south to accumulate funds to continue the journey. In Urepetiro, the repatriates used engines to power water wells, build an electric lighting system for a school, and make other improvements to the town. Some of the families Lomeli helped resettle, in the Anáhuac and Cuauhtémoc colonies, such as those of Cristobal and Juan Escorsa, David Perez, and Jose Simental, ended up staying long term in the *ejido* communities due to their ability to commercialize the crops.[79]

The National Repatriation Board replaced the National Repatriation Committee in 1934 and redoubled its colonization efforts with the support of the newly elected President Lázaro Cárdenas. Colonization was a small piece of Cárdenas's larger land reform agenda. Cárdenas was familiar with the problems of Mexican migration from his time as governor and believed returning Mexicans had skills that would help the rural economy.[80] Although a large population of destitute repatriates was already in Mexico, his government turned to new repatriates from the United States.

In 1938, Manuel Gamio became chief of the demographics department in the *Secretaría de Gobernación*, a role that empowered him to make his vision of colonization a reality. In 1935, Andrés Lana y Piña, head of the *Departamento de Migración*, had published a plan that called for the creation of more agricultural colonies as part of the *Ley de Población* of 1936. Based on this report and his observations of difficulties at earlier colonies at Acambaro, Gamio created a plan that could remedy previous problems and succeed. As laid out his in book *Hacia una México Nuevo: Problemas Sociales*, he believed that previous repatriates went to large cities, increasing urban unemployment, social ills, and crime. Those who did go to rural areas were regressing back to Mexican peasant life, so he proposed a model for a new type of colony with new migrants. Only returnees with agricultural experience and enough capital to start new lives without much help would be eligible. This new colony would be set up near the US border, next to a previous colony and away from the general Mexican population. It eventually became *18 de Marzo*.[81]

Named after the date of President Cárdenas's nationalization of the oil industry, it was a symbol of national independence intended to signal that the government could offer returning Mexicans a new start. The government spent 13,819,268 *pesos* establishing the community, by far the largest investment in a colony during the repatriation period. Approximately 4,000 individuals comprising 627 families settled in the colony, which grew to 5,000 people over a few years. However, its operation proved anything but smooth. The colony was delayed, its location was changed, and at one point, the colonists went on strike. Conditions were so difficult in the first years that repatriated families depended on wages from the United States; some migrated back to work in Texas to raise money.[82] Others left the colony permanently within a few years.[83] The colony managed to survive, however, and by the 1940s, it formed the core of the Tamaulipas cotton district.

With enough investment, especially in water dams and irrigation, and proximity to markets, at least a few colonies were able to grow into prosperous towns during this period.[84] These successful examples notwithstanding, the region did not act as a permanent settlement for large numbers of migrants. By the 1950s, most of the cotton was picked by migrant farm workers who were on their way to the United States, reinforcing the migrant economy rather than acting as a bulwark against it.[85] Throughout this period when pro-repatriation views dominated the Cárdenas government, very few questioned how the promises of the president would be carried out. The Mexican consul in Detroit was one of the few to object to the recruiting of new repatriates to move to colonies. The most serious objections came from those tasked with implementing the policy within *Gobernación*, one of whom was quoted as stating it would be better if "*que se queden allá* [they should stay there]," though these concerns were never voiced publicly.[86] Most colonies lacked the resources to succeed; the exceptions survived only through significant investment.[87]

Overall, the plan to settle repatriates in colonies as a basis for building a modernized rural Mexico failed. Funds regularly ran out long before any project got off the ground. The last repatriation program for colonies, in 1939, ran short of money in just two months.[88] Yet across the country, colonies were established. Some, like *El Centinela*, were as large as four million acres, while others were only a few hundred acres. The government never committed the resources that were needed, and to a large extent, it never planned to. Colonies and the rhetoric of return around them were a way for the government to publicly respond to the crisis of repatriation, a way to deflect criticism and raise the banner of patriotism. Antonio Mendez Lomeli came to believe that the government's pro-repatriation campaign had encouraged people to return when they should have stayed in the United States. He said, "Many Mexicans would get tired and become enthralled by promises like the ones made by Cárdenas, that returning to the homeland they would lack for nothing, but they found that the way people in Mexico lived was very difficult. Arriving there they had to become agricultural workers, they had to learn to live without mobility."[89] A detailed look at one colony's experience illustrates the limits of support for those who headed the government's call.

Pinotepa Nacional, Oaxaca

In 1931, in Detroit, Michigan, Diego Rivera—who was working on the Ford River Rouge murals at the time—encouraged Mexicans there to return home. In speeches and through donations to the cause, Rivera promoted return as bringing progress and development to rural Mexico.[90] At the behest of the Mexican consulate, he helped to organize and fund the *Liga Obreros Campesinos Mexicanos Organizados*, which arranged the repatriation of dozens of families to San Luis Potosí, Nuevo Laredo, Oaxaca, and other places where the Mexican government was providing land for colonies. Echoing the government's rhetoric, the *Liga* made patriotic appeals to Mexicans to rebuild their nation. The return voyage was celebrated in communities, with departure and welcome parties and events featuring speakers. While some went to the Don Martin colony in Coahuila, others ended up at Pinotepa Nacional.[91]

The colony at Pinotepa Nacional in Oaxaca was planned as a model colony, the focus of the government's campaign. Highly skilled workers from the Midwest were meant to boost agricultural development, but conditions rapidly deteriorated. In theory, repatriates would be sold unused lands on favorable terms, along with water, tools, animals, and other essentials. Loans and land titles would be structured to promote financial independence. However, most of the funds went to pay the costs of establishing the colony and soon ran out.[92] A good number of the colonists were unemployed former factory workers from Detroit, not experienced farmers. After writing increasingly desperate letters to the government about the problems at the colony, including forced labor under Municipal President Jose F. Grialva, families abandoned the project en masse.[93]

Rafael Garcia told President Rodríguez about how he had been caught up in Diego Rivera's words, joined the *Liga de Obreros y Campesinos*, and had "left my job in order to relocate to my beloved homeland, now I find myself unemployed."[94] Destitute in Mexico City, he begged the president for help. Garcia was not alone. A group of former colonists at the Colonia Pinotepa Nacional and *El Coloso* formed the *Confederación Nacional Obreros Pro-Trabajo*. They wrote a series of petitions to President Rodríguez in which they drew attention to corruption, lack of funds, and forced labor. The largest contingent returned to Mexico City, formed the *Unión de Repatriados Mexicanos*, and demanded that the government spend more.[95] They also wrote a series of petitions describing their families' situations and demanding jobs and land.[96] When that did not work, they carried out a sit-down protest at the National Palace in the hopes of drawing attention to their plight. After a protracted standoff, the protests slowly dissipated. Mexico City in particular became the final destination of former colonists, but cities across the country experienced similar crises.

Within the Mexican government through the 1930s, it was believed that repatriation might be re-fashioned to serve Mexico's economic development. Successive administrations took the public position that it was the duty of every Mexican to return to the homeland. Colonies were to be the answer. Migrants' return was sometimes marked by joyous events, with speeches and receptions, during which Mexican government officials welcomed them back. But without enough funds devoted to return and resettlement, thousands of people found themselves in Mexico without resources and internally displaced. Showing the limits of their vision, the government continued to build colonies even as previous ones failed. The Mexican state had no place for repatriates, economically or politically.[97]

Urban Repatriation

In Mexico City alone, unemployment jumped from 90,000 in 1930 to 339,378 in 1932. While few Mexican migrants were originally from the capital, a large number of repatriates migrated there in search of work.[98] *El Universal* and other newspapers published reports of large numbers of these repatriates in Mexico City, and *Excélsior* urged repatriated people to organize and present their situation to the *Secretaría de Gobernación.*[99] Mexico City established soup kitchens and emergency aid services for returnees. More than 10% of the workforce in most cities was unemployed, but in some sectors like mining, employment decreased by 50% between 1929 and 1932.[100] While the bulk of migrants continued on to rural hometown destinations, these railroad junctions in central Mexico were also major receiving points of repatriates trying to build new lives.[101] At least 15% of all repatriates went to cities.[102] However, the number could have been as high as 25%, as many repatriates migrated to cities after initially going to rural hometowns.[103] Having lived in American cities, some repatriates preferred urban life, while others found better work opportunities there.

Families came back with cars full of goods, and in some cases, repatriate groups organized the sending of large quantities of goods across the border.[104] Returnees rarely brought back the tractors or agricultural machinery Mexican officials dreamt of; more often, they brought back goods like sewing machines, radios, records and record players, and automobiles. While these consumer goods were not what the government had in mind, they made a profound difference for the individual families that took the trouble to bring them. More women petitioned the SRE for certificates of residence for their sewing machines than for any other household object.[105] These machines greatly cut down the workload of women as most clothing was still homemade and women were expected to do all domestic work.

Enrique Vega's family had saved enough to take a truck with all their belongings back to Zacatecas. His father bought a ranch and horses with money he had saved working in the United States and started a new life, though his US-raised children had mixed feelings about settling down permanently in Mexico.[106] One man drove two Ford trucks when he remigrated and used them to start a business hauling animals and produce to market: "Now I own a house and two trucks; it makes me a living. I was a laborer here, and never could have bought trucks (with my wages) here."[107] Observers at the border often remarked on the number of cars filled with all kinds of goods, including chickens.[108] One extended family of nine drove from Colorado to Chihuahua in a 1926 Chevrolet with "100 pounds of beans, a gas stove, a sewing machine, and 200 pounds of flour."[109]

Small businessmen took the tools of their trades with them. One man, who had been working at Chicago, returned in 1931 with a car and tool-making machines to start a new life, but the car broke down in San Luis Potosí. He abandoned the car there but managed to get his machinery to his hometown, where he used it to establish a business.[110] Similarly, "barbers, repairmen, plumbers, tailors, leather workers, musicians, carpenters, mechanics, and other journeymen insisted on taking their equipment with them in hopes of being able to reestablish themselves in Mexico."[111] For repatriates, accustomed to the US cash economy, urban spaces in Mexico represented their best option.[112] This was particularly true of migrants from urban centers and those from the Midwest, whose experience in factories and skilled trades enabled them to create new small businesses and achieve greater financial stability.

In Guanajuato, Isidro López, Elías Calderón, and Luis Sandoval joined together to bring various automobiles to Silao, where they established a trucking business. Pénjamo, an agricultural town that supplied goods to larger cities via its rail link, saw its economy devastated by the Great Depression. It was a double blow as much of the income came from migrants aboard, who returned in great numbers. Pénjamo's plaza was filled with cars that people had brought back, and repatriates came to dominate the agricultural trucking business, replacing the mules that had been used. People also returned with tools and small mechanical equipment. Nearly every returnee lived with a relative in the city. Despite efforts to create jobs, migrants had to leave the area in search of work.[113]

Repatriation rhetoric celebrated the new skills, democratic beliefs, and most importantly, capital returnees were thought to possess that would help industrialize agricultural production. There were some reasons to be optimistic. Mexicans in California had withdrawn seven million dollars cumulatively from banks in 1931, though most accounts were rather modest in size. *El Universal* estimated that Mexicans repatriated twenty million dollars' worth of cash and property, while Balderrama put his own estimate at twice that.[114] Tens of thousands had taken advantage of duty exemptions. Accounts from the period and government records suggest that the reality was at best mixed. Some returnees had funds; some had materials, such as food, luggage, and goods; others had only the clothes on their backs. In the end, not enough people returned with substantial capital to make a meaningful difference to the economy.

Even when repatriates did have skills, they encountered entrenched opposition. Manuel C. Téllez, *Secretaría de Gobernación*, encouraged state governors to create employment programs for workers who had acquired skills in the United States. While the federal government encouraged the use of repatriates in large infrastructure projects, they were not employed in any meaningful sense. The labor board, *Junta Federal de Conciliación y Arbitraje*, was opposed to hiring repatriates in government projects because they competed against existing laborers, while the union *Confederación de Trabajadores de México* believed repatriates increased unemployment and labor competition. When the government did create large infrastructure projects, jobs went to union members instead of repatriates. Most returnees, however, had neither worked in skilled trades in the United States nor accumulated capital. For them, moving to urban Mexico was much more difficult.

Jesus Grimaldo arrived in Mexico City after being repatriated from Los Angeles. By August of 1932, he was without a job and starving on the streets, as he told Consul Ricardo Castro Sainz. The Consul in Los Angeles, Rafael de la Colina, received many such letters from former repatriates.[115] Jose R. Grejeda told President Rodríguez that, after being repatriated, he had been unable to establish himself in Zamora, Michoacán, and was in poverty and unable to send his children to school; he asked for railroad passes to Mexico City to search for work.[116] Like these men, thousands of people expected to be able to make money in Torreón, Monterrey, or Mexico City but were disillusioned and desperate.[117] The government turned away most who wrote letters seeking work or transportation to other parts of the nation.

Even when aid was forthcoming, its recipients did not always fare well. Daniel Martinez explained, "Me and my mother are repatriated, and came to this city [Monterrey], with scarce resources, and without a home where to stay." They were given tickets to Torreón, where he had a sister and aunt, only to find that these relatives had died and that "our presence has served to increase the number of the unemployed who have gathered in this population, waiting for help that federal authorities have promised."[118] Such stories were far too common in these years. Throughout the 1930s, large numbers of repatriates continued to be internally displaced.

Adjusting to Rural Life

Tens of thousands returned to rural northern or central Mexico, primarily to the communities where they had once lived, and they brought along children who had never lived there. By going to their home regions, repatriates relied on their communities, hometowns, and extended families. A few bought land, others worked on *haciendas*, and a larger number acquired *ejido* land. While those with capital were sometimes able to secure upward mobility, the majority resumed agricultural work. Children frequently found the transition much more difficult than their parents. Stories of rural return underscore that pathways continued to be shaped by migrants' pasts.

Francisco Castañeda's return to Mexico did not go well. His mother was from San Luis Potosí and his father from Durango, and the family had gone to the north with extended family. His father worked as a miner and his uncle as a carpenter. The family did well until the Great Depression, when his father lost his job and his mother became the sole breadwinner. When the family went to Los Angeles County charities for help, they were persuaded to repatriate, though it is unclear if they were coerced. They returned to Mexico in 1937, late in the Depression and after the peak wave of repatriation. They took trains to his father's hometown of Palacio, Durango, and eventually settled on a farm. There, his mother died, and Francisco and his US-born siblings worked on the farm from a young age, growing corn and later picking cotton.[119]

Returning to rural towns meant being dependent on relatives to make a new life. Bernardo Moreno, who returned to San Luis Potosí, worked for his brother. Pastor Ortiz, returning to Michoacán, relied on his family for support until he found work.[120] Some reported having misspent their earnings in the United States or being forced to abandon items like cars when they repatriated. In Arandas, Jalisco, the bulk of those who had returned did not find their lives had permanently changed as a result. One landowner reported that the migrants asked for higher wages than before. But otherwise, most simply picked up their former rural clothing, work, and lifestyles. As one person put it, "Our business is *agricultor*, before and after."[121] This confirms the findings of the migration study (see Appendix) that most repatriates worked in agriculture.

In Pénjamo, Guanajuato, repatriating families who came with few resources ended up working on shares of land, renting small patches of a hillside to eke out a living. In Purépero, Michoacán, and nearby villages, returnees struggled to adjust to small village life, telling interviewers they planned to return to the United States as soon as possible. There were some exceptions. In one study, those who were able to access family networks to obtain loans to start over fared the best, especially those who created small businesses, but this was a distinct minority. The majority were "now no better off economically than before they went north."[122] In other words, the success

Figure 7.2 Map of central Mexico, with Brownsville, Monterrey, Torreón, Zacatecas, San Luis Potosí, Aguascalientes, Guanajuato, Leon, Celaya, Guadalajara, Morelia, and Mexico City shown.

of repatriates depended heavily on how much capital they brought back and the extent to which they could rely on their communities.

For Fernando Pérez and his family, return was a pathway to a better life in Mexico. They went to Encarnación, Jalisco, where Fernando's father's savings allowed him to buy a farm near his hometown. He had saved for years to return to Mexico, so when offered a chance to do so at the Mexican government's expense, he took it.[123] Families like Pérez's made use of the language, social connections, and farming skills they had gained to create stable lives in Mexico. A select number of repatriates became independent farmers, deploying their knowledge of American farming techniques to plant new crops and sell to markets.[124]

About half of the total number of people who "repatriated" were underage minors, comprising more than 200,000 children. Some had been born in Mexico, but about 40% of repatriates were US-born. For them, Mexico was a foreign land. While there are significant data on repatriates' destinations, there has been limited research into what happened to those children over time. Most of the extant accounts of repatriation from the viewpoints of children are from those who migrated back to the United States. In their stories, *El Retorno* did not mean going back to Mexico but to the land of their birth. These accounts omit the majority of people who settled in place.

Differences in material conditions, compounded by cultural, language, and religious differences, posed challenges for children. Women in particular had a difficult time adjusting to the more patriarchal, conservative expectations of family members in Mexico. Hortencia Martinez de Benitez's family took the train from Los Angeles to Juárez and from there to "*la villa*," which had no roads, at the encouragement of family members. They moved in with her aunt. However, her father became ill, and the family was forced to sell most of the belongings they had brought back to Mexico. After being unable to find work in town, they moved to a rural farm, where her father worked the land. He was only able to send her to the first three years of school. Hortencia struggled to adjust to rural life with its limited opportunities, lack of roads, no access to running water, and absence of shops. She missed the relative social freedom of the United States compared to the patriarchal norms in rural Mexico.[125]

Castañeda Valenciana and her family did not have much when they arrived in Mexico and moved to a rural ranch with only six other inhabitants. There, they began a far different life than the one she had known in California as a child. The children struggled in the local schools but eventually became fluent in Spanish and adjusted to life in Durango.[126] Schools were a gateway to adjustment for children like Castañeda. In a few towns with large amounts of repatriates, schools began programs to "Mexicanize" the students. Some children rejected their new homes. Gregorio Gonzalez and his wife, Juana Carmona, were repatriated from Pennsylvania to Tarimoro, Guanajuato. Their US-born children struggled to adjust to their new lives in Mexico, which they saw as a foreign country.[127] One young migrant who had returned with his parents to Pénjamo, Guanajuato, from the Midwest was pessimistic about the situation he faced in Mexico, remarking, "I can't understand how many of these people live here. There's no industry, nothing but agriculture. And that's no good—no irrigation, just raising corn once a year."[128]

Despite what they had been told, repatriates were not universally welcomed by Mexican society. Intellectuals analyzed the situation of the *pocho* (US-born of Mexican ancestry) as early as the 1930s. While Manuel Gamio saw them as redeemable through return, writing in 1936 José Vasconcelos saw them as rejecting their Mexican-ness and irredeemable.

Later, intellectuals such as Octavio Paz picked up their arguments to illustrate the alienation of Mexican *pachucos*[129] in the United States. Throughout the 1930s, newspapers pointed to destitute migrants as sources of danger and suspect morals. The arrival of tens of thousands of children into towns and villages made these abstract debates much more real. Many saw them as taking jobs and driving down wages. In a survey of repatriates, most of those who had worked high-skilled factory jobs were not using their skills in Mexico, having been kept out of factories.[130] While some writers, such as Enrique Flores Magón, argued that migrants were compatriots, in villages across the country people doubted the Mexican-ness of the new arrivals. Flores Magón reported meeting a man who discarded his American clothing as people thought it made him look pretentious. Flores Magón also found that children's Spanish was often mocked, especially in small towns.[131] Old words were reinterpreted as new slang spread to describe the repatriates. It was common to hear them called *Americanizados, ayancados, pochis, pochos, agringados,* and *pachucos*—that is, no longer proper Mexicans.[132] In Rioverde, San Luis Potosí, people called those who were returning *los despatriados*, meaning they had no homeland.

While children struggled to adjust, the majority of them did at least settle in their home regions. One study found differences by age, with younger children of repatriates adjusting better to rural life than older children.[133] A study of families that returned to Guanajuato showed that most people eventually settled into life in these communities and could be found there in the 1940s and 1950s, as husbands, wives, and parents. Making use of repatriation and local parish rolls, Escoto Molina found that, of those families who returned, most of the children were under 15 years, which may indicate that older children did not follow their parents. Most repatriating families returned in groups with other families from the same region, which indicates that they continued to rely on networks. While many did not stay in their hometowns permanently, they tended to live in the general vicinity. Of the approximately 172 child returnees found in records, 80 were female. The majority eventually married locally. Most of the men also married women from the area, but a substantial minority returned to the United States after some time, in keeping with the emerging pattern of men working in the north to support families in Mexico. These findings suggest that, even though acculturation was difficult, people were able to make the transition, but it also suggests the endurance of decades-long migration patterns.[134]

Tierra y Libertad: Land Reform in Rural Central Mexico

Returning migrants entered a nation undergoing political transformation. Despite a new constitution in 1917, a relatively stable government after 1920, and an official peace agreement with the Cristeros in 1929, violence from local uprisings, Cristero groups, and bandits continued, especially in the highlands of central Mexico. Most importantly, the problem of land distribution remained unresolved. After the revolution, the Constitution of 1917 re-established the right to communal lands. In the 1920s, the government codified the land seizures that had already taken place but limited new divisions. In the late 1920s, Presidents Calles and Rodríguez promoted small private ownership over collective property. However, a cadre of governors strongly supported large-scale redistribution and *ejido*, including Cedillo in San Luis Potosí and Cárdenas in Michoacán. Supported by *agraristas*, these governors continued to dismantle *haciendas*.

Focusing on the 1933 election, thousands of local groups organized and even armed themselves to pressure the government into act on land redistribution. The resulting 1933 Agrarian Land Reform Law and election of Lázaro Cárdenas to the presidency greatly expanded access to land reform. After his election, Cárdenas outmaneuvered Calles, forcing him into exile, and instituted large-scale agrarian reform. In six years, more than forty million acres of land were redistributed to *ejido* communities. Having been left out of previous agrarian reforms, former migrants exacerbated the tensions that drove redistribution. Returning migrants were just a small fraction of the hundreds of thousands seeking land through their communities, but their invisibility within this movement was perhaps a sign of how fully they integrated into rural society. Most migrants who petitioned for land did not do so as repatriates going to colonies but as Mexican citizens rooted in their agrarian communities.

The states of the Bajío region of Mexico, where the bulk of repatriates returned to, were still dominated by large landholdings. The region had seen far less land redistribution than other parts of Mexico in the 1920s, and the influx of hundreds of thousands of returnees raised tensions, making reform more urgent. In many places, repatriates were seen as competition for land; in Michoacán and San Luis Potosí, workers on *ejidos* land voiced disapproval of the new arrivals, arguing that they should not be entitled to land.[135] Newspapers argued that redistributed land should go to those who had stayed in the country rather than those who had left.[136] Despite these objections, migrants joined the movement across central Mexico.

Statistical data on land redistribution and migration patterns show how repatriation spurred land redistribution throughout much of central Mexico. Migration depressed land redistribution through much of the 1920s. Taking into account land-ownership concentration, areas of high outmigration had less land redistribution than comparable places that did not. This is because migration offered ways for men to earn money without challenging social relations. Those who left tended to be young, landless, literate single men—the people who traditionally supported *agrarismo*. Those left behind faced considerable risks and social costs of pressing for economic reform. This also made successful redistribution much harder for those who tried to enact it, because government officials could find that there was not enough agrarian demand from the local population.[137] Land petitions in central Mexico were undermined by high levels of outmigration from a community.[138]

In the 1930s, the situation reversed. The large number of returnees to rural villages in central Mexico simultaneously closed off avenues of escape and ended the large-scale remittances that had been supporting families. With migration no longer an option and new people pouring into these areas,

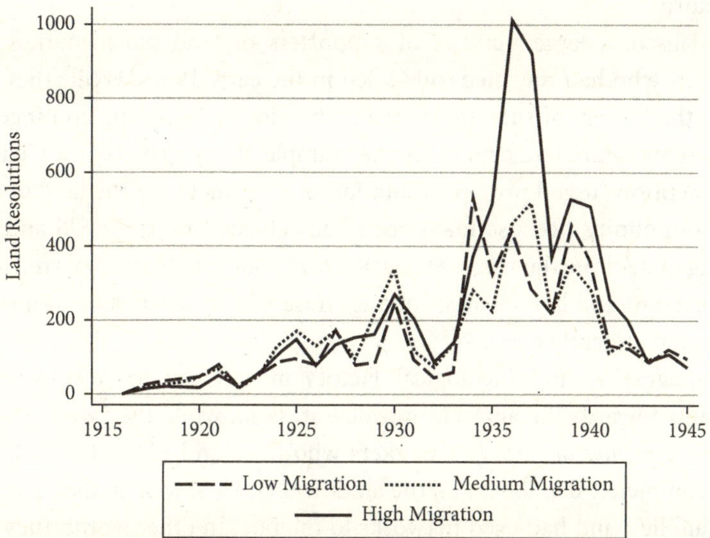

Figure 7.3 Land reform petitions by migration intensity and year, 1915–1945. Emily Sellars, "The Politics of Exist: Emigration, Collective Action, and Agrarian Reform in Mexico" (unpublished manuscript, September 2022), ch. 4.

pressure increased to redistribute land. Land redistribution increased in general across the nation, but its relative rate was highest in areas that had been dependent on migrant remittances.[139] The areas with the highest level of outmigration were now disproportionately represented in land redistribution, as interviews of returning families illustrate.

Cipriano Barbosa left for the United States in 1918, when his older brother sent him thirty dollars to join him. He worked in fourteen different states before returning to Mexico at the end of 1930. He credited his firsthand observations of the two societies for his involvement in the *ejido* movement. "The large landowners, what they wanted was to have people enslaved. To have them work for nothing, and to be hungry. Lots of people claimed that if the poor laborer were hungry, he would work more. But in the US, one learned that a man with a full stomach . . . works willingly if he is paid for his work."[140] Ernesto Rodriguez was a barber before going to the United States in 1922. He returned to Mexico in 1930, was reunited with his brother who was "a revolutionary," and joined the land redistribution group *Sindicato de Oficios Varios* in 1932. He credited his US union experience as his reason for joining the *agraristas*.[141] Jon Oliva's family returned to Mexico in 1932 after fifteen years in the United States. While outside the country, he learned about agrarian reform from other migrants and joined the movement upon his return.[142]

In Jalisco, a large number of supporters of land redistribution were migrants who had returned to Mexico in the early 1930s. While they were rarely the leaders of such movements, they formed a strong contingent of support for agrarian reform.[143] In one example, the *ejido* of Paso de Cuarenta in its petition "urged prompt resolution of a conflict over the land grant to that community, because many men had returned from the US and were hoping to dedicate themselves to agriculture." Some petitions referred to unemployment and landlessness among those who had returned as a reason *ejidos* were urgently needed.[144]

Demographic and ideological factors intertwined to steer returning migrants towards the agrarian movement. First, while they were landless, few were *peones acasillados* (workers who lived and worked on a plantation, completely dependent on the landowner). Most were in their twenties, had families, and had used networks to migrate. In other words, they were similar to most of the young men leaving central Mexico.[145] But the experience of migration had changed them. As one migrant put it, "Here they have always paid really miserable, very low wages, and so those of us who were accustomed to earning more money there (in the US) and another life, well, how could we come back here to work the same way?"[146] They had also liberalized their views on a wide variety of issues, from religion to support for unions, and many had become more educated and literate. Some had direct organizing experience and had participated in US strikes. As a result, local leaders specifically recruited returned migrants, knowing they would be the most enthusiastic.[147]

In Guanajuato, returnees joined agrarian movements already in place. Victor Hernández from Romita, Guanajuato, migrated to Chicago in the 1920s, where he became a union organizer and traveled to Mexico as a delegate of Chicago for the *Casa del Obrero Mundial.* When the Depression began, he returned to Mexico. His wife, Natividad, supported their family by operating a grocery store, he joined the local agrarian movement. By 1932, Hernandez had become president of the *Comité Particular Ejecutivo Agrario de Silao* and oversaw the establishment of *ejidos* throughout the area. Likewise, Primo Tapia came back to Michoacán from Los Angeles, where he had been involved with the PLM and Industrial Workers of the World before joining the agrarian movement upon his return.[148] At the *hacienda de Guarancha* in Michoacán, observers noted how returning migrants didn't conform to the worldview of the closed *hacienda*, but instead demanded land.[149]

Not all returning migrants were eager to join the *agrarista* movement, however. In Jalisco, some repatriates were sympathetic to the Cristero movement, which was wary of land redistribution. In Guanajuato, a violent altercation between rural police and *agraristas* made repatriates suspicious. Repatriates often voiced their preference for buying individual land rather than joining collective *ejidos*, though few could afford to do so. On the other hand, these positions were not mutually exclusive. In Etúcuaro, Michoacán, repatriates joined the agrarian movement to claim *ejidos* while also borrowing funds to buy and cultivate land from the local *ejido* organization.[150] In seeking to own land or join *ejidos*, they were willing to push back against the power of local *hacendados*.

The experience of repatriates in Baja California shows how migrants could force the Mexican government's hand. In 1934, the Colorado River Land Company (CRLC) began to sell land to small farmers, and in 1935, repatriates established the *Colonia México Libre*. However, the process was slow and mostly helped small farmers rather than establishing communal lands, pitting repatriates who could afford to purchase lands against those who could not. In 1936, hundreds of armed *agraristas* began to seize company-owned and small farmer land. The standoff forced President Cárdenas to expropriate the CRLC's lands in 1937. In turn, the Agrarian Commission sent large shipments of farm machinery and tools. It then resettled 5,000 on the land. Continuing federal support, such as for irrigation projects, helped these communities survive. Later, Lazaro Cárdenas made a farewell tour of Mexico, visiting *colonias* at Baja and other places. He held up the land seizure as an example of his policies, but it was returnees who had forced his hands to make it happen.[151] While repatriates played an obvious role here, they were not so visible in most places.

That the government did not put much comparable effort into appeals from those claiming repatriate status but was attentive to appeals from landed villages is telling. Migrants were not a significant political constituency, but farmers were. Landed communities carried political legitimacy. Repatriates generally acculturated into the general population and didn't gain land based on their status, but there were a number of instances of repatriates taking the lead in local *ejido* petitions or being cited as a reason *ejidos* were so urgently needed. In making the rural unemployment problem more urgent in central Mexico, repatriates pushed these areas into creating a disproportionate number of new *ejidos*.[152]

Toward a Mixed Economy in San Luis Potosí

Land reform took on a different character in San Luis Potosí. While the state has a relatively small population, it disproportionally sent migrants north, and in the 1930s, tens of thousands of people returned to the Zona Media and the small towns in the valley. Although the governor offered land to settle 1,000 families on colonies and additional land for 500 destitute families, these efforts were dwarfed by the large number of people returning to their home villages, adding to the population and the pressure for land reform.[153] In the 1930s, a new round of land reform added to the redistribution that had already occurred.

Following the Mexican Revolution, the breakup of large *haciendas* was much more vigorous in San Luis Potosí than in most of Mexico. At Guaxcama, many of the buildings were destroyed, though the *hacienda* as a unit of production continued to exist. But it was unclear who had claim to the land. In 1929, the *hacendados* told the families living on the land that they were selling the land to them, but the transaction was deceptive, meant to give the impression of a sale while keeping ultimate legal control in the hands of the *hacendados*. In 1935, during the Cárdenas administration, the families who lived on the land brought their claim to the *Comisión Agraria*, which finally broke it into *ejidos* for the workers. However, the use of the water from the aqueduct remained contested, and claims were not fully settled until the 1940s.[154] To the northeast, the great *Agostura hacienda* was divided in the 1920s, and the surrounding towns were granted *ejido* land. At *Bosques y Caldera* outside of Cerritos, the townspeople acquired a legal claim to parts of the *hacienda* in 1925, and so did many more people across the valley.[155]

Records from across San Luis Potosí and Illinois in the 1930s demonstrate a growing culture of family migration. *Salvaconducto* requests show that close to 30% of those migrating were spouses and children, and groups often included extended families. At the Saint Francis of Assisi Parish in Chicago, a

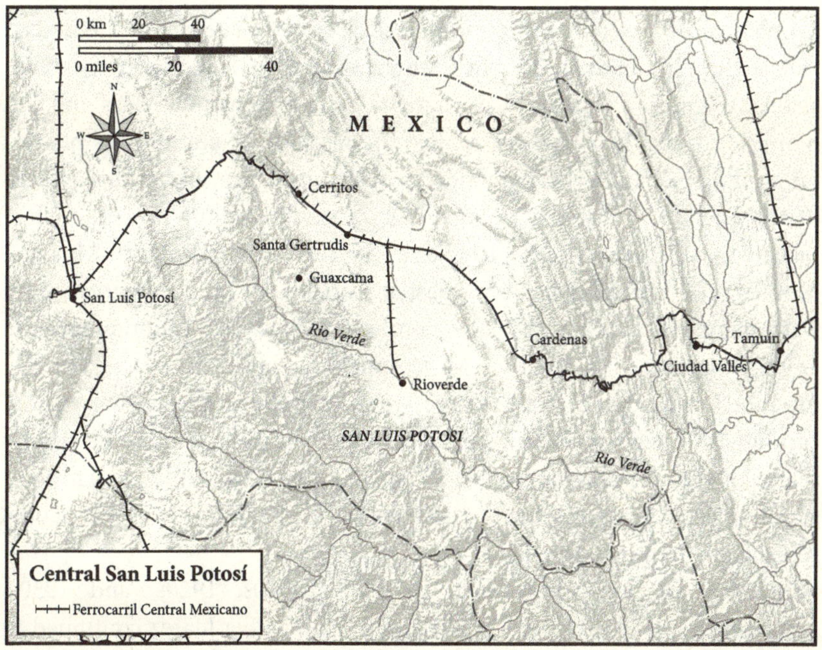

Figure 7.4 Map of central San Luis Potosí, with the locations of San Luis Potosí, Cerritos, Santa Gertrudis, Guaxcama, Rioverde, Cardenas, Ciudad Valles, and Tamuín marked in between. San Luis Potosí Railroad Map.

significant number of the marriages between 1930 and 1935 involved people from San Luis Potosí, and they mostly wed women from San Luis Potosí or nearby states. Even in a migrant-sending state like San Luis Potosí, towns' participation in migration varied greatly. Of the men who married before 1935, the portion who had spent time in the United States from each county varied from as low as 1% in Cedral to as high as 55.4% in Matehuala, giving a sense of the range of integration into the migrant economy. In 274 weddings in villages across the state, 152 involved one spouse who had been to the United States, and their locations were as varied as California, Texas, Illinois, Louisiana, Colorado, and New York. Most people had spent between one and five years out of the country and had often migrated back and forth multiple times. It appears that young men (and some women) saw migration as a cultural expectation and a way to gain maturity, adventure, skills, and status. People left but returned to their hometowns to marry, having saved up for a wedding, house, or farmland. In doing so, they expanded where people lived and worked to include a transnational conception of community.[156]

In Cerritos, San Luis Potosí, migration became embedded in local practice. Even after the county was split in 1917, the train station at Cerritos drew people from the surrounding municipalities as the gateway to the United States. Throughout the 1920s, the Catholic Church had taken a strong stance against migration, arguing that migrants gained dangerous vices and immoral ideas that turned them against the Church. Migration was blamed for eroding the family, keeping men from settling down, and enabling them to abandon their responsibilities. When years of warning proved ineffective, some clergymen began to take a different stance. Roberto Murrieta Montoya used his position as a priest at Cerritos to shape migration, both welcoming migrants and acting as a broker. He promoted traditional values among migrants to ensure they were supporting family structures. His role expanded significantly in the 1940s, when he became one of the primary conduits through which braceros in Cerritos and Villa Juárez, the county seats, got migrant labor contracts. He favored men with families and in good standing in the Church, which he believed improved the chances that people returned with money saved.[157]

Building on long experience from the 1910s, 1920s, and 1930s, communities in central Mexico like Cerritos and Villa Juárez continued to disproportionately participate in circular migration despite large-scale land redistribution. While some of these new migrants did not have access to their own land, many did. The Mexican government didn't have anything like the

Figure 7.5 Generations of families have used the train station at Cerritos in San Luis Potosí to migrate between there and the United States. Daniel Morales, Cerritos Train Station, 2013. Photograph by the author.

New Deal state and its vast agricultural subsidies. however. Without broad access to credit, fertilizers, machines, or even animals, a large number of *ejitarios* (people who held a claim to ejido lands) and small landowners found that their yields were not enough.[158] A period of droughts starting in the late 1930s made it difficult for families to stay on the land without other sources of income.[159] Earlier decades had established a precedent for sons to participate in migrant labor and send back remittances to their families who stayed and cultivated the land. These actions brought about a mixed economy in which extended families worked land while getting remittances from northern Mexico, Mexico City, or the United States. The mixed migrant-agrarian economy became a critical component of life across the region.[160]

Land reform was not enough to end migration, at least not in central Mexico. The redistribution of six million acres of land ended the rural violence that had been ongoing since the Mexican Revolution, broke the power of large landholders, and established the Institutional Revolutionary Party's vision of a nationalist cooperative capitalism as the predominant political and economic model of the country. In the years after land redistribution, the Mexican economy grew at a fast pace, and it continued to do so until the 1960s. However, this did not alter the basic conditions that made people migrate, especially the high levels of poverty in the countryside, which persisted due to the limited amount of arable land with a water source and the small crop yields.[161]

Renewed Migration

Valente Benavides Rendon had originally migrated to support his wife, Regina, and their twelve children. When the Great Depression began, he took advantage of the Mexican government's program to return to Mexico. Without his US earnings supplementing their income, however, the family began to suffer. Valente also did not enjoy farm work. So in 1934, at the height of the Depression, he decided to hire a coyote to smuggle him and his sons across the border. The family lived *la vida de inmigrantes* as farm workers across the United States, traveling from California to Louisiana depending on the season and wages. This pattern continued for several years until Valente was arrested for being undocumented. He told his son Reynaldo, "If they throw me to Mexico I will come back one way or another."[162] Desperate circumstances pushed some back into a life of migration. The family of Ramon Espinosa was repatriated from California to La Llama, Sinaloa, but they made their way back to Mexicali and then to California to resume migrant agricultural work.[163] Enrique Vega decided he wanted his own children to grow up in the United States. As he told a researcher, "If I had to do it over again, I would have stayed [in the US]." He arranged for papers for his family and returned within six weeks.[164]

Even during the height of the Depression, which has been emphasized as an era marked by a lack of migration, people found ways to return to the United States.[165] As early as 1932, there were reports of people seeking to cross in significant numbers, something both governments tried to prevent.[166] Regardless, the children of previous migrants used the resources at their disposal—information, legal status, and language skills—to recreate practices of transnational migration. Families who returned to Mexico in the early 1930s participated in renewed migration in the late 1930s or, more commonly, in the 1940s.

Many of those who repatriated in the early 1930s found the path to return legally blocked. One migrant wrote to US officials that he wished to return because his US-born children "do not like the Mexican customs and wish to return to the US," but his request was denied.[167] His was not an isolated case. Consular officials usually rejected the visa claims of US-born Mexicans who wished to return.[168] During the repatriation campaigns, authorities told people that, if they departed voluntarily, they would be eligible to return in the future. This was not true. Having accepted help from private or government agencies, they were excluded on the grounds that they were Liable to be a Public Charge. As a result, families decided to migrate without documents.

When Ramón Sánchez and his family found it difficult to readapt to life in San Julian, Jalisco, they decided to return to the United States. However, he was denied legal entry even though ten of his children were US-born. The family languished in Juárez as they appealed their case, and their youngest daughter died of malnutrition there. Frustrated, Mr. Sánchez "borrowed money to buy a secondhand suit, shaved off his mustache, and relying on his fair skin and green eyes, he simply walked across the border." He later paid a coyote to smuggle in the rest of his family.[169] The Castañeda family followed the same pattern. Francisco Castañeda and his siblings sought to return to the United States, but when they had previously left, the Castañedas had failed to secure papers to prove US birth. They were denied entry at the border. In the late 1940s, some of the family members began to cross without documents. Francisco crossed and funded the journeys of relatives in subsequent years.[170]

The family of Lauro Vega shows how families were led back to the United States even in the mid-1930s. The father, mother, children, and grandfather had moved from Jalisco to Southern California during the revolution. By the 1930s, the family had several US-born members. Lauro remembers that "even when we were born here they (the US government) wanted to send us all to Mexico . . . they made a propaganda [*sic*] . . . said that the people who want to volunteer to go to Mexico, they will [pay] everything, transportation free, and there will be free land and all that." His father was enthusiastic about returning to Mexico. However, enthusiasm for repatriation soon turned into cynicism, and most of the family members returned to the Los Angeles area within a few years.[171]

The Martinez family was in a similar situation. Their migratory journey continued, from Mexico to Arizona to California back to Mexico, and then back to Los Angeles when the Depression hit. Leonaides and Agapito moved to El Monte, where they had more stable employment than most of their neighbors. Their siblings, on the other hand, joined the repatriation movement and went back to Michoacán. However, they didn't like it there, and they all came back to Los Angeles by the end of the 1930s.[172] Jose Lopez, who had been repatriated with his parents in 1931 at the age of 5 years, returned to the same place his father had worked—the Ford Motor Company in Detroit. He used family connections with those who had stayed behind to resettle in the Motor City. By maintaining close contacts across the border, many eventually sought to turn those connections to their advantage.

The Venegas family was in a stable economic position in Los Angeles at the start of the Depression, but their desire to return to Mexico eventually led them to join the waves of repatriates. Miguel and Dolores Venegas were grocery store owners who had fled the Cristero War in Jalisco. As his business suffered, Miguel wrote to his brother in Jalisco about his desire to return, described the financial pressures on the family, and asked about the possibility of coming back.[173] In 1932, Miguel went back to Zapotlanejo after the death of *cacique* (municipal political chief) Rosario Orozco. He came to the conclusion that conditions were worse there than in the United States. But he did not give up on his dream, and in 1938, he moved the whole family to Guadalajara, where he established a glass shop alongside his brother's store.[174]

When Miguel and Dolores Venegas moved to Guadalajara, their oldest son stayed behind to manage the grocery store in Los Angeles. The other children, who accompanied them, experienced a culture shock. While in the United States, the parents had cultivated a utopian vision of Jalisco, which the children imagined as a place of farms, horses, and family that they were excited to move to. Thus, they were not prepared for the realities of Mexican life. Miguel struggled to support his family with his glass business. Meanwhile, the store in Los Angeles was doing well during the war years, and so the family returned to the city in 1942.[175] Families like the Venegases developed deep transnational ties to both countries with members living on both sides.

Even when returnees grew up, married locally in Mexico, and settled down, they could be drawn back towards migration. Hortencia Martinez de Benitez settled in Mexico until she became an adult, at which point she returned to the United States. But that was not the case for all of her fifteen siblings. Some went north temporarily to work and send back money, and others migrated permanently. Other siblings got married in Mexico and settled there permanently.[176] Thousands of these migrant families ended up in border towns, expanding the populations of Tijuana and Mexicali.[177]

Mariana Gonzalez, who was US-born and whose story began this chapter, fit this mold. She wanted to go north to join her sister, despite her husband's desire to stay in La Barca, Jalisco. Her desire to return home continued even after her sister's death in the 1940s. When she decided to return to the United States, this proved a more difficult process than she had imagined. She was unable to secure papers for her husband Fermin and children. Following the advice of another relative, she instead settled the family in Tijuana until an opportunity arose to take them across the border with or without documents. Such an opportunity did not come until 1960. For two decades, Mariana, fluent in two languages, crossed daily at San Ysidro to work as a house cleaner in San Diego while raising nine children in Tijuana. Her US citizenship afforded her the relative freedom of movement that most migrants lacked at the border. As the primary wage earner, her income allowed her children to live a middle-class life in Tijuana even as Fermin's business struggled. Most of her children eventually crossed the US border without documents, and she moved north to East Los Angeles, and then to Azusa, to live near her late sister's family.[178]

While repatriation has been painted as a rupture, the two worlds north and south of the border were never truly separate. Migrants stayed in contact with relatives in Mexico, and most returned to their hometowns. The Great Depression is usually thought of as ending the first era of mass Mexican migration and breaking up communities, but even at the height of these developments, Mexicans still made up a majority of field workers in California, and two-thirds of the workers in the beet fields of the Midwest and the cotton fields of Texas through the 1930s. Along the Rio Grande Valley, the cross-border seasonal migration of cotton field workers continued.[179] Migrants, especially of the second generation, were returning in small numbers to California, Texas, and Illinois even before the World War II economy started to draw in a whole new generation of migrants.

The resumption of large-scale migration is not surprising considering migrants' active stance through the Great Depression and repatriation crisis of the 1930s and the limits of the rural economy. While most returned as a direct result of hardship in the United States, many saw it as an opportunity to come home. They contributed to making return a reality by sending letters, joining organizations, and demanding land. After going back to their hometowns and region, they called on their relatives, acquaintances, and organizations to help them restart their lives. As groups and as individuals, they used these networks to become involved in local repatriate organizations, set up businesses, join the agrarian movement, and migrate to other parts of Mexico and the United States. That they used their social capital to migrate again should not be surprising given how meager their earnings and lack of resources were. It was especially unsurprising for the estimated 40% of "repatriates" who were US-born children and for whom Mexico was never home. Those who maintained links in the United States had an existing infrastructure for migration that enabled them to make new choices in the 1940s.

Mexican society did not have a language to describe the world and practices of circular migration that became entrenched in these decades. While intellectuals had looked at returning Mexicans as an opportunity, the reality of return had made many in Mexico pessimistic about the ability of these migrants, especially the US-born generation, to assimilate into society. However, returning migrants insisted they were part of Mexican society, citizens deserving of aid and land as farmers, if not as repatriates. They organized and sometimes took up arms for land. Their actions contributed to forcing the government's hand. They raised tensions, spurring land redistribution across central Mexico. The structural limits of the rural economy still made migration an attractive option, whether it was to the rapidly expanding cities or the United States. Leaving the country eventually became a way to prop up small agriculture. Migrants continued to see themselves as Mexicans even as they found new reasons to leave, and some children realized for the first time how American they were. Thus, a new generation began to reestablish practices of transnational migration.

Epilogue

The Persistent Political Economy of Migrant Labor

Ricardo Villalobos's father was a citizen of the United States, born in Rockdale, Illinois. His grandfather had been a migrant and railroad worker. During the Great Depression, the family, including his father, was forcibly repatriated to Mexico. Like many others, his father was unable to prove that he had been born in the United States and had a right to stay, so he returned to the country the only way he knew how: as a Mexican bracero, a guest worker.[1]

The bilateral Bracero Program was the culmination of twenty years of efforts by intellectuals, government officials, and agricultural interests. Since the early 1900s, the US Bureau of Immigration had been improvising immigration exceptions and looking for ways to formalize the recruiting and hiring of workers.[2] On the Mexican side, presidents going back to Porfirio Díaz had proposed ways to regulate migration. Mexican anthropologist Manuel Gamio, along with American intellectuals, charities, and migrant assistance organizations, had long believed that a formalized labor program was the way to avoid most of the abuses that befell workers.[3] Through the 1920s Mexican officials in the SRE inspired by French and Italian migrant agreements at a series of international conferences, developed their ideas for a bilateral labor program. Gamio participated in these conferences as he developed his own proposal.[4] In 1929, *Secretaría de Relaciones* Genaro Estrada sought to make a formal labor arrangement with the US government, as did Consul Enrique Santibañez.[5] All of these efforts failed because American growers felt no need to deviate from their practice of informal recruitment. World War II changed this dynamic.

The formal entry of the United States into the conflict and the resulting growth of the wartime economy and armed forces quickly led to labor shortages and calls to renew World War I era policies that allowed for temporary Mexican laborers. Signed in August 1942, the Mexican Farm Labor Agreement was the largest bilateral labor program in US history. It

Between Here and There. Daniel Morales, Oxford University Press. © Oxford University Press 2024.
DOI: 10.1093/oso/9780197612590.003.0009

implemented changes to Mexican migration that had long been sought: control of migration by both federal governments, guaranteed labor for employers, and some protections for workers. It was part of a turn in Mexican politics toward accommodation with the United States after Manuel Ávila Camacho became president of Mexico and consolidated the Institutional Revolutionary Party (PRI). Despite their fears that the program would hurt migrants or cause flight from the agricultural fields of northern Mexico, Mexican officials promoted it alongside a larger set of agreements between the two governments that covered debt, oil, and wartime investment. The program was created just in time for the 1942 sugar beet harvest, and its participants originally worked in sugar beets, cotton, vegetable and fruits, and other agricultural industries. Later, the program was opened to railroad workers. All of these industries had been dependent on Mexican labor for decades.

On paper, the program established a systematic way to recruit and organize migrant labor. The Mexican government established recruiting stations in Mexico City, but later opened them in several other major cities. Only landless men could apply; *ejidatarios* (those who worked communal land holdings) could not qualify. Workers applied locally, were selected, and then waited at recruiting centers to receive a contract outlining conditions. They were then taken by train to the border, where the US government acted as their employer. Workers were inspected and disinfected in a communal shower before being sent on to their individual employers. Wages were pegged to the prevailing rate as certified by the US Department of Labor and were set at no less than thirty cents per hour. Employers were required to pay for transportation, housing, and food. Ten percent of wages were supposed to go to Mexico's Agricultural Credit Bank, which braceros would receive on their return to Mexico. To enforce these provisions, the Mexican government placed inspectors who could press claims. Discrimination and abuses were banned and could cause a company to be blacklisted. Texas, notorious for its poor conditions and segregation, was at first deemed ineligible for the program. From 1942 to its conclusion in 1964, some 4.6 million Mexicans participated.

In Mexico, the program was heavily promoted as a modernizing project, part of the Allied war effort and Roosevelt's Good Neighbor Policy. Mexican bracero migrants were said to be defeating the Axis Powers through work while their wages supported families and built the rural economy. The skills they learned in the United States would make Mexicans, especially indigenous people, into modern citizens and consumers. The program became a

(a)

(b)

Figure E.1a and b In 1942, the Bracero Program was created between Mexico and the United States; the program institutionalized migration between both societies. First Braceros, Dorothea Lange, 1942. © The Dorothea Lange Collection, the Oakland Museum of California.

new way to create the post-revolutionary mestizo citizen.[6] Echoing earlier rhetoric on migration, President Camacho and the Mexican government believed that migrants working in the United States would enable rural Mexico to advance socially and technologically.

Control over choosing braceros quickly devolved to the local level as federal efforts to run a centralized recruiting program faltered. Originally, people could only sign up in Mexico City, but bribery and exploitation ran rampant, leading to a riot. The government turned over control of selection to the states, who, also not equipped, turned over control of the program to local municipal presidents. Local officials were encouraged to recruit landless farm workers, men with families as single men were thought to be more likely to skip out on contracts. Towns were each given set targets for recruitment. In letters to municipal presidents, President Camacho used the language of civilizational uplift to enlist them in recruiting and organizing the program across rural and central Mexico. In practice, local officials used the program for political ends, giving contracts to those who had a particular hardship (like a natural disaster), were well connected, were agitating for land, were a threat to the PRI because of their Cristero ties, were political opponents of the local party boss, or were simply willing to pay a bribe. All of this reinforced the local nature of the Bracero Program, entrenching the dominance of central Mexico in migration to the United States.[7]

In theory, the Bracero Program was separate from previous labor arrangements, but in practice, it operated along the same local and transnational migrant networks established in the preceding decades. The largest sending areas of braceros were the same places that had sent workers north before. Local officials, including clergy, acted as brokers that chose who did and did not receive a contract.[8] As time passed, this new wave of migration grew to a massive scale and became increasingly difficult to control. In San Luis Potosí for example, undocumented migration was as numerous by the end of the war as braceros. This high proportion of undocumented workers characterized the program across Mexico.

In San Luis Potosí, state and local interests aligned to support the Bracero Program. After the program's creation, the Southern Pacific and Santa Fe railroads lobbied the US government to add railroad workers to the agreement, and the program began to recruit them in 1943. Governor Gonzalo N. Santos saw the program as a way to alleviate unemployment at minimal cost and put the experience of former migrants to use. After lobbying the government, the railroad recruiting center was moved to the state capital, and later to Querétaro.[9] Braceros were understood to be emigrating for many of the same reasons as an earlier generation. *El Heraldo*, a newspaper in San Luis Potosí, stated: "They go with the desire to obtain enough money to 'build a future' for themselves and their families. Emigrating to work in order to provide for their families 'those pressing needs that have been denied to them,' they leave 'full of faith' and hope that they will improve their living conditions." A good number went north because of a lack of land or low agricultural productivity. Others went to pursue new job opportunities. For example, one worker quit his work at the American Smelting and Refining Company (ASARCO), the copper giant in Mexico, to work as a bracero.[10] By 1945, 65,000 Mexicans worked across the United States as railroad section labor workers.[11]

In the town of San Martin de Hidalgo in Jalisco, the program depended on the organizational efforts of communities, families, and especially women to function. The municipal president, Gabino Preciado, pushed residents to sign up, and many of them did. More importantly, they were encouraged to lend money to working-class residents who wanted to participate but could not afford to. While men migrated, women worked back home, took care of families, ran businesses, and oversaw the finances of community organizations. Braceros and their families also benefited from the experience of former migrants and repatriates. Former migrants cautioned against being too optimistic about working in the United States, noting that it could be accompanied by discrimination, hardship, and practical challenges such as saving money and avoiding bad behavior. They warned migrants that transitioning from the bracero lifestyle back to long-term settlement at home with their families was difficult, and that "careful planning would be necessary for dealing with family separation, increased debt, and tense ethnic, gender, race, and class relations."[12] Manuel Ricardo Rosas, an ex-migrant and administrator of the San Martin de Hidalgo Bracero Program, facilitated agreements and loans, wrote letters of recommendation, and offered advice about journeying and working in the north.[13] Communities harnessed the resources and the experience of former migrants like Rosas to carry out the Bracero Program.

Scholars have critiqued the Bracero Program for importing workers without granting them rights and for breaking most, if not all, of its promises. The ten inspectors initially assigned by the Mexican government to the program were not enough to keep employers from violating the terms of the agreement. The US Department of Labor allowed growers' associations to determine the prevailing wage, which was set at lower rates than domestic laborers would work for, creating shortages of willing American laborers and necessitating the use of braceros. Wages were frequently lower than the legal minimum and were often paid late. Workers were often charged for their poor housing, transportation, and food when this was supposed to be covered by employers. Complaints often went unheard, injured workers were sent away untreated, and braceros' attempts to organize were met with violence. Thousands of growers, especially in Texas, hired workers at the border, undermining the program to such an extent that the Immigration and Naturalization Service (INS) took to legalizing undocumented workers at the border to keep people officially in the program. In doing so, they effectively acquiesced to the growers' practices, encouraging a migration that, by the late 1940s, was greater than those who came via the official program. The US agencies running the Bracero Program—the INS, State Department, and Department of Labor—worked toward different and contradictory goals.[14]

After the war, the Mexican government lost the ability to shape the program and increasingly bowed to demands that sacrificed migrants' working conditions. As prospective braceros had to get letters of support from local municipal presidents, state officials, and federal officials, as well as identification and medical checks, more resorted to bribery to obtain selection cards. As more recruiting stations were added, the process was even more difficult to regulate.[15] Many workers suffered psychological trauma and injuries, sometimes fatal, in the fields. Medical care was often inadequate or nonexistent. Workers frequently came back to Mexico with nothing, and it was easy to fall victim to coyotes, scams, or Mexican *Departamento de Migración* agents who committed abuses.[16] The 10% of earnings that were supposed to be returned to braceros upon their return home was never paid. Braceros who failed to save enough money had to migrate north again.

Braceros themselves, however, often saw the program differently. Turned into transnational subjects by their time in both places, braceros pursued their own ends, making the program their own. Their goals varied from saving money, seeking adventure, and buying consumer goods to raising large families and remaking their lives.[17] Women and families built separate lives while apart and challenged traditional notions of family and gender roles.[18] Braceros defied the Mexican government's efforts to control the narrative of the program, the official *política de la dignidad* that portrayed braceros as idealized Mexican men, instead opposing the PRI, seeking a transnational labor union, maintaining indigenous identities, or freeing themselves from conservative social norms.[19]

These two interpretations of the Bracero Program—as an imported neocolonial labor project, or as an opportunity for millions of rural families—are two sides of the same coin. Workers and communities fought to pursue opportunities from the realistic options available to them, be it bracero or undocumented worker, and found ways to expand the realm of possibilities. The formal mechanisms of labor migration were controlled by the US and Mexican states, ending an era when migration was almost entirely a social phenomenon. Yet the practical organization of the program at the local level and the realities of undocumented migration outside of official channels show that migration remained a social phenomenon dependent on interpersonal networks. Municipal presidents, parish priests, and hometown associations chose who migrated and funded them. It was because of migrants' strong ties to their communities that, even when migration was co-opted by government bureaucracies, they continued to come overwhelmingly from the same towns in central Mexico that had previously been sending people. In this sense, migrants were able to build social structures outside of the official state.

From the early 1940s to 1968, Mexico's economy lifted millions out of poverty as the country industrialized and pursued import substitution. The PRI solidified its hold on power and created an image of a new, modern Mexico, one that fulfilled the promise of the Mexican Revolution. Yet the golden age of Mexico's economic miracle was accompanied by permanent migration as part of the political economy of rural Mexico. There was never a time when Mexico's economy was strong enough to dissuade people from leaving for *El Norte*. Critics of Mexico's government on both the left and the right pointed to the Bracero Program as a new colonialism, the selling of Mexico's people to the United States. Officials within the government and critics alike associated continuing migration with the limits of land reform.[20] Yet even if the Mexican public and critics were not reconciled to migration, the political elite was. The Bracero Program marked the acceptance of mass migration as part of the political economy of Mexico, at least by the PRI. In the 1920s and 1930s, the Mexican elite saw Mexico as the rightful place for all Mexicans; they viewed migration as desertion and sought the return of migrants. The Bracero Program, once underway, created its own dynamics, driving more people, both documented and undocumented, across the border. Officials increasingly saw migration as economically and politically necessary, a political safety valve, and used it to bolster their state-building project. The program formalized and provided state sanction for the political economy of migrant labor between the two countries while drawing a distinction between "legal" migration (migration organized by the Bracero Program) and "illegal" or undocumented and unsanctioned labor migration.

The movement of people between Mexico and the United States is the largest migration between two states in modern history. Both societies have been changed by this reality. This book can only partially explore how migration became a deeply embedded reality in the lives of millions of families on both sides of the border, as well as an entrenched part of the social and political structures of both countries.

Expanding on the Manifest Destiny of settler colonialism, the US economy reshaped the Southwest and Mexico simultaneously. The United States came to rely heavily on non-white, non-citizen labor in the American West during these years. Nowhere was this more true than in Mexico, where conquest was followed by economic neo-colonialism. The widespread violence of the early twentieth century, both state and private, served to establish the limits of Mexicans' rights, labeling them politically and racially as non-white and outside the polity. The mostly open border and welcoming legal system was replaced by physical markers of exclusion. Small ports of entry were replaced by walls and fencing, the border patrol, and raids. Most legal avenues to migration were cut off. The modern legal conception of nation-states made it possible to imagine a border, separation across the borderlands, and the existence of the "illegal alien." Layered over racial divides, this distinction between alien and citizen made possible, in the 1930s, the largest expulsion of people in US history up to that time. In the 1940s, the mostly self-organized social phenomena of migration was replaced with the unfree vision of the migrant laborer. Devoid of rights and excluded from the political communities of both the United States and Mexico, the bracero and the undocumented came to symbolize the inequality of power between the two societies. Mexican migrants constituted an internal colony of American empire. The migrant economy is, then, the material manifestation of this imbalance of power.

The political economy of migration could then be understood as a phenomenon that leaves people with little agency over their own lives. Yet this interpretation does not account for the motivations and experiences of migrants themselves. It does not mesh with what migrants themselves had to say about their actions and motivations. While state policies and major political and military events framed migration, they do not explain why migration continued after the end of various crises, or how circular migratory routes were encouraged, guided, and sustained on both sides of the border. They do not clarify how communities formed and operated. And they do not elucidate the various acts of organizing and resisting, under various competing political visions, that Mexican migrants undertook in this era. At every turn, they defied the expectations of elites in both countries. They protested for better working and living conditions, joined political movements, and pushed back against Mexican and American officials using the tools they had access to. Their actions were often at the center of political debate in both nations. By looking at how migrant culture took on a life of its own and began to change expectations in Mexico, this book underscores how the creation of a political economy is profoundly influenced by its participants.

The construction of the political economy of migration was both a top-down and a bottom-up process. Migrants and the state interacted on a daily level in numerous ways, but only a tiny portion of their direct communications are preserved in the institutional historical record. Reading against the grain of institutional records in both countries illuminates how state agents were acting, reacting, and negotiating with migrants, which in turn shows how migrants were acting and reacting to state agents and institutions. What they said and did demonstrate that migrants had more agency than is commonly believed; they shaped the creation of the structure of migration as much as policymakers did.

Migrants pushed back against efforts to control them. What emerges is a story of local negotiation, as governments, businesses, labor contractors, and various other intermediaries contended with the interests and actions of migrants. While most of the resistance of migrants was small scale—quitting, migrating, and seeking out other opportunities—there was much overlap with larger forms of resistance. Labor organizing and strikes were highly public reactions to exploitative conditions, perhaps not the most common ones but not rare either. Equally important, labor organizing and labor organizations acted as vehicles of cross-border politics and networks.

Interpersonal networks operated in conjunction with a social world of organizations that advanced migrants' interests in Mexico and the United States. Some networks, like those of the *Partido Liberal Mexicano* (PLM), enabled successful cross-border organizing, inspired a revolt in southern Texas, and created the conditions for strikes in the 1910s. Others, such as *mutualistas*, businesses, newspapers, and consulates, were critical in the formation of a cultural and political community known as *México de Afuera*. Simultaneously, Mexican American organizations were articulating a claim to rights based on US citizenship and were the backbone of the country's largest wave of agricultural strikes in the 1930s. The circulation of ideas followed from the circulation of people.

Mass migration created a large diaspora of Mexicans in a land that had once been part of Mexico. There, they lived and worked amongst pre-existing Mexican American communities that had their own long histories of struggle. The transnational economy and culture of migration that arose by the 1920s posed a challenge to US and Mexican society. In the United States, the "Mexican Problem" became a major political issue, while in Mexico, official discourse saw migration as a problem to be curtailed, repatriated, and brought under control. Both countries saw migrants as "Mexican" and acted accordingly to keep them out or to force them to return. Although neither country saw a place for circular migrants in its conception of the nation, individuals nonetheless continued to build migrant lives. Some migrants began to articulate an expansive vision of transnational belonging, including through the PLM, communist-backed unions, and other radical organizations. However, most did not, at least not explicitly. Before the 1940s, migrants generally thought of themselves as Mexican, or *México de Afuera* (a political identity based on Mexican nationalism), and did not seek a radical departure from their country of birth. Instead, they saw themselves as continuing to be part of their families and home communities even as their practices challenged those definitions.

Interactions between migrants, US and Mexican governments, employers, and communities show how circular migrant pathways were laid down and, once established, reproduced over time. As migration increased, it increased tensions and became a major political issue in both countries. Policies were enacted in response to migrants' actions as officials sought to channel and, ultimately, curtail this movement. Yet migration was never fully determined by capital or the state. It was sustained by migrants' familial and village ties in Mexico, by their own networks of information and support, by their resistance to American employers and immigration agents, and by their own desires and agendas for economic and political improvement. Migrants organized and pushed both states for recognition, for land in Mexico, for labor rights in the United States.

The growth of modern global capitalism has unleashed new waves of migration even as walls have gone up around the world. Efforts to build the border began in the late nineteenth century but took on a new urgency during the Mexican Revolution (1910–1920). During the 1920s, the United States tried to close off migration, began to fortify the border, and established a border patrol. In the 1930s, it forced 425,000 people to repatriate to Mexico. The desire for labor continued after the Bracero Program ended in 1964, but in its wake, people were forced to migrate without documents, outside the bounds of governmental protection, and without legal rights. Despite the obstacles, migration became normalized across Mexico as millions of new families came to participate in circular migration and forge transnational lives. More and more barriers to block their activity have been built. Starting in the 1970s, fences were erected along the US-Mexico border. More were constructed in the 1990s, and hundreds of miles went up after 9/11. This has made the journey far more costly and dangerous, pushing people to stay in the United States longer and forcing migrants into remote deserts. The fences injure and maim hundreds of people every year. Since 1994, more than 10,000 have died trying to cross the border.

The creation of hard borders and the regulation of people have occurred at the same time the neo-liberal policies have lowered the barriers to the free movement of capital. Free trade has not brought the free movement of people, even though nineteenth-century classical liberalism took seriously the right of people to choose their country. As global capitalism has transformed labor and migration patterns, nation-states have worked in the interest of capital to limit people's ability to claim belonging and rights. The North American Free Trade Agreement (NAFTA) undermined local agriculture and small industries. This led to increased migration north from a broader area, including regions that had sent few migrants previously, such as southern Mexico, and especially from indigenous communities. More than eleven million people from dozens of nationalities are now living undocumented in the United States and are shut out of the nation's official social and political institutions.[21]

The US interventions in Latin America continue to reverberate as migration and refugee crises. From colonial projections to the Cold War to the War on Drugs, US policy has often destabilized nations and fueled cycles of violence and poverty. Present-day difficulties of local governance have created new waves of migration, especially from the Northern Triangle countries of Guatemala, Honduras, and El Salvador; from the Caribbean; and increasingly from South America. These crises continue to challenge both US officials at the border and antiquated legal definitions of refugees.

Within the United States, the building of these barriers is driven by anti-immigrant politics. The machinery of deportation has spread across the country and has grown across successive administrations from both parties. In 1996, the Illegal Immigration Reform and Immigrant Responsibility Act greatly expanded penalties for undocumented immigration, cutting off pathways to legalization and expanding the number of offenses considered criminal. The law also banned police and local governments from prohibiting officials from reporting the status of immigrants to federal agents. The federal government and states have moved to limit the rights of migrants, both documented and undocumented, especially since 2001. Since then, successive expansions have made the Border Patrol the largest federal US law enforcement agency. Taking advantage of the growth of the criminal justice system, the Border Patrol, along with Immigration and Customs Enforcement (ICE), has worked with local law enforcement and with programs such as Secure Communities and 287(g) to detain and deport around 400,000 people per year in the mid-2010s. The Trump administration expanded enforcement to new levels, including policies that separated thousands of children from their families, forced asylum seekers to wait for lengthy periods in refugee camps in Mexico, and used Public Health Title 42, which dates to the early twentieth century, to summarily expel most asylum seekers due to their supposed COVID-19 risk. Biden kept the "stay in Mexico" policy and Title 42 into his term out of a fear of a backlash. Since 2022 the administration has opened some new avenues for refugees but that created a political backlash. Deportations today dwarf the repatriations of the 1930s even before the threatened actions of a second Trump Administration that promise to be the largest deportations in American history.[22]

New movements have arisen, led by migrants themselves, to challenge the politics of exclusion. In 2006, the largest protest marches in American history up to that point culminated in May Day marches that drew millions across the country. These public events were instrumental in defeating HR 4437, the most anti-immigrant law yet attempted in Congress. But the political battles moved to the states over the following year. The immigrant rights movement evolved. Students pushing for the Dream Act for undocumented minors became a potent force in American politics, pressuring President Obama to enact the Deferred Action for Childhood Arrivals (DACA) program in 2012, which offers temporary protected status but not legal permanent residency. A new sanctuary movement has grown in churches, college campuses, and cities, echoing that of the 1980s. Latino organizations have advocated for more power and rights as Latino Americans have been elected across the country.

In Mexico, public perceptions of migrants shifted in the early 2000s, when President Vicente Fox called them "heroes" for their tireless work. This was the culmination of narratives that saw migrants, including braceros, as good, patriotic, family-centered people who sacrificed for their children, communities, and nation.[23] In 2008, the federal government decriminalized the undocumented in Mexico, and in 2011, it passed a new *Ley de Migración* that brought Mexican law into accordance with the International Convention on the Protection of Rights of All Migrant Workers and Members of their Families (ICMW). Since then, the arrival of a wave of Central American refugees, mostly children and families, has called this commitment into question as Mexican policymakers have struggled to respond. Meanwhile, rejecting older forms of nationalism, Mexican immigrant rights activists have embraced a new language of human rights, joining with other social movements to call for a just society based on rights for all. The Mexican government recently adopted the UN Global Compact for Migration, enshrining human rights for migrants in law, though actual follow-through remains to be seen.

The discourse of human rights has not gained as much traction in the United States, but activists are challenging longstanding norms. They reject the framework that justifies the inequality of rights. They have pointed out that, while the Universal Declaration of Human Rights recognizes the right of people to leave the country, it should also oblige nation-states to allow people to enter. They move beyond narratives of deserving and non-deserving immigrants that have long dominated public debate and reject attempts to determine who is deserving of being in the country based on participation in capitalist systems, instead advocating for a system based on universal human rights. Yet this rhetoric co-exists with immigrant rights campaigns that put labor at the center, seeking to stress the importance of those who labor in the factories and fields to the functioning of our society. Unions and non-governmental organizations need to campaign for equal rights for all workers, whether their legal status is that of citizen, permanent resident, H-2A visa holder, or undocumented. The labor of those at the edges of society should not remain invisible, especially after having been deemed essential workers in the US economy during the COVID-19 pandemic.

Over a century of mass migration, Mexican and US societies have deeply shaped each other. The efforts of states to keep people out have made transnational migration and migrants' lives difficult, but they are unlikely to stop this movement. Far more people, from more diverse origins, crossed back and forth in the twentieth century than in the nineteenth, and the borderlands of the Southwest remain a fluid zone of exchange for ideas, politics, and culture. The regions of exchange extend well beyond the borderlands, as this book has shown. Mexico and the United States are home to each other's largest foreign populations, are each other's largest investors, and are nearly each other's top trading partners. The foremost transnational tie between communities in these two countries remains the people who have built lives in between. Latin Americans are now the largest minority in the United States, at 18% of the country's population. Of the fifty-five million Latinos in the US, thirty-six million, or 63%, are Mexican or Mexican American. As migration from Mexico decreases due to demographic changes, migration from Central America has grown. In Villa Juárez, San Luis Potosí, as in many other towns, a new generation is migrating even as another returns. These transnational ties, tested by governments, the Great Depression, and too much violence and tragedy throughout the twentieth century will continue to shape lives well into the twenty-first century.

APPENDIX

Counting the Uncounted

The Mexican Migrant Study, 1910–1940

The graph in Figure A.1 obscures more than it illuminates.[1] Official numbers of Mexican migration from this era peaked at 89,000 in 1924. Although the actual immigration figures are much larger when accounting for all types and forms of Mexican migration, the trends are relatively correct.[2] However, the official data do not capture the nature of the back-and-forth movement between the two countries (see Figure A.1). More importantly, Figure A.1 only includes official "legal immigrants"—people who came through the Bureau of Immigration's checkpoints who stated their intention to live permanently in the United States and met all corresponding regulations and fees. After 1917, this included a literacy test and an eighteen-dollar head tax, not an insubstantial amount for a migrant to pay, especially if he brought a family.

The graph also does not include the 73,000 workers who were brought in from 1919 to 1921 under exclusions to the 1917 Immigration Act and Alien Contract Labor Law of 1885 as temporary workers. More importantly, it does not include non-statistical aliens—people who were not considered immigrants because they did not intend to live permanently in the United States. These could range from a border town resident crossing for a day to migrant workers who said their visit would be for less than six months. The largest percentage of these non-statistical crossers were refugees who fled the violence of the

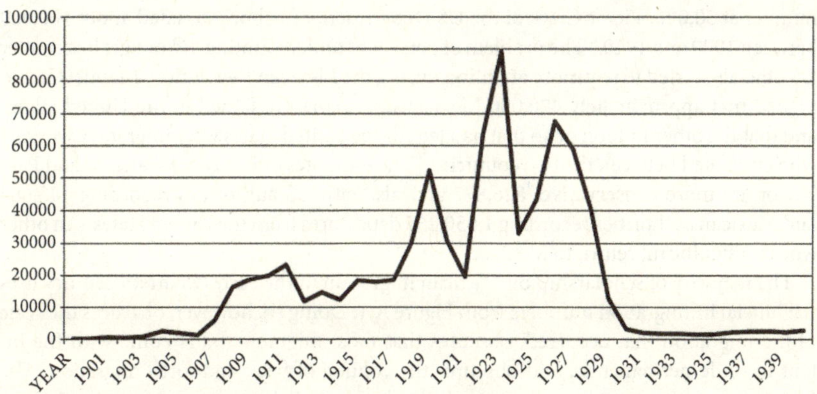

Figure A.1 Official numbers of Mexican immigrants to the United States, 1900–1940. US Census.

Mexican Revolution while intending to return to Mexico soon after. Most non-statistical aliens who crossed in the 1910s stayed longer than six months. While not counted as official immigrants, they were a key demographic, especially among people who would later develop circular migration patterns.

While the Bureau of Immigration didn't keep official non-statistical migrant data until the 1920s. Linda Hall and Don M. Coerver's work on non-statistical migrants gives us a better picture. Between 1911 and 1920, 628,672 non-statistical Mexicans crossed, dwarfing the 261,699 legal immigrants. In most years during this era, non-statistical aliens were about double the number of statistical ones. The exception was the height Mexican Revolution, when 123,484 refugees in 1917 ballooned the non-statistical category. The flow shifted from individuals seeking to flee the violence of the revolution to large family groups by the end of the decade.[3]

Finally, Figure A.1 also does not include the people who simply walked over the border. A major source of the problem in counting how many migrants came to the United States is that many were going back and forth without any documentation. The Bureau estimated from 10% to upwards of 50% of the total number of Mexicans crossing the border simply never presented themselves to a border station, depending on the year. Officials estimated that the number who went back to Mexico every year was more than half of the total number who arrived. To give one example, the US Census reported a total 927,000 immigrants from Mexico between 1910 and 1928, yet Mexican authorities had 1,085,222 returnees reporting themselves as coming back within a *shorter* time period. Mexican anthropologist Manuel Gamio, in describing the circular and unreliable nature of migration between 1920 and 1925, noted that "329,269 Mexicans departed for the United States, and—surprising fact—in the same period not only that number returned to Mexico, but 228,449 more!"[4]

While the Bureau of Immigration did not count many sources of migration, scholars have been able to use Mexican government data to substantiate a greater volume of migrations. Gamio used these records to offer his own estimate of 890,000 Mexicans in the United States in 1926, including 438,000 "immigrants" and 230,000 transients who were staying a short time for work.[5] More recently, Fernando Saul Alanís Enciso found that Mexican officials counted 22,000 Mexicans leaving for the United States in 1906, about ten times the number of entries recorded by the United States. In 1908, more than 16,000 people passed into El Paso alone, and in 1910, Mexican officials pegged the number at 50,000. Victor Clark of the US Department of Labor estimated about 100,000 between 1900 and 1910.[6] The problem of persistent undercounting did not get better after US officials started to pay more attention during the Mexican Revolution. Manuel Gamio argued that approximately 470,000 Mexicans permanently settled in the United States, and that the other million or so that had left for the United States were migratory workers who circulated between the two countries.[7] The estimates of Lawrence Cardoso and Paul Taylor are more conservative: 826,877 arrivals, with US authorities recording 145,684 and Mexican authorities recording 1,050,256 departures from the United States—in other words, a significant return to Mexico.[8]

The majority of scholarship on Mexican migration in the early twentieth century uses the official immigration numbers from Figure A.1. Doing so, however, obscures the scale of the migration that occurred, obscures that most migrants didn't come with the intent to settle permanently, and obscures the volume of back-and-forth migration. The flow is far too large to account for traditional non-statistical migrants who lived along the border and crossed back and forth regularly. The figures should include a significant proportion of people who were going north to work. While the sheer volume of traffic and the large number of people going through as non-statistical migrants make it hard to pin down how many people were going back and forth, it appears that at least half of the non-statistical crossers should be considered labor migrants, and that at least as many were crossing back into Mexico every year. In other words, the distinction between immigrant and non-statistical aliens is not useful for the case of Mexican migrants, and both should be considered when talking about this movement.

The Mexican Migrant Study

The goal of the study that is the focus of this Appendix was to address these problems and trace the contours of migration, to see where people were going and when, and to identify what changed over time. As such, it is not designed to answer the question of how many people participated in migration or went back to Mexico. Other scholars have considered these questions, and I believe it is more fruitful to examine the migrants themselves rather than revisiting that issue. The study is thus designed to track migrants over time, not in the aggregate because that changes over time as people entered and left the country, but as individuals, in order to see where they went and how they fared. Thus, the study follows a random sample of Mexican migrants over thirty years, with smaller checks in the years before and after the period.

The sample is drawn from a random selection of the US population in 1920. I chose 1920 because it was the first year for which a large number of Mexican migrants first appeared in the US Census.[9] The overall random selection was 0.5% of the US population from IPUMS, from which I eliminated everyone except those born in Mexico. This yielded a random sample of about 6,000 people born in Mexico and about 800 US born children of migrants, residing in the United States in 1920. Using the US Census is not without problems. Minorities and migrants are undercounted in most historical censuses, Mexican migrants even more so. A large number didn't have stable homes and moved frequently, especially those who lived in boarding houses. They were also suspicious of US government agents asking questions, especially in the 1930 census, which occurred during repatriation and a large anti-Mexican backlash. The 1930 census also designated Mexicans a separate race, a possible prerequisite for restriction. As a result, the census tends to have a selection bias, with more and better results regarding those who are more stable, have families, are skilled, and live in single-family housing, and less data with less reliability for those who are single, migrants, and work in agriculture, railroads, and mines—the three largest industries for Mexicans in the 1920s. To counteract this, I sought a large initial sample. This approach captures a greater number of individuals who are underrepresented in the census data. With a larger sample, the data will be better, although the bias is not eliminated and still needs to be addressed in the analysis.

In order to show changes over time among a migrant population, one where the composition of neighborhoods and locations were changing constantly, a normal census study that looks at changes in a given location is inadequate. Instead, this study looks at each household so that, instead of an aggregate study that suggests an anonymous stand-in for all Mexicans, my sample comprises a cohort that is followed over a period of time. I tracked the cohort from 1920 back in time to the 1910 US Census and forward to the 1940 US Census and the 1930 Mexican Census. When possible, information was gathered from border crossing cards. This involved a laborious process of looking up each individual's census card across four decades.[10] In the 1910 census, about 320 people from the 1920 census were identified, and in the 1930 and 1940 censuses, 1,100 people were identified from the original list, or approximately 600 households. I used Geographic Information Systems (GIS) to track the special mobility of the sample migrants from 1920 to 1930, allowing us to see where people were living relative to each other and to the general population.[11]

This study used the definitions and categories that have been used in the histography of immigration. These studies used census, nationalization, and other government records to show the acculturation, spread, and economic mobility of selected immigrant populations. I use their definitions when I believe they shed light on how Mexican migrants adjusted to life in the United States, but not when I don't think the methods would help. Scholars, going back to Stephan Thernstrom in his classic work on the immigrant working class of Boston, have run into a particular problem in following a cohort across time—that is, working-class men (often from immigrant backgrounds) disappear from census and official records. This is especially the case in studies that look at only one city or region, and it was a major reason I undertook a national and transitional study. The only other major study of return migration was undertaken by Zachary Ward, who found that return migration was very common in the pre-Great Depression era among European and Mexican migrants. He discovered that while the bulk of European migrants who returned home were those who had done worse in the US labor market, Mexicans who returned had the exact same characteristics as those who stayed (among single men). Corroborating my arguments elsewhere, he also found that people from the Bajío central states of Mexico were the most likely to return home. My results were the same, but with a larger share of workers disappearing from the records. I argue that this is largely a result of the migratory nature of the work that Mexican migrants undertook. It is also consistent with the high levels of return migration scholars of European migrants found in this era as well, especially the migrants from southern Europe.[12]

Where Were Mexican Migrants Living in 1920?

By 1920, Mexican migrants had already spread out from the borderlands and across the United States. The railroad, cotton, vegetable, fruit, and sugar beet migration routes that were just coming into existence in 1910 were solidly in place by 1920. Mexicans in the sample were found in most states in the United States by 1920, although still heavily concentrated in the borderlands, where they worked in agriculture, especially cotton. Significant populations lived in the fruit- and vegetable-growing areas of California, the mining region of Arizona and Colorado, the sugar-beet region stretching across the entire Midwest from Colorado to Michigan, and along the major railroad routes in the West that concentrated in Chicago. Large communities also existed in places as far removed as Louisiana and Florida, where Mexican migrants worked on plantations, and Pennsylvania, where they worked in mills for Bethlehem steel.[13] For the most part, however, Mexicans lived and worked along transportation and agricultural corridors. In major hubs like Los Angeles, San Antonio, and El Paso, migrants were spread across the metropolitan region but concentrated in specific neighborhoods. In other places, such as the Rio Grande Valley, Kansas, Oklahoma, and Arizona, they were concentrated along agriculture, railroad, and mining corridors.

Table A.1 Eight US States with the Largest Mexican Population, 1920

State	Number (Percentage)	State	Number (Percentage)
Texas	3,179 (53%)	Kansas	163 (2.7%)
California	989 (17%)	Colorado	145 (2.4%)
Arizona	754 (12.5%)	Oklahoma	66 (1.1%)
New Mexico	275 (4.6%)	Illinois	64 (1.06%)

Source: Daniel Morales, sample of Mexican population in the United States, from US population census, 1920.

Looking at the total number of people in each place, however, reminds us how much migration out of the borderlands was a new process in 1920. The 1920 base group allowed for a large picture of the Mexican population in the United States as a whole. This population was overwhelmingly based in Texas. More than three times as many Mexicans lived in Texas than in any other state in the sample, followed by California, Arizona, and New Mexico (Table A.1). Only then do Midwestern states show up in the totals. The US Census has a well-known bias towards stable families in immigrant populations, and it is probable that this is changing the results. This is especially the case with housing, where 4,733 people were reported living in single-family homes and only 202 in official boarding houses. Yet of that 4,733, about 700 were single men boarding with other families. Mexican families often had various sources of income; taking in borders was a common way for families to decrease the risks of the migrant labor market.

Characteristics of Population

The sample cohort is consistent with the demographic knowledge we have of Mexican migration in this period. While scholars had thought that Mexican migrants before 1965 were overwhelmingly single young men, recent studies have shown that a significant number of families and women migrated as well, that most men were in their twenties rather than just entering adulthood, and that significant numbers were married and had families in Mexico. These trends are all true of the sample population. There were 2,111 heads of households in the 1920 sample. The majority were men without families, though this could just mean their families were in Mexico, and a third of households consisted of families. The sample population does have more men than women (55% to 45%), and a majority are also single, but not overwhelmingly so (52% to 42% married). The sample population had spent an average of eight years in the United States, longer than anticipated. Likewise, the average age was 26.25 years, older than people normally assume, but younger than the 29 year average age that Ward found in his own study of this population.[14] About 60% could read while 58% could write, which makes them more educated than the Mexican population in Mexico in general. However, only 32% could speak English; 68% spoke Spanish only. Overall, these trends do some reflect a bias towards more settled people; however, it is much less than in the 1910 census and 1930 census, with a large population of single male workers that isn't captured in the other censuses.[15]

Where Were Migrants Working in 1920?

While the literature has focused on agricultural workers, the majority of Mexicans in the study did not work directly in the fields. The 1920 sample indicates that of the 53% of Mexicans working in agriculture, only about a third worked directly in the fields, with an additional 20% of Mexicans in ancillary roles. The people in the sample were employed in a much broader set of jobs and industries than the literature would indicate, with railroad workers and industrial workers together making up a slightly higher number than those in the fields. Railroads, manufacturing, and mining were the largest industries after agriculture, and the rest were spread among other industries.

When it came to skill level, most tended to be at the bottom, and there were almost as many skilled laborers as semiskilled ones. Making use of the same categories previous studies of migrants have done in order to make sense of the hundreds of different jobs migrants performed, Table A.2 breaks down the sample into levels of skill required for each job. These are skill indicators, correlated, but not direct indicators of socioeconomic status. For example, a clerk is white collar, but not well off. Yet in general, skill levels are indicators of job type, location within the larger economy, and settlement. When looking at the Mexican migrants in the sample, more than 90% worked in some sort of blue-collar job, with "laborer" being by far the most common job description. This was true in both agricultural jobs and industrial jobs. There was also a significant minority who were skilled workers, a sixth of the sample, with skilled mining jobs and heavy industrial jobs leading the way.

Overall, none of the demographic descriptions of the Mexican sample population in the United States in 1920 are surprising in light of recent literature or recent studies. There is an oversampling of large families and white-collar workers because the US Census in general did a better job of tracking them.

Not in the US Census

In following people and families from 1920 in 1930 and 1940, it quickly became clear that the most significant result would be what was missing rather than what was found. Two-thirds of the sample in 1920 were not found again in the US or Mexican Census. This included most of the single male agricultural labor workers and nearly all the railroad workers (see Table A.7). Of those found again, 578 families were in the United States, and a further 58 were in Mexico, in 1930. This figure, however, is misleading. While most people could not be completely identified again in either census, they were much more likely to have candidates in the Mexican Census. For example, for a

Table A.2 Skill Level Among Mexican Workers, 1920

Unskilled	60%	White Collar	5.5%
Semiskilled	16.6%	Professional	2%
Skilled	15%		

Source: Daniel Morales, sample of Mexican population in the United States, from US population census, 1920.

male who was without a family in the 1920 US Census, there might be a dozen people with his name and age in Mexico in 1930, making it impossible to positively identify them with any confidence. There were about 200 such cases. We could not narrow the choices, especially among young men of similar names. This was also sometimes the case in the United States, but it occurred at a much lower rate because of the availability of other supporting documents like city directories or border crossing cards. A significant proportion of these workers were also living migratory lives in the United States, where the census could not capture them. This reasoning led me to conclude that even through most people completely identified again were in the United States, not Mexico, the majority of the people in the overall sample were migrant workers, with no fixed home.[16]

The findings given here must be interpreted in light of the fact that most people could not be positively located again ten years later. There is still the issue of those who were identified in 1930 and 1940. In 1940, 640 families were found, but many of these were children starting new families. This is enough to draw patterns and trends from, especially in the United States.

Where Were the Migrants Living?

The majority of people in most major cities were not living in the same city in 1930 as they were in 1920. To prove this, we also ran the sample names through city directories. In a majority of cases, people only showed up once around 1920 and not in later years. In the United States, while Texas was still home to the largest concentration of people in the sample, various trends are worth noting. California's share of the Mexican sample population increased from 17% to 29% in 1930, while Arizona's share decreased (Table A.3). Of the people in the cohort who lived in Missouri, Montana, Nebraska, Nevada, Minnesota, and Michigan, none still lived in those states a decade later. Kansas had five families stay the whole ten years, while Oklahoma had two families and Iowa had one. This illustrates the precarious nature of the migrants in the Midwest, especially among single men who worked for railroads. Illinois, Michigan, and Indiana had their share of the total cohort grow substantially by 1930. Those in Louisiana were recruited by farmers to replace African American labor that was going north, but they were less successful in keeping Mexican families.

With regard to locational mobility among families, the majority of those who were found again stayed in the same state (Table A.4). Only a fifth had changed states; however,

Table A.3 Eight US States with the Largest Mexican Populations, 1930

State	Percentage	State	Percentage
Texas	50%	Oklahoma	2.8%
California	29%	Illinois	1.3%
Arizona	7.8%	Michigan	1%
New Mexico	4.0%		

Source: Daniel Morales, sample of Mexican population in the United States, from US population census, 1930.

Table A.4 Locational Mobility Among Heads of Household

Same Area	Moved in State	Changed State
42.3%	36.8%	21%

Source: Daniel Morales, sample of Mexican population in the United States, from US population census, 1930.

among those who had moved, the majority had moved to California, Texas, and the Midwest (Table A.5). The most common move was from Arizona to California, followed by from Texas to California. This is in keeping with the general trends in the literature that show California's proportion of the Mexican population rising quickly in the 1920s. This also appears to show that this was not only new migration from Mexico but people who had been in other parts of the country moving to California.

In 1930, Mexico conducted its first census since the end of the revolution. Its previous census in 1921 was extremely unreliable because of the disorder in the countryside and the weak state of the central government at the time. It is thus a unique source in Mexican historical studies. Fifty-eight distinct families who appeared in the sample group in 1920 were positively identified as living in Mexico in 1930. This is not a large number of people, but some 200 more from the 1920 sample were identified who were men whose name and age was the same as other men in Mexico but could not be positively identified by corroborating data. Nevertheless, the simple fact remains that very few people from the 1920 sample could be positively identified in the 1930 Mexican Census. This is not completely surprising, both because the major repatriations had not started by the time the 1930 census began and because single men, who make up such a large percentage of the total in 1920, are nearly impossible to find in any census sample due to the lack of detailed information. As stated earlier, more than two-thirds of the entire 1920 sample group does not appear again in government records in either the United States or Mexico.

The limited sample of individuals and families that could be positively identified again in 1930 in Mexico gives us less data to work with than the US sample (Table A.6). However, several trends are worth noting. A small majority of migrants were in central Mexico, with almost as many living in northern Mexican states and with Chihuahua and Sonora having the most families overall. The second notable trend is the disproportionate number of men and families that were living in Arizona and were found in Mexico in 1930. This is not surprising given the more mobile nature of mining and railroad work that prevailed in Arizona. Texas had the largest mobile population, with families going to northern and central Mexico.

Table A.5 Top Places to Move Among Mexican Migrants (number of households)

	California	Texas	US Midwest	US West	US East	US South
1930	45	3	10	16	4	0
1940	57	8	5	16	2	5

Source: Daniel Morales, sample of Mexican population in the United States, from US population census, 1910–1940.

Table A.6 Locations of Families in Mexico in 1930 Compared to 1920

	Northern States	Central States	Southern States
Arizona	8	10	3
California	2	2	1
Colorado	2	1	
Kansas	1	1	
New Mexico	1	2	
New York			1
Texas	13	8	1
Wyoming	1		

Source: Daniel Morales, sample of Mexican population in the United States, from Mexican census 1930

Survivor Bias

With the bulk of migrant working men not identifiable, the 1930 sample weighs heavily towards those who have families, those who are settled, and those who are of the middle class. In other words, the known biases of the census assert themselves very powerfully in both the US Census and the Mexican Census. The way the census gathered information favored these demographic groups over migrant workers, the poor, and single men.

This bias was strongest in those who were found living in the United States, where almost everyone was living in single-family dwellings. Likewise, nearly the entire population of single migrant men is gone, with only 180 heads of household accounting for the 958 individuals found again, with an average of six family members in each household. The gender gap does not exist with the 1930 group; there is almost exactly as many women as there are men in the Mexican sample group. Given that these are people who have been at least ten years in the United States, and that almost all are part of families that are living in the United States and, on average, their time was closer to twenty years by 1930, it is not surprising that they are better educated than the 1920 cohort. In fact, 79% of those in the sample could read and write, while 64% of people could speak English. Most of the migrants who were in the 1930 Mexican Census had families; on average, each family was 3.5 persons, which is smaller than the large, settled families found on the US side. This is not surprising given the fact that these were often single men in the United States ten years previously and were usually younger than those who stayed in the United States. Like the US sample, it was about equal in gender composition overall.

As mentioned earlier, the major finding of the study is just how transitory most workers' paper trails were in the United States. This was especially the case with railway and agricultural workers, who were the most migratory of all. Looking at Table A.7, the dominance of the agricultural, railroad, and mining industries declines over time, especially railroad workers. One in ten families took in boarders; some even took in many boarders. Some of these families were operating boarding houses, and others were taking in a person or two as a source of extra income. This form was especially common among families headed by women. This was part of a larger strategy used by migrant families of all types in creating multiple income (and goods) streams to

Table A.7 Largest Industries/Types of Labor Performed by Sample

	Agriculture	Railroad	Mining	Meat Packing	Steel	Automobile	Grocery
1910	116	9	12	6	0	1	4
1920	893	461	202	60	42	12	49
1930	281	43	49	16	10	17	30
1940	195	23	16	10	4	6	30

Source: Daniel Morales, sample of Mexican population in the United States, from US population census, 1910–1940

protect themselves against the uncertainty of the market, especially in the agriculture industries.

On employment and economic mobility, it at first appears as if there is some mobility into higher wage occupations and away from unskilled labor in basic industries like railroads, where only 2.3% of workers held jobs, and agriculture, which fell to 44%. While this was the case for some workers, it appears that this was primarily the result of selection bias. It was very difficult to find people in railroad, agriculture, and other types of general laborers again in the census, or really any government records. These workers tended to be in industries with volatile employment, industries dependent on migrant labor. Therefore, Table A.7 should not be taken as a reflection of upward mobility among the Mexican migration population as a whole.

The data do show, however, the slow emergence of a stable working and middle class, mostly in urban centers. Table A.7 shows a growth in the automobile and steel industries, and the remarkable stability of grocery store owners and small proprietors. Among those in white collar occupations, the most common occupation was those of clerk, small business owner, and grocer. The other large change over time occurred in the large growth of semiskilled workers (Table A.8), and this was in fact the result of many unskilled workers moving up over time. The most common was for laborers to become employed in a specific industrial job. These were low-wage jobs but offered much more stability than unskilled work. It was the only place this trend was observed; selection bias accounted for the other changes over time. The results for 1940 are not directly comparable, both

Table A.8 Skill Level Among Mexican Workers in Sample

	Unskilled	Semiskilled	Skilled	White Collar and Proprietors	Professional	Farmers (owners)	Other
1910	63%	13%	5%	7%	>1%	10%	>1%
1920	63%	13%	5%	12%	>1%	7%	>1%
1930	42%	19%	9%	19%	>1%	7%	4%
1940	59%	10%	5%	19%	>1%	5%	1%

Source: Daniel Morales, sample of Mexican population in the United States, from US population census, 1910–1940.

because many workers had retired by then and because a large number of the observed workers were people who were children in 1920.[17]

An important exception to these trends is agricultural workers in Texas, in particular tenant farmers. Fifteen percent of the total number of families were farmers. They were tenant farmers, ranch workers, or owners, and their trajectory was distinct. Unlike other agricultural workers, where migration and mobility from place to place was a central characteristic, almost all of them were living in the same place in 1930 as in 1920. If they did move, it was within the same city or county rather than far away like most of the sample. They also showed the lowest occupational mobility of any group, with only two heads of family holding a better occupation than they had in 1920. Together, this group represents the largest single socioeconomic bloc within the 1930 sample. That said, it must also be noted that most people who were agricultural workers in Texas in 1920 are either not found at all or are living somewhere other than Texas in 1930, especially single men without families.

Some other patterns emerge in Tables A.9 and A.10. While there were more skilled and white-collar occupations as a proportion of the sample, unskilled workers were still dominant. A significant number of unskilled workers became their own bosses, starting businesses, though about half of these were young farmers buying land or tenancy. Proprietors and landowners were also the least likely to move, so they are disproportionately represented in the 1930 and 1940 results. Some business owners and landowners lost their positions over time and became wage laborers. Most of the larger moves into skilled labor, ownership, or white-collar work was done by workers who were in their early twenties in 1920. Older workers tended to stay close to their original occupation level. Of those who has changed jobs since 1920, most also changed industries. And while most of those who changed jobs moved up to higher skilled or better-paid positions, those who stayed in the same industry did so at a slightly higher rate. Of those that did move up into higher skilled work, the largest group moved from unskilled to semiskilled jobs.

Turning to those who went back to Mexico, a direct comparison to the US Census is not easy because of the differences in the ways jobs were categorized in Mexico compared to the United States. There were fewer job categories in Mexico, with many under the name *jornalero* or *jornalero del campo* that could be distinct occupations in the US Census. However, some basic characteristics are visible. While the agricultural sector is well

Table A.9 1930 Occupational Skill Outcomes from Occupational Skill in 1920

1920	Unskilled 1930	Semiskilled 1930	Skilled 1930	Proprietor/ Owner 1930	White Collar 1930	Professional 1930
Unskilled	230	25	11	31	7	0
Semiskilled	15	37	2	1	4	0
Skilled	3	3	23	2	1	0
Proprietor/Owner	8	1	0	63	1	0
White Collar	2	1	1	1	17	1
Professional	0	0	0	0	0	4

Source: Daniel Morales, sample of Mexican population in the United States, from US population census, 1930.

Table A.10 1940 Occupational Skill Outcomes from Occupational Skill in 1920

1920	Unskilled 1940	Semiskilled 1940	Skilled 1940	Proprietor/ Owner 1940	White Collar 1940	Professional 1940
Unskilled	80	22	13	18	2	0
Semiskilled	3	16	4	2	4	0
Skilled	5	2	12	3	1	0
Proprietor/Owner	2	0	0	27	2	0
White Collar	2	2	0	2	16	1
Professional	0	0	0	0	0	2

Source: Daniel Morales, sample of Mexican population in the United States, from US population census, 1940.

represented, it is a much smaller factor than it is for the Mexican population as a whole, or even for the migrant population in the United States. A very high proportion of the workers who went to the United States were engaged in non-agricultural labor when they returned to Mexico, and few were working in the railroad and mining industries. Many were skilled tradesmen like shoemakers, carpenters, or general laborers. Once a person did such a job in the United States, he was unlikely to go back to the fields in Mexico; indeed, he often established his own business when he returned. One common laborer in the United States even remade himself as a businessman in Mexico.[18] About half of returned migrants were working in unskilled jobs, but more than 43% were either skilled or semiskilled workers. Likewise, Ward's census study indicates that there were no major differences in skills and human capital between those who returned to Mexico and those who stayed in the United States.[19]

Occupational mobility among the Mexican migrants in Mexico in 1930 is more difficult to measure (Table A.11). A lot of the people did not have jobs lined up that were directly comparable between 1920 and 1930, either because they were too young, or they were women who did not work in Mexico or the United States, or they did not have an occupation in Mexico. There were comparatively few people who had the same job in 1930 that they had in 1920; in fact, 66% had changed occupation. The most single common

Table A.11 1930 Occupational Mobility in Mexico Among Those Who Had Occupations in 1920

	Same Occupation, Same Industry	Different Occupation, Same Industry	Different Occupation, Different Industry
Percentage of working people	33%	11%	55%
Among those who changed occupation, what percentage had better occupation?	N/A	100%	50%

Source: Daniel Morales, sample of Mexican population in the United States, from US population census, 1930.

change was from a specific unskilled US job to a farmer in Mexico, even if a higher proportion stayed outside agriculture than would be expected. Likewise, there are no clear trends in occupational mobility among skill levels other than that most people didn't change the skill level of their occupation even if they changed occupation and industry.

There are always individual examples that defy the trends, like the laborer turned businessman. There was also an automobile mechanic who became a white-collar employee of the Mexican federal government ten years later, two boarding house operators in the United States who returned to Mexico to own land, and a low-skilled railroad worker in the United States who became a skilled railway worker in Mexico. Some individuals appear to have experienced downward mobility. However, the sample size was simply too small to derive any general trends from these outcomes.

Conclusions

Scholars have argued that the labor market in the United States is not a unified whole, but a series of different markets with their own characteristics and development. This has important implications for issues of economic mobility, immigrant assimilation, and racial stratification.[20] The most important division is between the primary labor market and the secondary labor market. In the primary labor market, worker skill matters most. In the industrial world, these are skilled and often unionized positions. In the secondary labor market, jobs are labor intensive, usually unskilled and low paid, and traditionally not unionized. Historical studies have found large social, racial, and economic gaps between these two types of jobs even in the same company, such as the railroad workers in Chapter 3, and little to no mobility into the primary market for unskilled workers. Skilled workers had a vested interest in maintaining the hierarchy, especially if overlain on racial differences. Alejandro Portes found many of these factors at play in limiting intergenerational socioeconomic mobility among US-born Mexican Americans in the 1990s. He also proposed the ethnic enclave as something in-between the two labor markets, where ethnic/racial minorities could move up.[21]

I believe much of the labor dynamics in this book and in the census study are the result of segmented labor markets that Mexican migrants found in the United States during the first half the twentieth century. Segmented labor markets were not entirely limiting; they helped guide Mexicans into many industries and locations in the United States and opened up opportunities. In the railroad, steel, and meat packing industries, they helped migrant newcomers get jobs, but the same logic also limited their mobility once they were in those positions, unable to move up or into different industries. Similar dynamics occurred in agriculture; by the 1920s, Mexican migrants were the largest source of field labor in cotton, vegetables, sugar beets, and citrus fruits in the West and Midwest. Agriculture workers had the least economic mobility in the census cohort.

The study shows that Mexican migration during these years was not a single predictable process, but rather included a wide range of behaviors and patterns that followed different trajectories. Residential and job patterns from the study show that while a significant minority were settling in rural farms or urban spaces, the majority were not. These two significant exceptions to the main trajectories in the study say a lot about the way Mexican migration operated. The first of these exceptions is farm workers who had access to land, the majority of whom were tenants in Texas. They had the highest rates of stability, with a significant portion staying within several miles of where they had been in 1920. The second exception was the emerging urban middle class. These were semiskilled industrial workers, skilled craftsmen, and small proprietors: boarding house owners, newspapermen, skilled tradesman working with other migrants, teachers in migrant communities, and grocers who sold Mexican goods as far as Michigan. They played a particular role in migrant communities. Their livelihood depended on Mexican migration, and in turn, they were a key part of the structure of immigrant life. This relatively stable class of migrants arose from the migrations of the 1910s, and those who were primarily migrant laborers lived in the same neighborhoods, worked in the same spaces, and were often members of the same families. The stable migrants were those that successfully climbed within the migrant economy rather than separated from it into the mainstream American economy. They were a minority of Mexicans in every location studied, and even in the largest, most diverse cities, the tendency for the non-middle class was to leave after some amount of time.

With the exception of tenant farmers and the emerging middle class, ongoing migration was a fact of life for the vast majority of Mexicans in the United States. They moved according to the particulars of the industry that employed them, or between industries and regions. While the trajectories of settling in a location and migrating between different places could be thought of as counterexamples of assimilation and identity formation in both countries, I argue that this is not how scholars should look at the relationship between these migrants. Most Mexican migrants did not have the option of a stable job and the ability to settle down. Socioeconomically, the cohort showed limited economic mobility among Mexican migrants. Migrants were likely to have a type of job similar to what they had twenty years earlier. This is likely because migrants in this era were coming to work in only a few industries, where they were segmented into a separate labor and economic market than the US population in general. Migration often seemed a better option than staying in a bad situation. Migration from place to place in the United States and back to Mexico was itself a critical strategy, and so was moving from job to job. Workers frequently left for higher wages, better conditions, or flexibility even if they stayed in the same occupational category. This is especially important when looking at migration inside the United States, where migrations across regions and industries was normalized.

Notes

Introduction

1. There are many histories of this region, but historians have generally ignored migration and its impact. Exceptions include Alanís Enciso, *Voces de la repatriación*; Alanís Enciso, *Que se queden allá*; and Cohen, *Braceros.*
2. I use the term *Mexicans* to include people who are Mexicans by birth or ancestry, regardless of legal status. Depending on the circumstances, they could have been called *Tejano*, Mexican American, Hispanic, or Chicano. There were and are significant differences among and within Mexican communities. I have used the term *Mexican* to avoid extended discussions on terminology. All terms are historically constructed.
3. Sanchez, *Becoming Mexican American*; Ruiz, *From Out of the Shadows*; Gutiérrez, *Walls and Mirrors*; Pitti, *The Devil in Silicon Valley*; Garcia, *A World of Its Own*; Molina, *How Race Is Made in America.*
4. Examples include Massey, *Return to Aztlan*; Massey, Durand, and Malone, *Beyond Smoke and Mirrors*; Minian, *Undocumented Lives*; Cohen, *Braceros*; Rosas, *Abrazando el espíritu*; Smith, *Mexican New York*; Stephen, *Transborder Lives.*
5. Sanchez, *Becoming Mexican American*, 188–206.
6. Labor scholars have argued that a separate immigrant labor market for migrants operates with a different set of jobs with their own logics, apart from the native-born workforce. Telles and Ortiz, *Generations of Exclusion*; Portes and Rumbaut, *Legacies*; McDonald and Solow, "Wages and Employment," 1115–1141.
7. To rephrase Michel-Rolph Trouillot. Trouillot, *Silencing the Past*, 88.

Chapter 1

1. "Vidas de Manuel Perez," 1927, no. 1, interview, BANC FILM 2332 REEL 2, GNEG Box 2569, Manuel Gamio Papers, Bancroft Library, University of California, Berkeley.
2. Hale, *The Transformation of Liberalism in Late Nineteenth-Century Mexico*; Knight, *The Mexican Revolution*, Vol. 1; Katz, *The Secret War in Mexico*; Hart, *Empire and Revolution*; Coatsworth, *Growth Against Development.*
3. Hart, *Empire and Revolution*, ch. 1.
4. González, *Culture of Empire*, 103–112.
5. Coatsworth, *Growth Against Development.*
6. Kuntz Ficker, *Empresa extranjera y mercado interno.*
7. Coatsworth, "Railroads, Landholding, and Agrarian Protest in the Early Porfirato," 48–71.
8. Ankerson, *Agrarian Warlord.*
9. Knight, *The Mexican Revolution*, Vol. 1, 79, 343.
10. Monroy and Unna, *Breve historia de San Luis Potosí*; Knight, *The Mexican Revolution*, Vol. 1, 107–109.
11. Tutino, *From Insurrection to Revolution in Mexico*, 285–287.
12. Knight, *The Mexican Revolution*, Vol. 1, 79.
13. Ibid.
14. Local histories in "Asi es San Luis. Y asi es Villa Juarez"; Ankerson, *Agrarian Warlord*, 50–53.
15. Tutino, *Making a New World.*
16. One mine—the Cubo mine—went from zero production (it was believed to be exhausted) to making 150 tons of ore per day, employing 672 people and earning a 50% profit rate in 1910 while paying among the highest wages in the country. Thousands of people flocked either to work in the mines or in many of the ancillary industries that existed in such mining towns. Hart, *Empire and Revolution*, 145.
17. Knight, *The Mexican Revolution*, Vol. 1, 92–93.
18. Kuntz Ficker, *Empresa extranjera y mercado interno*, 354.

19. Durand, *Más allá de la línea*, 193-195.
20. Ankerson, *Agrarian Warlord*, 22.
21. Sanguino, "The Origins of Migration Between Mexico and the United States," ch. 2.
22. Knight, *The Mexican Revolution*, Vol. 1, 90.
23. Fitzgerald, "Inside the Sending State," 259–293.
24. Confidential Report by Frank R. Stone to Supervising Inspector, June 23, 1910, Bureau of Immigration, 52546/31 B, INS RG 85, US National Archives and Records Administration (NARA), Washington, DC.
25. Paul H. Foster, US Consul, Piedras Negras, Coahuila, November 28, 1928, Folder 10.4, Carton 10, Paul S. Taylor Papers, Bancroft Library, University of California, Berkeley.
26. Confidential Report by Frank R. Stone to Supervising Inspector, June 23, 1910, Bureau of Immigration, 52546/31 B, INS RG 85, NARA, Washington, DC.
27. Interview with Alvaro Ruis, April 20, 1929, Folder 10.4, Carton 10, Paul S. Taylor Papers, Bancroft Library, University of California, Berkeley.
28. "Vidas la de DeGregorio Vazques," interview, BANC FILM 2332 REEL 2, GNEG Box 2569, Manuel Gamio Papers, Bancroft Library, University of California, Berkeley.
29. Coatsworth, *Growth Against Development*; Hale, *The Transformation of Liberalism*; Hernandez, *Mexican American Colonization During the 19th Century*; Brown, *Oil and Revolution in Mexico*; Cerutti, *El Norte de Mexico y Texas*; Hart, *Empire and Revolution*; Melendez, *Capitalism and Development.*
30. US companies established separate colonies for white Americans, creating separate legal and social structures and reserving the highest-paid jobs for Americans. The discrepancy in wages between US workers and Mexicans was 20 to 1 in mines and 30 to 1 on plantations. Hart, *Empire and Revolution*, 261.
31. Ibid., 265; Benton-Cohen, *Borderline Americans*; Gordon, *The Great Arizona Orphan Abduction.*
32. Katz, *The Life and Times of Pancho Villa*, 1–56.
33. Knight, *The Mexican Revolution*, Vols. 1–2; Katz, *The Life and Times of Pancho Villa*; Katz, *The Secret War in Mexico*; Tutino, *From Insurrection to Revolution*; Schryer, *The Rancheros of Pisaflores*; Womack, *Zapata and the Mexican Revolution*; Gonzales and Johnson, *The Mexican Revolution.*
34. Lomnitz, *The Return of Comrade Ricardo Flores Magón.*
35. Katz, *The Life and Times of Pancho Villa.*
36. Manuel Gamio, Preliminary Report, "Antecedents on the Mexican Immigration in the United States," BANC FILM 2332 REEL 3, GNEG Box 2570, Manuel Gamio Papers, Bancroft Library, University of California, Berkeley.
37. Knight, *The Mexican Revolution*, Vol. 1, 191–193.
38. Ankerson, *Agrarian Warlord*, 39.
39. Ibid., 53.
40. Knight, *The Mexican Revolution*, Vol. 2, 50.
41. Knight, *The Mexican Revolution*, Vol. 1, 271, 343–344.
42. Ankerson, *Agrarian Warlord*, 44–66.
43. Local histories in "Asi es San Luis. Y asi es Villa Juarez"; Dotacion, Poblacion Guxcama, Villa Juárez, San Luis Potosí, Mexico, 23/21221, Archivo del Registro Agrario, México DF.
44. Dotacion, Poblacion Guxcama, Villa Juárez, San Luis Potosí, Mexico, 23/21221, Archivo del Registro Agrario, México DF.
45. Tutino, *From Insurrection to Revolution*, 276–349; Knight, *The Mexican Revolution*, Vol. 1, 100–101; for a counterexample, see Schryer, *The Rancheros of Pisaflores.*
46. Knight, *The Mexican Revolution*, Vol. 2, 395.
47. Knight, *The Mexican Revolution*, Vol. 1, 210.
48. Knight, *The Mexican Revolution*, Vol. 2, 400–401.
49. Rudy Hernandez, OH 3828, Orange County Colonias Oral History Project, California State University, Fullerton.
50. Trini Gamez went from a migrant farm worker to an important labor organizer and legal advocate in the 1960s and 1970s. Romero, "Trini Gamez and the Texas Farm Workers: Toil and Trouble on the Texas Plain."
51. "Locario Lopez," interviews, Folder 11.34, Carton 11, Paul S. Taylor Papers, Bancroft Library, University of California, Berkeley.

52. "Vidas la de Jesus Gonzalez," interview by Luis Felipe Recinos, BANC FILM 2332 REEL 1, GNEG Box 2568, Manuel Gamio Papers, Bancroft Library, University of California, Berkeley.
53. "Vida de Luciano Herrera," interview, BANC FILM 2332 REEL 2, GNEG Box 2569, Manuel Gamio Papers, Bancroft Library, University of California, Berkeley.
54. "El Case de Jesus Franco," interview by Manuel Gamio, BANC FILM 2332 REEL 2, GNEG Box 2569, Manuel Gamio Papers, Bancroft Library, University of California, Berkeley.
55. "Serino Medina, Mary Lee Nolan," February 3, 1973, Archivo de la Palabra: Revolución Mexicana, Biblioteca Central, Instituto Nacional de Antropología e Historia (INAH), México DF.
56. "Vidas la de José Rocha," interview, BANC FILM 2332 REEL 2, GNEG Box 2569, Manuel Gamio Papers, Bancroft Library, University of California, Berkeley.
57. "Interviews, Manuel Santa Cruz," Field Notes, Folder 10.8, Carton 10, Paul S. Taylor Papers, Bancroft Library, University of California, Berkeley.
58. "Interview, F. Huerta," June 8, 1928, Field Notes, Folder 11.32, Carton 11, Paul S. Taylor Papers, Bancroft Library, University of California, Berkeley.
59. "Romulo Munguia, Mary Lee Nolan," July 12, 1973, Archivo de la Palabra: Revolución Mexicana, Biblioteca Central, INAH, México DF.
60. "Vidas, Jose Lanides Gonzales," interview, BANC FILM 2332 REEL 1, GNEG Box 2568, Manuel Gamio Papers, Bancroft Library, University of California, Berkeley.
61. "Vidas la de Pedro G. de la Lama," interview, BANC FILM 2332 REEL 1, GNEG Box 2568, Manuel Gamio Papers, Bancroft Library, University of California, Berkeley.
62. "Vidas, Sr. Jose M. Ramires M.," May 4, 1927, BANC FILM 2332 REEL 1, GNEG Box 2568, Manuel Gamio Papers, Bancroft Library, University of California, Berkeley.
63. "Interview with Antonio Mendez Lomeli," OH 1297, August 24, 1972, Mexican American Oral History Project, California State University, Fullerton.
64. Report, Bureau of Immigration, April 10, 1913, 53108/71 A-Q, INS RG 85, NARA, Washington, DC.
65. Varios, *El ir y venir de los norteños*, 112–113.
66. Numbers based on the Bureau of Immigration and Manuel Gamio's estimate in 1929. Gamio, *Mexican Immigration to the United States*.
67. Letters by Supervising Inspector F. W. Berkshire, Bureau of Immigration, 53108/71 A-Q, INS RG 85, NARA, Washington, DC; Zamora, *The World of the Mexican Worker*, 70–72.
68. Investigaciones Acerca de la entrada legal e ilegal de Mexicanos a Estados Unidos de N. America, Luis Felipe Recinos, BANC FILM 23322 REEL 4, GNEG Box 2571, Manuel Gamio Papers, Bancroft Library, University of California, Berkeley.
69. Report, Bureau of Immigration, 1913, 51463 A-C, INS RG 85, NARA, Washington, DC.
70. "Al Gral. Don Albaro Obregon," Leonido Acuna, July 19, 1920, Fondo Álvaro Obregon, MFN 2920, serie 030500, inventario 2886, Archivo Plutarco Elias Calles, México DF.
71. Varios, *El ir y venir de los norteños*, 117.
72. Confidential Report by Frank R. Stone to Supervising Inspector, June 23, 1910, Bureau of Immigration, 52546/31 B, INS RG 85, NARA, Washington, DC.
73. Investigaciones Acerca de la entrada legal e ilegal de Mexicanos a Estados Unidos de N. America, Luis Felipe Recinos, BANC FILM 23322 REEL 4, GNEG Box 2571, Manuel Gamio Papers, Bancroft Library, University of California, Berkeley.
74. "En Torreón se hace un inmoral negocio con los emigrantes," El Siglo, 4-352-2-1926-9A El Agente de Migración en Torreón Coah, in Archivo Histórico del Instituto Nacional de Migración, México DF.
75. Alanís Enciso, *El primer programa bracero y el gobierno de México*, 26.
76. Report from Inspector in Charge to Supervising Inspector, June 16, 1915, Bureau of Immigration, 53108/71 A-Q, INS RG 85, NARA, Washington, DC.
77. "Old Resident in the Harbor," interviews, Folder 11.33, Carton 11, Paul S. Taylor Papers, Bancroft Library, University of California, Berkeley.
78. "Aguilera," interview by Robert C. Jones, July 29, 1928, Folder 11.71, Carton 11, Paul S. Taylor Papers, Bancroft Library, University of California, Berkeley.
79. "Unnamed Picker," Bermuda, Texas, April 24, 1929, Folder 10.5, Carton 10, Paul S. Taylor Papers, Bancroft Library, University of California, Berkeley. Translations by Paul Taylor.
80. "Necesito desenraizadores para ir a Three Rivers, Texas, para deseraizar 2,000 races [*sic*]. Precio de $12.00 hasta $40.00 por acre. pago con pura plata . . . C. M. Posey (El Pason),"

Migrant Border Ballads Project, "Migrant Border Ballads Project Records, 1979," Benson Latin American Library, University of Texas, Austin, 38.

81. "Old Resident in the Harbor" and "Man Who Was Waiting for the Ice Man," interviews, Folder 11.33, Carton 11, Paul S. Taylor Papers, Bancroft Library, University of California, Berkeley.
82. "Sr. Caribales," interviews, Folder 11.33, Carton 11, Paul S. Taylor Papers, Bancroft Library, University of California, Berkeley.
83. Sarafin Sanchez, interview, August 13, 1929, Folder 10.7, Carton 10, Paul S. Taylor Papers, Bancroft Library, University of California, Berkeley.
84. Notes, "Three Men at Hull House," interviews, Folder 11.33, Carton 11, Paul S. Taylor Papers, Bancroft Library, University of California, Berkeley.
85. Letter to Commissioner-General of Immigration, Berkshire, May 11, 1916, Bureau of Immigration, 55609/551, INS RG 85, NARA, Washington, DC.
86. Martinez, "Mexican Emigration to the US," 42.
87. Alanís Enciso, *Que se queden alla*, 46–48.
88. Martinez, "Mexican Emigration to the US," 40–43.
89. Ibid., 40–48.
90. Alanís Enciso, *Que se queden alla*, 41.
91. Martinez, "Mexican Emigration to the US," 42.
92. Cardoso, *Mexican Emigration to the United States*, 96–118.
93. Diario de los Debates, April 20, 1921, in Varios, *El ir y venir de los norteños*, 158.
94. Hernandez, *Migra!*
95. "Auraliana, Aguilera," interview by Robert C. Jones, July 29, 1928, Folder 11.70, Carton 11, Paul S. Taylor Papers, Bancroft Library, University of California, Berkeley.
96. "Sam Ramirez," interview, July 1929, Folder 10.6, Carton 10, Paul S. Taylor Papers, Bancroft Library, University of California, Berkeley.
97. "Inspector W. C. Nester and Yard Master Trinidad Romero," November 1928, Folder 10.4, Carton 10, Paul S. Taylor Papers, Bancroft Library, University of California, Berkeley.
98. Scholars have argued that *corridos* were critical in creating a working-class borderlands culture in the late nineteenth and early twentieth century. The popular music told stories that spoke to people, or through popular singers in the borderlands. The songs were reflections of borderlands culture.
99. "Puro Mexico," 1939, Mexican Folklore Survey, Federal Writers Project, Box 187, Folder 3, 306, Special Collections, University of California, Los Angeles. Translation by Daniel Morales.
100. "Songs of the Mexican Migration," Mexican Folklore Survey, Federal Writers Project, Box 187, Folder 3, 306, Special Collections, University of California, Los Angeles. Translation by Daniel Morales.
101. "My Voy Para el Norte," Music by Manuel Esquivel, Libro de Oro la Cancion, found in home of Sostenes Martinez, Thelma, Texas. Migrant Border Ballads Project, "Migrant Border Ballads Project Records, 1979," Benson Latin American Library, University of Texas, Austin, 387. Translation by Daniel Morales.
102. "Vidas la de Pedro Macias," interview, BANC FILM 2332 REEL 2, GNEG Box 2569, Manuel Gamio Papers, Bancroft Library, University of California, Berkeley.
103. "Unknown Mexican," interview, August 1928, page 28, Folder 10.8, Carton 10, Paul S. Taylor Papers, Bancroft Library, University of California, Berkeley.
104. La Epoca 3, num. 148 (September 12, 1920), in Sanguino, "The Origins of Migration Between Mexico and the United States," 99. While the phrase comes from the Archbishop of Guadalajara, the "fever" was not isolated to his diocese. Jose Moya illustrates the way "migration fever" was used by contemporaries across the world in the late nineteenth century and describes the way interpersonal networks grew from the ground up. Moya, *Cousins and Strangers*, 95–120.
105. Durand, *Más allá de la línea*, 316.
106. "Martinez, Onorio," oral interview, December 19, 2013, San Luis Potosí, Villa Juárez.
107. See Appendix.
108. Hernandez, *Migra!*
109. San Miguel de Hidalgo in Jalisco seems to be such a case; Rosas, *Abrazando el espíritu.*

Chapter 2

1. Andrews, *Killing for Coal*, 150.
2. Deutsch, *Making a Modern US West*, 13.

3. James Scott's concept of weapons of the weak is very influential in this chapter. Scott, *Weapons of the Weak.*
4. Labor history has traditionally privileged local histories, neglecting the transnational aspects of labor. Yet focusing on migrants shows a rich history of connections. Peck, *Reinventing Free Labor*, 1–6.
5. Weber, "Wobblies of the Partido Liberal Mexicano," 188–226.
6. Ankerson, *Agrarian Warlord*, 7.
7. Truett, *Fugitive Landscapes*, chs. 3–4.
8. Hart, *Empire and Revolution*, 137.
9. Ibid., 136–148.
10. Calderón, *Mexican Coal Mining Labor in Texas and Coahuila*, 23–99.
11. Ibid., 83.
12. Weber, "Wobblies of the Partido Liberal Mexicano," 205.
13. Acuña, *Corridors of Migration*, 128–138.
14. Lomnitz, "Chronotopes of a Dystopic Nation," 102–138.
15. Beckert, *Empire of Cotton.*
16. Knight, *The Mexican Revolution*, Vol. 1, 109–111.
17. Catarino Lermo, September 21, 1929, Folder 10.7, Carton 10, Paul S. Taylor Papers, Bancroft Library, University of California, Berkeley.
18. Zamora, *The World of the Mexican Worker in Texas*, 16–17.
19. Acuña, *Corridors of Migration*, 78; Weber, "Wobblies of the Partido Liberal Mexicano," 207.
20. Deutsch, *Making a Modern US West, 125.*
21. Martinez, "Mexican Emigration to the US 1910–1920," 5.
22. Acuña, *Corridors of Migration*, 125.
23. McWilliams, *Ill Fares the Land*, 231–232, in Montejano, *Anglos and Mexicans in the Making of Texas.*
24. Camarillo, *Chicanos in a Changing Society*; Hernández, *City of Inmates*; Montejano, *Anglos and Mexicans*; Montoya, *Translating Property*; Reséndez, *The Other Slavery.*
25. Montejano, *Anglos and Mexicans.*
26. "Gil, Pete, Paul Ortis," 43, 44, 46, 46, VOCES Oral History Project, Benson Latin American Library, University of Texas, Austin.
27. Foley, *The White Scourge.*
28. See Appendix.
29. Zamora, *The World of the Mexican Worker*, 17.
30. Ibid., 18.
31. Foley, *The White Scourge*, 43.
32. "El Consulado en Pheonix, proporciona dato relatives a la Coonia Mexican en ese lugar," February 24, 1930, Archivo Histórico Diplomático de Secretaria de Relaciones Exteriores, México DF.
33. Deutsch, *Making a Modern US West*, 125.
34. Perales, *Smeltertown.*
35. Ibid., 61.
36. Benton-Cohen, *Borderline Americans.*
37. Calderón, *Mexican Coal Mining Labor*, 171–175.
38. Ibid., 93–104.
39. Lindquist, "The Jerome Deportation of 1917"; 4-532-1930-615, "Gobernado de Aguascalientes: Informa Sobre Emigration," Archivo Histórico del Instituto Nacional de Migración, México DF.
40. Calderón, *Mexican Coal Mining Labor*, 123.
41. "Colonias Mexicanas en Rio Verde, Visita del Consul," January 10, 1929, IV-76-59, Archivo Histórico Diplomático de Secretaria de Relaciones Exteriores, México DF.
42. Acuña, *Corridors of Migration*, 170–172.
43. VIDAS, la de Pedro Silva, doc. 20, no. 101, BANC FILM 2322 REEL 1, GNEG Box 2568, Manuel Gamio Papers, Bancroft Library, University of California, Berkeley.
44. VIDAS, la de Bra Teresa de Guerrero, no. 31, BANC FILM 2322 REEL 1, GNEG Box 2568, Manuel Gamio Papers, Bancroft Library, University of California, Berkeley.
45. Peck, *Reinventing Free Labor*, 40.
46. Confidential Report by Frank R. Stone to Supervising Inspector, June 23, 1910, Bureau of Immigration, 52546/31 B, INS RG 85, US National Archives and Records Administration (NARA), Washington, DC.

47. Martinez, "Mexican Emigration," 20.
48. Hernández, *Migra!*, 17–69.
49. Limerick, *The Legacy of Conquest*; Montejano, *Anglos and Mexicans*; Montoya, *Translating Property*; St. John, *Line in the Sand*; Kang, *The INS on the Line*.
50. Inspector Seraphic Report and Letters, Bureau of Immigration, 51423/1-A, INS RG 85, NARA, Washington, DC.
51. Goodman, *The Deportation Machine*, 32.
52. Confidential Report by Frank R. Stone to Supervising Inspector, June 23, 1910, Bureau of Immigration, 52546/31 B, INS RG 85, NARA, Washington, DC.
53. Ibid.
54. Bureau of Immigration 1908–1911, 52546/31 A-C, INS RG 85, NARA, Washington, DC.
55. Trejo Terreros, "Los Coyotes," 75–77.
56. Peck, *Reinventing Free Labor*, 15–48.
57. Trejo Terreros, "Los Coyotes," 92–94.
58. 52546/031 D-H, To the Commissioner General of Immigration in DC, November 25, 1911, 52546/031 D-H, INS RG 85, NARA, Washington, DC; Peck, *Reinventing Free Labor*, 102–114.
59. Perkins, *Border Patrol*, cited in Sanchez, *Becoming Mexican American*, 52.
60. Sanchez, *Becoming Mexican American*, 51–54; McKeown, "Ritualization of Regulation," 377–403.
61. Memorandum by Berkshire for the Secretary, Commissioner General, March 12, 1913, Bureau of Immigration, 52546/31-G, INS RG 85, NARA, Washington, DC.
62. Kang, *The INS on the Line*, 1–35.
63. This is what historian Laurencio Sanguino misunderstood about the nature of migration. He points to labor agents as the primary cause of Mexican migration and the prime instigator in where they went. Sanguino, "The Origins of Migration Between Mexico and the United States."
64. Peck, *Reinventing Free Labor*, 131.
65. October 29, 1917, BSI 1602, Manifest 1600-1, Zamorano Family, Board of Special Inquiry Cases, 54281/36 A-Q, INS RG 85, NARA, Washington, DC.
66. A. J. Milliken, October 1929, Folder 10.4, Carton 10, Paul S. Taylor Papers, Bancroft Library, University of California, Berkeley.
67. July 3, 1917, BSI 1439, Manifest 19–20, Trinidad and Beatriz Orrellana, Board of Special Inquiry Cases, 54281/36 A-Q, INS RG 85, NARA, Washington, DC.
68. July 24, 1917, BSI 996, Manifest 147, Micaela Quintero, Board of Special Inquiry Cases, 54281/36 A-Q, INS RG 85, NARA, Washington, DC.
69. December 19, 1928, BSI 1152, Manifest 403-304, Juana and Jesus Mendoza, Board of Special Inquiry Cases, 54281/36 A-Q, INS RG 85, NARA, Washington, DC.
70. Historian Yolanda Chávez Leyva has argued that women and children outside of the control of the nuclear family were seen as possible threats to the nation. Leyva, "Cruzando la linea."
71. Canaday, *The Straight State*.
72. Leyva, "Cruzando la linea," 79.
73. February 3, 1918, BSI 1038, Rosas Quijada; July 22, 1919, BSI 1213, Manifest 55-56, Catalina and Guadalupe Lopez; June 1919, BSI 1901, Manifest 2704, Dolores Morales, Board of Special Inquiry Cases, 54281/36 A-Q, INS RG 85, NARA, Washington, DC.
74. Leyva, "Cruzando la linea," 72–75.
75. Ibid., 70–86.
76. February 21, 1919, BSI 1176, Manifest 565-570, Feliciano Mendoza and Family, Board of Special Inquiry Cases, 54281/36 A-Q, INS RG 85, NARA, Washington, DC.
77. Folders 11.8 to 11.25, Carton 11, Paul S. Taylor Papers, Bancroft Library, University of California, Berkeley.
78. Ibid., 97.
79. Deutsch, *No Separate Refuge*, 87–126.
80. Francisco Guerra, 265, VOCES Oral History Project, Benson Latin American Library, University of Texas, Austin.
81. Trejo Terreros, "Los Coyotes," 77–78.
82. Mayers, interview, December 1929, Folder 10.5, Carton 10, Paul S. Taylor Papers, Bancroft Library, University of California, Berkeley.

83. Mexican in Manheim Camp, June 1928, Folder 11.33, Carton 11, Paul S. Taylor Papers, Bancroft Library, University of California, Berkeley.
84. *La Prensa*, America's Historical Newspapers.
85. Trevino, "Prensa y patria," 451; Garcia, "Class, Consciousness, and Ideology," 42–43.
86. *La Prensa*, "Los trabajadores Mexicanos en El Estado de Michigan."
87. *La Prensa*, America's Historical Newspapers.
88. Zamora, *The World of the Mexican Worker*, 36.
89. Acuña, *Corridors of Migration*, 160–165.
90. Calderón, *Mexican Coal Mining Labor*, 88-92.
91. Letters by Supervising Inspector F. W. Berkshire, Bureau of Immigration, 53108/71 A-Q, INS RG 85, NARA, Washington, DC; Zamora, *The World of the Mexican Worker*, 70–72.
92. VIDAS, la de Jesus Luis Acuna, no. 12, April 28, 1927, BANC FILM 2322 REEL 1, GNEG Box 2568, Manuel Gamio Papers, Bancroft Library, University of California, Berkeley.
93. VIDAS, la de Conrado Martinez, no. 39, BANC FILM 2322 REEL 1, GNEG Box 2568, Manuel Gamio Papers, Bancroft Library, University of California, Berkeley.
94. VIDAS, la de Daniel Aguilar y Maria Dolores de Aguilar, May 23, 1927, Folder 2, BANC FILM 2322 REEL 1, GNEG Box 2568, Manuel Gamio Papers, Bancroft Library, University of California, Berkeley.
95. Zamora, *The World of the Mexican Worker*, 65.
96. Knight, *The Mexican Revolution*, Vol. 1, 447.
97. Weber, "Wobblies of the Partido Liberal Mexicano," 188–226.
98. Ibid., 199.
99. Foley, *The White Scourge*, 64–140.
100. Ibid., 104–117.
101. Zamora, *The World of the Mexican Worker*, 77.
102. Ibid., 145–146.
103. Foley, *The White Scourge*.
104. Zamora, *The World of the Mexican Worker*, 133–161.
105. In the nineteenth century, this atmosphere produced several rebellions, including a revolt led by Juan Cortina in 1859 and Catarino Garza's revolt in 1891. Montejano, *Anglos and Mexicans*, 118; Young, *Catarino Garza's Revolution*.
106. Johnson, *Revolution in Texas*; Sandos, *Rebellion in the Borderlands*.
107. Sandos, *Rebellion in the Borderlands*, 189.
108. Ibid., 133, 175.
109. Ibid., 178; Ray, Arizona, is disproportionally represented in the census study, possibly because of its long-established connections.
110. Benton-Cohen, *Borderline Americans*, 203.
111. Acuña, *Corridors of Migration*, 195.
112. Letters to Secretary of Labor, June, August 1918, 54261/202-D, INS RG 85, NARA, Washington, DC; Cohen, *Borderline Americans*, 1–18.
113. Acuña, *Corridors of Migration*, 207.
114. Ibid., 210.
115. Ibid., 1–3.
116. Ibid., 220–238.
117. Ibid., 206.
118. FEC, MFN 87, Series 0202, Exp 35, Fondo Elías Calles, Archivo Plutarco Elías Calles, México DF.
119. Calderón, *Mexican Coal Mining Labor*, 149–196.
120. Ibid., 152–167.
121. Acuña, *Corridors of Migration*, 214.
122. Pedro Gómez, in Acuña, *Corridors of Migration*, 216.
123. Acuña, *Corridors of Migration*, 216.
124. Weber, "Wobblies of the Partido Liberal Mexicano," 223.
125. Many letters can be found in 54261/202, INS RG 85, NARA, Washington, DC.
126. Kang, *The INS on the Line*, 20–35.

127. Most of those were non-statistical entrants. Harris, Immigration Service, Washington, Folder 35, Carton 11, Paul S. Taylor Papers, Bancroft Library, University of California, Berkeley; Alanís Enciso, *El primero programa bracero y el gobierno de México.*
128. Martinez, "Mexican Emigration," 19.
129. This was the first use of the mechanics of the US state to control the recruitment, distribution, and conditions of Mexican workers in the United States. Alanís Enciso, *El primer programa bracero y el gobierno de México.*
130. May 31, 1917, W. B. Wilson to Senator John Burnett, 54261/202, INS RG 85, NARA, Washington, DC.
131. Ibid.
132. September 18, 1917, Letter to Bureau of Immigration, 54261/202, INS RG 85, NARA, Washington, DC.
133. March 30, 1918, Commissioner of Conciliation to A. Caminetti, Commissioner-General DC, 54261/202, INS RG 85, NARA, Washington, DC.
134. July 27, 1918, NO 502/767, Supervising Inspector Berkshire to all Inspectors in Charge, 55301/217, INS RG 85, NARA, Washington, DC.
135. January 28, 1920, NO 5002/769, Acting Supervising Inspector to Commissioner General of Immigration DC, and 54261/202 Box I, II, III, IV, INS RG 85, NARA, Washington, DC.
136. Herrera; stockyards, Chicago, June 30, 1929, Folder 10.6, Carton 10, Paul S. Taylor Papers, Bancroft Library, University of California, Berkeley.
137. May 30, 1917, Murrell Buckner Superintendent of the Union Terminal to Senator Chas. A Culberson, 54261/202, INS RG 85, NARA, Washington, DC.
138. April 23, 1919, No 6008/1, Berkshire to Commissioner General of the Bureau of Immigration DC, 54261/202, INS RG 85, NARA, Washington, DC.
139. Farmers meeting at Corpus Christi, July 14, 1920, Folder 12.32, Carton 12, Paul S. Taylor Papers, Bancroft Library, University of California, Berkeley.
140. Correspondence in 54261/202, INS RG 85, NARA, Washington, DC.
141. 54731/76, 54731/77, and 54647/69, Special Board of Inquiry, INS RG 85, NARA, Washington, DC.
142. Series of Telegrams, July 1920, W. F. Berkshire, 54261/202, INS RG 85, NARA, Washington, DC.
143. March 14, 1918, No 6002/1, Supervising Inspector Berkshire to Commissioner General of Immigration DC, 54261/202, INS RG 85, NARA, Washington, DC.
144. July 8, 1918, No 6002/1, Response by the Inspector General to the Commissioner General, 54261/202, INS RG 85, NARA, Washington, DC.
145. They could also be in this category before 1921 if they didn't get a wartime exemption, but after a certain amount of time, they could not be deported. Mexican Consulates began issuing certificates to prove their residency in the United States before 1921.
146. Deutsch, *Making a Modern US West*, 170.
147. Montoya, *Risking Immeasurable Harm*, 123–243.
148. Ngai, *Impossible Subjects*, 58–71.
149. Noel, *Debating American Identity*; Webber, "Homing Pigeons, Cheap Labor, and Frustrated Nativists," 167–186.
150. Garcia, *Rise of the Mexican American Middle Class*, 56.
151. Correspondence in IV-111-12, IV-111-13, IV-111-17, and IV-111-18, San Antonio Consulate Files, Archivo Histórico Diplomático de Secretaría de Relaciones Exteriores, México DF.
152. 383 Augustine Martinez, VOCES Oral History Project, University of Texas, Austin.
153. L. A. Ethridge, Micolith, Texas, sixteen miles south of Van Horn, Texas, November 25, 1928, Folder 10.4, Carton 10, Paul S. Taylor Papers, Bancroft Library, University of California, Berkeley.
154. Louis Baily, Farmer near Agua Dulce, August 13, 1929, Folder 10.7, Carton 10, Paul S. Taylor Papers, Bancroft Library, University of California, Berkeley.
155. P. Butts, Bishop, Texas, August 1929, Folder 10.7, Carton 10, Paul S. Taylor Papers, Bancroft Library, University of California, Berkeley.
156. Mr. Wilkinson, County Agricultural Agent, Kleberg County, Kingsville, Texas, November 1928, Folder 10.4, Carton 10, Paul S. Taylor Papers, Bancroft Library, University of California, Berkeley.
157. Montejano, *Anglos and Mexicans*, 205.
158. Rosales, *Pobre Raza!*, 157.

159. Maston Nixon, CC, August 19, 1929, Folder 10.7, Carton 10, Paul S. Taylor Papers, Bancroft Library, University of California, Berkeley.
160. Henry Baldwin, Guarantee Title Company, Corpus Christi, August 1929, Folder 10.7, Carton 10, Paul S. Taylor Papers, Bancroft Library, University of California, Berkeley.
161. "12,000 Smuggled Aliens Captured," *El Paso Times*, November 19, 1927, 55598/459, INS RG 85, NARA, Washington, DC.
162. Mr. Stillwell, Spear and Stillwell Ranch, November 13, 1928, Folder 10.4, Carton 10, Paul S. Taylor Papers, Bancroft Library, University of California, Berkeley.
163. Hernandez, *Migra!*, 19–44; Ngai, *Impossible Subjects*, 60–71.
164. Kang, *The INS on the Line*.
165. Ngai, *Impossible Subjects*, 131.
166. Zamora, *The World of the Mexican Worker*, 67.
167. Taylor, *Mexican Labor in the United States*, Vol. 1, 346.
168. Ibid., 139.
169. Commission on Industrial Relations, Final Report, 10:9258, in Zamora, *The World of the Mexican Worker*, 67.
170. Grossman, *Land of Hope*.
171. Valdes, *Al Norte*.
172. Mexican merchant, Bishop, Texas, August 1929, Folder 10.7, Carton 10, Paul S. Taylor Papers, Bancroft Library, University of California, Berkeley.
173. Taylor, *An American-Mexican Frontier*, 121.
174. Másquez, Mexican on Byrd Ranch, July 1929, Folder 10.7, Carton 10, Paul S. Taylor Papers, Bancroft Library, University of California, Berkeley.
175. The Villarreal Family, 1929, Folder 10.5, Carton 10, Paul S. Taylor Papers, Bancroft Library, University of California, Berkeley.
176. Mexicans at the Employment Office in Chicago, July 1928, Folder 11.33, Carton 11, Paul S. Taylor Papers, Bancroft Library, University of California, Berkeley.
177. Mexican from Michoacán, Bermuda, Texas, April 24, 1929, Folder 10.5, Carton 10, Paul S. Taylor Papers, Bancroft Library, University of California, Berkeley.
178. Alvaro Ruís, Contractor, Ehler Brother Ranch, April 20, 1929, Folder 10.5, Carton 10, Paul S. Taylor Papers, Bancroft Library, University of California, Berkeley.
179. Mexican in Manheim Camp, June 1928, Folder 11.33, Carton 11, Paul S. Taylor Papers, Bancroft Library, University of California, Berkeley.
180. "Man Who Was Waiting for the Ice Man," August 1928, Folder 11.33, Carton 11, Paul S. Taylor Papers, Bancroft Library, University of California, Berkeley.
181. See Appendix.
182. Taylor, *Mexican Labor in the United States: Migration Statistics III*.
183. Ibid., 39.
184. Ibid.
185. Ward discounts the role of migrant networks as he looks only at whether relatives were meeting migrants at the border, using border crossing cards. Ward, "The Circular Flow: Return Migration from the United States in the Early 1900s."
186. Taylor, *Mexican Labor in the United States: Migration Statistics III*.
187. Interview by author with Felipe Morales, December 1, 2013.
188. Sayer, "Everyday Forms of State Formation," 367–377.

Chapter 3

1. Baba and Abonyi, *Mexicans of Detroit*, 43, in García, *Mexicans in the Midwest*, 15.
2. The Mexican Consulate estimated 60,000, while Paul Taylor estimated 110,000. IV-343-19, Recortes de Periodicos, Consulate Records, Archivo Histórico Diplomático de Secretaría de Relaciones Exteriores, México DF.
3. Garcilazo and Ruiz, *Traqueros*, 35–40.
4. García, *Mexicans in the Midwest*, 6.
5. General Offices, Topeka, Kansas–Los Angeles, California, Mexican Labor in the United States Railroad Studies, Atchison, Topeka & Santa Fe, Folder 12.46, Carton 12, Paul S. Taylor Papers, Bancroft Library, University of California, Berkeley.
6. Mexican Laborers Shipped from El Paso, Texas, to the Atchison, Topeka & Santa Fe Co., Western Lines by the Hanlin Supply Company, Folder 12.46, Carton 12, Paul S. Taylor Papers, Bancroft Library, University of California, Berkeley.

7. Monthly Shipments of Mexican Railroad Laborers from El Paso, Texas, by the Holmes Supply Company, Folder 12.46, Carton 12, Paul S. Taylor Papers, Bancroft Library, University of California, Berkeley.
8. Monthly Statements of the Zarate & Avina Company and L. H. Manning Company, Folder 12.46, Carton 12, Paul S. Taylor Papers, Bancroft Library, University of California, Berkeley.
9. Garcilazo and Ruiz, *Traqueros*, 57.
10. Ibid., 92–93.
11. F. Huerta, June 8, 1928, Folder 11.32, Carton 11, Paul S. Taylor Papers, Bancroft Library, University of California, Berkeley.
12. Mr. Williams, Chief Clerk to Engineer, Baltimore & Ohio, Chicago terminal, June 1928, Folder 11.32, Carton 11, Paul S. Taylor Papers, Bancroft Library, University of California, Berkeley.
13. Mr. T. E. Pratt, Special Agent, CB&Q Railway, Chicago terminal, June 1928, Folder 11.32, Carton 11, Paul S. Taylor Papers, Bancroft Library, University of California, Berkeley.
14. John Generella, Employment Agent and Commissary for C&NW Ry., Chicago terminal, July 11, 1928, Folder 11.32, Carton 11, Paul S. Taylor Papers, Bancroft Library, University of California, Berkeley.
15. Garcilazo and Ruiz, *Traqueros*, 61.
16. Ibid., 78.
17. Mexicans in the Employment Office, Chicago, June 9, 1928, Folder 11.33, Carton 11, Paul S. Taylor Papers, Bancroft Library, University of California, Berkeley.
18. Garcilazo and Ruiz, *Traqueros*, 111–136.
19. Santa Fe Memo, November 27, 1914, in Garcilazo and Ruiz, *Traqueros*, 140.
20. George Edson, "Mexicans in Sugar Beet Work in the Central West: A Summary of Local Reports," Interviews with Labor Contractors, BANC-MSS-74/187c, Folder 40, Carton 13, Paul S. Taylor Papers, Bancroft Library, University of California, Berkeley.
21. Mr. W. H. Talbot, Los Angeles, December 20, 1928, Folder 10.4, Carton 10, Paul S. Taylor Papers, Bancroft Library, University of California, Berkeley.
22. Benito Rodriguez, November 22, 1928, Folder 10.4, Carton 10, Paul S. Taylor Papers, Bancroft Library, University of California, Berkeley.
23. *Daily Free Lance* of El Centro, Imperial County, CA, March 1, 1910, 52546/31, INS RG 85, US National Archives and Records Administration (NARA), Washington, DC.
24. General Offices, Topeka, Kansas–Los Angeles, California, Mexican Labor in the United States Railroad Studies, Atchison, Topeka & Santa Fe, Folder 12.46, Carton 12, Paul S. Taylor Papers, Bancroft Library, University of California, Berkeley.
25. Mexican Labor in the United States Railroad Studies, Santa Fe Railroad, August 1928, Folder 12.53, Carton 12, Paul S. Taylor Papers, Bancroft Library, University of California, Berkeley.
26. J. R. Silva, November 17, 1828, Folder 10.4, Carton 10, Paul S. Taylor Papers, Bancroft Library, University of California, Berkeley.
27. Letters re Colorado Beet Workers, CB&Q and Great Western Sugar Company, Folder 11.32, Carton 11, Paul S. Taylor Papers, Bancroft Library, University of California, Berkeley.
28. D-18-b Barron, President Honorific Commission, Folder 11.15, Carton 11, Paul S. Taylor Papers, Bancroft Library, University of California, Berkeley.
29. Sarah Deutsch has argued that historians have focused too much on localities and not enough on regions. She showed the ways that people, families, and women in particular used different economic structures, including migration, to their advantage as part of multifaceted survival strategies. Deutsch, *No Separate Refuge*, 9–33.
30. Ibid., 90–93.
31. D-16 Labor History in Mines, Folder 11.15, Carton 11, Paul S. Taylor Papers, Bancroft Library, University of California, Berkeley.
32. Ibid.
33. D-21 Watson, Superintendent Ideal Mine, 1927, Folder 11.15, Carton 11, Paul S. Taylor Papers, Bancroft Library, University of California, Berkeley.
34. Andrews, *Killing for Coal*, 87–106.
35. Ibid.
36. Cottrell, *Sugar Beet Economics*, 23.
37. Mapes, *Sweet Tyranny*, 1–38.
38. Ibid., 39–64.
39. Cottrell, *Sugar Beet Economics*, 55.
40. Deutsch, *No Separate Refuge*, 125.

41. Mapes, *Sweet Tyranny*, 122–142.
42. This prompted an inquiry by the Bureau of Immigration. Microfilm T458, section 5, 56, 134–268, INS, NARA, Washington, DC.
43. Martinez, "Mexican Emigration to the US," 46.
44. Ibid., 37.
45. D-11 Robert Barr, Littleton, Colorado, 1927, Folder 11.14, Carton 11, Paul S. Taylor Papers, Bancroft Library, University of California, Berkeley.
46. Fred Holmes, Holly Sugar Company, Colorado Springs, 1927, Folder 11.19, Carton 11, Paul S. Taylor Papers, Bancroft Library, University of California, Berkeley.
47. Ibid.
48. Statistics: Beet Labor Report, December 15, 1926, Beet Labor Living in the Greeley Mexican, Folder 11.19, Carton 11, Paul S. Taylor Papers, Bancroft Library, University of California, Berkeley.
49. A-11 Chester Gear, 1927, Folder 11.8, Carton 11, Paul S. Taylor Papers, Bancroft Library, University of California, Berkeley.
50. Taylor, *Mexican Labor in the United States: Valley of the South Platte, Colorado*, 153.
51. E-39 Mexican Beet Workers in Eaton, October 1927, Folder 11.16, Carton 11, Paul S. Taylor Papers, Bancroft Library, University of California, Berkeley.
52. Deutsch, *No Separate Refuge*, 132–135.
53. J. R. Ruberson, Investigator, Industrial Commission of Colorado, September 8, 1931, Folder 10.3, Carton 10, Paul S. Taylor Papers, Bancroft Library, University of California, Berkeley.
54. Report on Child Labor in Agriculture in Colorado, January 1932, Folder 10.3, Carton 10, Paul S. Taylor Papers, Bancroft Library, University of California, Berkeley.
55. Wages of the Unskilled Workers in Colorado, Thomas F. Mahony, May 27, 1929, Folder 10.3, Carton 10, Paul S. Taylor Papers, Bancroft Library, University of California, Berkeley.
56. Boxes 2–3, Federico Idar Papers, and Boxes 8–9, Clemente Idar Papers, Benson Latin American Library, University of Texas, Austin.
57. Report: Mexican Welfare Committee of the Colorado State Council of the Knights of Columbus, Folder 11.21, Carton 11, Paul S. Taylor Papers, Bancroft Library, University of California, Berkeley.
58. Deutsch, *No Separate Refuge*, 155–161.
59. Mapes, *Sweet Tyranny*, 138–142.
60. Ibid., 156.
61. Ibid., 215–240.
62. Edson, "Mexicans in Our North Central States," 99–114.
63. Garcilazo and Ruiz, *Traqueros*, 45.
64. Juan Martinez, VIDAS, Doc. 15, No. 73, Appendix III, BANC FILM 2322 REEL 1, GNEG Box 2568, Manuel Gamio Papers, Bancroft Library, University of California, Berkeley.
65. A-19 on Employment, Folder 11.8, Carton 11, Paul S. Taylor Papers, Bancroft Library, University of California, Berkeley.
66. Valdes, *Al Norte*, 51–88.
67. American Beet Sugar Company, Folder 11.19, Carton 11, Paul S. Taylor Papers, Bancroft Library, University of California, Berkeley.
68. E-40 Phill Dale, October 1927, Folder 11.16, Carton 11, Paul S. Taylor Papers, Bancroft Library, University of California, Berkeley.
69. Mexican in the Office of J. R. Silva, April 29, 1929, Folder 10.5, Carton 10, Paul S. Taylor Papers, Bancroft Library, University of California, Berkeley.
70. Benito Rodriguez, November 22, 1928, Folder 10.4, Carton 10, Paul S. Taylor Papers, Bancroft Library, University of California, Berkeley.
71. Mr. Courtney, Chief Clerk to Engineer, Maintenance of Way, Illinois Central, June 1928, Chicago terminal, Folder 11.32, Carton 11, Paul S. Taylor Papers, Bancroft Library, University of California, Berkeley.
72. Mr. Williams, Chief Clerk to Engineer, Baltimore & Ohio, Chicago terminal, & Mr. T. E. Pratt, Special Agent. CB&Q Ry., Folder 11.32, Carton 11, Paul S. Taylor Papers, Bancroft Library, University of California, Berkeley.
73. Diego Campa, 336, VOCES Oral History Project, University of Texas, Austin.
74. Joe Jaime, 374, VOCES Oral History Project, University of Texas, Austin.
75. Mendoza, "The Creation of a Mexican Immigrant Community in Kansas City"; Laird, "Argentine, Kansas," 1–61.

76. Laird, "Argentine, Kansas," 105.
77. Valerie Mendoza followed these migrants back to Michoacán and found a whole world left behind. Men were leaving to support families in Mexico and were regularly circulating back. Their departure meant women were becoming heads of household, challenging traditional roles. Mendoza, "The Creation of a Mexican Immigrant Community in Kansas City," chs. 1–2.
78. Mendoza, "The Creation of a Mexican Immigrant Community in Kansas City."
79. Ibid.; Laird, "Argentine, Kansas."
80. IV-100-2, El Consul de Kansas City informa sobre visita hecha a la colonia Mexicana en Scottsbluff, Nebraska, IV/523973-25/6, March 29, 1930, Consulate Records, Archivo Histórico Diplomático de Secretaría de Relaciones Exteriores, México DF.
81. George Edson, January 1, 1926, Interviews with Labor Contractors BANC-MSS-74/187c, Paul S. Taylor Papers, Bancroft Library, University of California, Berkeley.
82. Valdes, *Barrios norteos*, 26.
83. Valdes, *Barrios norteos*.
84. García, *Mexicans in the Midwest*; Valdes, *Al Norte*; Valdes, *Barrios norteos*; Vargas, *Proletarians of the North*.
85. Valdes, *Al Norte*, 13.
86. García, *Mexicans in the Midwest*, 18.
87. Valdes, *Al Norte*, 25.
88. Javier Tovar, interview, July 30, 1928, Folder 11.70, Carton 11, Paul S. Taylor Papers, Bancroft Library, University of California, Berkeley.
89. Vargas, *Proletarians of the North*, 1–85.
90. Francisco Mares, VIDAS, BANC FILM 2322 REEL 1, GNEG Box 2568, Manuel Gamio Papers, Bancroft Library, University of California, Berkeley.
91. Mexicans in the Employment Office, Chicago terminal, June 9, 1928, Folder 11.33, Carton 11, Paul S. Taylor Papers, Bancroft Library, University of California, Berkeley.
92. Taylor, *A Spanish-Mexican Peasant Community*, 42.
93. Antonio Herrera, June 1928, Folder 11.33, Carton 11, Paul S. Taylor Papers, Bancroft Library, University of California, Berkeley.
94. Craig, *First Agraristas*, 190–193.
95. La Vida de Jesus Gonzalez, VIDAS, Folder 2, Appendix 1, Manuel Gamio Papers, Bancroft Library, University of California, Berkeley.
96. Dan Rios, E-9 Employment, 1927, Folder 11.16, Box 11, Paul S. Taylor Papers, Bancroft Library, University of California, Berkeley.
97. Francisco Carpio, 1042, April 1928, Folder 10.8, Box 10, Paul S. Taylor Papers, Bancroft Library, University of California, Berkeley.
98. Cronon, *Nature's Metropolis*.
99. Vargas, *Proletarians of the North*, 36–37.
100. Joseph John Diaz, 352, VOCES Oral History Project, University of Texas, Austin.
101. Garcilazo and Ruiz, *Traqueros*, 125.
102. Arredondo, *Mexican Chicago*, 37–38.
103. Cohen, *Making a New Deal*, 1–98.
104. George Edson, Mexicanas in Fort Mason, Iowa, 1927, Folder 13:30, Carton 13, Paul S. Taylor Papers, Bancroft Library, University of California, Berkeley.
105. Innis-Jiménez, *Steel Barrio*, 33.
106. Vargas, *Proletarians of the North*, 47.
107. It is estimated that the actual Mexican population of the city in 1920 was closer to 3,000 than to the 1,310 found by the US Census; this is small compared to Chicago's largest ethnic groups, including the Polish (137,000), the Germans (112,000), and the Russians (107,000). Burgess and Newcomb, *Census Data of the City of Chicago 1920*, 21.
108. Burgess and Newcomb, *Census Data of the City of Chicago 1920*; Burgess and Newcomb, *Census Data of the City of Chicago 1930*.
109. Vargas, "Armies in the Fields and Factories," 47–71; Fujigaki, "Mexican Steelworkers and the United Steelworkers of America in the Midwest."
110. Jones, "Conditions Surrounding Mexicans in Chicago."
111. Laborers, helpers, and "hands" were placed into the unskilled category, while machine operators, waiters, and cutters were placed in the skilled category. Electricians, butchers, and carpenters were placed in the skilled category. Clerks, teachers, and government workers were

placed in the white-collar category. Doctors, engineers, lawyers, and business owners were placed in the professional category.

112. Burgess and Newcomb, *City of Chicago 1920*, 23.
113. Burgess and Newcomb, *City of Chicago 1920*.
114. Ibid., 13.
115. Jones, "Conditions Surrounding Mexicans in Chicago."
116. A direct comparison in rates of boarders with European immigrants and African Americans could not be made, because the census reports measured different criteria that negated the difference between apartments and houses.
117. South Chicago Studies, Old Resident, June 15, 1928, Chicago, Folder 11.33, Carton 11, Paul S. Taylor Papers, Bancroft Library, University of California, Berkeley.
118. Julian Samora and Richard Lamanna, "Mexican-Americans in a Midwest Metropolis," p. 230, Box 120, Folder 13, Julian Samora Papers, Benson Library, University of Texas, Austin; Innis-Jiménez, *Steel Barrio*, 84.
119. Arredondo, *Mexican Chicago*, 48; Fujigaki, "Mexican Steelworkers."
120. Guerra Employment Agency, San Antonio, Folder 10.5, Carton 10, Paul S. Taylor Papers, Bancroft Library, University of California, Berkeley.
121. Val Martinez, 385, VOCES Oral History Project, University of Texas, Austin.
122. Unknown Mexican, p. 28, Folder 10.8, Carton 10, Paul S. Taylor Papers, Bancroft Library, University of California, Berkeley.
123. Worker at Inland Steel, August 1928, Folder 11.33, Carton 11, Paul S. Taylor Papers, Bancroft Library, University of California, Berkeley.
124. Arredondo, *Mexican Chicago*, 26.
125. Inland Steel Company, Indiana Harbor, Mr. D. P. Thompson, May 31, 1928, Folder 11.32, Carton 11, Paul S. Taylor Papers, Bancroft Library, University of California, Berkeley.
126. Samora and Lamanna, "Mexican-Americans in a Midwest Metropolis," 230.
127. Innis-Jiménez, *Steel Barrio*, 20.
128. Ibid., 28.
129. Ibid., 37.
130. Old Man from Colorado, Indiana Harbor, August 1928, Folder 11.33, Carton 11, Paul S. Taylor Papers, Bancroft Library, University of California, Berkeley.
131. Innis-Jiménez, *Steel Barrio*, 34.
132. Ibid., 37.
133. Circular of Obreros Catolicos, Chicago, June 15, 1928, Folder 11.33, Carton 11, Paul S. Taylor Papers, Bancroft Library, University of California, Berkeley.
134. Buitron, 3927 Evergreen Street, Indiana Harbor, August 5, 1928, p. 36, Folder 10.8, Carton 10, Paul S. Taylor Papers, Bancroft Library, University of California, Berkeley.
135. Rev. Galindo, Catherine House, Indiana Harbor, August 1928, Folder 10.8, Carton 10, Paul S. Taylor Papers, Bancroft Library, University of California, Berkeley.
136. Innis-Jiménez, *Steel Barrio*, 53–64, 135–136.
137. South Chicago Studies, Old Resident, June 15, 1928, Chicago, Folder 11.33, Carton 11, Paul S. Taylor Papers, Bancroft Library, University of California, Berkeley.
138. Innis-Jiménez, *Steel Barrio*, 66, 130.
139. Mexican Picker, Fresno, September 10, 1928, Folder 10.8, Carton 10, Paul S. Taylor Papers, Bancroft Library, University of California, Berkeley.
140. Samora and Lamanna, "Mexican-Americans in a Midwest Metropolis," 20.
141. Fred Gomez, 367, VOCES Oral History Project, University of Texas, Austin.
142. Mr. Fernandez, June 1928, Folder 32, Carton 11, Paul S. Taylor Papers, Bancroft Library, University of California, Berkeley; also in Vargas, *Proletarians of the North*, 44.
143. Arredondo, *Mexican Chicago*, 25.
144. Unfortunately, accurate figures on jobs for non-Mexican groups could not be recreated using the 1930 census due to a change in the way employment figures were presented between the 1920 and 1930 reports.
145. The city of Chicago in general became much older in these 10 years. The demography charts became more of a "tree" than a pyramid. The bulge started at 20 years of age rather than at 10 and peaked at 44–50 years of age rather than the 25–30 of 1930. The population under 10 dropped from 10.08% to 7.56%. Burgess and Newcomb, *City of Chicago 1930*.
146. Other studies of immigrant neighborhoods have noted this tendency among new arrivals. Ferrie, *Yankeys Now Immigrants*.

147. The total number of Mexicans in Chicago in 1930 was 19,362, a major increase, though it still trailed African Americans at 233,903, followed by the Polish at 149,622, Germans at 111,366, and Russians at 78,462. Burgess and Newcomb, *City of Chicago 1930*, X–XIII.
148. 1920 and 1930 US Census of City of Chicago population, including East Chicago.
149. Taylor, *Mexican Labor in the United States: Chicago and the Calumet Region*, 209.
150. García, *Mexicans in the Midwest*, 59.
151. Innis-Jiménez, *Steel Barrio*, 59–61.
152. Gabriella Arredondo has argued that society in Chicago came to see them as non-white, creating space for European immigrants to position themselves as white. Arredondo, *Mexican Chicago*.
153. Much of the scholarship of Mexican communities has focused on acculturation and political development within the community. Arredondo focused on those who stayed in Chicago, using US citizenship applications even while noting how rare it was for people to become citizens. She does point out that the continual flow of people into and out of Chicago and back to Mexico meant that the community stayed culturally tied to Mexico. While critical, it doesn't fully capture how deep the ties to Mexico were.
154. Vargas, *Proletarians of the North*, 169–200.
155. Samora and Lamanna, "Mexican-Americans in a Midwest Metropolis," 230.
156. The Department of Protection within the consulate took on cases of Mexicans who faced the legal system in the United States.
157. Rosales, *Pobre Raza!*
158. Innis-Jiménez, *Steel Barrio*, 141.
159. Samora and Lamanna, "Mexican-Americans in a Midwest Metropolis," 242.
160. Innis-Jiménez, *Steel Barrio*, 5; Fernández, *Brown in the Windy City*.
161. Rev. Galindo, Catherine House, Indiana Harbor, August 1928, Folder 10.8, Carton 10, Paul S. Taylor Papers, Bancroft Library, University of California, Berkeley.
162. Innis-Jiménez, *Steel Barrio*, 44.
163. Jose Vasconcelos, "Speech before the mutualista Ignacio Zaragoza at Hull House, Chicago," June 2, 1928, BANC MSS 84/38, Folder 11.22, Carton 10, Paul S. Taylor Papers, Bancroft Library, University of California, Berkeley.

Chapter 4

1. "Defensa de los Nortenos," Mexican Folklore Survey, Federal Writers Project Papers, Box 187, Folder 3, 306, Special Collections, University of California, Los Angeles [Translation edited by Daniel Morales].
2. Vida de Daniel Aguilar, interview, No. 19, Folder 2, BANC FILM 2322 REEL 1, GNEG Box 2568, Manuel Gamio Papers, Bancroft Library, University of California, Berkeley.
3. Within the field of US history, scholars of migration have tended to focus on the structural forces shaping migration rather than micro-level social interactions. Early scholarship on European migration from Oscar Handlin, John Bodnar, and others focused on displacement due to large structural forces and did not give circular movement importance. Scholars like Thomas Kessner and Stephen Thernstrom focused on issues of assimilation and economic mobility after arrival. Later scholars illustrated the importance of merchants and businesses, immigrant brokers, and family networks in the context of Asian and European migration. This chapter builds on their work, showing how migration became socially embedded in Mexico. Handlin, *The Uprooted*; Bodnar, *The Transplanted*; Higham, *Strangers in the Land*; Taylor, *The Distant Magnet*; Kessner, *The Golden Door*; Thernstrom, *The Other Bostonians*; Wokeck, *Trade in Strangers*; Hsu, *Dreaming of Gold, Dreaming of Home*; Ngai, *The Lucky Ones*; Ward, "The Circular Flow."
4. Jorge Duránd, Rafael Alacron, and Douglass Massey have shown in their work on post-1965 Mexican migration that international migration is a sociological process that is embedded in communities across Mexico. They developed models and theory to explain ways information traveled and its relative importance in making decisions, migrating, and circulating back home. Their work arose to explain modern Mexico. I build on these ideas and bring them back in time, to the early twentieth century.
5. Cardoso, *Mexican Emigration to the United States*, 94–95.
6. 4-352-1929-472 El Gobierno del Estado de Guanajuato, Departamento de Estadísticas de Migración, Instituto Nacional de Migración, Archivo Migratorio Central, México DF.
7. The months in between these two periods are missing.

8. I further address this issue later in this chapter.
9. Detailed records are, unfortunately, only available for December 1929 to February 1930, a time when migration was slower than in the summer, but they still yield valuable information.
10. There was no advantage for indicating one location or another, though there is probably a bias towards returning migrants rather than first-time migrants. 4-352-1930-612 El Gobierno del Estado de Guanajuato, Departamento de Estadísticas de Migración, Instituto Nacional de Migración, Archivo Migratorio Central, México DF.
11. "Doublé Numero del Que Emigra a los EEUU Está Regresando," 4-352-1929-471 Al Gobernador del Estado de Aguascalientes, Instituto Nacional de Migración, Archivo Migratorio Central, México DF.
12. 4-532-1930-615 Gobernador De Aguascalientes Informa Sobre Emigración, Instituto Nacional de Migración, Archivo Migratorio Central, México DF.
13. Martinez, "Mexican Emigration to the US," 87.
14. These spaces could be said to be a transnational village, or transnational social space. For a more theoretical discussion, see Kyle, *Transnational Peasants*; Levitt, *The Transnational Villagers*; Özveren and Faist, *Transnational Social Spaces*.
15. Ochoa Serrano, *Viajes de michoacanos al Norte*, 83–95.
16. Durand, *Más allá de la línea*, 193–199.
17. "Report: Mexican Welfare Committee of the Colorado State Council of the Knights of Columbus," Folder 11.21, Carton 11, Paul S. Taylor Papers, Bancroft Library, University of California, Berkeley.
18. While this model was developed in sociology for modern Chinese migration, it closely aligns with Mexican migration. Giulietti, Wahba, and Zenou, "Strong Versus Weak Ties in Migration," 4.
19. Beals, *A Sierra Tarascan Village*, 4; Foster, *Tzintzuntzan*.
20. Circular, May 15, 1929, 4-352-1929-507 Inmigracion de Mexicanos a los EUA, Instituto Nacional de Migración, Archivo Migratorio Central, México DF.
21. "El Problema de la Emigración de Obreros y Campesinos Mexicanos," July 26, 1929, to the Governors of Zacatecas, Michuacan, Nayarit, Hidalgo, Colima, Gurango, San Luis Potosí, and Aguascalientes, 4-352-1929-530-540, Instituto Nacional de Migración, Archivo Migratorio Central, México DF.
22. Departamento de Migración Tecnica, March 8, 1930, 4-352-1930-607 Secretaría de Relaciones Exteriores, Instituto Nacional de Migración, Archivo Migratorio Central, México DF.
23. Letters, July 29, 1929, Departamento de Migracion de Estadisticas, 4-352-1929-472 Gobernado de Guanajuato, Instituto Nacional de Migración, Archivo Migratorio Central, México DF.
24. Granovetter, "The Strength of Weak Ties," 1360–1380.
25. "Unknown Mexican," interview, p. 28, Folder 10.8, Carton 10, Paul S. Taylor Papers, Bancroft Library, University of California, Berkeley.
26. Gamio, *Mexican Immigration to the United States*, 238.
27. Taylor, *An American-Mexican Frontier*, 104–105.
28. Ibid., 4–5.
29. Ibid., 163–165.
30. "Analysis of Mexicans Savings Accounts, Imperial Valley," Field Notes, Folder 10.20, Carton 10, Paul S. Taylor Papers, Bancroft Library, University of California, Berkeley.
31. Draft Article, Folder 10.36 Carton 10, Paul S. Taylor Papers, Bancroft Library, University of California, Berkeley.
32. George T. Edson, "Mexicans in Gary Ind," US Department of Labor, Bureau of Labor Statistics, Folder 13.28, Carton 13, Paul S. Taylor Papers, Bancroft Library, University of California, Berkeley.
33. Taylor, *Mexican Labor in the United States: Chicago and the Calumet Region*, 162–163.
34. Ibid., 32–41.
35. Cardoso, *Mexican Emigration to the United States*, 74.
36. Massey, *Return to Aztlan*; Massey, Durand, and Malone, *Beyond Smoke and Mirrors*.
37. Rosas, *Abrazando el espíritu*.
38. Mr. G and Mrs. G, Mexicans in Chicago Field Journal, 1928, p. 35, Folder 21, Robert Redfield Papers, Special Collections, University of Chicago.
39. La Videa de Manuel Perez, interview, Folder 2.4, BANC FILM 2322 REEL 1, GNEG Box 2568, Manuel Gamio Papers, Bancroft Library, University of California, Berkeley.
40. Vida de Jesus Gonzales, No. 17, Folder 2, BANC FILM 2322 REEL 1, GNEG Box 2568, Manuel Gamio Papers, Bancroft Library, University of California, Berkeley.

41. Vida de Manuel Lomeli, No. 24, Folder 2:14, BANC FILM 2322 REEL 2, GNEG Box 2569, Manuel Gamio Papers, Bancroft Library, University of California, Berkeley.
42. Pedro Flores, US Census 1920, US Census 1930.
43. This is a point historian Ana Rosas made of the migrants of San Martine de Hidalgo, Jalisco, in the middle of the twentieth century, and one that was true for an earlier generation in the 1920s. Rosas, *Abrazando el espíritu.*
44. Taylor, *A Spanish-Mexican Peasant Community*, 43.
45. Corn mix.
46. "Cancion del Interior (Song of the Interior)," Folder 26, Carton 1, Paul S. Taylor Papers, Bancroft Library, University of California, Berkeley. Translation by Paul S. Taylor.
47. "Locario Lopez," interviews, Folder 11.34, Carton 11, Paul S. Taylor Papers, Bancroft Library, University of California, Berkeley.
48. Ana Rosas has written of the role that pictures played in keeping migrant families together Rosas, *Abrazando el espíritu*, 112–143.
49. Venegas, *Letters Home.*
50. Ochoa Serrano, *Viajes de michoacanos al Norte*, 99–126.
51. "Vida de Jose Rocha," Folder 2, BANC FILM 2322 REEL 1, GNEG Box 2568, Manuel Gamio Papers, Bancroft Library, University of California, Berkeley.
52. "Ofelia Silva and Manuel Martinez," interview by Daniel Morales, January 15, 2015. East of East: Mapping Community Narratives in South El Monte and El Monte, SEMAP, El Monte, California.
53. Many of the contours of the public debate on migration have been studied by other scholars, such as Lawrence Cardoso, Francisco Balderrama, Laurencio Sanguino, and Kelly Hernandez.
54. Gamio, *Mexican Immigration to the United States*, 184.
55. Ibid., 185–196.
56. Balderrama and Rodríguez, *Decade of Betrayal*, 163–166.
57. Torres, *La patria perdida.*
58. Dennison, "Mexico de Afuera in Northern Missouri," 2.
59. Espinoza, *El sol de Texas.*
60. Venegas, *Las adventuras de Don Chipote.*
61. Cardoso, *Mexican Emigration to the United States*, 104–105.
62. Ibid., 78–82.
63. "Platica Entre Dos Rancheros," Mexican Folklore Survey, Federal Writers Project Papers, Box 187, Folder 3, 306, Special Collections, University of California, Los Angeles.
64. "Defensa de los Nortenos," Mexican Folklore Survey, Federal Writers Project Papers, Box 187, Folder 3, 306, Special Collections, University of California, Los Angeles. Translation edited by Daniel Morales.
65. Taylor, *A Spanish-Mexican Peasant Community*, 53.
66. Ibid., 42.
67. Ibid., 40.
68. "Dr W Rebeling interview," October 20, 1931, Folder 22, Carton 1, Paul S. Taylor Papers, Bancroft Library, University of California, Berkeley.
69. The region was not a hotbed of agrarian land revolts. While large *haciendas* did exist, they were outnumbered by the many independent rancherias in the region.
70. Venegas, *Letters Home*, 7–15.
71. Taylor, *A Spanish-Mexican Peasant Community*, 36–40.
72. "Mexican Interviewed," July 1928, Folder 12.1, Carton 12, Paul S. Taylor Papers, Bancroft Library, University of California, Berkeley.
73. "Rafael Orendain interview," October 18, 1931, Folder 22, Carton 1, Paul S. Taylor Papers, Bancroft Library, University of California, Berkeley.
74. Taylor, *A Spanish-Mexican Peasant Community*, 160.
75. Gonzalez, *San José de Gracia*, 158.
76. Julia Young has argued that as Cristero supporters formed a transnational diaspora in order to advance a common set of political and religious goals. Young, *Mexican Exodus.*
77. Ibid., 8.
78. Taylor, *A Spanish-Mexican Peasant Community*, 40.
79. Ibid., 44.
80. Fitzgerald, "Inside the Sending State," 259–293.
81. Ibid.

82. Taylor, *A Spanish-Mexican Peasant Community*, 32.
83. Agrarian Files 307 (La Barca, Municipio of La Barca, 1925) and 309 (Lagos de Moreno, Municipio of Lagos de Moreno, 1925), Historical Agrarian Archive of Jalisco; see Sellars, "Does Emigration Inhibit Reform?"
84. Sellars, "Does Emigration Inhibit Reform?"; Sellars, "Emigration and Collective Action."
85. Kelly Lytle Hernandez has argued that reaching the border was not the beginning of a migrant's evasion of border guards but rather the culmination of it, as migrants had to find ways around the Departamento de Migración's agents along railroad routes and the northern frontier. Hernandez, "Persecuted Like Criminals," 221–232.
86. El Visitador de Migración, March 2, 1927, "Se Solicita de gestión con los Ferrocarriles la expedición de tarjetas-pases anuales," 4-123-1927-2 Pases Personales de Ferrocarril Departamento de Migración, Instituto Nacional de Migración, Archivo Migratorio Central, México DF.
87. Cámara Nacional de Comercio de Nuevo Laredo, March 13, 1928, 4-352-1928-219, Cámara de Comerciado de Nuevo Laredo Los Braceros Emigrantes Los Coyotes, Instituto Nacional de Migración, Archivo Migratorio Central, México DF. Translations by Daniel Morales.
88. Hernandez, "Persecuted Like Criminals," 228.
89. Trejo Terreros, "Los coyotes," 84–104.
90. José Inez Pérez, December 14, 1928, José Inez Pérez to Secretaría de Gobernacion, 4-352-2-1928-52A Oficio Mayo, Instituto Nacional de Migración, Archivo Migratorio Central, México DF. Translations by Daniel Morales.
91. Cámara Nacional de Comercio de Nuevo Laredo, March 13, 1928, 4-352-1928-219, Cámara de Comerciado de Nuevo Laredo Los Braceros Emigrantes Los Coyotes, Instituto Nacional de Migración, Archivo Migratorio Central, México DF. Translations by Daniel Morales.
92. Yankelevich, "Corrupción y gestión migratoria en el México posrevolucionario," 451.
93. Trejo Terreros, "Los coyotes," 80–83.
94. Ibid., 84.
95. Ibid., 104.
96. Yankelevich, "Corrupción y gestión migratoria," 460.
97. "Memorándum para el Señor Presidente de la Republica," December 9, 1925, 4-123-1926-1, Para la Dirección de Ferrocarriles nacionales de México Anexo NA, Instituto Nacional de Migración, Archivo Migratorio Central, México DF. Translation by Daniel Morales.
98. "Ferrocarriles Nacionales de Mexico Oficina del Gerente General," March 8, 1926, 4-123-1926-1 Para la Direccion de Ferrocarriles Nacionales de Mexico Anexo, Instituto Nacional de Migración, Archivo Migratorio Central, México DF.
99. Secretaría de Gobernación, Al Adalberto Tejado, 4-352-2-1926-9A, El Agente de Migración en Torreón Coahila, Instituto Nacional de Migración, Archivo Migratorio Central, México DF.
100. Secretaría de Gobernación, February 22, 1926, 4-352-2-1926-10A, El Delegado de Migración en Matamoros, Instituto Nacional de Migración, Archivo Migratorio Central, México DF.
101. File 4-352-1925-1F, Agente del Servicio de Emigración en Saltillo Coahuila, Instituto Nacional de Migración, Archivo Migratorio Central, México DF. Translation by Daniel Morales.
102. Letters, January 11–21, 1926, 4-352-2-1925-7A, Agente de Migration en Saltillo Coah, Instituto Nacional de Migración, Archivo Migratorio Central, México DF.
103. Manuel Limon Maciel, August 25, 1926, 4-352-2-1927-24A Delegado de Migración Ciudad Juarez: Da cuentas con las medias que ha tomado para evitar la aglomeración de braceros emigrantes, Instituto Nacional de Migración, Archivo Migratorio Central, México DF.
104. Memorandum of Secretary of Migration, March 17, 1930, 4-352-1930-607 Secretaría de Ralaciones Exteriores, Instituto Nacional de Migración, Archivo Migratorio Central, México DF.
105. Ibid.
106. Letter to President of Mexican Railroad, March 24, 1930, 4-352-1930-607 Secretaría de Ralaciones Exteriores, Instituto Nacional de Migración, Archivo Migratorio Central, México DF.
107. Circular No. 5, Mexican National Railroad to all Passenger Agents, Departamento de Migración Letter, April 30, 1930, A Circular for Station Agents, 4-352-1930-607 Secretaría de Ralaciones Exteriores, Instituto Nacional de Migración, Archivo Migratorio Central, México DF.
108. "Participio que varios mexicanos se quejan contra el maltrato del celador norteamericano en Andrade, California—J. Brussel," 4-352-2-1925-6A El Agente de Migración en Algodones, Instituto Nacional de Migración, Archivo Migratorio Central, México DF.

109. January 29, 1927, 4-352-1927-77 Consulta Si Permite a Unos Mex ir a Trabaja a Terriotorio Americano Sin Llenar los Requisitos, Instituto Nacional de Migración, Archivo Migratorio Central, México DF.
110. "Informa como braceros burlas las disposiciones de migración para salir a EE UU y sugiere la forma de evitarlo," February 14, 1926, 4-352-2-1926-9A, El Agente de Migración en Torreón Coah, Instituto Nacional de Migración, Archivo Migratorio Central, México DF.
111. Jose Choren, July 1, 1929, 4-352-1929-523, Instituto Nacional de Migración, Archivo Migratorio Central, México DF.
112. R. Castaneda, 4-352-1926-2, Series 352 from 1926 to the mid-1930s, Instituto Nacional de Migración, Archivo Migratorio Central, México DF.
113. Cardoso, *Mexican Emigration to the United States*, 59–60.
114. Cardoso, *Mexican Emigration to the United States*, 66; *Diario Oficial* 14 (March 17, 1920): 1225; Aguirre Berlanga to Ramón P. Denegri, Consul Genderal, June 14, 1918, AHSRE, 16-24-25.
115. 4-352-1929-382, Fernando Frausto, Cd Victoria Tamps, Instituto Nacional de Migración, Archivo Migratorio Central, México DF.
116. Guadalupe Simental, April 23, 1926, 4-352-1626-4, Instituto Nacional de Migración, Archivo Migratorio Central, México DF.
117. 4-352-1926-45 Maria Dolores Mora, 4-352-1930-603 Serfina Garcia, 4-352-1928-313, Consulta si un Grupo de Mujeres Pueden Salir Solas a EEUU, Instituto Nacional de Migración, Archivo Migratorio Central, México DF.
118. 4-352-1927-132 Teodora Torres Ornelas, Instituto Nacional de Migración, Archivo Migratorio Central, México DF.
119. 4-352-1927-88 Jesús Cevallos, Instituto Nacional de Migración, Archivo Migratorio Central, México DF.
120. 4-352-1926-50 Rosario Hernandez, many more in Series 352 individual cases, Instituto Nacional de Migración, Archivo Migratorio Central, México DF.
121. Kang, *The INS on the Line*, 1–86.

Chapter 5

1. El Universal, June 14, 1939; Archive General de la Nation (AGN), APLC, r. 10, part 1, Letter from Castillo Najera to the President, Washington, DC, July 31, 1939, in Alanís Enciso, *They Should Stay There*, 174.
2. Ibid.
3. Morales, "*Tejas, Afuera de México.*"
4. Various scholars studying Mexican communities from this time period have examined *México de Afuera*. Emilio Zamora, David Montejano, Richard Garcia, Gilbert González, and F. Arturo Rosales, among others, have written about organizing *mutualistas* (Mexican mutual organizations), newspapers, and consuls as part of the history of particular communities. They have shown that, rather than being simple victims of international and domestic capitalism, Mexicans countered attempts to segregate and control them by organizing civic society. Yet they have often looked at the *México de Afuera* discourse that defined this era as an elite, conservative, backward-looking ideology. Zamora, *The World of the Mexican Worker in Texas*; Montejano, *Anglos and Mexicans in the Making of Texas*; Garcia, *Rise of the Mexican American Middle Class*; Gutiérrez, *Walls and Mirrors*; González, *Mexican Consuls and Labor Organizing*; Rosales, *Pobre Raza!*
5. Arendt, *The Origins of Totalitarianism*, 296.
6. For a history of US criminal justice response to Mexicans, see Rosales, *Pobre Raza!*
7. Anne Cloe Watson, "Mexican Families in Transit North Through the Inland Port of San Antonio," International Institute, YWCA, San Francisco 1929, Special Collections Research Center, University of Chicago.
8. Zamora, *World of the Mexican Worker*, 211.
9. Garcia, "Class, Consciousness, and Ideology," 30.
10. Garcia, *Rise of the Mexican American Middle Class*, 17.
11. Ibid., 48–49.
12. Ibid., 34.
13. Ibid.; González, *Redeeming La Raza*.
14. Acuña, *Occupied America*, 152.
15. Garcia, *Rise of the Mexican American Middle Class*, 52–57.

16. For a larger discussion of this, see Zamora, *World of the Mexican Worker*, 86–109; Sanchez, *Becoming Mexican American*; Garcia, *A World of Its Own*; Alamillo, *Making Lemonade out of Lemons*.
17. Sociedad Mutualist Melchor Ocampo Papers, Benson Latin American Library, University of Texas, Austin.
18. Garcia, *Rise of the Mexican American Middle Class*, 90; Zamora, *World of the Mexican Worker*, 66–81.
19. Gomez-Quinones, *Roots of Chicano Politics*, 312.
20. Cohen, *Making a New Deal.*
21. Zamora, *World of the Mexican Worker*, 86–87.
22. Gomez-Quinones, *Roots of Chicano Politics*, 312.
23. Box IV-100, San Antonio Consulate, Archivo Histórico Diplomático de Secretaría de Relaciones Exteriores, México DF.
24. Zamora, *World of the Mexican Worker*, 94.
25. Consulates routinely sent reports to the SRE about their activities and relations with the community. Informes Sobre Sociedades Felentropicas Mexicanas, 38-11-244, Box IV-100, and 6-13-70; Informes de Labores del Consulado en San Antonio, IV-15-8, San Antonio Consulate, Archivo Histórico Diplomático de Secretaría de Relaciones Exteriores, México DF.
26. González, *Redeeming La Raza*, 125–129.
27. Garcia, *Rise of the Mexican American Middle Class*, 90–92.
28. Gabriela González has argued that masonic orders and *mutualistas* were vehicles by which middle-class reformers sought to redeem *La Raza* (the Mexican people). González, *Redeeming La Raza*, 44–46.
29. Ibid., 193.
30. Gomez-Quinones, *Roots of Chicano Politics*, 314–320.
31. Zamora, *World of the Mexican Worker*, 166–168.
32. Rosales, *Pobre Raza!*, 145.
33. Ibid., 27.
34. González, *Redeeming La Raza*, 82–107.
35. Zamora, *World of the Mexican Worker*, 88–94.
36. Gomez-Quinones, *Roots of Chicano Politics*, 370–373.
37. Lozano, *An American Language.*
38. Meyer, *Speaking for Themselves*, 207–212.
39. Felix Gutiérrez has argued that these newspapers were instruments of social control and social activism, while offering literary reflections of Chicano life. Gutiérrez, "Spanish-Language Media in America," 37–38.
40. Miller, *The Ethnic Press in the United States*, 248.
41. Valencia, "Ricardo Flores Magón y el periodismo subversivo Mexican en EUA," 169–178.
42. Kent and Huntz, "Spanish-Language Newspapers in the United States," 446–456.
43. Miller, *The Ethnic Press in the United States*, 250–255.
44. Zamora, *World of the Mexican Worker*, 145. I read every other Sunday issue of *La Prensa* from 1920 to 1921 and 1929 as well as selected in-week editions when they were mentioned in the Mexican consulate's correspondence. These were accessed November 2016–March 2017. https://www.readex.com/products/hispanic-american-newspapers-1808-1980.
45. Stefano, "*Venimos a luchar*," 96–118.
46. Ríos-McMillan, "A Biography of a Man and His Newspaper," 136–149; Parle, "The Novels of the Mexican Revolution Published by the Casa Editorial Lozano," 163–168.
47. Garcia, *Rise of the Mexican American Middle Class*, 223.
48. Hinojosa-Smith, "*La Prensa*," 125–129; La Vida de Ricardo Sotero, Los Angeles, CA, April 3, 1927, Folder 2.15, BANC FILM 2332 REEL 2, GNEG Box 2569, Manuel Gamio Papers, Bancroft Library, University of California, Berkeley.
49. Riveras-Rodriguez, "Ignacio E. Lozano," 75–89.
50. This was similar to the lost and found family members listings that African Americans ran in newspapers after emancipation, but for migration.
51. Scholars have pointed out that the newspaper represented the voice of elite Mexicans rather than most of the Mexicans who were arriving to the United States. Trevino, "*Prensa y patria*," 451; Garcia, "Class, Consciousness, and Ideology," 42–43.
52. Medeiros, "*La Opinión*, a Mexican Exile Newspaper," 65–87.
53. Garcia, *Rise of the Mexican American Middle Class*, 224–225.

54. Habermas, *The Structural Transformation of the Public Sphere*; Aguirre, "Porfirista Femininity in Exile," 147–162.
55. Novoa, "*La Prensa* and the Chicano Community," 150.
56. Ríos-McMillan, "A Biography of a Man and His Newspaper," 136–149.
57. To see an example of this, see the issue of *La Prensa* from January 25, 1920. Accessed November 2016–February 2017, https://www.readex.com/products/hispanic-american-newspapers-1808-1980.
58. Aguirre, "Porfirista Femininity in Exile," 150.
59. Ibid., 152.
60. Ibid., 157.
61. *La Prensa*'s first women's and children's sections ran on January 11, 1920.
62. Garcia, *Rise of the Mexican American Middle Class*, 237.
63. Anderson, *Imagined Communities.*
64. Munguía, "*La Prensa*," 130–135.
65. Ríos-McMillan, "A Biography of a Man," 136–419.
66. The clinic campaign ran for many months. See "Necesitamos por lo menos vienticino mil dolares para construir la clinica," *La Prensa*, February 3, 1929.
67. Munguía, "*La Prensa*," 130–135.
68. Garcia, *Rise of the Mexican American Middle Class*, 108–130.
69. Ibid., 200.
70. Medeiros, "*La Opinión*," 65–87.
71. Ríos-McMillan, "A Biography of a Man," 136–149.
72. Ibid.
73. "Toda la frontera se halla interesada por la suerte de los braceros mexicano," *La Prensa*, April 28, 1929; "Vigorosa defensa de los braceros de nuestro pais," *La Prensa*, February 10, 1929.
74. "Otro Mexicanos atropellado por una locomotora," and "La vida mexicana en estados unidos," *La Prensa*, March 3, 1929.
75. Rosales, *Pobre Raza!*, 38.
76. "Protestan contra los Aaaltos que sufren los mexicanos," *La Prensa*, January 4, 1920.
77. "Por las cortes y de policia," *La Prensa*, January 11, 1920.
78. Rosales, *Pobre Raza!*, 144.
79. "Interviene el consulado en favor de un reo," *La Prensa*, November 18, 1930.
80. "Un mexicano asesinado en El Paso, Texas," *La Prensa*, February 3, 1929.
81. Rosales, *Pobre Raza!*, 42; Lee, "To the Seventh Generation," 1–50.
82. "El Paso and New York Most Important Consulate Posts of Mexico in the US: Advantages Outlined by Consul Ruiz," Consul General Enrique D. Ruiz in the El Paso Herald, October 13–14, 1923, 38-22-178, El Paso Consulate, Archivo Histórico Diplomático de Secretaría de Relaciones Exteriores, México DF.
83. Box IV-73, Protección a Mexicanos del Consulado en San Antonio, Archivo Histórico Diplomático de Secretaría de Relaciones Exteriores, México DF.
84. Several scholars have argued that consulates ignored the migrant's concerns, seeking to organize the community along collectivist-nationalist lines loyal to the government in Mexico City. González, *Mexican Consuls and Labor Organizing*, 197–228.
85. Rosales, *Pobre Raza!*, 38, 75–98.
86. Mexicanos Deportados, Consulado en San Antonio, IV-346-51, Box IV-345, San Antonio Consulate, Archivo Histórico Diplomático de Secretaría de Relaciones Exteriores, México DF.
87. Rosales, *Pobre Raza!*, 39.
88. Ibid., 78.
89. Ibid., 106.
90. Contractos a Mexicanos Para Trabajar, IV-76-31, El Paso Consulate Files, Archivo Histórico Diplomático de Secretaría de Relaciones Exteriores, México DF.
91. Rosales, *Pobre Raza!*, 110–115.
92. Manifestación de los sin trabajo en el Consulado en San Antonio, IV-260-36, San Antonio Consulate, Archivo Histórico Diplomático de Secretaría de Relaciones Exteriores, México DF.
93. Santibañez, *Ensayo sobre la inmigración mexicana.*
94. Ibid., 1–101.
95. Weise and Rass, "Migrating Concepts."
96. Riveras-Rodriguez, "Ignacio E. Lozano," 80.

97. Acusaciones contra el Servicio Consular, IV-348-63, Archivo Histórico Diplomático de Secretaría de Relaciones Exteriores, México DF.
98. Informes de Labores del Consulado en San Antonio, IV-15-8, San Antonio Consulate, Archivo Histórico Diplomático de Secretaría de Relaciones Exteriores, México DF.
99. "1929, Maltrato a Mexicanos residentes en McNary, Texas," IV-75-26, El Paso Consulate, Archivo Histórico Diplomático de Secretaría de Relaciones Exteriores, México DF.
100. Rosales, *Pobre Raza!*, 38.
101. "Se pide ayuda para los compatriotas deportados, que estan en la miseria en varias ciudades de la frontera," *La Prensa*, July 28, 1930, IV-256-1, San Antonio Consulate, Archivo Histórico Diplomático de Secretaría de Relaciones Exteriores, México DF.
102. Dificultaded con el Consul por supresion de Comisión Honorifica de la colonia mexicana de ese lugar, IV-99-46, Archivo Histórico Diplomático de Secretaría de Relaciones Exteriores, México DF.
103. Visita a las Comisiónes Honorificas en Charlotte y Rondo, Texas, IV-100-30, San Antonio Consulate, Archivo Histórico Diplomático de Secretaría de Relaciones Exteriores, México DF.
104. For the El Paso Consulate, Box VI-82, Archivo Histórico Diplomático de Secretaría de Relaciones Exteriores, México DF.
105. El Paso and San Antonio Consulates, Archivo Histórico Diplomático de Secretaría de Relaciones Exteriores, México DF.
106. "El Consul Santibañez da a conocer la Ley Sobre la Inmigracion," *La Prensa*, May 23, 1929; "El Consul recomienda a los mexicanos so se dejen explotar," *La Prensa*, June 25, 1929; "Una gran agrupaccion impedira la deportaciones de mexicanos," *La Prensa*, September, 4, 1929; "Compana contra la deportacion de mexicanos," *La Prensa*, September 5, 1929; "Los Estados Unidos de Norteamerica y los emigrantes," *La Prensa*, May 21, 1929; in 4-352-2-1929-56A, Jose Ines Perez, Instituto Nacional de Migración, Archivo Migratorio Central, México DF.
107. Garcia, *Rise of the Mexican American Middle Class*, 115.
108. Garza, "Framing Mexicans in the Great Depression Editorials," 26–48.
109. Alberto Rembao, "Las golondrinas de becquer," *La Prensa*, March 22, 1930, seen in Garza, "Framing Mexicans," 26–48.
110. McKay, "Texas Mexican Repatriation During the Great Depression," 105–109.
111. Ibid., 38.
112. Ibid., 65–97.
113. Ibid., 98–150.
114. San Antonio *La Prensa* (April 3, 1930): 3.
115. "1929, Sobre Requisitos a inmigrantes Mexicanos," IV-89-3, El Paso Consulate, Archivo Histórico Diplomático de Secretaría de Relaciones Exteriores, México DF.
116. For a longer discussion, see Hoffman, *Unwanted Mexican Americans in the Great Depression*; Velasco, *Los mexicanos que devolvio la crisis*; Katz, Stern, and Fader, "The Mexican Immigration Debate," 157–189.
117. Enciso, *Voces de la repatriación*, 310–312.
118. See Appendix; Morales, "The Making of Mexican America."
119. McKay, "Texas Mexican Repatriation," 65–98.
120. Ibid., 133.
121. "Se pide ayuda para los compatriotas deportados," *La Prensa*.
122. "Panico en El Paso, Tex. por las deporaciones," *La Prensa*, May 19, 1931.
123. McKay, "Texas Mexican Repatriation," 117.
124. Ibid., 139–141.
125. Ibid., 201.
126. Ibid., 162–219.
127. Ibid., 171–177.
128. Fox, *Three Worlds of Relief*, 55–155.
129. McKay, "Texas Mexican Repatriation," 220–256.
130. Ibid., 118.
131. Balderrama pointed out that the US State Department estimated a total of 345,000 Mexican repatriates between 1930 and 1935, while the SRE in Mexico put the official tally at 422,831 over the course of the 1930s. Mexican newspapers claimed much higher figures: *El Universal* counted 2,000,000, while *Excelsior* claimed 75,000 had arrived from just Los Angeles in three years. Balderrama and Rodríguez split the difference between the documented arrivals, and the numbers given by newspapers to arrive at their own estimate of a million people.

132. Balderrama and Rodríguez, *Decade of Betrayal*, 150–151; Hoffman, *Unwanted Mexican Americans*; Velasco, *Los mexicanos que devolvió la crisis*; Katz, Stern, and Fader, "The Mexican Immigration Debate," 157–189.
133. Carreras de Velasco, *Los mexicanos que devolvió la crisis, 1929–1932.*
134. Alanís Enciso, *Que se queden allá.*
135. Taylor, *Mexican Labor in the United States: Migration Statistics IV*, 24–30.
136. The demographers used census information to estimate the number of migrants that would be expected regardless of repatriation and compared this number against the actual population in the United States in 1940. They came up with 176,720 people, or about 14% of the ethnic Mexican population in 1930. When circular migration is included, the number of repatriates is 355,000. This analysis gives historians the best estimate yet on returning children and their citizenship, and its estimate is roughly in line with previous studies. Gratton and Merchant, "Immigration, Repatriation, and Deportation," 944–975.
137. My census study was geared towards following the paths taken by a random sample of Mexican migrants and, thus, showing how common geographic mobility was among them. As such, the study was not designed to estimate migration or repatriation numbers.
138. These numbers are different than the commonly accepted range of 500,000 to 1,000,000, 60% of whom are believed to have been citizens.
139. 1931, IV-346-51 and IV-346-51, Mexicanos Deportados, San Antonio Consulate Files, Archivo Histórico Diplomático de Secretaría de Relaciones Exteriores, México DF.
140. Garcia, *Rise of the Mexican American Middle Class*, 263.
141. Rodolfo Uranga, "Glosorio del dia," *La Prensa*, April 3, 1930.
142. "El Consul recomienda a los mexicanos so se dejen explotar," *La Prensa.*
143. IV-107-94, San Antonio Consulate issues CIRCULAR 7, Archivo de la Secretaría de Relaciones Exteriores, México DF.
144. McKay, "Texas Mexican Repatriation," 271–272.
145. IV-355-21, Repatriados Mexicanos en Detroit: Relativo su domicilio en el extranjero, Archivo de la Secretaría de Relaciones Exteriores, México DF.
146. "Facilidades a todoes los repatriados," *La Prensa*, February 2, 1930.
147. McKay, "Texas Mexican Repatriation," 274.
148. Ibid., 282.
149. Ibid., 115.
150. Ríos-McMillan, "A Biography of a Man," 136–149.
151. *La Prensa*, September 21, 1929: 3 and January 14, 1930: 7, in Garcia, *Rise of the Mexican American Middle Class*, 226.
152. "Mexicanos que desean colonizar en terrenos de la Hacienda Sautefa," IV-170-27, Archivo de la Secretaria de Relaciones Exteriores, México DF.
153. "El regreso a la patria," *La Prensa*, January 7, 1931, seen in Garza, "Framing Mexicans," 26–48.
154. McKay, "Texas Mexican Repatriation," 318–319.
155. Ibid., 285.
156. File 812.5511/105, INS RG 59, US National Archives and Records Administration (NARA),, Washington, DC.
157. McKay, "Texas Mexican Repatriation," 287.
158. "800 Familias Mexicanas se Disponen a Emprender a Pie su Viaje a la Patria," *La Prensa*, September 27, 1931.
159. *La Prensa*, October 19, 1931.
160. McKay, "Texas Mexican Repatriation," 331.
161. "Lo crea un decreto del presidente," *La Prensa*, June 27, 1930; "En Mexico no quieren a los repatriados," *La Opinión*, October 2, 1932, Informes Sobre Mexicanos Repatriados, IV-549-1.5, Archivo Histórico Diplomático de Secretaría de Relaciones Exteriores, México DF.
162. "El problema de los sin trabajo en Mexico es de gran importancia," *La Prensa*, September 30, 1930.
163. McKay, "Texas Mexican Repatriation," 321.
164. Memorándum Sobre Reparación, Repatriados Estados Unidos, Exp. 549.5/45, Caja 925, Fondo Cárdenas, Archivo General de la Nación, México DF.
165. McKay, "Texas Mexican Repatriation," 410.
166. Mensaje a la Colonia Mexicana de San Antonio, Texas, y Jurisdicción, January 1, 1939, Repatriados Estados Unidos, Exp. 549.51/17, Caja 935, Fondo Cárdenas, Archivo General de la Nación, México DF.

167. 55957, Repatriation of Mexican Nationals, INS RG 85, NARA, Washington, DC.
168. McKay, "Texas Mexican Repatriation," 112.
169. "Mexican Repatriation Project Outlines Here by Ramon Beteta," *Corpus Cristi Caller*, April 17, 1939, 27-9-164, Archivo de la Secretaría de Relaciones Exteriores, México DF.
170. "El Plan de la Repatriacion a Mexico," *La Prensa*, April 18, 1939, 27-9-164, Archivo de la Secretaría de Relaciones Exteriores, México DF.
171. Jose Guerrero, March 24, 1939, Repatriados Estados Unidos, Exp. 549.5/45, Caja 925, Fondo Cárdenas, Archivo General de la Nación, México DF.
172. Letter to Ramon Beteta, Pedro de la Cruz, May 28, 1939, Ernesto Hidalgo, June 1, 1939, 27-9-164, Archivo de la Secretaría de Relaciones Exteriores, México DF.
173. Tirso A. Valdez, May 20, 1939, Repatriados Estados Unidos, Exp. 549/19, Caja 925, Fondo Cárdenas, Archivo General de la Nación, México DF.
174. Reynaldo Osorio, May 6, 1939, Repatriados Estados Unidos, Exp. 549.5/45, Caja 925, Fondo Cárdenas, Archivo General de la Nación, México DF.
175. Jose M. Reyes, Janurary 14, 1936, Repatriados Estados Unidos, Exp. 549.51/8, Caja 935, Fondo Cárdenas, Archivo General de la Nación, México DF.
176. Jose Navarro, April 9, 1935, Repatriados Estados Unidos, Exp. 549.5/21, Caja 935, Fondo Cárdenas, Archivo General de la Nación, México DF. Translation by Daniel Morales.
177. For examples, see Joaquin F. Lopez, Elvira V. Perez, Seguno Botello, Exp. 549.51/17, Caja 935, Fondo Cárdenas, Archivo General de la Nación, México DF.
178. Enciso, *They Should Stay There*, 142.
179. This challenges F. Arturo Rosales, who has claimed that "México Lindo" (or *México de Afuera*) activism waned as the community naturally matured, and Richard Garcia, who pointed to the rise of a middle class in 1920s San Antonio as leading to the creation of a Mexican American identity in the 1930s. Garcia, *Rise of the Mexican American Middle Class*, 4; Rosales, *Pobre Raza!*, 4–5.
180. Ibid., 270–272.
181. Camacho, *Migrant Imaginaries*, 49–58.
182. Garcia, *Rise of the Mexican American Middle Class*, 62–64.
183. González, *Redeeming La Raza*, 155–157.
184. Leal, "The Spanish-Language Press," 157–162.
185. Garcia, *Rise of the Mexican American Middle Class*, 170–172.
186. González, *Redeeming La Raza*, 122–140.
187. Garcia, *Rise of the Mexican American Middle Class*, 292.
188. Trevino, "*Prensa y patria*," 451–472.
189. Hinojosa-Smith, "*La Prensa*," 125–129.
190. "El problema de irigación en México," *La Prensa*, September 24, 1930, from Weise, *Corazón de Dixie*, 1–150.
191. "El algunos campos agricolas se trata con suma dureza a los trabajadores mexicanos," *La Prensa*, June 5, 1924; "Centenares de mexicanos se encuentran sufriendo en los campos de trabajo," *La Prensa*, August 28, 1924.
192. "Una compatriota se queja de los enganchadores," *La Prensa*, March 31, 1926; "Varios mexicanos son aprehendidos en Clarksdale, Mississippi," *La Prensa*, November 4, 1925. "Una compatriota se queja de los enganchadores," *La Prensa*, March 31, 1926; "Las penalidades de los braceros mexicanos en el Mississipi," *La Prensa*, November 24, 1925.
193. Fraser, "Rethinking the Public Sphere," 56–80.
194. Garcia, *Rise of the Mexican American Middle Class*, 115.
195. Rosales, *Pobre Raza!*, 194–195.
196. Peck, *Reinventing Free Labor*, 235.

Chapter 6

1. Sanchez, *Becoming Mexican American*, 60–71.
2. "California Farm Labor Problems," in *The Commonwealth Party Two*, Vol. XII, April 7, 1936, in *Laborers in Imperial Valley*, 1934, Irving W. Wood Papers, BANK MSS 77/111C, Bancroft Library, University of California, Berkeley.
3. Hoffman, *Unwanted Mexican Americans in the Great Depression*.
4. Turner, "The Significance of the Frontier in American History," 199–227.
5. McWilliams, *Factories in the Field*, 61–133.
6. Ngai, *Impossible Subjects*, 95–127.

7. McWilliams, *Factories in the Field*, 7, 118, 152–172, 191–199.
8. Molina, *Fit to Be Citizens?*
9. Lewthwaite, *Race, Place, and Reform in Mexican Los Angeles.*
10. Ibid., ch. 1.
11. A significant portion of the literature is devoted to histories of particular communities, with an emphasis on how they were unique. This has led scholars to see these places as more isolated than they really were. For examples, see Garcia, *A World of Its Own*; Alamillo, *Making Lemonade out of Lemons*; Pitti, *The Devil in Silicon Valley.*
12. González, *Mexican Consuls and Labor Organizing*, 162.
13. "Interviews in Citrus Fields [of] Orange County: Santa Ana Folder," Folder 10.38, Carton 10, Paul S. Taylor Papers, Bancroft Library, University of California, Berkeley.
14. Taylor, *The Migrants and California's Future.*
15. "Section Report on Migratory Farm Labor," in *Laborers in Imperial Valley*, 1934, Irving W. Wood Papers, BANK MSS 77/111C, Bancroft Library, University of California, Berkeley.
16. Ibid.
17. "Imperial Valley," August 30, 1928, Folder 10.4, Carton 10, Paul S. Taylor Papers, Bancroft Library, University of California, Berkeley.
18. "A Small Farmer's Viewpoint," in *Laborers in Imperial Valley*, 1934, Irving W. Wood Papers, BANK MSS 77/111C, Bancroft Library, University of California, Berkeley.
19. González, *Mexican Consuls and Labor Organizing*, 128.
20. "Mr. Martinez," Clovis, California, September 5, 1928, Folder 10.9, Carton 10, Paul S. Taylor Papers, Bancroft Library, University of California, Berkeley.
21. Taylor, *The Migrants and California's Future.*
22. Carpio, *Collisions at the Crossroads*, 102–154.
23. Ibid., 74.
24. "Wiley B. Giffen," Giffen Ranch, September 7, 1928, 172, Folder 10.8, Carton 10, Paul S. Taylor Papers, Bancroft Library, University of California, Berkeley.
25. "Mexican Boy at Campomento Mejicano," Reedley, California, September 8, 1928, 180, Folder 10.8, Carton 10, Paul S. Taylor Papers, Bancroft Library, University of California, Berkeley.
26. "Servicio Que esta Banco Ofrece a Sus Clientes," Pacific Southwest Trust & Savings Bank, Field Notes 1927, Folder 10.10, Carton 10, Paul S. Taylor Papers, Bancroft Library, University of California, Berkeley.
27. "Paul Taylor Report on Citrus Fields," 19, Folder 10.36, Carton 10, Paul S. Taylor Papers, Bancroft Library, University of California, Berkeley.
28. Sanchez, *Becoming Mexican American*, 211.
29. Acuña, *Corridors of Migration*, 227.
30. Hoffman, *Unwanted Mexican Americans*, 42–45.
31. Ibid., 1–58.
32. Cybelle Fox disproved the claims, as there were too few Mexicans on relief to make a meaningful difference. Fox, *Three Worlds of Relief.*
33. For more detail on how repatriation was carried out across the United States, see Hoffman, *Unwanted Mexican Americans*; Balderrama and Rodríguez, *Decade of Betrayal*; Balderrama, *In Defense of La Raza*; Sanchez, *Becoming Mexican American*; Valdes, *Al Norte*; Fox, *Three Worlds of Relief*; Lewthwaite, *Race, Place, and Reform*; Guerin-Gonzales, *Mexican Workers and the American Dream.*
34. Hoffman, *Unwanted Mexican Americans*, 91–95.
35. Sanchez, *Becoming Mexican American*, 220.
36. Gutiérrez, *Walls and Mirrors*, 60.
37. "Ventura Martinez," Brawley, California, May 16, 1927, Folder 10.13, Carton 10, Paul S. Taylor Papers, Bancroft Library, University of California, Berkeley.
38. Gutiérrez, *Walls and Mirrors*, 39–152.
39. Hoffman, *Unwanted Mexican Americans*, 69.
40. Acuña, *Corridors of Migration*, 229.
41. For more information, see Los Angeles, Cal. Consulado, IV-343-19, IV-70-7-1, IV-71-1, IV-341-9; 36-16-309, IV-100-9, IV-109-100, IV-185-20, Archivo Histórico Diplomático de Secretaría de Relaciones Exteriores, México DF.
42. Hoffman, *Unwanted Mexican Americans*, 49, 72.

43. Song in the camps helped create a "shared system of knowledge," as historian Elisabeth Sine put it, that "nurtured a collective critique of prevailing power arrangements while validating the grievances of many agricultural workers." Sine, *Rebel Imaginaries*, 40–41.
44. Hagen, "Corrido de California," 110–113.
45. Andres, "Invisible Borders," 5–21.
46. McWilliams, *Factories in the Field*, 129.
47. Lopez, "The El Monte Berry Strike of 1933," 111.
48. Ruiz, *Cannery Women, Cannery Lives*, 48; "Section Report on Migratory Farm Labor," in *Laborers in Imperial Valley*, 1934, Irving W. Wood Papers, BANK MSS 77/111C, Bancroft Library, University of California, Berkeley.
49. Olmsted, *Right Out of California*, 6.
50. Flores, *Grounds for Dreaming*, 32–33.
51. Weber, *Dark Sweat, White Gold*, 83.
52. Acuña, *Corridors of Migration*, 225.
53. "Sr. Pesquierra, Mexican Consul," October 11, 1928, Folder 10.9, Carton 10, Paul S. Taylor Papers, Bancroft Library, University of California, Berkeley.
54. Gutiérrez, *Walls and Mirrors*, 103–105.
55. Weber, *Dark Sweat, White Gold*, 86.
56. For the Magón brothers in Los Angeles, see Lomnitz, *The Return of Comrade Ricardo Flores Magón*.
57. Acuña, *Corridors of Migration*, 35, 172.
58. Felix Gonzales, María Gonzales, Lupe Gonzales, Mariana Gonzales, 1930 US Census; "Interview of Felipe Morales on Mariana Gonzalez," by Daniel Morales, January 4, 2016, Azusa, California.
59. "Juan Martinez," Brawley, California, September 1928, Folder 10.8, Carton 10, Paul S. Taylor Papers, Bancroft Library, University of California, Berkeley.
60. Acuña, *Corridors of Migration*, 225–226.
61. Olmsted, *Right Out of California*, 41.
62. McWilliams, *Factories in the Field*, 212.
63. Weber, "Oral Sources and the History of Mexican Workers in the United States," 47–50; Weber, "Wobblies of the *Partido Liberal Mexicano*," 188–226.
64. Weber, *Dark Sweat, White Gold*, 9.
65. Acuña, *Corridors of Migration*, 170.
66. Sanchez, *Becoming Mexican American*, 237.
67. Ruiz, *Cannery Women, Cannery Lives*, 49.
68. Sanchez, *Becoming Mexican American*, 215–221.
69. Guzmán et al., eds., *East of East*.
70. Ruiz, *From Out of the Shadows*, 14.
71. Ibid., 44.
72. Daniel Morales, "El Monte's Hicks Camp: A Mexican Barrio," in Guzmán et al., eds., *East of East*, 149–162.
73. Interview, Felix Ramos, January 14, 2014, by Daniel Morales and Romeo Guzmán, South El Monte Arts Posse, El Monte, California.
74. "Hicks Camp Study: Outline of Camp Study," in the Papers of Ralph Leon Beals, National Anthropological Archives, Smithsonian Institution, Washington, DC.
75. Lopez, "The El Monte Berry Strike," 110.
76. Gutiérrez, *Walls and Mirrors*, 89.
77. Lopez, "The El Monte Berry Strike," 104.
78. González, *Mexican Consuls and Labor Organizing*, 92.
79. Lopez, "The El Monte Berry Strike," 104.
80. González, *Mexican Consuls and Labor Organizing*, 84.
81. Martinez and Hill disagreed bitterly about the strike and sent contradictory reports to the *Secretaría de Relaciones Exteriores*. See "Martinez, Alejandro V.," September 4, 1933 to February 1934, MFN 4416, Savveta 51, Expidiente 152, Inventario 35326, PEC; and "Telegrama de Viceconsul Ricardo G Hill al Gral PEC," September 4, 1933 to February 1934, MFN 3525, Gaveta 41, Expidiente 165, Inventario 2801, PEC, Archivo Plutarco Elías Calles, México DF.
82. Gilbert Gonzalez has argued that the Mexican government's ultimate goal was not to help the strikers. It sought to orient the strikers into a union along corporatist lines like unions in Mexico. González, *Mexican Consuls and Labor Organizing*, 92–98.

83. Ibid., 98–99.
84. Lopez, "The El Monte Berry Strike," 106.
85. Tokunaga, "Japanese Farmers, Mexican Workers, and the Making of Transpacific Borderlands," 165–197.
86. Ibid., 102–103.
87. Lopez, "The El Monte Berry Strike," 107–108.
88. Dr. Clements to Mr. Arnol, November 23, 1937, George C. Clements Collection, Box 80, Special Elections, University Research Library, University of California, Los Angeles, in González, *Mexican Consuls and Labor Organizing.*
89. Ibid.
90. Clements, Los Angeles Chamber of Commerce, in González, *Mexican Consuls and Labor Organizing*, 110.
91. Weber, "Wobblies of the *Partido Liberal Mexicano*," 224.
92. Sanchez, *Becoming Mexican American*, 237–238.
93. "Memo from W. B. Cunningham to J. H. Fallin, Assistant Director, United States Employment Service, Farm Labor Division," Los Angeles, July 19, 1933, Box 44, George Clements Collection, University of California, Los Angeles.
94. Weber, *Dark Sweat, White Gold*, 80.
95. Ibid., 80.
96. Weber, "Wobblies of the Partido Liberal Mexicano," 188–226.
97. Olmsted, *Right Out of California*, 14–17.
98. Ibid., 122.
99. Ruiz, *Cannery Women, Cannery Lives*, 49.
100. Olmsted, *Right Out of California*, 39–64.
101. González, *Mexican Consuls and Labor Organizing*, 12.
102. Ibid., 240–242.
103. Olmsted, *Right Out of California*, 55.
104. Sine, *Rebel Imaginaries*, 77–81.
105. Acuña, *Corridors of Migration*, 246–267.
106. Ruiz, *Cannery Women, Cannery Lives*, 49.
107. McWilliams, *Factories in the Field*, 214.
108. "Interview of Caroline Decker," CGOH-BAN, in Olmsted, *Right Out of California*, 51.
109. "Interviews with Pat Chambers and Caroline Decker," *Visalia Times Delta*, September 19, 1933, in Weber, *Dark Sweat, White Gold*, 82.
110. Ibid., 159–196.
111. Olmsted, *Right Out of California*, 107–150.
112. Weber, *Dark Sweat, White Gold*, 122.
113. Sanchez, *Becoming Mexican American*, 224.
114. McWilliams, *Factories in the Field*, 230–263.
115. Andres, "Invisible Borders," 5–21.
116. McWilliams, *Factories in the Field*, 224–225; Garcia, *A World of Its Own*, 36.
117. Garcia, *A World of Its Own*, 65–95.
118. Francisco Madrigal, "The Experience of Mexican Migrants," Box 2, FL 8, in David L. Clark LA Oral Histories, Collection 2080, Archives of University of California, Los Angeles.
119. McWilliams, *Factories in the Field*, 243–249.
120. Weber, *Dark Sweat, White Gold*, 159.
121. McWilliams, *Factories in the Field*, 250.
122. Sanchez, *Becoming Mexican American*, 236–238.
123. Garcia, *A World of Its Own*, 119; González, *Mexican Consuls and Labor Organizing*, 115–121.
124. González, *Mexican Consuls and Labor Organizing.*
125. Weber, *Dark Sweat, White Gold*, 163.
126. Acuña, *Corridors of Migration*, 280.
127. González, *Mexican Consuls and Labor Organizing*, 200–205.
128. Weise, *Corazón de Dixie*, 51–119.
129. Ruiz, *Cannery Women, Cannery Lives*, 9.
130. Ibid., 81.
131. Ibid., 1–123.
132. Sanchez, *Becoming Mexican American*, 241–243.
133. Ruiz, *Cannery Women, Cannery Lives*, 88–89.

134. González, *Mexican Consuls and Labor Organizing*; Balderrama, *In Defense of La Raza*; Guerin-Gonzales, *Mexican Workers and the American Dream.*
135. George Sanchez has pointed out how a distinctly Mexican American culture arose in these years as Mexican Americans looked more towards the United States, while David Gutierrez has shown how Mexican-based identity and the Mexican consulates still had power and wide appeal. Sanchez, *Becoming Mexican American*, 169; Gutiérrez, *Walls and Mirrors.*
136. Sine, *Rebel Imaginaries*, 87–89.
137. Weber, "Wobblies of the *Partido Liberal Mexicano*," 188–226.
138. "Interview with Ernie Gonzalez," January 15, 2015, East of East: Mapping Community Narratives, South El Monte Arts Posse.

Chapter 7

1. Felix Gonzales, María Gonzales, Lupe Gonzales, Mariana Gonzales, 1930 US Census.
2. Birth Certificates, Lupe Gonzales, Mariana Gonzales, Morales Family Papers.
3. Interview of Morales family members by Daniel Morales, January 4, 2016, Azusa, California.
4. Ibid.
5. *El Retorno*, or "The Return," suggests the difficulties of the concept of return. The same is true of the term *repatriation*, as it suggests that the "rightful" place of these people was Mexico. In many ways, the United States and Mexico could be people's homes and places of exile, sometimes at the same time. I chose to use the term *repatriation* because it is what this movement of people was called at the time and what most scholars have used to describe these events. Though the terminology has been challenged in recent years, it is still the primary signifier in the public sphere.
6. Mexican repatriates' journey in returning to Mexico did not stop at the border; yet most scholarship focuses on the US side of the experience. Francisco Balderrama and Raymond Rodriguez's account is primarily concerned with the injustices committed on the US side. This leads them to praise the Mexican government's efforts at assisting repatriates and establishing colonies. Abraham Hoffman likewise kept his inquiry to the US side and government sources. Lorenzo Cardoso wrote from the Mexican perspective but rarely departed from the Mexican government's sources, which gave him a similar perspective on the benevolence of the Mexican government's efforts. Overall, migration literature on repatriation assumes that the Mexican government attempted to protect the welfare of Mexican migrants. Balderrama and Rodríguez, *Decade of Betrayal*; Cardoso, *Mexican Emigration to the United States*; Alanís Enciso, *Voces de la repatriación*; Alanís Enciso, *Que se queden allá*; Escoto Molina, "Migrantes guanajuantenses y las repatriaciónes de 1929–1935."
7. Balderrama and Rodriguez's book focuses on colonies when examining the question of resettlement even though most of their interview subjects clearly did not go to resettlement colonies.
8. Alanís Enciso places the estimate between 1.25% and 0.75%. Alanís Enciso, *Voces de la repatriación*, 263–265.
9. Alanís Enciso, *Que se queden allá*, 56.
10. Most theoretical models developed to explain why migration starts, continues, and declines neglect the role of political and economic crisis in the host country. Causes and changes in Mexican migration were not just economic but political as a web of regulation went up in both countries. Hass, "Migration System Formation and Decline"; Massey et al., "Theories of International Migration," 431–466; Massey et al., "An Evaluation of International Migration Theory," 699–751.
11. *El Universal*, January 4, 1930, México DF.
12. For examples, see *Repatriados mexicanos en Los Angeles*, IV-357-12, Archivo de la Secretaría de Relaciones Exteriores, México DF.
13. Alanís Enciso, "Percepciones Ambivalentes," 192, 195.
14. Enrique Flores Magón, October 24, 1932, Repatriados Proyecto Colonias, Exp. 017/19, Caja 7, Fondo Abelardo L. Rodríguez, Archivo General de la Nación, México DF.
15. Ibid.
16. Snodgrass, "The Land of Great Tools."
17. Hagen, "Corrido de California," 110–113.
18. For examples, see IV-360-28, IV-354-34, IV-362-49, IV-363-2, IV-352-31, IV-360-14, IV-348-70, IV-360-7, IV-354-1, IV-356-31, IV-87-52, IV-187-18, IV-354-1, IV-364-53, IV-107-94, IV-256-1, IV-111-12, IV-360-23, IV-360-30, IV-360-35, Archivo de la Secretaría de Relaciones Exteriores, México DF.

19. 4-123-1933-44 Beneficenia Public en el Instituto Nacional de Migración, Archivo Migratorio Central, México DF.
20. Alanís Encinos, "Regreso a casa," 124.
21. IV-355-27 Barber Guild of El Paso, IV-349-35 Red Cross of Bisbee, IV-364-51 Sonora Arizona, IV-261-41 Comita de Beneficencia y Protection Mutual, Archivo de la Secretaría de Relaciones Exteriores, México DF.
22. For examples, see IV-354-40 Morley 1931, IV-350-20 Comisión Honorifica of Tulare, IV-109-30 Comisión Honorifica Cook County, IV-354-4 Comisión Honorifica Morely, IV-350-20 Comisión Honorifica Tulare, IV-351-13 Comisión Honorifica Mackay, IV-350-48 Comisión Honorifica Wiley Colorado, IV-350-13 Reparacion, Archivo de la Secretaría de Relaciones Exteriores, México DF.
23. Comisión Honorifica Mexicana, March 14, 1932, IV-361-25, Archivo de la Secretaría de Relaciones Exteriores, México DF.
24. Comité Reconstructor, San Antonio, Texas, Repatriados Estados Unidos, Exp. 244.1/71, Caja 25, Fondo Abelardo L. Rodríguez, Archivo General de la Nación, México DF.
25. Comisión Honorifica de Wiley Co. Solicita la Repatriación de Familias de lòs Citados, May 16, 1932, IV-350-48, Archivo de la Secretaría de Relaciones Exteriores, México DF.
26. Gustavo Del Rio, April 6, 1930, 5389, Exp. 49, Caja 31, Mexicanos en el Extranjero, Dificultades, Fondo Ortiz Rubio, Archivo General de la Nación, México DF.
27. IV-354-4 Rockdale, IL, Archivo de la Secretaría de Relaciones Exteriores, México DF.
28. Luz G. Salas, October 5, 1931, IV-358-14, Archivo de la Secretaría de Relaciones Exteriores, México DF.
29. Repatriation Petition, May 15, 1931, IV-353-38, and Repatriation Petition, October 5, 1932, IV-341-39, Archivo de la Secretaría de Relaciones Exteriores, México DF, related in Balderrama and Rodríguez, *Decade of Betrayal*, 189–193.
30. Balderrama and Rodríguez, *Decade of Betrayal*, 199–200.
31. For more examples, see IV-360-7, IV-354-34, IV-354-1, IV-349-1, IV-354-45 Manuel Salgado, I36-16-198 Tomasa Robles de Salcedo, IV-357-30 Francisco N Salcedo, IV-354-17 David Salcedo, IV-3554-44 Toas Salazar, IV-619-4 Srita Collins, IV-357-33 María Ester Reteria, IV-357-15 Luz Rendo de Urias, IV-362-57 Repatriation of Pedor Samano, IV-355-23, Archivo de la Secretaría de Relaciones Exteriores, México DF.
32. 4-123-1-1933-42 Trinidad Martinez, 1933, Instituto Nacional de Migración, Archivo Migratorio Central, México DF.
33. Memorandum, December 21, 1933, Delegado de Migración in Monterrey NL, 4-123-1933-44 Beneficenia Public en el DF Mexico, Instituto Nacional de Migración, Archivo Migratorio Central, México DF.
34. December 5, 1933, María C. Martinez, 4-123-1933-44 Beneficenia Public en el DF Mexico, Instituto Nacional de Migración, Archivo Migratorio Central, México DF.
35. Tepoxina Pintado vda. de Ferrer, June 18, 1934, Repatriados Estados Unidos, Exp. 244.1/84, Caja 25, Fondo Abelardo L. Rodríguez, Archivo General de la Nación, México DF.
36. Maria F. Zamarripa, July 13, 1933, Repatriados Estados Unidos, Exp. 244.1/55, Caja 25, Fondo Abelardo L. Rodríguez, Archivo General de la Nación, México DF.
37. Sra. Carmen Rivera, December 2, 1933, Repatriados Estados Unidos, Exp. 244.1/20, Caja 24, Fondo Abelardo L. Rodríguez, Archivo General de la Nación, México DF.
38. Hortensia Vallejo, May 12, 1939, Repatriados Estados Unidos, Exp. 549.5/45, Caja 925, Fondo Cárdenas, Archivo General de la Nación, México DF.
39. Juan T. Zamarripa, December 4, 1933, 244.1/67, Caja 25, Fondo Abelardo L. Rodríguez, Archivo General de la Nación, México DF.
40. Jose G. Saldana, February 25, 1932, El citado solicita repatriación de su familia, IV-355-23, Archivo de la Secretaría de Relaciones Exteriores, México DF.
41. Apolinar E. Espinosa, 1137, February 21, 1930; Victor V. Gomez, February 18, 1930; Exp. 9, Caja 24, Fondo Ortiz Rubio, Archivo General de la Nación, México DF.
42. Ignacio, Herreras, December 22, 1933, Repatriados Aguascalientes, 244.1/23, Caja 24, Fondo Abelardo L. Rodríguez, Archivo General de la Nación, México DF.
43. Primitico Rodriguez, October 16, 1932, Repatriados Estados Unidos, Exp. 244/3, Caja 24, Fondo Abelardo L. Rodríguez, Archivo General de la Nación, México DF.
44. Manuel de Valle, May 9, 1934, Repatriados Estados Unidos, 344.1/1251, Caja 74, Fondo Abelardo L. Rodríguez, Archivo General de la Nación, México DF.

45. Maros Perez, September 21, 1935, Repatriados Estados Unidos, Exp. 549.51/7, Caja 935, Fondo Cárdenas, Archivo General de la Nación, México DF.
46. "A Plutarco Elías Calles," November 14, 1927, 4-352-1927-190, Melchor Sala Hidalgo, Instituto Nacional de Migración, Archivo Migratorio Central, México DF. Translation by Daniel Morales.
47. Solicita Informes para su Emigracion a EUA, 4-352-1929-591, Carlos Bastien, Instituto Nacional de Migración, Archivo Migratorio Central, México DF. Translation by Daniel Morales.
48. Mauricio F. Gonzalez, February 26, 1930, 2174, Exp. 9, Caja 24, Fondo Ortiz Rubio, Archivo General de la Nación, México DF.
49. Zeferino Ramirez, September 19, 1930, 12854, Exp. 299, Caja 41, Fondo Ortiz Rubio, Archivo General de la Nación, México DF.
50. Aduardo Aragon, Brandy, CA, November 21, 1930, 14228, 299, Caja 41, Fondo Ortiz Rubio, Archivo General de la Nación, México DF.
51. Ramon Sierra, Soc. Juárez Mutualista Mexicana, Arvin, CA, November 29, 1939, 14561, 299, Caja 41, Fondo Ortiz Rubio, Archivo General de la Nación, México DF.
52. Mariano Moreno, June 11, 1934, San Benito Texas, Repatriados Estados Unidos (Impuestos), Exp. 533.21/19-11, Caja 155, Fondo Abelardo L. Rodríguez, Archivo General de la Nación, México DF.
53. Land has been underappreciated as a motivator in the scholarly writings on repatriation.
54. Zerino Dominguez, June 25, 1930, 7833, Exp. 49, Caja 31, Mexicanos en el Extranjero, Dificultades, Fondo Ortiz Rubio, Archivo General de la Nación, México DF.
55. 4-123-1933-44 Beneficenia Public en el DF Mexico, Memorandum, December 9, 1933, Instituto Nacional de Migración, Archivo Migratorio Central, México DF.
56. Adalberto Ojeda, April 7, 1934, Repatriados Estados Unidos, Exp. 244.1/80, Caja 25, Fondo Abelardo L. Rodríguez, Archivo General de la Nación, México DF.
57. Rodolfo B. Benavides y Otros, June 1930, 6844, Exp. 49, Caja 31, Mexicanos en el Extranjero, Dificultades, Fondo Ortiz Rubio, Archivo General de la Nación, México DF.
58. Martin T. Valles y Otros, July 27, 1930, 9357, Exp. 49, Caja 31, Mexicanos en el Extranjero, Dificultades, Fondo Ortiz Rubio, Archivo General de la Nación, México DF.
59. (1932) 3765 T.-finch 13, Exp. 0-0706, Caja 126, Fondo Ortiz Rubio, Archivo General de la Nación, México DF.
60. For examples, see IV-350-14 Repatracion: San Angelo. Tomas Chavarris, Archivo de la Secretaría de Relaciones Exteriores, México DF; 4-123-1-1932-1 to 4-123-1-1932-33, Instituto Nacional de Migración, Archivo Migratorio Central, México DF.
61. Consul Foster to Department of State, January 27, 1931, Piedras Negras, INS RG 59, 812.5511/105, US National Archives and Records Administration (NARA), Washington, DC.
62. Hoffman, *Unwanted Mexican Americans in the Great Depression*, 128.
63. Alanís Enciso, *Voces de la repatriación*, 142–150.
64. Tres Memorándums, Cámara Nacional de Comercial C. Juárez, January 25, 1933, Repatriados Chihuahua, 07/10, Caja 3, Fondo Abelardo L. Rodríguez, Archivo General de la Nación, México DF.
65. Alanís Enciso, "Precepciones Ambivalentes," 202.
66. 4-123-1-1932-38 Jose A Rico, December 24, 1932, Instituto Nacional de Migración, Archivo Migratorio Central, México DF.
67. 4-123-1-1933-41 Luis Gonzales Medina CD Juárez, January 3–6, 1933, Instituto Nacional de Migración, Archivo Migratorio Central, México DF.
68. Rose y Maria Castillo, April 28, 1938, Repatriados Chih., Exp. 121/7, Caja 73, Fondo Cárdenas, Archivo General de la Nación, México DF.
69. Maria Ramiez, July 18, 1940, Repatriados Chih., Exp. 121/7, Caja 73, Fondo Cárdenas, Archivo General de la Nación, México DF.
70. Paz Zamarripa S. Y. Socorro Quinero, June 16, 1940, Repatriados Chih., Exp. 121/7, Caja 73, Fondo Cárdenas, Archivo General de la Nación, México DF.
71. Pedro Valdez Peza, Repatriados Estados Unidos, Exp. 549.2/3, Caja 922, Fondo Cárdenas, Archivo General de la Nación, México DF.
72. Balderrama and Rodríguez, *Decade of Betrayal*, 177.
73. Alanís Enciso, *Voces de la repatriación*, 155–169.
74. Hoffman, *Unwanted Mexican Americans*, 140–141.
75. Alanís Enciso, *Voces de la repatriación*, 234–243.
76. Ibid., 249–250.
77. McKay, "Texas Mexican Repatriation During the Great Depression," 500–517.

78. Hoffman, *Unwanted Mexican Americans*, 145.
79. Interview with Antonio Mendez Lomeli, OH 1297, Mexican American Oral History Project, California State University, Fullerton.
80. Balderrama and Rodríguez, *Decade of Betrayal*, 179.
81. Alanís Enciso, *They Should Stay There*, 88–126.
82. Walsh, *Building the Borderlands*, 135–153.
83. Alanís Enciso, *El Valle Bajo del Río Bravo, Tamaulipas, en la década de 1930.*
84. Walsh, *Building the Borderlands*, 135–153.
85. Ibid., 154–173.
86. Alanís Enciso, *Que se queden allá.*
87. Escoto Molina, "Migrantes Guanajuantenses," 45–56.
88. By the mid-1930s, the US government openly questioned whether repatriation colonies existed at all. Letters, April 17, 1936, October 26, 1937, December 1937, Bureau of Immigration, 55957, INS RG 85, NARA, Washington, DC.
89. Interview with Antonio Mendez Lomeli, OH 1297, Mexican American Oral History Project, California State University, Fullerton.
90. Alanís Enciso, *Voces de la repatriación*, 175–176.
91. Repatriados Estados Unidos, Exp. 244/2, Caja 24, Fondo Abelardo L. Rodríguez, Archivo General de la Nación, México DF.
92. Campana Medio Million 1933, Repatriados, 244.15, Caja 24, Fondo Abelardo L. Rodríguez, Archivo General de la Nación, México DF.
93. Colonizacion de Terrenos Nacionales, (1931) 3713-3748-4072-4758-5542, Exp. 77, Caja 119, Fondo Ortiz Rubio, Archivo General de la Nación, México DF.
94. Rafael Garcia, December 9, 1933, 6703, Repatriados, Exp. 344/409, Caja 59, Fondo Abelardo L. Rodríguez, Archivo General de la Nación, México DF. Translation by Daniel Morales.
95. Repatriados DF, Exp. 244.1/36-2, Caja 24, Fondo Abelardo L. Rodríguez, Archivo General de la Nación, México DF; Balderrama and Rodríguez, *Decade of Betrayal*, 250–252.
96. C. Iberra, Enrique Guerreso y Demoas firmantes. Union Repatriados Mexicanos, Repatriados, Exp. 344/409, Caja 59, Fondo Abelardo L. Rodríguez, Archivo General de la Nación, México DF.
97. Téllez, Secretary of the Interior, expressed his reservations about both the colonies and Ramón Beteta's efforts. McKay, "Texas Mexican Repatriation," 410–411.
98. Gilbert, "A Field Study in Mexico of the Mexican Repatriation Movement," 28.
99. Balderrama and Rodríguez, *Decade of Betrayal*, 241.
100. Alanís Enciso, "Precepciones Ambivalentes," 199–202.
101. McKay, "Texas Mexican Repatriation."
102. Alanís Enciso, *Voces de la repatriación*, 150–151.
103. Gilbert, "A Field Study in Mexico," 27.
104. For example, see IV-130-7, IV-348-73 Laredo Texas, IV-354-40 Morley 1931, Archivo de la Secretaría de Relaciones Exteriores, México DF.
105. IV-70-7-1 Protección a Mexicanos del Ano 1930, Anastasio Pérez, Secretaría de Relaciones Exteriores, México DF.
106. Ibid., 246.
107. Taylor, *A Spanish-Mexican Peasant Community*, 62.
108. Hoffman, *Unwanted Mexican Americans*, 128–129.
109. Balderrama and Rodríguez, *Decade of Betrayal*, 128.
110. Taylor, *A Spanish-Mexican Peasant Community*, 69.
111. Balderrama and Rodríguez, *Decade of Betrayal*, 140.
112. Ibid., 248.
113. Gilbert, "A Field Study in Mexico," 50–53.
114. *El Universal*, April 28, 1932, in Balderrama and Rodríguez, *Decade of Betrayal*, 241.
115. Jesús Grimaldo, August 29, 1932; Jose Diaz, November 15, 1932, IV-348-57, Archivo de la Secretaría de Relaciones Exteriores, México DF.
116. Jose R. Grajeda, January 6, 1933, Repatriados, Exp. 344/409, Caja 59, Fondo Abelardo L. Rodríguez, Archivo General de la Nación, México DF.
117. 4-123-1-1932-1 to 4-123-1-1932-33, Instituto Nacional de Migración, Archivo Migratorio Central, México DF.
118. 4-352-1929-565 Daniel E. Martinez, Pide Informes Sobre Entrada a EEUU, Instituto Nacional de Migración, Archivo Migratorio Central, México DF. Translation by Daniel Morales.

119. Interview with Francisco Castaneda, OH 1301, Mexican American Oral History Project, California State University, Fullerton.
120. Alanís Enciso, *Voces de la repatriación*, 316.
121. Taylor, *A Spanish-Mexican Peasant Community*, 59.
122. Gilbert, "A Field Study in Mexico," 55–131.
123. Balderrama and Rodríguez, *Decade of Betrayal*, 279.
124. Interview with Antonio Mendez Lomeli, OH 1297, Mexican American Oral History Project, California State University, Fullerton.
125. Interview with Hortencia Martinez de Benitez, OH 1298, Mexican American Oral History Project, California State University, Fullerton.
126. Balderrama and Rodríguez, *Decade of Betrayal*, 242.
127. Ibid., 239.
128. Gilbert, "A Field Study in Mexico," 37.
129. *Pachucos* refers to Mexican youth in the United States who are thought to be improper—alienated, disrespectful, flashy, gang members, etc.
130. Ibid., 134.
131. Balderrama and Rodríguez, *Decade of Betrayal*, 190–197.
132. *Americanizados, ayuntados,* and *agringados* mean "became American" or "became white" while *pocho* means rotten.
133. Gilbert, "A Field Study in Mexico," 140.
134. Escoto Molina, "Migrantes Guanajuantenses," 58–82.
135. Ibid., 208; Gilbert, "A Field Study in Mexico," 150–158.
136. Ibid., 109.
137. Sellars, "Does Emigration Inhibit Reform?," 7.
138. Sellars, "Emigration and Collective Action," 1210–1222.
139. Ibid., 20.
140. Ibid., 203.
141. Ibid., 189–193.
142. Ibid., 202–203.
143. Craig, *First Agraristas*, 92–93.
144. Ibid., 93 (see also, expedientes ejidales, Archivo del Registro Agrario [ASRA]).
145. Ibid., 178–180.
146. Ibid., 180.
147. Ibid., 181.
148. Friedrich, *Agrarian Revolt in a Mexican Village*; Escoto Molina, "Migrantes Guanajuantenses," 82–90.
149. Heriberto Moreno, *Tiempos Viejos, Tiempos Nuevos*, in Durand, *Más allá de la línea*, 260–261.
150. Gilbert, "A Field Study in Mexico," 65–102.
151. Andres, "Invisible Borders," 5–21.
152. Alanís Enciso has countered that repatriates were not a significant factor in land reform as they did not lead efforts, were mostly not politically active, and their supposed liberalism didn't lead to a crisis or changes in local society. Alanís Enciso, *Voces de la repatriación*, 262–284.
153. Balderrama and Rodríguez, *Decade of Betrayal*, 214.
154. Dotacion, Poblacion Guxcama, Villa Juárez, San Luis Potosí, Mexico, 23/21221, Archivo del Registro Agrario, México DF.
155. Dotacion, Bosques y Caldera, Cerritos, San Luis Potosí, Mexico, 23/11967, Archivo del Registro Agrario, México DF.
156. Isabel Monroy Castillo used these findings to show that a community of migrants from San Luis Potosí was settling in the city and within that parish. Castillo, "Los Rastros de una Migración Antigua," 13–40.
157. Ibid., 75–94.
158. Durand, *Más allá de la línea*, 262–263.
159. People interviewed in Cerritos and Villa Juárez often claimed the land became drier, as does Montoya, "El Cura y Los Braceros," 77–78.
160. Robert, "Agrarian Structure and Labor Mobility in Rural Mexico," 299–322.
161. Mexico's post-World War II, large-scale increase in crop yields, known as the Green Revolution, did not extend to the *ejido* and small landholder class.
162. Interview, Rendon, Reynaldo Benavides, VOCES Oral History 436, Benson Latin American Library, University of Texas, Austin.

163. Alanís Enciso, *Voces de la repatriación*, 334–335.
164. Balderrama and Rodríguez, *Decade of Betrayal*, 257.
165. Alanís Enciso, *Voces de la repatriación*, 306.
166. IV-355-21, Repatriados Mexicanos en Detroit, Relativo su Domicilio en el Extranjero, Archivo de la Secretaría de Relaciones Exteriores, México DF.
167. Hoffman, *Unwanted Mexican Americans*, 149.
168. Ibid, 149.
169. Balderrama and Rodríguez, *Decade of Betrayal*, 258–259.
170. Interview with Francisco Castaneda, OH 1301, Mexican American Oral History Project, California State University, Fullerton.
171. Interview with Lauro Vega, VOCES Oral History 113, Benson Latin American Library, University of Texas, Austin.
172. Manuel Martinez and Ofelia Silva, interview by Daniel Morales, January 15, 2015, East of East: Mapping Community Narratives, South El Monte Arts Posse.
173. Venegas, *Letters Home*, 95–121.
174. Ibid., 1–24.
175. Ibid.
176. Interview with Hortencia Martinez de Benitez, OH 1298, Mexican American Oral History Project, California State University, Fullerton.
177. Years later, many of these border residents would become transnational residents, crossing daily to work in the United States. In the 1940s and 1950s, both towns would provide housing to braceros and undocumented migrant workers who crossed the border each day.
178. Interview with Felipe Morales, January 4, 2016; interview, Morales Family Members, December 2019, Azusa, California.
179. Valdes, "South from the United States," 180.

Epilogue

1. Ricardo Villalobos, "Come or Go," Bracero History Archive, Item #3208, accessed August 5, 2013, University of Texas at El Paso Oral History Project, http://braceroarchive.org/items/show/3208.
2. In an early example, Porfirio Díaz and William Taft came to an agreement to send Mexicans under contract to hoe sugar beets in the Midwest shortly before the Mexican Revolution.
3. García and Griego, "The Importation of Mexican Contract Laborers to the United States," 51.
4. Weise and Rass, "Migrating Concepts."
5. Cardoso, *Mexican Emigration to the United States*, 117.
6. Loza, *Defiant Braceros*, 23–60.
7. Garcia, *Abandoning Their Beloved Land*, 1–156; "Manuel Avila Camacho to Town Presidents in Jalisco, August 9, 1942," Governmental Correspondence, 1940–1950, Archivo Municipal, San Martin de Hidalgo, Jalisco, Mexico, in Rosas, *Abrazando el espiritu*.
8. Montoya, "El cura y los braceros," 71–90.
9. Alanís Enciso and Puente, *Nos vamos al traque*, 1–42.
10. *El Heraldo*, April 7 and April 28, 1944, in Alanís Enciso and Puente, *Nos vamos al traque*, 59. Translation by Daniel Morales.
11. García and Griego, "The Importation of Mexican Contract Laborers," 51.
12. Rosas, *Abrazando el espiritu*, 28.
13. Ibid., 31.
14. Calavita, *Inside the State*; Hernandez, *Migra!*
15. García and Griego, "The Importation of Mexican Contract Laborers," 47.
16. Gutierrez, "Health Care and Deportation During the Bracero Program."
17. Cohen, *Braceros*.
18. Rosas, *Abrazando el espiritu*, 215–224.
19. Loza, *Defiant Braceros*, 1–171.
20. González Navaro, *Poblacion y sociedad*, 154–156, in García and Griego, "The Importation of Mexican Contract Laborers," 64.
21. Baker and Warren, "Estimates of the Unauthorized Immigrant Population Residing in the United States," https://www.dhs.gov/sites/default/files/2024-05/2024_0418_ohss_estimates-of-the-unauthorized-immigrant-population-residing-in-the-united-states-january-2018–january-2022.pdf.
22. Goodman, *The Deportation Machine*.
23. Loza, *Defiant Braceros*, 1–171.

Appendix

1. For more detailed analysis of 1920 census and 1930 census, see Morales, "The Making of Mexican America."
2. A large migration occurred right before the Mexican Revolution, made up of mostly men going to agriculture in Texas, railroads, and mining zones across the southwest. This was followed by a drop in the early years of the revolution, and then a large increase in the later years of the revolution, especially after the start of World War I. The recession of 1921 triggered the first large-scale repatriations of Mexicans, but it was followed by a boom in the late 1920s. The drops in 1925 and starting in 1928, however, are primarily due to increasing enforcement and attempts to limit legal migration; the drop in 1925 in particular is unlikely to reflect a drop in actual migration.
3. Hall and Coerver, *Revolution on the Border.*
4. Gamio, *Mexican Immigration to the United States*, new ed., 9–10.
5. Preliminary Report, "Antecedents on the Mexican Immigration in the United States," Folder 3.1, BANC FILM 2332 REEL 3, GNEG Box 2570, Manuel Gamio Papers, Bancroft Library, University of California, Berkeley.
6. Alanís Enciso, *Que se queden alla*, 36.
7. Manuel Gamio, "Quantitative Estimates: Sources and Distribution of Mexican Immigration to the United States," BANC FILM 2332 REEL 3, GNEG Box 2570, Manuel Gamio Papers, Bancroft Library, University of California, Berkeley.
8. Taylor, *Mexican Labor in the United States: Migration Statistics*; Cardoso, *Mexican Emigration to the United States.*
9. Data came from the University of Minnesota Population Center, IPUMS-USA.
10. Ancestry.com was used to find individuals.
11. This proved more accurate in urban settings, where people were more likely to have exact addresses; rural migrant workers were the most difficult to pinpoint.
12. Thernstrom, *The Other Bostonians*; Ferrie, *Yankeys Now*; Kessner, *The Golden Door*; Ward, "The Circular Flow."
13. Taylor, *Mexican Labor in the United States*, Vol. 1.
14. Ward, "The Circular Flow," ch. 4.
15. The demographics of the Mexicans and their families in the sample are within a few percentages of the general Mexican-born population of the United States in 1920. This gives me some confidence in arguing that they are a representative sample of the Mexicans in the United States with the exception of an oversampling of middle-class families. This will be important when looking at how these families fared afterwards. 1930 US Census.
16. Ward comes to a different conclusion in his study of Mexican migrants and argues that only 44% of migrants returned to Mexico by 1930. This is based on the belief that transcription errors and Anglicization is more likely in the United States than in Mexico. However, I was able to find many of the people who had changed their name or other markets of identification, so while it did happen, I don't believe it was common enough to change the sample. The 1930 Mexican Census was much more likely than the 1930 US Census to miss people, however, and the large amounts of potential people in Mexico convinced me that the opposite was more likely. Ward, "The Circular Flow."
17. The numbers for 1940 also included second-generation children of the original migrants that were followed.
18. As per rules for using the University of Minnesota IPUMS Census Data, I am refraining from using individual's names in this census study. Original census data can be made available upon request.
19. Ward, "The Circular Flow."
20. Doeringer and Piore, *Internal Labor Markets and Manpower Analysis*; Beck, Horan, and Tolbert, "Stratification in a Dual Economy," 704–720; Massey and Magaly Sanchez, *Brokered Boundaries*, illustrated ed., 1–25.
21. Portes and Rumbaut, *Legacies.*

Bibliography

US Archival Sources

National Anthropological Archives, Smithsonian Institution, Washington, DC

University of Minnesota, Integrated Public Use Microdata Series
United States Census 1910, 1920, and 1930

California State Archives & State Library
Earl Warren Papers
Clarence Lininger Papers

Orange County Colonias Oral History Project, California State University, Fullerton
Mexican American Oral History Project, California State University, Fullerton

New York Public Library
Library Maps Division

Stanford University Archives
Bert Corona Papers
Manuel Ruiz Papers

US National Archives and Records Administration
US Immigration and Naturalization Service

Bancroft Library, University of California, Berkeley
Manuel Gamio Papers
Paul S. Taylor Papers
Irving W. Wood Papers
Federal Writers Project Papers
Californians of Mexican Descent Collection

University of California, Los Angeles, Archives
David L. Clark LA Oral Histories
Railroad Publicans from the United States, Mexico, and Panama

Special Elections, University Research Library, University of California, Los Angeles
Chicano Studies Library, University of California, Los Angeles
Pedro J. Gonzalez Papers

Special Collection Research Center, University of Chicago
National Conferences of Social Work Records
Department of Anthropology Records
Robert Redfield Papers
Annetta M. Dieckmann Papers
George Ellsworth Hooker Papers
Ernest Watson Burgess Papers

Special Collections, University of Southern California
Emory Bogardus Papers

Benson Latin American Library, University of Texas, Austin
Eleuterio Escobar Papers
George I. Sanchez Papers
Gustavo Garcia Papers
Jovita González Mireles Manuscripts
José de la Luz Sáenz Papers
Julian Samora Papers
Federico Idar Papers
Clemente Idar Papers
Migrant Border Ballad Project
VOCES Oral History Project
Sociedad Mutualist Melchor Ocampo Papers

Oral History Project, University of Texas, El Paso
Bracero History Archive
El Paso del Norte Entrepreneurship Oral History Project
Oral History Digital Commons

La Historia Society of El Monte
Oral History Project, South El Monte Arts Posse (SEMAP)
East of East: Mapping Community Narratives in South El Monte and El Monte, SEMAP, El Monte, California

Mexican Archival Sources

Mexican Census 1930

Instituto Nacional de Antropología e Historia

Biblioteca Nacional de Antropología e Historia
Colección Revolución de México

El Archivo General de la Nación
Francisco I. Madero Papers
Lázaro Cárdenas Papers

Archivo Histórico del Instituto Nacional de Migración
Vales, Pases, y Cortes de Cuentas Mensuales
Solicitudes de Pases y Vales para Empleados y Repatriado
Movimientos y Quejas de Mexicanos que Cruzan la Frontera con y sin Documentación
Informes de Movimiento Migratorios en la Republica

Archivo Histórico Diplomático de la Secretaría de Relaciones Exteriores, México DF.
Mexican Embassy Papers
Mexican Consulate Papers

Archivo Plutarco Calles
Archivo Plutarco Elías Calles
Fondo Elías Calles
Fondo Álvaro Obregon
Fondo Fernando Torreblanca
Fondo Joaquin Amaro

Archivo del Registro Agrario
Dotaciones de Ejidos en San Luis Potosí y Guanajuato

Archivos Municipales de Villa Juárez y Cerritos San Luis Potosí
"Asi es San Luis. Y asi es Villa Juárez" (unpublished, 1996)
Historical Agrarian Archive of Jalisco

Oral History Interviews

Abram Martinez, December 13, 2013
Caterina Martinez, December 14, 2013
Jovoca Martinez Cruz, December 14, 2013
Onorio Martinez Martinez, December 10, 2013
Felipe G. Morales, January 4, 2016
Ofelia Silva and Manuel Martinez, January 15, 2015
Tules Silva Reyes, December 10, 2013

Published Material

Acuña, Rodolfo. *Corridors of Migration: The Odyssey of Mexican Laborers, 1600–1933.* Tucson: University of Arizona Press, 2007.

Acuña, Rodolfo. *Occupied America: A History of Chicanos.* Boston: Longman, 1972.

Aguirre, Nancy. "Porfirista Femininity in Exile: Women's Contributions to San Antonio's *La Prensa*, 1913–1929," in *Women of the Right: Comparisons and Interplay Across Borders*, ed. Kathleen Blee. University Park: Pennsylvania State University Press, 2012, 147–162.

Aguilar Camín, Héctor, and Lorenzo Meyer. *In the Shadow of the Mexican Revolution: Contemporary Mexican History, 1910–1989*, 1st ed. Austin: University of Texas Press, 1993.

Alamillo, José. *Making Lemonade Out of Lemons: Mexican American Labor and Leisure in a California Town 1880–1960.* Urbana: University of Illinois Press, 2006.

Alanís Enciso, Fernando Saúl. *El primero programa bracero y el gobierno de México 1917–1918.* San Luis Potosí: Colegio de San Luis, 1999.

Alanís Enciso, Fernando Saúl. *El valle bajo del Río Bravo, Tamaulipas, en la década de 1930: El desarrollo regional en la posrevolución a partir de da irrigación, la migración interna y los repatriados de Estados Unidos.* Ciudad Victoria, Tam.: El Colegio de Tamaulipas, 2003.

Alanís Enciso, Fernando Saúl. "Precepciones ambivalentes: Los repatriados Mexicanos procedentes de Estados Unidos," in *El ir y venir de los norteños: Historia de la migración a Estados Unidos*, ed. Fernando Saúl Alanís Enciso and Rafael Alarcón Acosta. Tijuana, B.C.: El Colegio de la Frontera Norte, AC, 2016, 189–206.

Alanís Enciso, Fernando Saúl. *Que se queden alla: El gobierno de México y la repatriación de mexicanos en Estados Unidos 1934–1940.* San Luis Potosí: El Colegio de la Frontera Norte/El Colegio de San Luis, 2007.

Alanís Enciso, Fernando Saúl. *They Should Stay There: The Story of Mexican Migration and Repatriation During the Great Depression.* Chapel Hill: University of North Carolina Press, 2017.

Alanís Enciso, Fernando Saúl. *Voces de la repatriación. La sociedad mexicana y la repatriación de mexicanos de Estados Unidos 1930–1933.* San Luis Potosí: Colegio de San Luis, 2015.

Alanís Enciso, Fernando Saúl, and Rafael Alarcón Acosta, eds. *El ir y venir de los norteños: Historia de la migración a Estados Unidos.* Tijuana, B.C.: El Colegio de la Frontera Norte, AC, 2016.

Alanís Enciso, Fernando Saúl, and Carlos Alberto Roque Puente. *Nos vamos al traque: la contratación de braceros ferroviarios en el ámbito regional durante la Segunda Guerra Mundial: el caso de San Luis Potosí, 1944.* San Luis Potosí: Colegio de San Luis, 2007.

Anderson, Benedict. *Imagined Communities: Reflections on the Origin and Spread of Nationalism.* New York: Verso, 2006.

Andres, Jr., Benny J. "Invisible Borders: Repatriation and Colonization of Mexican Migrant Workers along the California Borderlands During the 1930s," *California History* 88, no. 4 (2011): 5–21, 63–65.

Andrews, Thomas. *Killing for Coal: America's Deadliest Labor War.* Cambridge, MA: Harvard University Press, 2008.

Ankerson, Dudley. *Agrarian Warlord: Saturnino Cedillo and the Mexican Revolution in San Luis Potosí.* DeKalb: Northern Illinois University Press, 1985.

Arendt, Hannah. *The Origins of Totalitarianism.* New York: Harcourt Brace Jovanovich, 1973.

Arredondo, Gabriela F. *Mexican Chicago: Race, Identity and Nation 1916–1939.* Urbana and Chicago: University of Illinois Press, 2008.

Baba, Marietta Lynn, and Malvina Hauk Abonyi. *Mexicans of Detroit.* Detroit, MI: Wayne State University, Center for Urban Studies, 1979.

Baker, Bryan, and Robert Warren. Estimates of the Unauthorized Immigrant Population Residing in the United States: January 2018–January 2022. April 2024. Office of Homeland Security Statistics. https://www.dhs.gov/sites/default/files/2024-05/2024_0418_ohss_estimates-of-the-unauthorized-immigrant-population-residing-in-the-united-states-january-2018–january-2022.pdf

Balderrama, Francisco E. *In Defense of La Raza, the Los Angeles Mexican Consulate, and the Mexican Community, 1929 to 1936.* Tucson: University of Arizona Press, 1982.

Balderrama, Francisco E., and Raymond Rodriguez. *Decade of Betrayal: Mexican Repatriation in the 1930s.* Albuquerque: University of New Mexico Press, 1995.

Beals, Ralph. *Cheran: A Sierra Tarascan Village.* Washington, DC: Smithsonian Institution, Institute of Social Anthropology, 1946.

Beck, E. M., Patrick M. Horan, and Charles M. Tolbert. "Stratification in a Dual Economy: A Sectoral Model of Earnings Determination," *American Sociological Review* 43, no. 5 (1978): 704–720.

Beckert, Sven. *Empire of Cotton: A Global History.* New York: Vintage, 2015.

Benton-Cohen, Katherine. *Borderline Americans: Racial Divisions and Labor War in the Arizona Borderlands.* Cambridge, MA: Harvard University Press, 2011,

Bodnar, John. *The Transplanted: A History of Immigrants in Urban America.* Bloomington: Indiana University Press, 1987.

Brown, Jonathan C. *Oil and Revolution in Mexico.* Berkeley: University of California Press, 1993.

Novoa, Bruce. "*La Prensa* and the Chicano Community," *The Americas Review* 17, no. 3–4 (September 1989): 150–156.

Burgess, Ernest W., and Charles Newcomb, ed. *Census Data of the City of Chicago 1920.* Chicago, IL: University of Chicago Press, 1931.

Burgess, Ernest W., and Charles Newcomb, ed. *Census Data of the City of Chicago 1930.* Chicago, IL: University of Chicago Press, 1933.

Calavita, Kitty. *Inside the State: The Bracero Program, Immigration and the INS.* New York: Routledge, 1992.

Calderón, Roberto R. *Mexican Coal Mining Labor in Texas and Coahuila, 1880–1930.* College Station: Texas A&M University Press, 2000.

Camacho, Alicia Schmidt. *Migrant Imaginaries: Latino Cultural Politics in the US-Mexico Borderlands.* New York: NYU Press, 2008.

Camarillo, Albert. *Chicanos in a Changing Society: From Mexican Pueblos to American Barrios in Santa Barbara and Southern California, 1848–1930.* Cambridge, MA: Harvard University Press, 1979.

Canaday, Margot. *The Straight State: Sexuality and Citizenship in Twentieth-Century America.* Princeton, NJ: Princeton University Press, 2011.

Cardoso, Lawrence A. *Mexican Emigration to the United States 1897–1931.* Tucson: University of Arizona Press, 1980.

Carpio, Genevieve. *Collisions at the Crossroads: How Place and Mobility Make Race.* Oakland: University of California Press, 2019.

Carreras de Velasco, Mercedes. *Los mexicanos que devolvió la crisis, 1929–1932.* México: Secretaría de Relaciones Exteriores, 1974

Castillo, Isabel Monroy. "Los rastros de una migración antigua," in *La emigración de San Luis Potosí a Estados Unidos pasado y presente*, ed. Fernando Saúl Alanis Enciso. San Luis Potosí: El Colegio de San Luis, 2001, 13–40.

Cayton, Horace R., and St Clair Drake. *Black Metropolis*. London: Jonathan Cape and Weidenfeld & Nicolson, 1946.

Cerutti, Mario. *El norte de México y Texas: 1848–1880*. México, DF: Instituto Mora, 1999.

Coatsworth, John H. *Growth Against Development: The Economic Impact of Railroads in Porfirian Mexico*. Dekalb: Northern Illinois University Press, 1981.

Coatsworth, John. "Railroads, Landholding, and Agrarian Protest in the Early Porfiriato," *Hispanic American Historical Review* LIV (February 1974), 48–71.

Coerver, Don M. "Ethnicity, Identity, and Nationalism in 'México de Afuera,'" *Journal of American Ethnic History* 20, no. 3 (April 1, 2001): 133–137.

Cohen, Deborah. *Braceros: Migrant Citizens and Transnational Subjects in the Postwar United States and Mexico*. Chapel Hill: University of North Carolina Press, 2010.

Cohen, Lizabeth. *Making a New Deal: Industrial Workers in Chicago, 1919–1939*. Cambridge, UK York: Cambridge University Press, 1990.

Cottrell, R. H., ed. *Beet Sugar Economics*. Caldwell, ID: The Caxton Printers, Ltd., 1952.

Craig, Ann L. *First Agraristas: An Oral History of a Mexican Agrarian Reform Movement*. Berkeley: University of California Press, 1983.

Cronon, William. *Nature's Metropolis: Chicago and the Great West*. New York: W. W. Norton & Company, 1991.

Dennison, Craig. "Mexico de Afuera in Northern Missouri: The Creation of Profiriato Society in Americas Heartland," *Rupkatha Journal on Interdisciplinary Studies in Humanities* 2 (2010): 257–267.

Deutsch, Sarah. *No Separate Refuge: Culture, Class and Gender on an Anglo-Hispanic Frontier in the American Southwest, 1880–1940*. New York: Oxford University Press, 1987.

Deutsch, Sarah. *Making a Modern US West: The Contested Terrain of a Region and Its Borders, 1898–1940*. Lincoln: University of Nebraska Press, 2022.

Doeringer, Perter B., and Micheal J. Piore. *Internal Labor Markets and Manpower Analysis*. Oxfordshire: Routledge & CRC Press, 1985.

Durand, Jorge. *Más allá de la línea: Patrones migratorios entre México y Estados Unidos*, 1st ed. México, DF: Consejo Nacional para la Cultura y las Artes, 1994.

Durand, Jorge, Douglas S. Massey, and Mexican Migration Project. *Crossing the Border: Research from the Mexican Migration Project*. New York: Russell Sage Foundation, 2006.

Edson, George. "Mexicans in the North Central States," *Perspectives in Mexican American Studies* 2 (1989): 99–114.

Escoto Molina, Georgina. "Migrantes guanajuantenses y las repatriaciónes de 1929–1935." MA thesis. Escuela Nacional de Antropologia e Historia, 2010.

Espinoza, Conrado. *El sol de Texas*. Reprint. Houston, TX: Arte Publico Press, 2007.

Fernández, Lilia. *Brown in the Windy City: Mexicans and Puerto Ricans in Postwar Chicago*. Chicago: University of Chicago Press, 2012.

Ferrie, Joseph P. *Yankeys Now: Immigrants in the Antebellum United States, 1840–1860*. New York: Oxford University Press, 1999.

Fitzgerald, David. "Inside the Sending State: The Politics of Mexican Emigration Control," *International Migration Review* 40, no. 2 (Summer 2006): 259–293.

Flores, Lori A. *Grounds for Dreaming: Mexican Americans, Mexican Immigrants, and the California Farmworker Movement*. New Haven, CT: Yale University Press, 2016.

Foley, Neil. *The White Scourge: Mexicans, Blacks and Poor Whites in Texas Cotton Culture*. Berkeley: University of California Press, 1997.

Foster, George M. *Tzintzuntzan: Mexican Peasants in a Changing World*. Boston: Little, Brown and Company, 1967.

Fox, Cybelle. *Three Worlds of Relief: Race, Immigration, and the American Welfare State from the Progressive Era to the New Deal*. Princeton, NJ: Princeton University Press, 2012.

Fraser, Nancy. "Rethinking the Public Sphere: A Contribution to the Critique of Actually Existing Democracy," *Social Text* 1, no. 25/26 (1990): 56–80.

Friedrich, Paul. *Agrarian Revolt in a Mexican Village.* Chicago: University of Chicago Press, 1977.

Fujigaki, Jorge Hernandez. "Mexican Steelworkers and the United Steelworkers of America in the Midwest: The Inland Steel Experience 1936–1976." PhD dissertation. University of Chicago, 1991.

Gamio, Manuel. *Mexican Immigration to the United States: A Study of Human Migration and Adjustment.* Chicago: University of Chicago Press, 1930.

Gamio, Manuel. *Mexican Immigration to the United States: A Study of Human Migration and Adjustment,* new ed. New York: Dover Publications, 1971.

Gamio, Manuel. *The Mexican Immigrant, His Life-Story.* Chicago: University of Chicago Press, 1930.

García, Alberto. *Abandoning Their Beloved Land: The Politics of Bracero Migration in Mexico.* Berkeley: University of California Press, 2023.

García, Juan R. *Mexicans in the Midwest, 1900–1932.* Tucson: University of Arizona Press, 1996.

Garcia, Matt. *A World of Its Own: Race, Labor and Citrus in the Making of Greater Los Angeles, 1900–1970.* Chapel Hill: University of North Carolina Press, 2001.

Garcia, Richard A. "Class, Consciousness, and Ideology—The Mexican Community of San Antonio, Texas: 1930–1940," *Aztlán: A Journal of Chicano Studies* 9 (1979): 23–69.

Garcia, Richard A. *Rise of the Mexican American Middle Class: San Antonio, 1929–1941.* College Station: Texas A&M University Press, 1991.

García y Griego, Manuel. "The Importation of Mexican Contract Laborers to the United States, 1942–1964," in *Between Two Worlds: Mexican Immigrants in the United States,* ed. David Gutiérrez. Wilmington, DE: Scholarly Resources, 1996, 45–85.

Garcilazo, Jeffrey Marcos, and Vicki L. Ruiz. *Traqueros: Mexican Railroad Workers in the United States, 1870–1930.* Denton: University of North Texas Press, 2012, 35–40.

Garza, Maria M. "Framing Mexicans in the Great Depression Editorials: Alien Riff-Raff to Heroes," *American Journalism* 34, no. 1 (February 2017): 26–48.

Gilbert, James. "A Field Study in Mexico of Mexican Repatriation Movement." PhD dissertation. University of Southern California, 1934, 50–53.

Giulietti, Corrado, Jackline Wahba, and Yves Zenou. "Strong Versus Weak Ties in Migration," Forschungsinstitut zur Zukunft der Arbeit Institute for the Study of Labor No. 8089 (2014).

Gomez-Quinones, Juan. *Roots of Chicano Politics, 1600–1940.* Albuquerque: University of New Mexico Press, 1994.

Gonzales, Michael J., and Lyman L. Johnson. *The Mexican Revolution, 1910–1940.* Albuquerque: University of New Mexico Press, 2002.

González, Gabriela. *Redeeming La Raza: Transborder Modernity, Race, Respectability, and Rights.* New York: Oxford University Press, 2018.

González, Gilbert G. *Culture of Empire: American Writers, Mexico, and Mexican Immigrants, 1880–1930.* Austin: University of Texas Press, 2010.

González, Gilbert G. *Mexican Consuls and Labor Organizing: Imperial Politics in the American Southwest.* Austin: University of Texas Press, 1999.

Gonzalez y Gonzalez, Luis. *San José de Gracia: Mexican Village in Transition,* trans. John Upton. Austin: University of Texas Press, 1982.

Goodman, Adam. *The Deportation Machine.* Princeton, NJ: Princeton University Press, 2020.

Gordon, Linda. *The Great Arizona Orphan Abduction.* Cambridge, MA: Harvard University Press, 1999.

Granovetter, Mark S. "The Strength of Weak Ties," *American Journal of Sociology,* 78 (1973): 1360–1380.

Gratton, Brian, and Emily Merchant. "Immigration, Repatriation, and Deportation: The Mexican-Origin Population in the United States, 1920–1950," *International Migration Review* 47, no. 4 (December 1, 2013): 944–975.

Grossman, James R. *Land of Hope: Chicago, Black Southerners, and the Great Migration.* Chicago: University of Chicago Press, 1989.

Guerin-Gonzales, Camille. *Mexican Workers and the American Dream: Immigration, Repatriation, and California Farm Labor, 1900–1939.* New Brunswick, NJ: Rutgers University Press, 1994.

Gutiérrez, David G. *Walls and Mirrors: Mexican Americans, Mexican Immigrants, and the Politics of Ethnicity.* Berkeley: University of California Press, 1995.

Gutiérrez, David Gregory, ed. *Between Two Worlds: Mexican Immigrants in the United States.* Wilmington, DE: Scholarly Resources, 1996.

Gutiérrez, Felix. "Spanish-Language Media in America: Background, Resources, History," *Journalism History* 4 (Summer 1977): 34–68.

Gutiérrez, Laura D. "Health Care and Deportation during the Bracero Program." Paper presented at the annual meeting of the American Historical Association, Atlanta, GA, January 7–10, 2016.

Guzmán, Romeo, et al., eds. *East of East: The Making of Greater El Monte.* New Brunswick, NJ: Rutgers University Press, 2020.

Habermas, Jürgen. *The Structural Transformation of the Public Sphere: An Inquiry into a Category of Bourgeois Society.* Cambridge, MA: MIT Press, 1989.

Hagen, Carla J. "Corrido de California," in *Migrant Border Ballad Project.* PhD dissertation. University of Texas, Austin, 1979.

Hale, Charles A. *The Transformation of Liberalism in Late Nineteenth-Century Mexico.* Princeton, NJ: Princeton University Press, 1989.

Hall, Linda B., and Don M. Coerver, *Revolution on the Border: The United States and Mexico, 1910–1920.* Albuquerque: University of New Mexico Press, 1988.

Handlin, Oscar. *The Uprooted: The Epic Story of the Great Migrations that Made the American People.* Boston: Little, Brown and Company, 1973.

Hart, John Mason. *Empire and Revolution: The Americans in Mexico Since the Civil War.* Berkeley: University of California Press, 2002.

Hass, Hein de. *Migration System Formation and Decline: A Theoretical Inquiry into the Self-Perpetuating and Self-Undermining Dynamics of Migration Processes.* Oxford: International Migration Institute, 2009.

Hayes, Joy Elizabeth. *Radio Nation.* Tucson: University of Arizona Press, 2000.

Heriberto Moreno, Guarcha. *Tiempos Viejos, Tiempos Nuevos.* Morelia, MI; Zamora, MI: Colegio de Michoacán, 1980.

Hernandez, Jose Angel. *Mexican American Colonization During the 19th Century: A History of the US-Mexico Borderlands.* Cambridge, UK: Cambridge University Press, 2012.

Hernández, Kelly Lytle. *City of Inmates: Conquest, Rebellion, and the Rise of Human Caging in Los Angeles, 1771–1965.* Chapel Hill: University of North Carolina Press, 2017.

Hernandez, Kelly Lytle. *Migra! A History of the US Border Patrol.* Berkeley: University of California Press, 2010.

Hernandez, Kelly Lytie. "'Persecuted Like Criminals': The Politics of Labor Emigration and Mexican Migration Controls in the 1920s and 1930s," *Aztlán: A Journal of Chicano Studies* 34, no. 1 (Spring 2009): 232.

Higham, John. *Strangers in the Land: Patterns of American Nativism, 1860–1925.* New Brunswick, NJ: Rutgers University Press, 1988.

Hinojosa-Smith, Ronaldo. "*La Prensa*: A Lifelong Influence of Hispanics in Texas," *The Americas Review* 17, no. 3–4 (September 1989): 125–129.

Hoffman, Abraham. *Unwanted Mexican Americans in the Great Depression: Repatriation Pressures, 1929–1939.* Tucson: University of Arizona Press, 1974.

Hsu, Madeline. *Dreaming of Gold, Dreaming of Home.* Redwood City, CA: Stanford University Press, 2000.

Innis-Jiménez, Michael. *Steel Barrio: The Great Mexican Migration to South Chicago, 1915–1940 (Culture, Labor, History Series).* New York: New York University Press, 2013.

Johnson, Benjamin Heber. *Revolution in Texas: How a Forgotten Rebellion and Its Bloody Suppression Turned Mexicans into Americans.* New Haven, CT: Yale University Press, 2005.

Jones, Anita. "Conditions Surrounding Mexicans in Chicago." MA Thesis. University of Chicago, 1928.

Kang, S. Deborah. *The INS on the Line: Making Immigration Law on the US-Mexico Border, 1917–1954.* New York: Oxford University Press, 2017.

Katz, Friedrich. "Labor Conditions on Haciendas in Porfirian Mexico: Some Trends and Tendencies," *Hispanic American Historical Review* 54, no. 1 (1974): 1–47.

Katz, Friedrich. *The Life and Times of Pancho Villa.* Redwood City, CA: Stanford University Press, 1998.

Katz, Friedrich. *The Secret War in Mexico: Europe, The United States and the Mexican Revolution.* Chicago: University of Chicago Press, 1981.

Katz, Michael B., Mark J. Stern, and Jamie J. Fader. "The Mexican Immigration Debate: The View from History," *Social Science History* 31, no. 2 (Summer 2007), 157–189.

Kent, Robert B., and Maura E. Huntz. "Spanish-Language Newspapers in the United States," *Geographical Review* 86, no. 3 (1996): 446–456.

Kessner, Thomas. *The Golden Door: Italian and Jewish Immigrant Mobility in New York City, 1880–1915.* New York: Oxford University Press, 1977.

Knight, Alan. *The Mexican Revolution, Vol. 1: Porfirians, Liberals, and Peasants.* Lincoln: University of Nebraska Press, 1990.

Knight, Alan. *The Mexican Revolution, Vol. 2: Counter-Revolution and Reconstruction.* Cambridge, UK: Cambridge University Press, 1986.

Kuntz Ficker, Sandra. *Empresa extranjera y mercado interno.* México, DF: El Colegio de México, 1995.

Kyle, David. *Transnational Peasants: Migrations, Networks, and Ethnicity in Andean Ecuador.* Baltimore: Johns Hopkins University Press, 2000.

La Prensa, January 8, 1920, America's Historical Newspapers, accessed 11/2016-03/2016, https://www.readex.com/products/americas-historical-newspapers.

La Prensa, "Los trabajadores Mexicanos en el Estado de Michigan," January 4, 1920, accessed 11/18, http://infoweb.newsbank.com.ezp-prod1.hul.harvard.edu/iw-search/we/HistArchive?p_action=keyword&f_pubBrowse=11F30FF2F63C9976#coverageMap.

Laird, Judith F. "Argentine, Kansas: The Evolution of a Mexican-American Community, 1905–1940." PhD dissertation. University of Kansas, 1975.

Leal, Luis. "The Spanish-Language Press: Function and Use," *The Americas Review* 17, no. 3–4 (September 1989): 157–162.

Lee, Jessica Harriet. "To the Seventh Generation: Italians and the Creation of an American Political Identity, 1921–1948." PhD dissertation. Columbia University, 2016.

Levenstein, Harvey A. "The AFL and Mexican Immigration in the 1920's: An Experiment in Labor Diplomacy," *The Hispanic American Historical Review* 48 (1968): 206.

Levitt, Peggy. *The Transnational Villagers.* Berkeley: University of California Press, 2001.

Lewthwaite, Stephanie. *Race, Place, and Reform in Mexican Los Angeles: A Transnational Perspective, 1890–1940.* Tucson: University of Arizona Press, 2009.

Leyva, Yolanda Chávez. "Cruzando la Linea: Engendering the History of Border Mexican Children during the Early 20th Century," in *Memories and Migrations: Mapping Boricua and Chicana Histories*, ed. Vicki L. Ruiz and John Chávez. Urbana-Champaign: University of Illinois Press, 2008, 71–92.

Limerick, Patricia Nelson. *The Legacy of Conquest: Unbroken Past of the American West.* New York: W. W. Norton & Co, 1987.

Lindquist, John H. "The Jerome Deportation of 1917," *Arizona and the West (Journal of the Southwest)* 11, no. 3 (1969): 233–246.

Lomnitz, Claudio. "Chronotopes of a Dystopic Nation: The Birth of 'Dependency' in Late Porfirian Mexico," in *Clio/Anthropos: Exploring the Boundaries Between History and*

Anthropology, ed. Andrew Wilford and Eric Taggliatozzo. Redwood City, CA: Stanford University Press.

Lomnitz, Claudio. *The Return of Comrade Ricardo Flores Magón*. Brooklyn, NY: Zone Books, 2014.

Lopez, Ronald W. "The El Monte Berry Strike of 1933," *Aztlán: A Journal of Chicano Studies* 3 (1972): 101–155.

Lopez, Mark Hugo, Jeffery Passel, and D'Vera Cohn. "Key Facts About the Changing US Unauthorized Population." Pew Research Center, 2021.

Loza, Mireya. *Defiant Braceros: How Migrant Workers Fought for Racial, Sexual, and Political Freedom*. Chapel Hill: University of North Carolina Press, 2016.

Lozano, Rosina. *An American Language: The History of Spanish in the United States*. Oakland: University of California Press, 2018.

Mapes, Kathleen. *Sweet Tyranny: Migrant Labor, Industrial Agriculture, and Imperial Politics*. Urbana: University of Illinois Press, 2009.

Martinez, John. "Mexican Emigration to the US 1910–1920." PhD dissertation. University of California Berkeley, 1957.

Massey, Douglas S. *Return to Aztlán: The Social Process of International Migration from Western Mexico (Studies in Demography) (No. 1)*. Berkeley: University of California Press, 1986.

Massey, Douglass S., Joaquin Arango, Graeme Hugo, Ali Kouaouci, Adelana Pellegrina, and J. Edward Taylor. "An Evaluation of International Migration Theory: The North American Case," *Population and Development Review* 20, no. 4 (1994), 699–751.

Massey, Douglass S., Joaquin Arango, Graeme Hugo, Ali Kouaouci, Adelana Pellegrina, and J. Edward Taylor. "Theories of International Migration: A Review and Appraisal," *Population and Development Review* 19, no. 3 (1993), 431–466.

Massey, Douglas S., Jorge Durand, and Nolan J Malone. *Beyond Smoke and Mirrors: Mexican Immigration in an Era of Economic Integration*. New York: Russell Sage Foundation, 2003.

Massey, Douglas S., and Magaly Sanchez R. *Brokered Boundaries: Creating Immigrant Identity in Anti-Immigrant Times*. New York: Russell Sage Foundation, 2010.

McDonald, Ian M., and Robert M. Solow. "Wages and Employment in a Segmented Labor Market," *Quarterly Journal of Economics* 100 (1985): 1115–1141.

McKay, R. Reynolds. "Texas Mexican Repatriation During the Great Depression." PhD dissertation. University of Oklahoma, 1982.

McKeown, Adam. "Ritualization of Regulation: The Enforcement of Chinese Exclusion in the United States and China," *The American Historical Review* 108, no. 2 (April 1, 2003): 377–403.

McWilliams, Carey. *Factories in the Field: The Story of Migratory Farm Labor in California*. Berkeley: University of California Press, 1935.

McWilliams, Carey. *Ill Fares the Land*. Boston: Little, Brown, 1942.

Medeiros, Francine. "La Opinión, a Mexican Exile Newspaper: A Content Analysis of Its First Years, 1926–1929," *Aztlán: A Journal of Chicano Studies* 11, no. 1 (1980): 65–87.

Melendez, Marcial E. Ocasio. *Capitalism and Development: Tampico, México 1876–1924*. New York: Peter Lang Publishing, 1998.

Mendoza, Valerie Marie. "The Creation of a Mexican Immigrant Community in Kansas City, 1890–1930." PhD dissertation. University of California, Berkeley, 1997.

Meyer, Doris. *Speaking for Themselves: Neomexicano Cultural Identity and the Spanish-Language Press, 1880–1920*. Albuquerque: University of New Mexico Press, 1996.

Miller, Sally M., ed. *The Ethnic Press in the United States: A Historical Analysis and Handbook*. New York: Greenwood, 1987.

Minian, Ana Raquel. *Undocumented Lives: The Untold Story of Mexican Migration*. Cambridge, MA: Harvard University Press, 2018.

Molina, Natalia. *Fit to Be Citizens?: Public Health and Race in Los Angeles, 1879–1939*. Berkeley: University of California Press, 2006.

Molina, Natalia. *How Race Is Made in America: Immigration, Citizenship, and the Historical Power of Racial Scripts.* Berkeley: University of California Press, 2014.

Monroy, María Isabel, and Tomás Calvillo Unna. *Breve historia de San Luis Potosí.* México, DF: Fondo de Cultura Económica, 1997.

Montejano, David. *Anglos and Mexicans in the Making of Texas, 1836–1986.* Austin: University of Texas Press, 1987.

Montoya, Benjamin C. *Risking Immeasurable Harm: Immigration Restriction and US-Mexican Diplomatic Relations, 1924–1932.* Lincoln: University of Nebraska Press, 2020.

Montoya, Maria. *Translating Property: The Maxwell Land Grant and the Conflict over Land in the American West.* Lawrence: University of Kansas Press, 2002.

Montoya, Ramón Alejandro. "El cura y los braceros," in *La Emigración de San Luis Potosí a Estados Unidos Pasado y Presente*, ed. Fernando Saúl Alanís Enciso. San Luis Potosí: El Colegio de San Luis, 2001, 77–78.

Morales, Daniel. "*Tejas, Afuera de México*: Newspapers, the Mexican Government, *Mutualistas*, and Migrants in San Antonio 1910–1940," *Journal of American Ethnic History*, 40, no. 2 (Winter 2021): 52–91.

Morales, Daniel. "The Making of Mexican America: Transnational Networks in the Rise of Mass Migration 1900–1940." PhD dissertation. Columbia University, 2016.

Moya, Jose C. *Cousins and Strangers*, 1st ed., Vol. 1. Berkeley: University of California, 1998.

Munguía, Rubén "*La Prensa*: Memories of a Boy . . . Sixty Years Later," *The Americas Review* 17, no. 3–4 (1989): 130–135.

Ngai, Mai M. *Impossible Subjects: Illegal Aliens and the Making of Modern America.* Princeton, NJ: Princeton University Press, 2005.

Ngai, Mae M. *The Lucky Ones: One Family and the Extraordinary Invention of Chinese America.* Boston: Houghton Mifflin Harcourt, 2010.

Noel, Linda C. *Debating American Identity.* Tucson: University of Arizona Press, 2014.

Ochoa Serrano, Alvaro. *Viajes de michoacanos al norte.* Morelia, MI; Zamora, MI: Colegio de Michoacán, 1998, 83–95.

Olmsted, Kathryn S. *Right Out of California: The 1930s and the Big Business Roots of Modern Conservatism.* New York: The New Press, 2015.

Özveren, Eyüp, and Thomas Faist. *Transnational Social Spaces: Agents, Networks and Institutions.* London: Routledge, 2004.

Parle, Dennis J. "The Novels of the Mexican Revolution Published by the Casa Editorial Lozano," *The Americas Review* 17, no. 3–4 (September 1989): 163–168.

Peck, Gunther. *Reinventing Free Labor: Padrones and Immigrant Workers in the North American West 1880–1930.* Cambridge, UK: Cambridge University Press, 2000.

Perales, Monica. *Smeltertown: Making and Remembering a Southwest Border Community.* Chapel Hill: University of North Carolina Press, 2010.

Perkins, Clifford Alan. *Border Patrol.* El Paso: Texas Western Press, 1978.

Pitti, Stephen J. *The Devil in Silicon Valley: Northern California, Race, and Mexican Americans.* Princeton, NJ: Princeton University Press, 2004.

Portes, Alejandro, and Rubén G. Rumbaut. *Legacies: The Story of the Immigrant Second Generation.* Berkeley: University of California Press, 2001.

Reséndez, Andrés. *The Other Slavery: The Uncovered Story of Indian Enslavement in America.* Boston: Houghton Mifflin Harcourt, 2016.

Ríos-McMillan, Nora. "A Biography of a Man and His Newspaper," *The Americas Review* 17, no. 3–4 (September 1989): 136–149.

Riveras-Rodriguez, Maggie. "Ignacio E. Lozano: The Mexican Exile Publisher Who Conquered San Antonio and Los Angeles," *American Journalism* 21 (2004): 75–89.

Robert, Kenneth D. "Agrarian Structure and Labor Mobility in Rural Mexico," *Population and Development Review* 8, no. 2 (June 1982): 299–322.

Romero, Yolanda García. "Trini Gamez, the Texas Farm Workers, and Mexican American Community Empowerment," in *Mexican American in Texas History*, ed. Emilio Zamora,

Cynthia Orozco, and Rondolfa Rocha. Austin: Texas State Historical Association, 2000, 143–155.

Rosales, F. Arturo. *Pobre Raza!: Violence, Justice, and Mobilization Among Mexico Lindo Immigrants, 1900–1936.* Austin: University of Texas Press, 1999.

Rosas, Ana Elizabeth. *Abrazando el Espíritu: Bracero Families Confront the US-Mexico Border.* Oakland: University of California Press, 2014.

Ruiz, Vicki L. *Cannery Women, Cannery Lives: Mexican Women, Unionization, and the California Food Processing Industry, 1930–1950.* Albuquerque: University of New Mexico Press, 1987.

Ruiz, Vicki. *From Out of the Shadows: Mexican Women in Twentieth-Century America.* New York: Oxford University Press, 1998.

Sandos, James. *Rebellion in the Borderlands: Anarchism and the Plan of San Diego 1904–1923.* Norman: University of Oklahoma Press, 1992.

Sanchez, George J. *Becoming Mexican American: Ethnicity, Culture and Identity in Chicano Los Angeles, 1900–1945.* New York: Oxford University Press, 1993.

Sanguino, Laurencio. "The Origins of Migration Between Mexico and the United States, 1905–1945." PhD dissertation. University of Chicago, 2012.

Santibañez, Enrique. *Ensayo sobre la Inmigración Mexicana en los Estados Unidos.* San Antonio, TX: The Clegg Co., 1930.

Sayer, Derek. "Everyday Forms of State Formation: Some Dissident Remarks on 'Hegemony,'" in *Everyday Forms of State Formation: Revolution and the Negotiation of Rule in Modern Mexico*, ed. Gilbert M. Joseph and Daniel Nugent. Durham, NC: Duke University Press, 1994, 367–378.

Sellars, Emily. "Does Emigration Inhibit Reform? Evidence from the Mexican Agrarian Movement, 1916–1945." PhD dissertation. Yale University, August 2017.

Sellars, Emily. "Emigration and Collective Action," *The Journal of Politics* 81, no. 4 (July 2019): 1210–1222.

Schryer, Frans J. *The Rancheros of Pisaflores: The History of a Peasant Bourgeoisie in Twentieth-Century Mexico.* Buffalo, NY: University of Toronto Press, 1979.

Scott, James C. *Seeing Like a State.* New Haven, CT: Yale University Press, 1998.

Scott, James C. *Weapons of the Weak: Everyday Forms of Peasant Resistance.* New Haven, CT: Yale University Press, 1985.

Sine, Elizabeth E. *Rebel Imaginaries: Labor, Culture, and Politics in Depression-Era California* Durham, NC: Duke University Press Books, 2021.

Smith, Robert. *Mexican New York: Transnational Lives of New Immigrants.* Berkeley: University of California Press, 2005.

Snodgrass, Michael. *Deference and Defiance in Monterrey: Workers, Paternalism, and Revolution in Mexico, 1890–1950.* Cambridge, UK: Cambridge University Press, 2003.

Snodgrass, Michael. "'The Land of Great Tools': How Two Generations of Labor Migrants Transformed Mexico's Emigrant Heartland," *Migration in Wirtschaft, Geschichte & Gesellschaft.* Göttingen: V&R Unipress, 2021, 141–162.

St. John, Rachel. *Line in the Sand: A History of the Western US-Mexico Border.* Princeton, NJ: Princeton University Press, 2012.

Stefano, Onofre di. "'Venimos a Luchar': A Brief History of *La Prensa*'s Founding," *Aztlán: A Journal of Chicano Studies* 16, no. 1–2 (1987): 95–118.

Stephen, Lynn. *Transborder Lives: Indigenous Oaxacans in Mexico, California, and Oregon.* Durham, NC: Duke University Press Books, 2007.

Stern, Alexandra Minna. *Eugenic Nation: Faults and Frontiers of Better Breeding in Modern America.* Berkeley: University of California Press, 2005.

Taylor, Paul Schuster. *An American-Mexican Frontier, Nueces County, Texas.* Chapel Hill: University of North Carolina Press, 1934.

Taylor, Paul Schuster. *A Spanish-Mexican Peasant Community: Arandas in Jalisco, Mexico.* Berkeley: University of California Press, 1933.

Taylor, Paul Schuster. *Mexican Labor in the United States.* Vol. 1, [no. 1] *Imperial Valley*; [no. 2] *Valley of the South Platte, Colorado*; [no. 3] *Migration Statistics I*; [no. 4] *Racial School Statistics, California, 1927*; [no. 5] *Dimmit County, Winter Garden District, South Texas*—Vol. 2, [no. 6] *Bethlehem, Pennsylvania*; [no. 7] *Chicago and the Calumet Region*—Vol. 3, [no. 8–10] *Migration Statistics, II–IV.* Berkeley: University of California Press, 1932.

Taylor, Paul Schuster. *The Migrants and California's Future: The Trek to California, and the Trek in California.* San Francisco: Resettlement Administration, California Commonwealth Club, 1935.

Taylor, Philip A. M. *The Distant Magnet: European Emigration to the USA.* London: Eyre & Spottiswoode, 1971.

Telles, Edward E., and Vilma Ortiz. *Generations of Exclusion: Mexican Americans, Assimilation, and Race.* New York: Russell Sage Foundation, 2009.

Thernstrom, Stephan. *The Other Bostonians: Poverty and Progress in the American Metropolis, 1880–1970.* Cambridge, MA: Harvard University Press, 1973.

Tokunaga, Yu. "Japanese Farmers, Mexican Workers, and the Making of Transpacific Borderlands," *Pacific Historical Review* 89, no. 2 (2020): 165–197.

Torres, Teodoro. *La patria perdida.* México DF: Ediciones Botas, 1935.

Trejo Terreros, Abraham. "Los coyotes. Migración y negocios en la frontera norte de México 1920–1964." PhD dissertation. El Colegio de Mexico, 2020.

Trevino, Roberto R. "Prensa y Patria; The Spanish-Language Press and the Biculturation of the Tejano Middle Class, 1920–1940," *The Western Historical Quarterly* 22 (1991): 451–472.

Trouillot, Michel-Rolph. *Silencing the Past: Power and the Production of History.* Boston: Beacon Press, 1995.

Truett, Samuel. *Fugitive Landscapes: The Forgotten History of the US-Mexico Borderlands.* New Haven, CT: Yale University Press, 2006.

Turner, Frederick Jackson. "The Significance of the Frontier in American History," *American Historical Association Annual Report for the Year 1893* (1894), 199–227.

Tutino, John. *From Insurrection to Revolution in Mexico: Social Bases of Agrarian Violence, 1750–1940.* Princeton, NJ: Princeton University Press, 1987.

Tutino, John. *Making a New World: Founding Capitalism in the Bajío and Spanish North America.* Durham, NC: Duke University Press Books, 2011.

Valdes, Dennis Nodin. *Al Norte: Agricultural Workers in the Great Lakes Region, 1917–1970.* Austin: University of Texas Press, 1991.

Valdes, Dionicio Nodin. *Barrios Norteos: St. Paul and Midwestern Mexican Communities in the Twentieth Century.* Austin: University of Texas Press, 2000.

Valdes, Dionicio Nodin. "South from the United States: Mexican Migration During the Great Depression and the Unfolding of a Neocolonial Relationship," in *El ir y venir de los norteños: Historia de la migración a Estados Unido*, ed. Fernando Saúl Alanís Enciso and Rafael Alarcón Acosta. Tijuana, B.C.: El Colegio de la Frontera Norte, AC, 2016, 167–188.

Valencia, Tita. "Ricardo Flores Magón y el periodismo subversivo Mexican en EUA," *Journalism History* 4 (Summer 1977): 169–178.

Vargas, Zaragosa. "Armies in the Fields and Factories: The Mexican Working Classes in the Midwest in the 1920s," *Mexican Studies-Estudios Mexicanos* 7 (1991): 47–71.

Vargas, Zaragosa. *Proletarians of the North: A History of Mexican Industrial Workers in Detroit and the Midwest, 1917–1933.* Berkeley: University of California Press, 1993.

Velasco, Mercedes Carrera de. *Los Mexicanos que devolvió la crisis, 1929–1932.* México DF: Secretaría de Relaciones Exteriores, 1974.

Venegas, Daniel. *Las adventuras de Don Chipote.* Houston, TX: Arte Publico Press, 2000 (original 1928).

Venegas, María Teresa. *Letters Home: Mexican Exile Correspondence from Los Angeles, 1927–1932.* [The Author], 2012.

Walsh, Casey. *Building the Borderlands: A Transnational History of Irrigated Cotton Along the Mexico-Texas Border.* College Station: Texas A&M University Press, 2008.

Ward, Zachary A. "The Circular Flow: Return Migration from the United States in the Early 1900s." PhD dissertation. University of Colorado at Boulder, 2014.

Webber, John. "Homing Pigeons, Cheap Labor, and Frustrated Nativists: Immigration Reform and the Deportation of Mexicans from South Texas in the 1920s," *The Western Historical Quarterly* 44 (2013): 167–186.

Weber, Devra. *Dark Sweat, White Gold: California Farm Workers, Cotton, and the New Deal.* Berkeley: University of California Press, 1996.

Weber, Devra. "Oral Sources and the History of Mexican Workers in the United States," *International Labor and Working Class History* 23 (Spring 1983): 47–50.

Weber, Devra Anne. "Wobblies of the Partido Liberal Mexicano: Re-envisioning Internationalist and Transnational Movements through Mexican Lenses," *Pacific Historical Review* 85, no. 2 (2016): 188–226.

Weise, Julie M. *Corazón de Dixie: Mexicanos in the US South Since 1910.* Chapel Hill: University of North Carolina Press, 2015.

Weise, Julie M., and Christoph Rass. "Migrating Concepts: The Transatlantic Origins of the Bracero Program, 1919–42," *The American Historical Review* 129, no. 1 (March 2024): 22–52.

Wokeck, Marianne Sophia. *Trade in Strangers: The Beginnings of Mass Migration to North America.* University Park: Pennsylvania State University Press, 1999.

Womack, John. *Zapata and the Mexican Revolution.* New York: Vintage, 1970.

Yankelevich, Pablo. "Corrupción y gestión migratoria en el México posrevolucionario," *Revista de Indias* LXXII, no. 255 (2012), 451.

Young, Elliot. *Catarino Garza's Revolution on the Texas-Mexico Border.* Durham, NC: Duke University Press, 2004.

Young, Julia G. *Mexican Exodus: Emigrants, Exiles, and Refugees of the Cristero War.* New York: Oxford University Press, 2015.

Zamora, Emilio. *The World of the Mexican Worker in Texas.* College Station: Texas A&M University Press, 1993.

Zamora, Emilio, Cynthia Orozco, and Rondolfa Rocha, eds. *Mexican American in Texas History.* Austin: Texas State Historical Association, 2000.

Index

For the benefit of digital users, indexed terms that span two pages (e.g., 52–53) may, on occasion, appear on only one of those pages.

Tables and figures are indicated by an italic *t* and *f* following the page number